MW01027356

At The River I Stand

AT THE RIVER I STAND

Joan Turner Beifuss

St. Lukes Press
A Wimmer Company
Memphis, Tennessee

St. Lukes Press
A Wimmer Company

Library of Congress Cataloging-in-Publication Data

Beifuss, Joan Turner
At The River I Stand / Joan Turner Beifuss. -- 2nd ed.
  p. cm.
ISBN 0-918518-80-6 : $19.95
1. Sanitation Workers Strike, Memphis, Tenn., 1968. 2. Memphis
(Tenn.) -- Officials and employees. 3. AFSCME. 4. King, Martin
Luther, Jr., 1929-1968--Assassination.   I. Title.
HD5325.S2572   1968M46   1990
331.89'28136372'0976819--dc20   90-30713
                                                  CIP

Copyright © 1990 Joan Turner Beifuss

For information address:
St. Lukes Press
4210 B.F. Goodrich Boulevard
Memphis, Tennessee 38118

Published privately in a limited edition:
First Printing   October 1985
Second Printing   November 1985
Third Printing   June 1986

Published by Carlson Publishing, Inc., April 1989 as
Volume 12 of MARTIN LUTHER KING, JR.
AND THE CIVIL RIGHTS MOVEMENT:
An Eighteen-volume Series of Major Studies
Edited by David J. Garrow

Revised Trade Edition:
First Printing   April 1990

DEDICATION

Keepers of history flatly record that Dr. Martin Luther King, Jr., was shot to death in Memphis in 1968 in the midst of a strike of public works employees seeking recognition of their union.

Sometimes the keepers of history say that the Memphis movement was the end of an era, the last great nonviolent civil rights campaign in the South.

Sometimes they see it as a prototype fusion of organized labor and minority groups for economic independence.

Sometimes they tell it simply as a tale of labor organizing—with variations.

Or they note that the Memphis campaign was an example of how power began to shift in a major southern city.

All of these approaches are true.

But the stark statements do not tell how the larger-than-life figure of Dr. King would come to brood over this place. It will be the mythmakers who tell of the flawed and fallen hero, the storytellers who script the inexorable move toward tragedy.

Nor do the statements tell what it was like in Memphis, the texture of that southern spring, warm winds sweeping up from the Gulf with azalea, the freak snow that offered a moment of false respite, the fear which gripped both blacks and whites. The strike did not so much happen in Memphis as engulf it.

This book is simply an attempt to fill in the empty spaces of that story of strike and assassination. It is told by garbagemen and their union organizers, by people who loved Dr. King and those who did not, by government, civic, and religious leaders, and by ordinary people caught in the events.

None of these were dispassionate observers. They were at times angry and frightened, at times brave and compassionate. At times truth was other than they perceived it.

This is the book of those days.

It is dedicated to those who cared then and care even now.

Contents

Prelude
Gather at the River

On Jordan's Stormy Banks
  1. Fertile Ground 23
  2. Garbage Is Going To Be Picked Up 45
  3. Contempt in My Heart 73
  4. Planted by the Waterside 93
  5. Nothing but the Strike 123

River Is Chilly and River Is Wide
  6. No Easy Riders Here 145
  7. Down Where We Are 183
  8. Mats and Spittoons 217
  9. Here Comes Dr. King 253

Through the Deep Waters
  10. Situation out of Control 277
  11. Mission Accomplished 319
  12. Jericho Road 343
  13. Darkest Day 371
  14. Greater Laws 413
  15. Concourse of Witnesses 435
  16. I Am a Man 451

On Making the Book 461

Notes 465

Sources 473

Additional Bibliography 478

PRELUDE

In the ten years from Montgomery to Selma, Martin Luther King, Jr., and the nonviolent civil rights movement of which he had become symbol forced more changes in the status of black Americans than any actions since the Emancipation Proclamation freed the slaves.

Segregation laws and even customs fell—to congressional legislation, federal court decisions, or local agreement, all pushed and pressured by legal brief and by those masses of marching blacks and their supporters, almost, it seemed, by endless verses of "We Shall Overcome."

It was a potent gospel King preached—the power of nonviolent resistance to injustice in a context of active Christian love and Gandhian tactics.

Still, all was not well. King had early said that racism was like a big boil. If it were lanced and opened to light and air, the poison would be drawn. Now the lancing was done. Racism lay open for all to see. Legal segregation was dying.

Yet fever persisted among black Americans, still poor, ill-housed, ill-fed, ill-educated. De facto segregation remained. Five months after Selma and the winning of voting rights came the Watts riots. The economic condition of America's poor was now lighted on television sets by ghetto flames from Newark, Detroit, Harlem. President Lyndon Johnson's Great Society program launched aid and self-help plans to bring the poor into the mainstream of the economy. But it was not broad, deep, or quick enough.

Over in South Vietnam, the war widened. "The Great Society has been shot down on the battlefields of Vietnam," King cried out at New York's Riverside Church in April 1967. His concern was both practical and theological. Money used for guns could not be used to help the poor. The war not only violated Christian love but it was an unjust war. King took his 1964 Nobel Peace Prize seriously.

The Southern Christian Leadership Conference's unsuccessful foray into Chicago in the summer of 1966 had convinced him that a new kind of campaign was needed to help those blocked from the economic mainstream. Government action on behalf of the poor needed to be forced as it had been in the area of segregation.

If he could bring together across racial lines a coalition of the unemployed and working poor, exemplified by domestics, garbagemen, migrant farm laborers, if they could agree on a common set of goals for jobs and aid and on a coordinated method, could the political structure afford to ignore their demands?

Such a coalition touched on the old dreams of the populists, labor organizers, socialists, even revolutionaries. Yet such a coalition of the poor and dispossessed had never been attempted in this country on the scale and within the context that King now considered—power without violence, revolution without overthrow of the existing government.

Throughout 1967 he worried with the idea, ignoring protests that he was shifting from race to class struggle. Late in the year his staff began to work on the actual logistics. On December 4, an announcement was made from his Atlanta headquarters.

He would lead a Poor People's Campaign. The first phase would take place in the spring. It would bring to Washington some three thousand blacks, Puerto Ricans, Appalachian whites, American Indians, Hispanics, representatives of the poor around the country. They would set up a tent city and engage in tactics of massive civil disobedience if necessary to get the attention of Congress and government agencies. They would call for an economic bill of rights, whose estimated cost was around twelve billion dollars.

The problems of the Poor People's Campaign, even early in the planning, were serious. Elements of support that had always rallied behind King were hesitant or no longer there. There had been too much northern ghetto violence in the past two years for many of his white liberal supporters to be enthusiastic at the thought of mass protests in the nation's capital. His shift in emphasis from integration to economics bothered segments of the black middle class and the black church. Organized labor disagreed with him on Vietnam. Young blacks were bewitched by Black Power. Whether these were defections or signs that the movement he led was growing up and further defining itself, he felt somehow hurt by the actions. He brooded over them.

Still, King pressed on. Contacts were being cemented with poverty groups. Yet he seemed to face in the Poor People's Campaign a situation that truly would either make or break his prestige. And he faced it on the shifty ground of economics, pressed from behind by more and more articulate militants, and facing directly a public and government that for the first time seemed almost totally unsympathetic.

It was a long way back to Montgomery where he had led one black community toward one simple goal.

King did not know early in 1968 that a variant of the coalition for economic gain he envisioned was already coming into being in Memphis.

Gather at the River

Ed Gillis

Ed Gillis marched with thirteen hundred other workers in the strike that Memphis spring of 1968. He was an old man, near to seventy by his own reckoning, twenty years an employee in the public works department. Sometimes the sign he carried read

AFSCME

Or

BOYCOTT

Or sometimes

I AM A MAN

"I was born and raised up at Savannah, Tennessee. Eight miles from the old Shiloh battlefield....stand on that hill at Shiloh and see the steeple on the courthouse at Savannah. The last cannon loaded there in that Civil War...is setting there loaded now, pointing right off the bank of the Tennessee River....

"I can't tell you all that was in my family. There were so many of us. I wasn't raised by my family. My mother give me to some white people when I was a year old and they raised me from the cradle up until I was twenty-one. My mother worked for them, but she didn't have no say over me. I stayed with the white people, slept right in the house with them....A whole lot of white folks back there raised colored children. The white folks that raised me raised three or four colored boys and girls and two or three white children besides their own....

"I was told that at the time the Civil War ended—surrendered—the family had forty little baby slaves, excusing the grown slaves. Old man Luke and old man Jim were both rebel captains in the rebel war. Old man John, he didn't fight. He got papers to stay at home and see after the family while his brothers were in the army.

"I had fun, plenty of fun. You know, I was a great hand to work calves, break them to harness, and we had slides for them....I was a pretty good bull trainer. I had my calf, trained him to where he'd stand up on his hind feet...put his front feet up on a block, stand up there, and then I'd make him kneel down and say his prayers. He'd get down on his knees and bellow and before he'd eat, he'd ask the blessing. He'd bellow and butt that trough before he'd eat...And I'd ride him. My wife can testify now that I can take a rope and catch a cow or a mule by any foot I want to catch him by. I know a cow as well as anybody. Fact of the business, I got my loops back there in the house now, come out of my lariat....I got three bull rings back there now....That clamp I haven't used since I left Savannah. That's fifty years ago....

"They didn't try to school me at all...When I was ten, I went to plowing...cultivating the garden, tending to the hogs, cattle...I used to get up there in the morning before day and milk twenty, twenty-one cows...I'd load up my wagon, go to town and peddle milk and butter....Then I made up their beds, swept the house. I tended to the poultry, fed them, watered them, and turned them out. I strained the milk. I hauled water from the creek to water the hogs. I hauled water to set out all the plants. In February and January we be done setting out ten thousand cabbage plants, five thousand a month of frostproof plants. Then later on when the frost lighten up, we plant our beans and everything like that. They sold a lot of chickens. I catch their chickens and carry them up there where they weigh them...They tie them up, put them in the pen and carry them to town.

"I left them folks at twenty-one—because I was a grown young man and they didn't want to pay me for my labor.

"I got big enough to want pay for my work. And they didn't want to pay me. They wanted me to work for my board and clothes. Well, I done got too large for that.

"I thought once I wanted to be a big farmer. And then I thought I wanted to be a horse trader. Well, horses commence running out. Later I got to the place where I thought I didn't want anything—just work....

"So I left there in 1917...in March, when spring commence approaching. I went to Arkansas. I been gone ever since, and I never been back to Savannah. I didn't never care to go back.

"When I first started, everybody tell me, 'You better not go out there. You'll die with the Arkansas Chills.' I studied over it. They said, 'They carried Lige Dixon away from there and brought him back in a box.' The Arkansas Chills is malaria and fever. It's what folks get out there running around in those swamps and, I reckon, drinking a lot of whiskey and not taking no medicine....But I was more healthy in Arkansas than I was in Tennessee."

He moved from job to job throughout the area. He worked on the railroad section at Lepanto and at a sawmill. "Things got dull. I got my first wife." He worked at Mississippi River flood control levee camps at Caruthersville and Alton and New Madrid. "I worked on the river for a while, on the willow boat, cutting willow and making mats." He went back to the railroad, dynamiting for cuts on a line between St. Louis and Springfield. "I left after there was a kind of riot between the colored and the whites....they said all the Negroes had to leave." Between jobs, he sharecropped.

For seven years he was at Weona. "I worked on the track. See that scar on my arm? That big muscle was cut in two...We was cutting a stump out of the dummy line track in mud and water...so the train could go over it without wrecking....The mud and water were so bad...and this young kid didn't want it in his face. He jumped back a little too quick and hit me in the arm. I run my hand down in mud and water and I commenced laughing until he got reconciled....I showed him how to bandage it...so you couldn't see a drop of blood. That's what made my arm jump...like it was going to jump off. I worked another two hours in the mud and water making the track safe…but every once in a while my arm look like it just jump off, and I'd lay flat on my back on a log till I got ease….I was in the hospital in Jonesboro. If I hadn't had a good doctor my hand would have been paralyzed…never would have been no more good. To see me working you wouldn't think there was anything the matter with this arm. I just can't run a hammer, but I can shovel, pick….

"I got acquainted with this wife while I was at Neuhardt…I was a hired hand on the farm, and my wife sharecropped. I had a crop for her. I worked by the day, but I plowed her crop, done all her cultivating….The farmers didn't want to work no white people. They didn't want nothing but colored on their farms. A white man don't want to work no white cropper; he don't want to deal fair.

"Course now, I raised hogs. I raised cows. I would sell them. He was fair with me on my stock. I could have sold the corn if I'd wanted to. But the cotton I couldn't touch. Nobody touched the cotton."

He left off sharecropping after a heated dispute with the farm's new owner over his right to sell his cows and over his refusal to buy at the company store.

"I got three wagons and hauled myself out of there. I come on here to Memphis and I walked around here two or three weeks trying to get a job….Mr. Crump was the big dog….

"Then old Charlie Sour—I think they called him that—he got me a job with the city. I give him two dollars to get me a job. He was a colored fellow that had been with the city a long time. The job was with the asphalt department in the public works. I said to him, 'I'll give you two dollars if you'll give me a job.' He said, 'Gillis, I know a foreman over there who wants a certain man to work for him. He can't keep none of them youngsters. Them youngsters don't stay on the job long. We always shorthanded.' I said, 'Tell him I'm just the man. Tell him I'll be there every day.' So he carried me out there and they put me to work that morning. That was the latter part of 1948 when I went to work….I got sixty-five cents an hour and we worked forty-eight hours a week then….

"I joined Mr. T.O. Jones and the union in 1966 cause we just wasn't getting justice. A lot of the men were scared to join and a lot of them wouldn't join….But we had to get better satisfaction."

On Jordan's Stormy Banks

Fertile Ground

1

"The ground is fertile beyond belief."
Jerry Wurf

Public works employee L. C. Reed caught the bus and went on to his job that Monday morning in Memphis. He had not been at a specially called union meeting the night before.

"The union stewards met me at the gate and said, 'Don't work.' I asked one of them what it was all about and he tried to tell me. I don't think he knowed exactly, but he knowed to tell us not to go to work. And I told him, 'Well, it suit me because they didn't pay me for that rainy day when they should have.' I took heel and turned around."

Charles Blackburn, the city's public works director, knew as soon as he drove up to the Scott Street installation at 7:00 A.M. that he had a work stoppage in sanitation. From cars parked around the entrance to the yard, workers were calling and urging others not to report. Many men had already checked in, but they were moving back out through the gates and clustering in little groups to find out what to do next. Union stewards circulated. The sun was barely up, and it was a bitter twenty-two degrees.

The extent of the stoppage was hard to assess so early. There were five sanitation yards—once they had been mule barns—

plus the sewers and drains and the asphalt divisions, and reports were coming in that the men were walking out at all of them. From the sanitation installation off Crump Boulevard, Blackburn called the mayor, Henry Loeb, and spent the morning trying to piece together enough crews to keep some of the garbage trucks rolling.

When accurate figures began coming in, the situation was far worse than Blackburn had expected. Nine hundred thirty workers out of 1,100 in sanitation, handling twenty-five hundred tons of garbage daily, had gone out. Over in asphalt and in sewers and drains, 214 men out of 230 were gone. The director managed to get 38 trucks, manned by 5 men each, out onto the streets, leaving some 150 trucks sitting idle. But some of the trucks came back in, the drivers claiming fear and harassment on the streets.

It was the size of the initial work stoppage that stunned both knowledgeable city and labor people. "To tell me you could get that many people out is unbelievable," said local AFL-CIO labor council secretary Bill Ross. "With no assurance whatsoever that they would have any support or that they would even have their jobs or would have any welfare, any assistance whatsoever. And the ones that came out, stayed out."

The hallway at the old Labor Temple on South Second was filled with public works men when Ross reached his office there. Former garbageman T. O. Jones, who had been struggling for years to get a union going, came in.

"I got a strike on my hands."

"It looks like it," replied Ross dryly.

They moved to try to get some order out of the chaos in the halls. The Temple's largest meeting hall held only five hundred, so by midmorning part of the crowd jammed in there. Others milled around in smaller meeting rooms. Now they were actually out, the men became braver. Ross called the Firestone Tire and Rubber plant to ask for use of their big auditorium, and then went in to encourage the men.

"I have never seen a group more determined," he said. "I have no idea what I said that morning....probably that everything was going to be all right and that we were going to win this—the typical speech."

It was almost noon by the time the international headquarters of the American Federation of State, County, and Municipal Employees (AFSCME) in Washington learned that its Local 1733 had walked off the job. A Memphis newsman got to the international first.

"God Almighty," moaned field services director P. J. Ciampa privately. "I need a strike in Memphis like I need a hole in the head." He held off the reporter with a statement about resolving the issue at the conference table and not in the streets, though Ciampa wasn't sure what was going on. He finally reached T. O. Jones, whom he reportedly chewed out. But he also promised aid.

Ciampa then got a plane for Memphis. But he was gloomy on the flight. "I wouldn't have called that strike—not in February, sir. I just don't believe...you sell snow to Eskimos...And, my God, what in the hell am I going to do with a strike in the South? I'd heard so many horror stories about them." But then, he brightened, "We'd been ready for organization a couple of times in Memphis. We'd muffed the opportunity. This time I thought, 'Well, maybe we can.' "[1]

The actual walkout also caught the city off balance, even those who suspected that something was in the wind. Assistant City Attorney James Manire learned of the action while talking to Memphis City Attorney Frank Gianotti on the phone. "Well, they went out this morning," said Gianotti. "How was it?" asked Manire. "It looks like most of them," Gianotti answered.

Even then Manire could not believe the men themselves would take such drastic action. "They needed strong leadersh to incite them to strike. They were men who were easily That was apparent. The strike was brought on by leadership from the union."

Surprise was also the reaction of the new city co had only been in office six weeks. Members felt t'

unfairly *hit* on their unsuspecting heads by the walkout at a time
when they *were* still trying to get themselves organized. "If they
had given us a *little* time, they would have gotten a fair and just
hearing and, if *possible,* their grievances settled," said Councilman Billy Hyman. The *mayor* had promised all city employees
there would be raises, but he *just* did not have the funds at that
time, noted Councilman Tom *Todd.*

In the mayor's office, Henry *Loeb* canceled all outside
appointments, figuratively opened his *door* wide, and waited
for representatives of the strikers to arrive. At *6:00* P.M. he was
still waiting, and had issued a statement that if the *workers* did
not "return to work immediately," others would be *fired.*

In Mayor Loeb's mind, some things were already quite *clear.*
A strike in the city's public works department had been *called*
because the city's new form of mayor/council government was
just starting out and strike leaders therefore assumed that it was
weak. He himself had not had time to be unfair to organized
labor or to anyone else. He had been all tied up with trying to
straighten out the mess of a budget left from the former
administration. The new Loeb administration knew it was
facing a probable operating deficit of some $65,000. But the
grim forecast at the end of January was that it faced a total deficit
of $2.2 million by June, end of the fiscal year, if the current
expenditure rate continued. There was little to be done about
the immediate deficit except to throw on tight fiscal controls and
try to pare expenses. Loeb froze all hiring and began an
economy crusade that brought jokes about recycling rubber
bands and paper clips. But concern over the anticipated budget
overrun would influence administration thinking throughout
the period.[2] National union leaders had played a big part in
calling the strike, the mayor believed. Employees had a right to
join a union, but nobody had the right to go beyond the law,
and a strike by employees against a city was obviously illegal. The
workers had a direct way of negotiating their grievances. "All
they had to do was come in the door." Finally, he regarded
taxpayers' money as trust money and had serious doubts

whether such monies should be subject to bargaining in the same way that private enterprise monies or profits were.

"Bravo, Henry," said the wife of one Memphis business executive as she listened to the local news. "To most people in Memphis, a strike against the city equalled rebellion," remarked an advertising man.

The evening newspaper, the *Memphis Press-Scimitar*, ran an editorial "Garbage Mess—New York and Here," which stated that government employees had no "moral right" to strike though they were entitled to a "fair deal" from public officials.

But there was not much public response to the initial walkout. If the strike were real, then it would be settled immediately because quite obviously garbage had to be collected. The hows, whys, and wherefores were not particularly important. That was why officials were elected—to handle such problems. The city's Republican U.S. Congressman (9th District) Dan Kuykendall shrewdly observed, "There is something inherent in the nature of a region that has had a long period of labor peace, inherent in a region that has never had any such thing as a strike of public employees of any kind and has a law against it. People just didn't think this could happen because they weren't attuned to it."

National staff members of the AFSCME began coming into Memphis that night. P. J. Ciampa was met by local leader T. O. Jones at the airport and taken to meet some of the men. "The thing that impressed me when I moved in there was the suspicion that I saw in these men's eyes…As I was talking to them they looked at me with such intentness, such 'Why is he here? Where is he from? What does he represent? Is he with us or isn't he?' I was very uneasy all that night."

Bill Lucy, associate director of legislation for AFSCME's community affairs department, was in Detroit when he got a call from Jerry Wurf, the international's president. It looked as if the walkout could be resolved easily, said Wurf from Washing' but he felt some of the headquarters staff people should hand. Lucy, who had spent his early childhood in M headed to Memphis. So did Joe Paisley, AFSCME's Tennessee representative in Nashville. Union organizer Jesse Epps was going to Little Rock when he, too, was rerouted to Memphis.

The union field staff was accustomed to unexpected situations and quick decisions. The men who came into Memphis were part of the field staff of seventy, operating on a 1968 organizing budget of $1.7 million and faced with requests for organizing assistance all across the country.

AFSCME had begun among groups of government employees in Wisconsin and Ohio in the thirties, a time when government jobs were considered political plums and there was periodic fear of firing when new administrations came into power. These first locals organized for legislative lobbying and were concerned about job security and the patronage system. For a short time AFSCME existed as a separate unit under the American Federation of Government Workers, but in 1936 it obtained a charter as an independent union in the American Federation of Labor. By its tenth anniversary in 1946, AFSCME had seventy-three thousand members.

The entire picture of labor relations between government management and public employees, federal, state, county, or municipal, had been one of confusion for years. Public employees ran the gamut from teachers, engineers, librarians, nurses, and postmen to gravediggers, streetcleaners, and garbage collectors. Their conditions of employment ran from civil service protection to none at all. If there was one constant in consideration of the rights of public employees, it had been announced by Governor Calvin Coolidge of Massachusetts to labor leader Samuel Gompers during the 1919 Boston police strike. "There is no right to strike against the public safety by anybody, anywhere, anytime."

While organized labor in the private sector fought, mounted strikes, bargained, forced legislation and court decisions, and became a workable, if not always stable, concomitant of the national economy, attempts to organize employees in public service and to obtain some sort of bargaining leverage were spotty and often unsuccessful. In 1962 President John Kennedy, in an executive order, gave the green light for federal workers to organize and bargain. But 9.5 million of the 12 million public workers were not employed by the federal government at all but by states, counties, and municipalities. Their salaries, benefits, and job protection lagged far behind those of private industry and they were not covered under the National Labor Relations statutes. As local governments had expanded their services between 1947 and 1967, the number of these local employees had increased 145 percent.

The situation was clearly an open invitation for union organizing, and a variety of unions and professional groups were working the territory. But union organizing was not orderly, for it ran afoul of many different state and local laws about the legality of public employees unions and of negotiating with them. Organizing was also influenced by the strength of local labor unions in the private sector, so organizing public employees went more smoothly in the industrial centers of the North, upper Midwest, and West Coast than it did in the South which had no strong union tradition.

As AFSCME continued to organize—membership topped one hundred thousand by 1955 and two hundred thousand by 1963—it became more aggressive, aiming at collective bargaining as opposed to improved civil service. In 1964, Jerry Wurf, executive director of the New York City District Council 37, won the presidency of the international. He was one of the oldest of the group of Young Turks who sought to turn AFSCME in a more aggressive direction. In power, Wurf and his aides began to reshape the union both along philosophical and pragmatic lines.

The stance that would be taken by AFSCME's representatives in Memphis had been publicly and clearly spelled out in the previous two years both in the AFSCME executive board policy statement on "public employee unions: rights and responsibilities" of July 1966 and by Wurf himself in a speech to the U.S. Conference of Mayors, meeting in Honolulu in June 1967.

"Unions would be unable to sign up a single employee if he were satisfied, if his dignity were not offended, if he were treated with justice," Wurf told the assembled mayors. "What is important is not the motives of union officials in organizing public employees, but the astonishing rapidity and success of their efforts. Barren ground yields poor crops, but here the ground is fertile beyond belief...All that we are we owe to you," he added wryly. "You represent our best organizers, our most persuasive reason for existence, our defense against membership apathy and indifference, our perpetual prod to militancy, and our assurance of continued growth."

The executive board statement warned that "Public officials must recognize that they must deal with the problems of their employees, not sweep them under the rug and hope they will stay out of sight." Union recognition and the setting up of orderly collective bargaining processes which brought administrators and workers to the table as equals, the methods used in private industry, were held to be the only sensible and democratic blueprints for good labor management relations.

The policy statement also set forth the controversial right of public employees, except those in law enforcement, to strike. And Wurf spoke quite frankly of the use of the strike, even where it was against the law. The mayors hearing him had cause to be concerned. In 1966 nationwide there had been 142 work stoppages of public employees and in 1967 the number of such strikes reached 150. Although the two most publicized public employees' strikes of early 1968, New York garbage workers and Florida teachers, did not involve AFSCME, Wurf's union had participated in some seventy-five illegal walkouts in the two preceding years.

Later, Wurf would say privately that a strike was a tactic in impressing upon the employer the need for communication with his employees. "The right to strike is critical and important at times, but much more fundamental than that is the right to bargain. Bargaining is the essential issue, but that's not nearly as lurid as the right to strike."

At the point when its staff members headed toward Memphis, AFSCME was the fastest growing union in the country with a membership pushing four hundred thousand, and registering new members at the rate of about a thousand a week. There were nineteen hundred locals in forty-five states, the District of Columbia, the Canal Zone, and Puerto Rico.

The bulk of membership was in the subprofessional ranks—parks and recreation, hospitals, sanitation, seventy percent blue collar. Estimates were that about thirty percent of the national membership was black. Local units, some of them small and barely surviving, did exist in southern states. But there had been no large, significant, publicized breakthrough in the unionizing of public employees in the South.

Local 1733 in Memphis was one of those small struggling units. Its president, short, chunky T. O. Jones, had become a garbageman in 1959. But he was never satisfied with the job, not the working conditions, not the dead-end quality of it. He began grumbling openly and learned that a lot of other men felt the same way. When he started talking back to drivers and supervisors, he was tagged a troublemaker. He began to talk about organizing.

Even before the Great Depression, mechanization, and land concentration had driven rural blacks into Memphis to become the urban rather than the rural poor, the street repair, drainage, asphalt and sanitation departments had been the working ground of uneducated blacks.[3] They were nonclassified, hourly laborers with no job protection other than what they could manage by keeping in good with drivers and foremen.

If public works jobs were reasonably steady they were also tough and physical. Back injuries were common. In bad weather when they could not work, the men were not paid. An optional pension plan was available, paid half by the city, but as late as 1964 fewer than half of the Memphis public works employees were in it. The men hung onto their small earnings. The pay scale was haphazard and the settlement of job grievances also haphazard.

Job turnover was high, but throughout the years the department did hold on to a segment of hard-working men who
stuck with it. It was not unusual to find employees who had been
there fifteen, twenty, twenty-five years. They were men who
knew, as T. O. Jones found out, that hauling garbage was as far
as they could go.

In other parts of the country public works departments had
modernized, mechanized, even unionized. In Memphis, with
the same dogged acceptance that drove their friends and kin out
in the country to plant the cotton year after year, knowing all the
while that in the end there would be no profits, no change,
public works men kept on toting.

But a small group of men began to listen to T. O. Jones.
Encouraged by leaders of the Retail Clerks, Local 1529, they
began to hold small meetings. In the summer of 1963 Jones led
thirty-two men on a disorganized walkout that caused a minor
stir and resulted in their firing. Eventually the men were allowed
to return to work. Jones did not go back, but he continued to
work with a hardcore group, to go out to other employees'
homes to push the need for a union.

In January 1964 Jones and his small group of men set up a
formal Independent Workers Association, complete with rules
and bylaws. Throughout that year there was minor agitation in
the department. The new independent union barely stayed
alive, its membership fluctuating from gripe to gripe. Pete
Sisson, then public works commissioner, began to make some
changes. He began unofficially to deal with the organized group
of men. The pay scale was standardized; the starting wage rose
from $1.27 to $1.60 an hour and some workers were up to
$1.80. Moves began to bring city employees under Social
Security.[4] Sisson began to apply civil service standards on
vacations and sick leave.

That fall of 1964, Jones asked local labor council secretary Bill
Ross if he could find an international union that might be
interested in his group. Ross carried Jones' request to AFSCME
headquarters in Washington. AFSCME was interested and the

local voted to merge with it. Jones went on the AFSCME payroll as a union organizer at a couple of hundred dollars a month. AFSCME began to pick up other union expenses, and a union staff member worked with Jones on an off-and-on basis.

In late August 1966, at a hot and emotional meeting, a sizable number of public works men agreed to go out on strike. But their action was blocked by a chancery court injunction and fell apart before picket lines were even in place. A later court decision decreed: "All city employees may not strike for any purpose whatsoever...." The decision was not appealed to a higher court nor was the injunction dissolved.

In Washington an angry Jerry Wurf had learned of that abortive Memphis strike only after the fact. He was angry that a strike had been called in the first place without adequate preparation and equally angry that it had folded so easily. "So Memphis was lying there on my conscience, yeah, and a lot of other places. I always had places," he would say.

In Memphis Commissioner Sisson continued his reforms. He got the open tubs used to move garbage from yards to trucks off the men's backs by purchasing three-wheeled pushcarts. He replaced the open-bed trucks with mechanical packers. For rainy days Sisson established the policy that the department would continue to work but the choice was up to the men. If they worked in the rain, they would be paid. If they chose, however, to return home, they would not be paid.

Jones continued as president of the local. He acted unofficially as a go-between with the director and he struggled to hold the union together. Dues were a dollar a week, but he hardly ever got it. "The men knew how the city felt about the union," he said. "They didn't want the boss to know they were supporting it. Their fear was still there."

That January of 1968 the weather was severe. Snow is rare in Memphis but ice is not. The dismal, dripping winter rains freeze at night, covering the streets and viaducts with a thin sheet of ice which vanishes by midmorning. Over in public works,

Charles Blackburn, the new director, had his crews out at night
scattering cinders on the main streets. Blackburn was conscientious and conscious that he had a great deal to learn about the
public works department. This was his first city job; he had been
in insurance and spent eight years as the manager of a linen
supply company.

Early in the month T. O. Jones dropped by to see the new
director. Blackburn knew little about the union except that it
was weak. He regarded the visit from Jones as a simple courtesy
call.

A little later he got another call from Jones about a worker who
had been suspended for three days for coming to work drunk.
And toward the end of the month Jones again called to see if
Blackburn would meet with the AFSCME director of field
services who was coming to Memphis. Blackburn agreed and
the meeting was set for February 1. Still, none of these contacts
seemed very important to Blackburn.

L. C. Reed reported for work at the Sewers and Drains
Division of public works on High Street at 7:15 A.M. Tuesday
morning, January 30, as he had been doing every working day
for fourteen years since he gave up sharecropping down in
Mississippi and moved to Memphis. Memphis was better than
Mississippi. Reed and his wife, who worked in a reducing salon,
were buying their small house. They had a married daughter up
in Indiana and a baby at home. And they had their son, Oscar,
the "Golden Shoes" boy of Booker T. Washington High
School. Oscar was in his senior year at Colorado on a football
scholarship and would soon be drafted by the Minnesota
Vikings pro football team. The Golden Shoes he had won for
rushing 155 yards and making four touchdowns in one game
were displayed in the high school trophy case. L. C. Reed liked
that.

In the Sewers and Drains Division the elder Reed helped lay
sidewalks and pipes, dig sewers and lay broken-up rocks in
concrete to prevent erosion on hillsides or drainage areas.

But that morning, said Reed, "There come a shower of rain

and it rained about half an hour after we checked in and they told us to wait a while and then they come out and call it cuttin' down. So many goed home. So many stayed. The superintendent sent us home. And after they sent us leaving, the sun come out. There wasn't anything new. They cut the crew and 'fore the crew leaves the barn the sun would be shining pretty, but still us go home. White men worked shine, rain, sleet, or snow. Them supervisors just sit there till 4 o'clock and then get up and go home ever since I been here. This is not the way to do things. It just been going on.

"Well, our union president is T. O. Jones and he got wind of this day. He have some stewards there so that if anything happen to any of the mens on our trucks, you're supposed to report it to the stewards and they report it to T. O. So they did report this."

Twenty-one of the men were sent home. There was nothing new about this "cutting down." Garbage collectors could work in the rain, but outside construction work such as digging sewers presented difficulties. Recent practice had been to devise some other type of work for rainy days, and to cut the crews because fewer laborers were needed. Since they were then paid only two-hours show-up time if they didn't work, the men who were cut or laid off for the day were rotated. Supervisors and truck drivers were not cut.

The new director Blackburn knew nothing of the men being sent home until he got a phone call at his office the next morning telling him that T. O. Jones was holding the sewer and drainage crews at the barn and "would not let them go out on the trucks to work." When he arrived at the barn, Blackburn found the union leader perched on a table in the middle of the men. T. O. agreed to send the men on to work and he would talk to Blackburn for them. In all, several hours of work were lost.

Jones and Blackburn talked for another half hour, somewhat at cross-purposes. Jones wanted a full day's pay for the men sent home, but was willing to settle for less. Blackburn was irritated over the work delay and over the fact that Jones had held the men off the trucks without attempting to solve the grievance.

"Actually, the union had a grievance procedure," Blackburn observed. "It was not a written procedure, but if one of their members had a grievance, he could go, probably with the union steward, to the department superintendent with this problem. If it could not be resolved there, it would be brought to the director of public works. Mr. Jones had made no attempt to handle this in the proper manner. He was actually holding our people there, to keep them from going to work!"

Blackburn reported telling Jones flatly that the men would not be paid for hours they did not work, but he did agree that the department policy of cutting men who wanted to work should be studied and possibly changed. Jones was under the impression that Blackburn would also get the twenty-one men more money than the two hours show-up pay. But when the next paycheck was issued the following week, T. O. Jones checked among the men. They reported they had not received any extra pay.

Blackburn worked on the "rainy day" guidelines for several days before posting them in final memorandum form on the employee bulletin boards. The memo stated that Sewers and Drains would try to see that all men got a full workweek even in bad weather. It might not always be possible, but the superintendents would do their best.

He also kept his scheduled meeting with visiting AFSCME field services director P. J. Ciampa and Jones on February 1. Ciampa brought up the need for establishing a grievance procedure, which Blackburn dismissed by saying there already was one even though it was not written. Ciampa also brought up the question of a payroll checkoff of union dues and offered to send information about other cities in Tennessee which had dues checkoff systems for city employees. Blackburn was not sure what his opinion of a dues checkoff was, but he was sure that any decision on it would exceed his authority. They chatted about other matters, but all three men expected a continuing dialogue and their parting was cordial.

T. O. Jones drove Ciampa out to the airport. It had been raining off and on all day and it was after working hours as he drove back toward town. Then he saw one of the department assistants in a city car racing toward the Democrat Road sanitation installation. Jones followed to see if anything was wrong.

"You haven't heard?" asked the assistant when Jones caught up.

"No. What?"

"Two men have been killed. On one of the garbage packers."

"He was standing there on the end of the truck, and suddenly it looked like the big thing (the compression unit) just swallowed him," said a woman who had been looking out her kitchen window. "He was standing on the side and the machine was moving. His body went in first and his legs were hanging out."

"The motor started racing and the driver stopped and ran around and mashed that button to stop that thing," said one of the crew riding in the cab of the truck. "I didn't know what was happening. It looked to me like one of them almost got out, but he got caught and just fell back in there."

"I didn't know at the time someone else had already been crushed in the thing," the woman told the newspaper. "It was horrible."

No one ever said whether it was Echol Cole, 35, or Robert Walker, 29, who almost made it out before the edge of his raincoat got snagged in the grinder.[5]

The truck, a barrel-type unit called wiener-barrel by the men, in which garbage thrown in the sides was mashed toward the back by a hydraulic ram, had completed the day's route and was heading toward the dump. The rain had been heavy. Cole and Walker had not worked as garbagemen for very long. Instead of using the steps and handholds on the outside of the truck, they were standing inside next to the ram. Somehow the electrical apparatus on the compressor shorted out, perhaps by a shovel shaking loose and falling across the wires. The mashing mecha-

nism began to work. Neither man could stop it. The stop button
was on the outside. These trucks, which had come into use ten
years before, were being phased out, but six were still in use.

"We had complained about faulty equipment," said T. O.
Jones. "We had told them."

There was no workmen's compensation. Neither man had life
insurance. The city paid the families back pay, an additional
month's salary and five hundred dollars toward burial expenses.
Mayor Loeb and Blackburn considered this a moral response;
it was not a legal necessity.

The union added "safety program" to the top of its list of
demands. The city began an investigation and held the trucks
out of use until they were cleared for safety. The public read the
story and shuddered. Down in Sanitation the men didn't talk
about it much, but the incident tugged at the periphery of their
thoughts like a nightmare on the edge of waking. They had seen
the hydraulic ram in action.

Several days after the men were killed, attorney James Manire,
who did part-time legal work for the city, got a phone call from
Mayor Loeb asking him to drop by his house. There seemed to
be some rumors of a strike in Sanitation, Loeb said, and he
wanted to explore some of the legal ramifications.

Manire was a member of the mayor's "kitchen cabinet," a
group of prominent men from families known for their services
to the city over the years, who met with Loeb every Wednesday
morning and discussed city problems. It was a practice the
mayor had begun during his earlier term in office. The "cabinet"
was thick with lawyers because Loeb himself had no legal
training and looked for advice on legal matters.[6]

Manire arrived at Loeb's house shortly after noon that Sunday
and found Public Works Director Blackburn and city legal staff
member Myron Halle. The problem of the sanitation department was discussed in general terms, with the acknowledgment
that there were a number of accumulated grievances and that
the men had been on the verge of a strike several years before.

All four men knew a little about the efforts to organize the department. In fact, T. O. Jones had been to see Loeb shortly before the mayoral election asking if he would be able to get in to see him in exchange for support. Loeb's answer had been, "Yes, but I am giving you nothing because anybody that wants to can get in to see me." In reply to Jones' question about a union-dues checkoff, Loeb's response was, "No. No deals. If you want one, you make one with somebody else."

The current agitation was assumed to be a continuation of the same effort to organize. Loeb's intention was to leave Blackburn free to handle matters in public works and to have Manire and Halle simply standing by for reference on legal matters.

Manire was later to remember that meeting. "Blackburn was at that time trying to work matters out with the employees and had what I would consider an extremely conciliatory attitude."

The general feeling of the meeting, as the four men sat around in the Loeb den, was that while the strike rumors might be true, only a small number of the men would go out. Manire personally felt that it would take very strong leadership to pull the workers off the job because many of the men had worked for the city for many years and were older, settled men used to a regular paycheck. The meeting lasted less than an hour.

But T. O. Jones, still unhappy over the rainy-day pay, wanted another discussion with Blackburn. It was set for Sunday night, February 11.

Jones also called for a special protest meeting of public works men that same night. Four to five hundred of them were packed into the Labor Temple meeting hall. Maybe fifty of these were dues-paying members of the union. Many had never even attended a union meeting before and the shabby old hall was a hubbub.

The voices cut across each other.

"I'm saying T. O. Jones is tired of it. He said here's the time for us to do something."

"These last cats that left here said, 'Well, we can't do nothing about it. You've got a new administration that takes care of it.'

Well, that's right. Lay it in their lap."

"They was edging us up all the time. Edging us up."

"We don't have anything no how, and there ain't no need in our standing around cuz we ain't gonna get anything under the situation that we have."

T. O. Jones led the meeting and laid it out. Rotten pay: Most of them were making less than seventy dollars a week. Safety: Two men flattened in a garbage truck. Pay for rainy days: Suppose it rained all week? Union recognition: Men scared shitless to join for fear they'd lose their jobs. Prospect for change under the new city government: None.

What could they do?

A few hardcore union members were calling for a walkout. But, for the most part, these were older men, with debts, with nothing to show for the years of work except that they still survived and their families with them. They edged toward a withholding of their services yet they held back at the brink, remembered the abortive walkout of a year-and-a-half before. They sent Jones to his scheduled meeting with director Blackburn with a list of their demands. T. O. Jones would negotiate for them. They would wait to hear what Blackburn had to say. They had waited before.

Blackburn and his assistants Maynard Stiles and Charles Woodall met with Jones and several union stewards who came with him in the director's office at 8:00 P.M. Blackburn, still thinking the meeting was to discuss the rainy-day pay, sat at his desk and made notes on a scratch pad.

"They had quite a list of demands," he would recall in some surprise later. "A pretty good little list of demands. I wrote them down as they mentioned them. They wanted $2.35 per hour for the laborers (scale was $1.65 to $1.85); $3.00 an hour for truck drivers (scale was $2.10); time-and-a-half for overtime over eight hours; deduction of union dues; participation in the safety program; sanitation trucks to drive more slowly. The next item was a charge of $6.97 to a man named Gene Faulkner for a replacement suit of rainwear. We never did finish that one. I don't know whether Mr. Faulkner lost his rainwear or tore it up. They were all issued rainwear....when they got a replacement suit they were charged for it.

"The next item was a newsletter. I believe that I misunderstood what Jones was thinking about there. I believe that he was thinking about a press release recognizing the union. I was thinking he wanted a newsletter put out by the public works department, an informational type of bulletin like so many businesses do. And again we got back to the six hours (rainy-day) pay they now wanted for the twenty-one men."

The demands were oral. Jones read them from a piece of paper in his hand. Blackburn's response was that he felt he had already stated his position on the rainy-day pay. He thought a department newsletter was a good idea, but that was not what Jones was after. He promised to check into the policy on lost or destroyed raingear. He welcomed the group's participation in any safety program, agreeing that sanitation trucks on the highway should not exceed forty miles an hour. He was hopeful that the department would some day be working with four-man crews and trucks with cabs that four men could fit into.

On granting union recognition and a union-dues checkoff, he told them that any such agreements or contracts were the mayor's prerogative, although he personally thought Tennessee law precluded a municipality from making a contract with a union. And he could not agree to raises or overtime when he had inherited a deficit in his department.

Response to his suggestion that union leaders go to see the mayor was short. "They didn't want to see any mayor in any plush office. They wanted an answer right then and there." Blackburn then agreed to present their demands to the mayor, but he insisted that he could not support all of them.

"You're not gonna do anything for us," said one of the union stewards. "It's the same old runaround."

Another of the stewards recalled, "I said, 'Well, the mens want an answer.' And they said, 'We are in the red. We ain't got no money, ain't seein' no raise in sight.' "

"I knew it was out to go back to the men and say, 'We didn't get anywhere but give me till tomorrow.' I knew that was out," said T. O. Jones.

He tried one last approach. Would Blackburn and his assistants return with him to the union hall and explain matters to the men? Union steward Nelson Jones chimed in, "We got to tell the men something when we get back down there because the men got their minds made up and they want an answer."

For the first time Blackburn realized that a group of workers were waiting for his answers. And that this meeting was not routine at all.

But he refused to go before the full meeting of the men. "There was no use in me going down to be presented with a bunch of demands that we could not possibly accomplish by the following morning."

At this point T. O. Jones left the meeting and returned in gray work khakis and jacket. "Call the chancellor," he said. "I'm ready to go to jail."

Blackburn was honestly bewildered. "Why are you going to jail?"

"I'll be in violation of the injunction."

Blackburn realized then that he must be referring to the 1966 strike injunction, theoretically still in effect. "That's not necessary," he said stiffly. "No one is going to be arrested."

The meeting began to break up. It was "like standing around at your house at night, when people stand in the door and don't go on and go," explained Blackburn.

Someone mentioned "tomorrow," and there was a mumble of "We're not gonna be there tomorrow."

"Even after all this," mused Blackburn, "I don't think I really believed that they would have a strike the next day, because I didn't see any great big grievance, any real reason to have caused a strike."

The large, noisy throng of men waited expectantly as one of the union stewards began his report on Blackburn's responses to their demands. Before he finished there were boos and catcalls. "He gives us nothing, we'll give him nothing," one of the men shouted. No work till they got an answer from City Hall, called another. There were yells of approval. No official strike vote was taken. They would simply work no longer. They would walk out. They would get the word around to their fellow employees.

They would not work.

T. O. Jones and several of his closest associates sat around throughout the night drinking coffee and talking. He did not notify the international AFSCME office. "I was not going to notify the international union because that international union wasn't going to do but one thing—tell those people to stay on that job and they'd come down and try to get a dialogue. And the dialogue had not worked, would not work. I made this decision....The men weren't thinking of strategy; they were thinking of justice and injustice."

That first night of the strike in Memphis, Ciampa continued meeting with Jones and the local stewards to assess the Memphis situation. From this first briefing he emerged pretty well convinced that he was dealing with a legitimate strike—that is, with a group of workers with valid complaints who were determined they would stay out of work rather than with some type of isolated wildcat action.

In terms of tactics, there were certain inherent weaknesses in the strike from the international's point of view. It was February, and it was cold. Garbage does not stink in the winter so, for a time at least, pressure on the city by individual citizens probably would not be great. A garbage strike in midsummer is quite another proposition. It also might be difficult to arouse public opinion against a mayor and city administration which had been in office only six weeks. The city would claim, and quite legitimately, that it had inherited much of the mess in public works. Memphis had a large pool of unemployed, unskilled workers, and there is little outside work available in February, so the city probably would be able to quickly hire replacement workers.

And the strikers themselves were something of an unknown quality to Ciampa. For all of their determination, how long would they be able to hold out if bills for food and rent really began piling up and if the city really began to apply pressure? They were southern blacks, generally uneducated and unsophisticated about unionism. They were older men supporting families. How much could realistically be asked, much less expected, of them? Obviously, the union's best strategy was to get some kind of initial agreement, get the men back to work, and continue negotiating.

Ciampa made an appointment to meet with Blackburn and Mayor Loeb in the morning.

Garbage Is Going To Be Picked Up

2

"Garbage is going to be picked up. Bet on it!"
Henry Loeb

They came into Mayor Loeb's office on Tuesday morning,
February 13, the union men P. J. Ciampa, Bill Lucy, Joe Paisley,
T. O. Jones, and the international's public relations man John
Blair. Blackburn, City Attorney Frank Gianotti, and his assistant
Myron Halle were there with Loeb. The office was like the
mayor, big and handsome. Its wood paneling looked rugged.
Loeb dominated it from the large desk at one end, where the
arrangement of fluorescent lighting, the slight elevation of the
desk, and the grouping of low couches and chairs around it
combined to give the visitor the feeling that he was always
looking up at the mayor—not only when the chief executive
was standing up to his full 6'5" height but even when he was
sitting down.

"He looked like he was about fifteen feet tall and he said in that
southern accent, 'Mister Chiampy, I heard a lot about ya. Glad
to see ya. Welcome to Memphis.' I said, 'I thank you, sir. Now
let's talk,' " related Ciampa, describing the first meeting.

"I didn't even know who the mayor of Memphis was when I
came in," said Bill Lucy. "But I thought that since we had such
a critical situation that it wasn't going to take a great deal of

time to point it out to him, whoever he was, and try to get our heads together to see what we could do to resolve the thing."

That was an optimistic assessment. For two days the citizenry of Memphis would witness, through newspaper stories and direct television coverage, the spectacle of the mayor and the union officials wrangling, shouting, pacing, stalking, in one instance even jostling over a microphone. But they would not see anything resolved.

Looking back, few people remembered the early issues of the strike, but everyone could recall that moment on television when Ciampa, roaring with Italian gusto, poked his finger under the mayor's nose and shouted, "Keep your big mouth shut!"

Loeb insisted that the meetings be open, that nothing be discussed behind closed doors. "By gosh," he later reported saying to Ciampa, "the meetings are going to be open. This is the public's business and you might as well make up your mind to like it."

The union people were appalled. Even City Attorney Gianotti was not entirely in favor of conducting all negotiations in a fishbowl. But there was nothing new about Loeb's insistence on open meetings. They had been his way of life as long as he'd been in politics.

A strange sort of negotiating dynamics came into effect. While the city and the union talked, reporters scribbled notes of exact quotes and the TV lights would suddenly come on, burn for a few minutes, and fade out. Instead of the normal initial assessing of the other side's positions and personnel that occurs when two sides in a labor dispute sit down together, both sides were forced into an image immediately. Outbursts of temper were frozen forever on the 10:00 P.M. telecast. It was inevitable that speaking to the public via the omnipresent media would become as important as speaking to each other.

Loeb was more of a master at this than Ciampa who lost his temper repeatedly. And as the hours went by, Loeb began to emerge as a combination Sunday-school teacher and western sheriff while Ciampa began to look like a Mafia hood sent into town to make off with the gold, the sheriff's wife, and whatever else was not nailed down.

Loeb, whose temper was well-known and given wide berth, kept cool. His classic rejoinder when pushed to the limit was "Chiampy, you son of a bitch!"—but never when the television cameras were grinding.

The mayor from the onset of the talks stood firm on his position that the strike was illegal. At the end, as at the beginning, he would say, "I was elected to represent the city and I did it....There wasn't any deviation in it or a sell out." He contended that elected officials had a special duty to protect the interests of citizens, "particularly those over sixty-five on limited income," who had no special group such as a union to represent them. Mayors of other cities might be influenced by money or votes to compromise in labor matters. He would go by the law.

Ciampa proposed that the men return to work temporarily if the city would recognize AFSCME as their bargaining agent while talks continued on a grievance system and union-dues checkoff. He offered to hold off on a discussion of money matters until some of the other issues were settled.

Loeb refused. "The mayor can't be in the position of bargaining with anyone who is breaking the law."

"What crime have they committed, Mr. Mayor?" demanded Ciampa. "They are saying they don't want to pick up stinking garbage for starvation wages. Is that a crime?"

"The facts are that you are breaking the law," Loeb answered.

"I am not breaking the law, mister," Ciampa retorted. "I don't want you to say that again unless you want to charge me with something." Loeb's frequent referrals to the strike's illegality caused the labor leader's strongest reactions.

"Come on, boss. It's a hell of a way to run a ship—standing in line on Thursday," Ciampa responded to Loeb's statement that any man with a grievance could come directly to see him during his regular Thursday afternoon open house for all citizens.

"This new administration is not going to be pushed around right off the bat in office. If it does, it's in for a mighty tough four years," Loeb said at one point.

"Oh, put your halo in your pocket and let's get realistic," was Ciampa's reply.[1]

Bill Lucy remained self-possessed and calm behind Ciampa's roaring rhetoric. He felt the mayor, who had characterized himself as stubborn as a mule and proud of it, thought there wasn't really much of a problem, that in a day or so the feeling of the men would die down and the strike would be over. And, said Lucy, "Loeb never could accept the idea that we (the international) had not planned the whole thing. He felt he was being taken a little bit."

Out at the Firestone auditorium thirteen hundred men had been gathering since late morning for their first mass strike meeting. Union steward Pete Parker, who would routinely manage the meetings until officials arrived, went over the points of the strike again and called for solidarity.[2]

Union officials arrived fresh from their meeting with Loeb to a roar of approval and T. O. Jones introduced Ciampa to all the men for the first time. "We've just come from meeting with the honorable mayor," Ciampa told them, "and the answer to the issues is still 'No!' We've got to stay together in the union to win the victory. Strength is in numbers. We must stay together for however long is necessary—a day, a week, a month."

Lucy also spoke to the men for the first time. They should go into the community and tell their neighbors and other citizens about their plight and that they should stand with the strikers and not seek or take their jobs. A person who would take a job that is yours is a thief, he continued.

Maybe T. O. Jones should lead a march of the men to City Hall that afternoon, he suggested. Both the mayor and the city council, which was meeting, would then see the strength of the union. There was another roar of approval.

The first march of the strike moved out onto the sidewalk into thin, cold, wintry sunlight. Joking and cheering, the men reached some sort of order, four or five abreast, and began the trek of several miles from the industrialized area of North Memphis to the new downtown City Hall. Motorcycle police moved in beside them in the street, strung out along the march.

At City Hall, Lucy and Ciampa went up to Loeb's office. "The men are here. You said 'Any men you want to bring down to talk to me, I'll talk to them.' Here they are."

"Bring them in," answered the mayor. Then, realizing hundreds of men were entering the building, he said, "Wait. We'll take them over to South Hall and I'll just address them, and we'll get the whole thing behind us."

The mayor, at the head of the moving crowd, was soon engulfed by men, already including several undercover policemen dressed as sanitation workers. Shouting and clapping, they swept into the auditorium building a block away, which hosted such events as the annual Metropolitan Opera tour, high school graduations, the Memphis Symphony, revivals, and the ballet.

A quick set of ground rules were agreed on. Loeb, Ciampa, and Lucy would each have a chance to talk to the men. The mayor must have known when he moved to the microphone what he was up against. He must have sensed that somehow this group of men was already beyond the old days.

But he tried the man-to-man approach that had worked so well when he himself was head of the public works department a decade before. "City employees can't strike against their employer. This you can't do. I have a responsibility as mayor to be fair to you, but I also have a responsibility as mayor to see that we don't have a health problem in Memphis. You are in effect breaking the law. Your work is essential to the health of the city and not doing your work constitutes a health menace to the city."

There was laughter and some heckling.

"It's time to go to work and it's time to talk. I suggested to these men (waving at the labor leaders) today that you go back to work. Go back to work!"

Cries of "No! No!" mingled with the laughter.

"Charles Blackburn…" the mayor began.

Loud "boos" interrupted him.

"He's a straight shooter," the mayor started again.

"Yeah, but he shoots the wrong way," someone yelled.

"They are going to have to come up with some bread and some decency or this city is going to smell a while," Ciampa told the cheering crowd.

("The crowd was naturally biased," he would comment later. "I could say nothing and they'd come screaming with me. And Loeb could be speaking some profound statement and they'd boo him.")

"After you've worked for the city for ten or fifteen years…what do you get?" asked Lucy rhetorically.

"A brand new garbage tub," promptly yelled one of the men.

The union's position was that Loeb must agree from the outset that the talks would result in actual changes. Loeb would only commit himself to a willingness to continue talking. A small jousting match between Lucy and Loeb over the microphone ensued. The mayor won. "If you go back to work, you'll be earning your salary, and we'll all be doing what we're supposed to do. And I want to remind you again that prior to this coming up we had a raise in there…"

More heckling.

Loeb, his jaw squared, was angry now, but still in control. "I have sat here and taken quite a bit of abuse and I don't appreciate it," he said in a loud, stern voice. "And I have not given any abuse back. Your jobs are important." He was almost shouting. "I promise you the garbage is going to be picked up. Bet on it!" And he stalked out of the meeting.

Not sure whether he was a little ahead in the game as a result of the auditorium meeting or decidedly behind as a result of Loeb's mounting ire, Ciampa again returned to the mayor's office to attempt further discussion. Rather surprisingly, Loeb was willing to continue talking. He knew now that only twelve garbage trucks had been manned that day, fewer than the day before, and that a direct appeal to the men obviously was not going to result in a stampede to the sanitation barns—at least not yet.

The same group began talking again and the same scenario was replayed.

"I don't care what Rockefeller did. I don't care what Lindsay did. You're talking to a country boy. This is not New York. This is Memphis. I live here and my kids live here and I am not going to play around with the health of this city," said Loeb.

"You try to put yourself in a sanctimonious little cubicle. You can't solve problems like that," retorted Ciampa.

The session closed late that night in mounting irritation. An exhausted T. O. Jones had fallen asleep on Loeb's couch.

Next morning the same group met again as scheduled. Mayor Loeb listened as the union officials spent another hour running through the issues. Then he said in effect, "Well, if there's nothing new that you have to say, I'm prepared to read to you a statement prepared by the city with reference to our position." If the workers were not back by 7:00 A.M. the next morning, the city would begin replacing those "who have chosen to abandon their jobs and their rights. I have no other choice in view of the danger to public health and welfare."

The first series of negotiations was over. Angrily, the union men left the mayor's office. Outside, four garbage trucks, manned by five regular workers and supervisors and trailed by police cars, were working their way through the downtown area. They were the only trucks out on the streets that day.

That afternoon the mayor met with Blackburn and with Frank B. Holloman, director of fire and police. Holloman canceled police officers' days off and vacations and put some of the men on ten-hour shifts. Plans were made to provide police escort for garbage trucks and police would be assigned to public works installations. Two days later Holloman was to bolster the police supply of walkie-talkie radios and of Mace, the temporarily disabling chemical spray then being touted as a crowd-control device. Against his protestations, Loeb was placed under police security. Unobtrusively and unannounced, several plainclothes policemen settled into his office and a police radio was installed. Police were also assigned to his home.

In public works, Blackburn began studying the maps and figuring how long it would take to cover the city if a small force of garbagemen worked in just one or two areas a day in addition to making emergency pickups at public institutions. Sewer, drain, and street maintenance could be handled with minimum effort for a while; garbage was the big problem.

Everyone was urged to seal organic food matter in airtight garbage bags or closed metal containers or bury it; flatten tin cans and other metal waste; and set aside papers and bottles which produced no health problems. It was against a city ordinance to burn waste or garbage.

Hiring replacement workers moved slowly, although the city was contacting every person in its job application file and Mayor Loeb went on radio to announce the city needed men. By the end of the first week, 111 replacements were ready to work and 23 trucks out of the 180 were in use.

But it was becoming apparent, as one reporter noted, that there was little chance to replace the entire public works force. "Most of the workers are Negro and the word has gone out in the Negro community."

The union began to dig in. Ciampa fired off a feisty telegram to the mayor reiterating union demands. He also hired local labor lawyer Anthony Sabella as legal consultant for the union. Among other things, Ciampa needed to be sure of his legal ground in relation to the 1966 injunction.

The city council, which had no intention of injecting itself into the dispute but which did want some first-hand information, met with first the mayor and then union leaders at the end of that first week. Loeb explained the city's position and the council expressed support. No actual vote was taken.

Union spokesmen did not fare so well. When Tommy Powell, head of the local AFL-CIO labor council, stated that Memphis, then twenty-second largest city in the nation, "has never been willing to sign a contract with any union," Councilman Tom

Todd shot back, "Why have you in the labor movement been keeping the Negroes out of your unions if you are so concerned about these poor, underpaid workers?"

"Because he knows that this union is all-Negro and he won't have to worry about taking them in," injected Councilman Bob James, taking a jab at Powell's Amalgamated Meat Cutters and Butcher Workers.

Bill Lucy stood up to say that the race question had never been raised by the union. "I'm sorry the council has seen fit to inject it now."

Councilman Wyeth Chandler, who had represented unions in his law practice, was especially incensed over the strike. "There are a lot of ways to handle the dispute," he said, "but one way *not* to....is to threaten this city with rabies or rats." Rats were one of the unspoken fears that lay just under the surface of talk about the strike. Memphis, lying along the Mississippi River, had a sizable rat population and was crisscrossed by a network of open drainage ditches to take the overflow during heavy rains. It was said that a rat could get from one end of the city to the other more quickly through the drainage ditches than a person could driving the streets. Rats would not begin multiplying during the February cold, but given a little warmer weather and piles of garbage to attract them, there was cause for apprehension.

Ciampa tried to focus on the issues of union recognition and the dues checkoff. "What would you lose by asking the men to go back to work?" Councilman James wanted to know.

"What would we gain?" answered Ciampa.

"The good will of the whole city."

"The good will of the whole city hasn't brought them any bread," Ciampa pointed out. "We are not here to coerce the city. We're not interested in alarming this city nor are we abdicating the rights of our people. We need to sit down and talk....This is not blackmail but a plea." The council thanked everybody for the testimony.

The strategy of the city was set by that first strike weekend. Clearly, if judgment of the highest court in Tennessee was to be supported, the strike was illegal. And the 1966 injunction against that abortive strike had never been wiped off the books. Just as clearly, the men were not at work; the garbage was not being picked up and the streets were not being repaired. And the way to return the work force to the job was through negotiation either directly with the men themselves or with their union representatives.

Loeb's immediate, forceful, and moralistic emphasis on the illegality of the strike brought the city into a real dilemma. How could it bargain with strike leaders who were acting illegally without itself becoming a party to the illegality? Conversely, how could the strike be settled if the city did not talk with the leaders of the men? The mayor's insistence that all negotiations be open painted him further into the corner. In private discussions both sides might have given a little. In the fishbowl atmosphere of the early talks neither side could give a thing.

Loeb sincerely thought he could reach the men on strike. He thought he could explain to them that the city government understood their problems and would take care of their gripes if they returned to work. It was this "we'll take care of you" attitude that cast him in the image of the old plantation master and this image was to be exploited by the opposition throughout the strike. What he failed to grasp early was that this group of men was groping toward more than bread and paid vacations, and when—or if—he did begin to understand, he was already too enmeshed in legalities and definitions to retrace his steps.

Loeb believed that union leaders were in town not to help the workers but to exploit them. And the city would not allow such exploitation—even if protection meant saving the men from themselves. More practically, the city was not going to allow any union to muscle in on its activities, upsetting the economic balance. The mayor was a novice on union bargaining, but there had been labor troubles in the family laundry business and he could remember his father saying that the way to fight a strike was to keep even just a little work going and gradually increase it. This gave the employer a psychological advantage as those off the job saw their work continuing without them. Some garbage was picked up every day of the Memphis strike.

And if he was a novice in labor relations, Loeb was no novice in politics. He knew that his support was centered in those classes of the city who innately distrusted unionism, in the older folks caught on fixed income in the mildly inflationary cycle of 1968, and in that cross section of the white community which longed for frugality in government, absolutist morality in leadership, and a surcease of the confusion caused by groups trying to redefine their status in the old structures of society. When he spoke, he spoke to them and for them, and they heard him loud and clear.

The two daily newspapers, both Scripps-Howard, the *Memphis Press-Scimitar* and the *Commercial Appeal,* came at once to his support, although neither had initially favored him for mayor in the fall election. In the first week of the strike a total of nine editorials appeared, all of them advising the men to return to work. In the editorials' perspective the strike, besides being illegal, was an effort by the union to strengthen its national power and to get money from the sanitation workers. The workers did deserve a raise in pay despite their obvious inability to determine who was really on their side. The city should take the strike leaders into court. The mayor's actions were fair and firm, but Ciampa was, at best, a boor. The entire city had been insulted by his behavior.

"The articles were more royalist than the king," commented Assistant City Attorney James Manire.

Supported by his associates in government and his advisors, by the newspapers, informally by the city council, the mayor now began to hear from ordinary citizens. By Saturday he announced to reporters that he was receiving "bushel baskets" of mail supporting his stand, and the claim was not much of an exaggeration.

Orange and black sticker strips began to appear around town—on car bumpers, on lamp posts, on trash collection baskets. They said bluntly:

CIAMPA GO HOME.

Ciampa had already had a long, rough-and-tumble career in organized labor. He grew up in the soft coal area of Pennsylvania where his father was a minor official in the United Mine Workers. "They have a strike and my father was part of the flying squad. And the Pinkertons rolled the car over and pretty well beat up Dad. Gouged out one of his eyes. He was just lying there. And people sent for me...." He was six years old then.

When he was grown he got into union organizing. Defense industries, construction, the United Auto Workers, finally AFSCME. He became director of field operations in 1967. "It's a professional profession...and I ply my trade as best I know how."

But, like the mayor, he made an important mistake in first assessing the Memphis situation. On the day of their first meeting, he misjudged the character of Henry Loeb. He had Bill Lucy and Jesse Epps, both southerners, on hand for advice on the tenor of the city. But he assumed Loeb was more sophisticated than the mayor actually was. Being strategy-minded himself, Ciampa initially looked upon the mayor's actions as some sort of strategic sparring before the two sides got down to the business of real negotiation. Some observers of the early talks between the two men thought Ciampa's rudeness was simply a tactic, intended to throw the mayor into the arms of the rational and unflappable Bill Lucy, the hard sell and the soft sell. But what the union was offering, Loeb wasn't buying under any packaging. Ciampa's bluster was Ciampa's way. Sometimes it worked. In Memphis it blew up a storm of controversy, but Loeb remained untouched.

In one of the most succinct comments on Ciampa, Loeb would say, "He used poor manners and poor strategy."

The workers had come off the job an unorganized group, loosely following T. O. Jones and his union stewards. Now professional leadership began to weld them into a cohesive unit. The first daily noontime meetings at the union hall were combination pep rallies and explanations of unionism and their part in it.

The men were ready to cheer, jeer, and laugh boisterously. Despite the breakdown of negotiations, the cause looked good that first week. They had crossed the line when they walked off their jobs; they had defied the city. They had even defied their cautious wives. They had not been struck by lightning nor put in jail nor cast out of their beds. And the garbage was not being picked up! They had help; the international union had come to their aid.

They cheered when Joe Paisley told them that Tennessee labor, thousands strong, was behind them and when the Memphis AFL-CIO labor council voted to support their demands.

They booed when Ciampa told them that their negotiating committee "had returned from Rome and the answer your emperor god Loeb sent to his Egyptians is still no!" and cheered and jeered together when Lucy said, "The honorable mayor, who calls himself your mayor, is going to take care of you. He's still treating you like children, and this day is over because you are men and must stand together as men and demand what you want."

"I'll bet you haven't got one honest-to-God orthodox union member in the whole crew," one labor man accused Jesse Epps. Epps just chuckled.

"Are you men going back to work?" one of the leaders would shout.

"No! No!" they would respond, on their feet and shouting back. "No! No!"

The union-dues checkoff was explained and counted as necessary for the strength of the union. They voted for the dues checkoff and filled out applications authorizing the city to deduct.

"There was a different feeling with these men than you normally feel at a union meeting," said Bill Lucy. "There was a sort of blind belief that the union and their goals were right for them, and that these things and their determination to stick with it were going to produce a victory. Victory, like beauty, is in the eye of the beholder…They felt that as long as they stood together that everything in the end was going to come out right regardless of what they had to go through in the meantime….

"Most of them were older men with a lot of time with the city, and these are usually the last to want to become involved with the union. They have the least to gain and the most to lose. But here many of the fifty and fifty-five-year-olds were more strong in their position than many of the younger men."

"They kind of reminded me of when I was a kid and my father was in the mines and he said, 'The hell with it. What have we got to lose!' " commented Ciampa.

The initial aid needed from the outside black community was in discouraging other workers from filling the now empty jobs as the city began hiring. The union also moved to apprise black community leaders of the aims of the strike. Forms volunteering aid were distributed by the men in their churches the first Sunday of the strike, and pamphlets, simple mimeographed sheets at first and then printed, were distributed along their former route, asking support for their cause.

"I did all kinds of checking," confessed Ciampa, "because I thought maybe there might be some who wouldn't distribute the pamphlets, suspicious they were laying off. After two hours of checking, well, I thought what a damn fool I was. This was a rainy, miserable day. But they said, 'Well, you said today's the day we put them out.' "

If the strike became any kind of a long haul, outside aid was going to be necessary. However, almost before it was asked, some help began to come in from the local black community, and the number of black community people appearing at the union meetings increased daily. The immediate concern of these first supporters was the gathering of food and some monies for the strikers. A group called the Concerned Citizens for Sanitation Department Workers and Families, headed by several small businessmen and ministers, held its first big rally of two thousand strikers, families and supporters at the Mason Temple Church of God in Christ six nights after the strike started. Donations of food, clothing, and household goods were called for, and a typical sack of food passed out to a striker that night contained sugar, meal, lard, coffee, canned milk, greens, potatoes, canned peas or beans, spaghetti, half a dozen eggs, and two loaves of bread.

The Concerned Citizens tackled the problem of the best way to distribute food, and at first any worker who turned up at Mason Temple was given a sack of whatever was available until supplies were depleted. It was a haphazard arrangement but everyone knew that the relief operation was only temporary and that the strike would end any day.

Union leaders, meanwhile, passed out forms to get some kind of economic profile. How many dependents did each striker have? How much money did he owe? What bills would have to be paid immediately? How many landlords could be talked into waiting for rent? Were any of them in danger of having utilities turned off? The union, said Ciampa, would call on businessmen to whom money was owed and ask for a moratorium on debt collections till the strike was settled.

By the third day of the strike banker Jesse Turner, president of the Memphis NAACP branch, which had risen to 11,502 paid memberships during that decade of civil rights, and dentist Dr. Vasco Smith, president of the black Shelby County Democratic Club, appeared at the union meeting.

"I let them know in no uncertain terms that the NAACP was behind them, that this was a racial matter and we were going to tackle it as such," said Turner.

Jesse Turner had been pushing for a long time: against his substandard Mississippi high school—"We might get no farther than halfway through a text book. What always bothered me was, what about the other part of the book? When were you supposed to learn the other part?"; after his graduation from LeMoyne College, against role casting in the U.S. Army in

World War II—"I told them I was not going to be a cook or a baker...so they made me a sergeant and put me in charge of a company of cooks and bakers!"; against segregation at Officers Candidate School where he integrated the swimming pool—"I couldn't swim! But I had to buy some trunks and just sit there in the water."

In the first black tank battalion, the 758th, he rose to captain and won the Bronze Star for bravery in the Italian campaign. Picking up a degree in accounting at the University of Chicago, he returned to Memphis in 1947 to set up an accounting office and later to join the all-black Tri-State Bank executive staff. His work with the NAACP had followed almost naturally.

Union leadership was somewhat nonplussed with Turner. They needed black support, but they were also making a try for the backing of the white community and of white labor. The current union pamphlet on the strike was calling it a matter of justice for the working man, not a problem of race. Was the NAACP willing to support the strike in a subsidiary role, on the union's terms?

The NAACP was not. "We said we had a responsibility to the men, to the sanitation workers, regardless of what the union did. So we took the position that we would go on our course whether they agreed with us or not," said Turner.

To make a distinction between blacks seeking justice and a union local made up of blacks seeking justice was whistling in the wind as far as the experience of the NAACP was concerned. Memphis was almost forty percent black. Every major public issue had a racial component. And Turner and Vasco Smith represented the fusion of political, legal, and civil rights action that had been forcing change in the city for the past dozen years.

In fact, civil rights history in Memphis was NAACP history. The local branch was large, active, sufficiently militant to hold the younger people yet established enough to keep the support of their elders.

The Memphis NAACP chapter had come into existence in 1917 in the wake of the last lynching to take place in Shelby

County.[3] Functioning at first as a verbal protest organization for the black middle class under black Republican leadership, it died out in 1928. It was reorganized in 1933 and managed to keep on an even keel up to the fifties, always a group to which black leaders paid lip service and where complaints could be brought.

Memphis' socially conscious black leaders, or "race leaders" as they were once called, had advocated varying cures for the continuous ills of the black community. There were always men who pinned their faith on education and on adopting the cultural values and business ethics of whites. By around 1920 several black businessmen were struggling to build strong economic institutions in the black community, believing that the accompanying accumulation of capital and employment that would follow held the key to success. But a series of business failures and the crushing effect of the Great Depression finally destroyed most of their hopes.

Economically, the segregated black community would remain almost totally dependent on the white. The small businesses that existed, such as mom and pop groceries, cafes, and beauty salons, served the segregated black community almost exclusively.[4] So did a few larger insurance companies and banks. Blacks employed by whites were generally in lower-paying, semi-skilled jobs. There were manufacturing jobs in the city, but whites held most of them. As late as the mid-sixties, some 47,500 families, and fifty-seven percent of the black families of Memphis and Shelby County, were estimated to have annual incomes below the $3,000 poverty level. Although the area had far more than its share of white poverty, the bulk of hunger, unemployment and underemployment, poor health and casual violence, illegitimacy and poor education were found among blacks.[5]

Politically the black community, like the rest of the city, had passed early in the century to the control of Edward Hull Crump, who built in Memphis and Shelby County one of the most powerful political organizations in the country. Crump was first elected mayor in 1910 and consolidated political control through subsequent county offices during the depression, two world wars, and the shift from rural to urban life. He remained in power, though not necessarily in office, for forty years.

The city was like Boss Crump himself, contradictory, raw below the edges of charm. Dominated early by the commerce of the river, Memphis was never the Old South of legend. In the years before the Civil War it had been a brawling, muddy, Mississippi River town, jumping-off place to the frontier Southwest, and then a railroad head. It became a cotton trade center as the hinterland farmers to the east and south began cotton planting on a large scale. There had always been slaves in the area but more and more were brought in and there was a small thriving slave market and auction square. Just beginning to recover from the Civil War, federal occupation, and a vicious race riot that began with Irish policemen and mustered-out black troops, and faced with a large influx of new black residents, the city was hit by four Yellow Fever epidemics moving up river from New Orleans between 1867 and 1880.

After the early epidemics the city began to clean up the open sewage runs, moldering wooden streets, rancid water, and mud. But there was not enough time. In 1878 fever was reported again, and by the first fever-breaking frost in October, another 5,150 Memphis residents were dead. Doctors had reported 17,000 cases of fever. At least 25,000 people had fled the city. Many never returned, including a sizable colony of Germans. The large Irish settlement along the river bottoms was devastated by the fever. Northern merchants departed and northern capital pulled back. Memphis was forced to declare bankruptcy, and for the next fourteen years remained a taxing district administered by the state.[6]

When people began moving into the city again, they came from the nearby areas of Mississippi, Arkansas, and West Tennessee. They were rural whites, Anglo-Saxon, fundamentalist Protestant, and rural blacks, uneducated and unskilled. Cotton and land would dominate the economy and the Memphis cotton aristocracy, brokers, bankers, and small industrialists, would trace their genealogical roots back to farmers and planters who moved to town. Blacks finally leveled off at about forty percent of the population, and Jim Crow laws at the end of the century only put legal sanctions on the separation of the races that already existed. Blacks had little power to affect the destinies either of the city or themselves.

Crump used the black vote. His ward men organized that vote, worked it through black lieutenants, herded it to the polls, disregarded or paid its poll taxes, and returned various small favors to the black community. The black vote would become a two-edged sword, but Crump would not live to see that. For while blacks were disenfranchised all over the South, Memphis blacks voted, never proportionate to their numbers, but enough that the precedent was set and the taste of it was on them.

Crump's legacy, on the whole, was an easily governable city, an almost sacrosanct low tax rate, a docile black population, and ingrained citizen belief in "letting Mr. Crump handle the government. He does it so well."

As the Crump machine finally faltered and began to fall apart in the early 1950s, individuals and different shifting coalitions began moving into the political void. And the black community, none of whose members had held elective public office since early Reconstruction, also began to organize politically.[7]

In 1955, there were thirty-five thousand blacks registered, nearly a fourth of the total registered vote. With the potential of a black vote beginning to show, a few blacks started filing for local offices. They always lost.

But in a circle of young black attorneys trained in northern law schools, among them Russell B. Sugarmon, A. W. Willis, and Rev. Benjamin L. Hooks, questions kept coming up. Who said the black vote couldn't be organized? Why couldn't it be organized not for the benefit of any political party but for the black community itself?

"Politics was one way of amassing a fund of power which could be used to produce some changes in the black community,"

Sugarmon would say. In 1959, with fifty thousand blacks now registered, he ran for public works commissioner in an election that thoroughly shook up the city's political processes. For it saw the creation of a black political coalition that cut across Republican and Democratic lines, the black bloc vote. Sugarmon lost, but he had polled more than thirty-five thousand votes, and the black political community had proved both to itself and to whites that the black bloc vote was a reality.

The Shelby County Democratic Club (SCDC) was its core organization, and Sugarmon estimated that by 1967 there were 125 functioning precinct groups. Blacks earned their political experience working with the SCDC. Black leaders emerged from it. White politicians even sought its endorsement.

Some gains were made. Black attorney Odell Horton was named an assistant U. S. attorney for West Tennessee. Rev. Ben Hooks was elected a judge of the criminal courts. A. W. Willis was elected to the Tennessee House of Representatives and Sugarmon and attorney J. O. Patterson, Jr., to the state senate. A few token blacks began appearing on appointed city boards and commissions.

Throughout this period the NAACP and the black political leaders fused their efforts. NAACP forces moved beyond their traditional dependence on legal moves into direct action against segregated facilities. The black lawyers worked on NAACP legal briefs; the NAACP threw its people into voter registration drives building black political power. So strong, in fact, were the NAACP and the leadership supporting it that none of the younger civil rights groups, the Congress on Racial Equality (CORE) and later the Student Non-Violent Coordinating Committee (SNCC) and even Dr. King's Southern Christian Leadership Conference (SCLC) ever gained any strong foothold in Memphis.

This NAACP pre-eminence in the growing civil rights area meant that leadership stayed in the hands of the black middle class. And in dealing with black demands, the white community had to negotiate with only one group of leaders, one organization.

For white Memphis did begin to deal with black demands, primarily through an unofficial group of business, civic, and religious leaders called the Memphis Committee on Community Relations (MCCR).[8] Its initial concern had not been with black progress but with keeping the city calm. Civic leaders had no desire to see their city become another Little Rock or Clinton. But as black pressure grew stronger, MCCR itself began working to facilitate some changes. Among its most active members were former-Mayor Edmund Orgill and attorney Lucius Burch, who both helped break the Crump machine; businessmen Arthur W. McCain and Carl Carson; the two newspaper editors Ed Meeman and Frank Ahlgren; religious leaders Dr. Paul Tudor Jones and Rabbi James Wax; and blacks such as LeMoyne College president Dr. Hollis Price as well as Turner and Vasco Smith.

The MCCR worked behind the scenes with little or no publicity. Black demands would be discussed, negotiated, and if the demands seemed appropriate and the time right—or, more commonly, if the NAACP had already filed court suits or was launching marches and more desegregation seemed inevitable—MCCR would work to satisfy them. Meetings were set up to defuse the situations, which often included not reporting in the media that more desegregation was in the offing till it actually happened.

Under federal court order, train, bus, and air terminals had desegregated early. The first suit to admit black students to Memphis State University, second largest university in the state, was filed in 1954, although it was the fall of 1958 before the first eleven students were enrolled. In the spring of 1960 the NAACP filed suit against a number of tax-supported institutions, such as parks and libraries, the city auditorium and museums, the fairgrounds and recreational facilities, playgrounds, tennis courts, and boat docks. Other targets would include rest rooms and water fountains, city buses, and the privately operated theaters, hotels, restaurants, and lunch counters.

The NAACP launched a direct-action campaign of weekly marches, picketing, and selective boycott. A newspaper boycott was called over the papers' racial identifications and refusal to use courtesy titles when referring to blacks. There were sit-ins at the fairgrounds, at libraries, at lunch counters, and there was picketing of stores.

The direct-action campaign went on for eighteen months. While numerous high school and college students were involved, control was in the hands of the adults who were always part of the demonstrations that remained nonviolent throughout. Some four hundred persons were arrested but the police, after an initial period of arrests, adopted a posture of keeping the peace rather than stopping demonstrations as long as they remained peaceful and as long as business owners did not swear out warrants. News reports of the campaign were kept low key. In November 1962, the NAACP called off the large campaign, convinced that a breakthrough had been accomplished and that progress was beginning in public facilities, and in May 1963, with the Supreme Court expressing impatience over the slowness of desegregation, Memphis public facilities were quietly desegregated, although as parks were opened, swimming pools were closed.

In private areas such as theaters, hotels, and restaurants, and in attempts to get blacks hired in places like department stores, progress was much slower.

In desegregation of the public schools, the NAACP relied almost entirely on the courts and progress was slow, each step a series of legal maneuvers. Thirteen black children entered four all-white schools under massive police protection and a news blackout in the fall of 1961. No crowds gathered; there were no incidents of violence even after all the facts were known. Under court directives the board of education speeded up its integration plans and was able to announce by 1966 that some black students were present in all formerly white "grade levels." Some 30,000 students, out of a total black and white enrollment of around 122,000, were in integrated classroom situations, some of the integration meaningful, most of it token. By 1968 the integrated-students figure was still rising and some token faculty integration had taken place, although NAACP figures still showed seventy-three percent of the students were in segregated school situations.

But Memphis had gained the reputation of a city which had gone through the difficult days of desegregation without trouble. Civic leaders spoke proudly both of racial progress and of law and order.

As the NAACP turned to the tougher problems involving the economics of black Memphis—unemployment, underemployment, lack of access to white-collar and higher paying jobs, discrimination on the job, and such issues as housing and health care—the role of the MCCR gradually tapered off. The white moderates of the coalition had never envisioned leading the kind of restructuring of community life that was required if real integration in every area was to take place.

Besides, by 1967 everyone was involved in politics. Memphis had voted in a new form of government—a mayor and thirteen-member city council—to replace the old mayor/commission form. This sealed the absolute break with the Crump years.

The mood was decidedly upbeat. Memphis, with a population approaching 540,000, stood on the bluffs above the river at the center of a rich agricultural region, once wedded to cotton but now diversifying into livestock, rice, corn, small grains, and soybeans. Lumber was a major business. It was the most important city in the wide area between St. Louis and New Orleans and its economic growth was tied to its position as a distribution center for the Mid-South.

There were many incentives to future expansion—available land, an artesian-well water supply, abundant and cheap TVA power, and a large source of labor (though much of it was as yet unskilled). From a business point of view, other incentives were low property taxes, a state right-to-work law, a low wage rate, and weak unions. Labor council secretary Bill Ross estimated that only twenty to twenty-five percent of potential union members were organized. Blacks made up less than a third of all union members.

Under the new government, seven of the thirteen city council members were to be elected from geographical districts, ensuring that blacks as well as Republicans, who were fast becoming the dominant white political party, would sit on the council. There were a mind-boggling 111 candidates for the council.

Seven candidates announced for mayor, but attention focused chiefly on three of them—the incumbent William Ingram; a former mayor, Henry Loeb; and black state representative A. W. Willis, of the Shelby County Democratic Club.[9]

Ingram announced for the "little man" and was riding a somewhat uneasy coalition of blacks and working-class whites. He had picked up black support when he had served as a city judge and had attacked certain casual and extralegal police practices and the support had continued through his mayoral term. Ingram was antagonistic to what he called the "white presidium" of the city, the chamber of commerce, the newspapers, the business and civic leaders who had, he felt, set the tone of city government and type of progress for too long. Personality aside, Ingram's tenure as mayor had not been very different from preceding ones. But there were members of the "presidium" who feared him. They did not see business and industry as consonant with populism. And leaders of the Shelby County Democratic Club feared his ability to break up the black bloc vote.

Henry Loeb had been mayor of Memphis from 1960 to 1963. He had pulled out of the office early because of problems in the family laundry business. He had also been public works commissioner from 1956 to 1960. A fourth-generation Memphian, he had graduated from Phillips Academy at Andover and from Brown University, commanded a PT boat during World War II, and married a former Queen of the Memphis Cotton Carnival. He was running under the slogan of "Be Proud Again. Elect Loeb Again."

Loeb was big, gregarious, bluntly outspoken. His years on the old city commission and as mayor had been those of the greatest push for desegregation, and while the commission as a whole was pushed by political considerations as well as private bent into opposition to integration, it was Loeb who made the strongest public statements against it.

Black political leaders had been outraged by his statements, more so, they would say, since they had supported Loeb at first. They had assumed he would help their cause because he himself was Jewish and a member of a minority. They assumed wrong. Loeb never denied his Jewish heritage, but he did not consider himself a member of a minority either. He came out of an assimilated Jewish culture; more than that, he was independent in a wide sense of the word. "Nobody owns a piece of me," he liked to say. He was independently wealthy. He was allied with no political organization. If the voters liked what he stood for, fine. If they did not, then they could find themselves another candidate. He would not compromise. He favored consolidation of city and county government, which was never achieved, through periods when it was not popular with most of his supporters. He supported the change in city government. He fought against the involvement of city employees in political campaigns. A balanced city budget was an article of high faith. He found the federal government suspect and spoke glowingly of love for flag and country. Like Ingram, he had fought at times with the newspapers, but they could not hurt him. He was more orthodox "old Memphis" than they.

There were attempts to find a white candidate acceptable to black politicians and to white moderates opposed to both Loeb and Ingram. Such attempts were abortive. In the end, the Shelby County Democratic Club leadership moved on its own and A. W. Willis came into the race. The registered black vote was around seventy-nine thousand, highest ever, although white registration was about twice that much.

In the state legislature Willis had initiated measures for minimum wage, reapportionment, and establishment of the

Office of Economic Opportunity. A member of the city's only interracial law firm, he had been involved in civil rights work for a decade and had fought for community control of the War on Poverty program. He was also president of a savings and loan company and of a mortgage and realty firm.

To many whites, of course, he was not a candidate but a symbol. Nor was his candidacy helped by a severe riot rumor that shook Memphis in midsummer of 1967, in the midst of the campaign. In June there had been widely reported racial trouble in Tampa, Cincinnati, and Atlanta, and in July heavy rioting had hit Detroit and Newark. In Memphis there were rumors that black militants were organizing; that blacks were flooding in from Chicago; that a white child had been killed in a park washroom. During a store robbery police had accidentally wounded a young black boy buying a loaf of bread, and another group of police trying to make an arrest had been confronted momentarily by a small black mob on a neighborhood street. A few Molotov cocktails were thrown and whites began buying guns. On July 28, with tension reaching its peak, Mayor Ingram and the city commission requested the National Guard. Between three and four thousand Guardsmen went on active alert that evening, brought in from their summer training camp, but the Guard was never sent into the streets. One-and-a-half inches of rain that night impartially quieted the whole affair. But a feeling of unease persisted.

And while Willis himself had entered the race with slim hopes, as the campaign went on he became convinced that with a base of black bloc votes he had a good chance at making the runoff. In the end, he wanted badly to win. And in the end, he lost in a crunching defeat that gave 47,771 votes to Loeb and 36,375 to Ingram, sending them into the November runoff. Willis got only 17,861 votes. The black voters had stayed with Ingram.

Reasons for the Willis rejection by blacks were endlessly analyzed. But whatever the reasons, the practical results were that the Shelby County Democratic Club was temporarily smashed as a political force that could deliver the vote in the black community.

In November, Henry Loeb was elected Mayor, defeating Ingram 78,740 to 66,628. Ingram had lost the white working-class areas. Loeb's black support had been infinitesimal, about two percent. No black leaders had worked for him. He had hardly campaigned in the black community at all.

A sense of bitterness and frustration swept leaders of the black community with Loeb's election, although three blacks had been elected to the city council. "You had the Negro community at a very critical point," said criminal court judge Rev. Ben Hooks. "They were disheartened. They were discouraged. And they had...a feeling that the political process is a fraud. We did what we were told to do if we wanted to have freedom. We registered. And we voted...We voted for the man that we believed was for the best interest of the city and he was defeated—by a segregationist!...After all these years of being cooperative citizens, there were not enough white people to join with us to give us a decent mayor...And the prospect was of four years of Henry Loeb."

So while early in the strike labor council secretary Bill Ross would say, "The strike is nothing more than the revolt of the public employees—call it race or civil rights or whatever you want to," the NAACP called a press conference to announce support for black strikers and the Shelby County Democratic Club steering committee did the same.

But out at the union meeting, Rev. S. B. (Billy) Kyles, as NAACP spokesman, was not allowed to read the group's support resolution to the strikers. He was told anything read at the meetings had to be checked first. The NAACP representative was understandably irked.

Contempt in My Heart

3

"And I even stood up and clapped for him—
with all the contempt in my heart."
Eddie Jenkins

Across the winter South, gray, wood-smoked and bare-branched, over in Atlanta, Martin Luther King, Jr., stayed close to the supportive center of his home, wife and four children, and the pulpit at Ebenezer Baptist church early in that new year. He had just turned thirty-nine years old.

He was in Washington early in February for a peace rally as grim news of the North Vietnamese and Viet Cong attacks across South Vietnam in the Tet offensive sent U.S. hopes for quick victory stumbling in retreat. The divisions over Vietnam War policy would intensify and color everything now—from the Oval Office through Congress and into the streets. He then began to move out of Atlanta on short trips to drum up enthusiasm for the Poor People's Campaign, now set for April.

In Memphis, while the main publicity swirled around City Hall and the union, the black clergy began to move quietly on the outside edges of the strike controversy. On the second day of the strike, Dr. Roy Love, president of the black Baptist Pastors Alliance, called a meeting.

These men were familiar with the past attempts of the sanitation workers to organize. Many of the workers were members of their congregations. And they knew the mayor. "He speaks with clenched teeth," one of them remarked. They were ready to move into their traditional role of interpreting the strikers' demands to the community at large.

Rev. James Jordan, pastor of the historic Beale Street Baptist Church, was appointed chairman of a committee to look into the strike. "Wouldn't it be nice," one of his group suggested, "to call in some of our white brethren to sit down and discuss this whole thing." Rev. Jordan was one of the few black ministers to have regular contact with his white counterparts. He belonged to the ecumenical Memphis Ministers Association.[1]

The ministers association was made up of some hundred ministers, most of them white. Its counterpart in the black community was a smaller, ecumenical Ministerial Alliance. A few blacks had integrated the white association several years before, about the same time some Catholic priests also became members. This year, as if proving the organization's diversity, a Jewish rabbi was president, a black Methodist vice president, and a Catholic priest secretary. There was no thought of merging the association and the alliance, but many of their members were acquainted with each other and there was a cordiality between the groups. An ecumenical and interracial agency for inner-city ministry was in the talking stage, and on the Sunday before, the day when the union decided to strike, the ministers association had celebrated "Race Relations Sunday." For the first time in that civil rights decade, the ministers of the association had issued a public joint statement on the immorality of racial prejudice. The greatest response, outside of members of their own congregations, was silence.

Yet Memphis was a church-oriented city, eighty-eight percent Protestant, ten percent Catholic, two percent Jewish. Newcomers were asked their church affiliation as casually as their names. The chamber of commerce listed 1,161 clergymen and was able to boast of more churches, some seven hundred, than gas stations. In white Memphis the larger churches rode the landscape easily, white-spired, buttressed, columned, languid on broad green lawns. They swept into view on nearly all of the main arteries leading east from the center of the city.

But religiously this was fundamentalist territory. This was the land the Southern Baptists had hewed out. There were some hundred thousand white Baptists in Memphis and the county and almost as many black Baptists. Most Baptist churches presented a far more utilitarian, red-brick, no-nonsense approach. They stood closer to the sidewalks. Their leaders knew the fight against sin was unending and deplored the cavalier attitudes of some of the more dilettante denominations toward the dog racing track just across the bridge in Arkansas or toward liquor.

Under church influence Memphis was still a "dry" city. The legal sale of mixed drinks, or "liquor by the drink," had been defeated in a referendum just the preceding summer.

There was no public anti-Semitism or anti-Catholicism. The most vigorous "anti" feeling was aimed at the "liberal" clergy-man, either theologically or on the scene of social issues. Memphis' fundamentalist believers, like those across the rest of the South, were in the tradition of that religion that had surged across the early Appalachian frontier with the somber Presbyte-rians, the Methodist circuit riders, several kinds of Baptists, the independents. They had preached the only kind of religion that made sense in the individualistic and often dangerous life of the early settlements, a highly personal, pietistic and provincial form of Christianity that placed pivotal importance on personal conversion, on being "saved." When sin was torn from the individual in particular, then it would be torn from society.

This concept of religion as a totally personal experience was so ingrained that those white southern ministers who did begin to get involved in social problems found themselves at best leaders without followers and at worst accused of subverting a mode of thought which their own culture had fostered.

Memphis' inner-city Methodist district superintendent Rev.
Frank McRae commented, "We're fine to give invocations at
football games and annual meetings. We have to have the
church as we have to have other parts of our culture. But as far
as being a dramatic, dynamic, motivating force in this community—I don't think we are...This is particularly true in social
matters where we're just generally forbidden to go. This has
been our history—to leave social issues alone."

The relationship of white to black churches in Memphis had
always been an ambivalent one. As the pastor of one very large
Baptist church explained, his congregation had no Negro
members. "But I go out and help our Negro churches and raise
money for them...when we have money in our treasury here and
they get in a jam, they come to me and we'll help them."
Negroes didn't want to come to his church anyway, he chuckled. Their own preachers were better. He thought the church
should take stands on social matters, but change had to be
gradual and it must not go to extremes.

"Some of our churches have quit preaching the Gospel of
Jesus Christ, the power of the Atoning Blood, His vicarious
suffering, the great fundamental truths of Christianity...and
have started majoring on social matters."

He spoke for a large segment of the white clergy in Memphis,
yet there were others with gnawing doubts, even though they
too encouraged black Christianity, did the right things for the
poor and needy. And there were a few who had broken through
tradition and congregational opinion in pursuit of a different
kind of understanding. But the country in which they moved
was uncharted and they were forced to almost feel their way.

However, prayer, being good wherever offered, went up
publicly from the pulpits, the schools, the political rallies, the
businessmen's breakfast, the chapel at the headquarters of
Holiday Inns of America, Inc.

Why, then, did the black ministers now call upon the white
ministers for help?

Even this early in the strike the ministers in Rev. Love's group knew that the sanitation workers would need all the help they could get. And they believed that the white clergy had a power to mold white opinion—that of the city administration and that of their congregations. They, too, had been treated for decades to the sight of the white ministers offering public prayer. Surely these white ministers were the moral force of the city. Surely they and the white clergy were brethren in some encompassing sense. Surely this time the white ministers, if they understood the importance of the strike, would help.

Some of the white ministers sensitive to race relations were already alerted to the strike's growing importance in black thinking. Rev. Ezekiel Bell, pastor of Parkway Gardens Presbyterian Church and the only black member of the Memphis Presbytery, had already come to a presbytery meeting to ask for strike support. But the ministers were worried about the legality of the strike and felt they needed more information. For a number of other white ministers the strike was raising disturbing questions.

When Rev. Jordan brought his small group of black and white ministers together all of them expressed concern about growing racial tensions. It was agreed to work through committees already set up in the Memphis Ministers Association and to try to bring the mayor and union officials back together to talk again.

Ciampa received their small committee at 10:00 P.M. that Friday night, February 16, in his hotel room.[2] The union leader had spent a harried day trying to reopen lines of communication with the city. On top of that, he was quartered at the famous Peabody Hotel, whose lobby was commonly called "the place where the Mississippi Delta begins" and where live ducks swam in the lobby fountain and with trumpet fanfares were escorted over a red carpet to their rooftop roost late every afternoon, a bit of local tradition that left Ciampa gasping. If he regarded the group of ministers in his room as a first sign that perhaps God was not quite as displeased with his servant P. J. as the week's events seemed to indicate, he was astute enough to remain casual.

Reform Rabbi James Wax, as president of the ministers association, led off in an explanation of their visit. The ministers, he assured Ciampa and Bill Lucy, had no desire to intrude unless they could be of service to both sides in the dispute, of service to the city. They did not represent the association, their congregations or denominations, but only themselves. They were concerned about the labor dispute, but their chief concern was over the race questions beginning to surface in the strike. "We have had in this city good race relations. We've worked long and hard at it."

The ministers proposed to provide a setting of "restraint and dignity" in which city and union leaders could again begin to talk. They would themselves sit in on the discussions, but they wanted to make clear that they were not taking sides. They were not offering to mediate the dispute.

Ciampa responded with a cordiality that had not appeared in his media image. "It is I," Ciampa said, "who am justly grateful for your presence here...I told the city councilmen this morning that I genuinely, sincerely, seriously want to find a solution to this problem." The union, he said, was willing to compromise on any of the points that had been under discussion; it was willing to completely abandon none.

"The management-owner-servant attitude—there's the real crux of the thing," he told them. "It's not Henry Loeb the man. It's Henry as the philosophy...And this is more than just 'do a thousand city workers get a contract?' "

He was sharply questioned as to why a simple labor-management dispute should slip into a racial issue at all, why was he allowing this to happen?

Ciampa tried to explain. He had already been told, he said, that the strike had united labor factions as nothing had for the past twenty years. "It has united many other groups, and whether the NAACP or the Urban League or the Sons of Africa or the Sons of Italy or somebody else, it's gonna create some furor...I suspect it is not gonna be too many days until the lid blows off some hothead, and away we go....

"I have warned all of the responsible community leadership I can think of," he said, "that I am as concerned over the community relations here as I am over the labor relations. I cannot sacrifice basic principles of one thing for another. I have to accept support where I can get it."

His answer was troubling. He also quickly refused to recommend that the men return to work for a three-week cooling off period, one of Rabbi Wax's conciliatory suggestions. The meeting lasted several hours and its outcome was that Ciampa agreed to meet with the mayor under the auspices of the ministers.

Next day the mayor also agreed to the talks. However, he stipulated that his position remained the same and that the news media were to be allowed to cover the entire proceedings.

The city council held a secret meeting late that Sunday afternoon, February 18, at the home of black councilman Fred Davis. There was a need to figure out what their role could—or should—be in attempts to settle the strike. Under the seven-week old city charter, they were the legislative branch—to pass laws, set the tax rate, approve the mayor's appointments. They could approve, disapprove, or make recommendations on the budget, but the mayor ran the city departments. There had been no prior unionization of city employees and no specific labor policy was spelled out. They had no precedents to fall back on.

Their immediate intention was to help Loeb reach a settlement quickly. At Davis' house they attempted to reach no agreement on formal union recognition, although the idea of some sort of indirect withdrawal of union dues from the workers' paychecks seemed to some of them to offer a way out for the mayor. Union scuttlebutt was that the men would go back to work if they were offered an immediate pay hike. So they hammered out a recommendation of an immediate ten cents an hour increase followed by another five cents on July 1, beginning of the new fiscal year. The proposal was to be subject to the mayor's approval.

Councilman Tom Todd left the meeting early and let Loeb know what was happening. The mayor expressed disbelief. And when Councilman Lewis Donelson reached him by phone at the close of the meeting to tell him of the council's action, Loeb refused to agree. "The city is going to beat this thing," he said. Furthermore, it was his responsibility and he didn't want the council getting involved.

The council attempt collapsed.

"I really felt like Henry could be right and I could be wrong," said Donelson. "There was a serious question at this point as to whether it was a council matter...From a strictly legal point of view, it really was his problem."

Since secret meetings rarely remain secret, word was soon out among union leaders about the council's ten-and-five-cent pay raise suggestion. "I think the three Negro councilmen contacted all their friends and told them," commented Councilman Todd irritably. "We had really gotten ourselves into a mess."

From then on, despite the city council's public statements that the dispute was outside their purview, pressure increased on the council to act.

As television cameramen positioned themselves and reporters settled back, two dozen men gathered around the long tables in one of the basement meeting rooms at St. Mary's Episcopal Cathedral that same Sunday evening.[3] In the late winter darkness the cathedral complex loomed an incongruous mass of Tudor stone above the urban renewal wasteland to the front and the neighborhood of small, poor homes to its back. Mayor Loeb, City Attorney Gianotti and legal staff member Myron Halle sat on one side. Facing them were Ciampa, Lucy, Paisley, T. O. Jones, and five representatives of the strikers. At the head of the U-shaped table were some of the ministers.

Rabbi Wax presided and William Dimmick, Dean of the Cathedral, gave the prayer. "Now, may we know we stand in God's presence." With a great deal of shuffling and chair scraping, the company settled itself for the Rabbi's opening remarks. "If there is a winner tonight...I earnestly hope it will be all the people of Memphis."

He suggested that the nine specific points that had been raised in the dispute, including union recognition, pay raises, union-dues checkoff, grievance procedure, and various other procedures and benefits, be examined one by one. If discussion got bogged down on one point, they would move to the next.

But the talks ran into difficulties immediately when the city restated its refusal to talk directly to union representatives across the table unless some promise was made to end the walkout. Father Nicholas Vieron, of the Greek Orthodox Church, tried to circumvent the problem by suggesting the chair ask all the questions.

Ciampa was already chafing. "Father, please! This is an exercise in futility...We're adults here. We're struggling with serious problems. Are we going to play it like children?"

Ciampa's voice was rising. "Mayor Loeb, will you discuss the matter of recognition with me? Mayor Loeb, will you discuss the matter of recognition with me? Mayor Loeb, will you discuss the matter of recognition with me?" Loeb answered calmly, "The point I made was simply this. I feel strongly about obeying the law...There's a very strong, inherent respect for the law in Memphis. I've gone about as far as I can go until we get to the point where the law is being obeyed...My position with the union is well known. Mr. Chiampy understands it. My position with you guys (ministers) is—ask."

"How can men talk when they're not here on an equal basis?" Ciampa persisted. "If we can't agree to sit down and recognize the existence of one another...."

"I have offered the union the same status as any union with whom the city deals now," countered Loeb. "I simply say that this union is breaking the law...but I recognize the fact that the ministers association called this meeting. The ministers association can get into anything it likes. There'll be no hesitation or reservation."

"Gentlemen," said Rabbi Wax, visions of the whole peace-making effort collapsing before him. "I think we are complicating our own procedure and we are in a sense defeating our own purpose. Let's start talking. And it might well be that when we talk and reach a certain point, the situation can be changed."

"The city's ready to talk," responded Loeb.

Ciampa refused to subside. "Rabbi, if I may, I am ready to talk with the city. I'd like to ask the question—what law would Mayor Loeb be violating if he discussed the problem at hand with the representatives of the people involved?"

City Attorney Gianotti now attempted to clarify for the ministers. "Let me just clear this thing up briefly. We have talked. There's no doubt about that. We talked a couple of nights ago till we were about to lose our voices...But there's a principle involved. Whether Mr. Ciampa or Mr. Lucy wishes to acknowledge that, that's not for us to say. The Supreme Court decision—I don't see how anybody can misunderstand. It may be partly my fault. I don't know. We discussed. But I thought we could sit down and show Mr. Ciampa and Mr. Lucy just what our position was. With all of their effective position with those men, they need to tell those men in no uncertain terms—not the way they've been telling them—that these men are violating the law!

"I personally know a number of them and worked with them for fifteen, twenty, or more years. I don't believe that these men appreciate the fact that they are violating the law of the state of Tennessee, as expressed by the Supreme Court in the Alcoa case....

"Will we discuss the problems of these men? Yes, we will discuss the problems of the men in the sanitation department—with these men here—if and when you men go back to work." He looked straight at the five workers, his voice loud and carrying. "Immediately! I mean now!" He pounded his fist on the table.

"Thank you for talking to our men!" bellowed Ciampa.

"I'm sure you haven't talked to them," answered Gianotti with equal sarcasm.

"Let's keep this on a high level," warned the Rabbi.

The high pitch subsided, whether because of the presence of so many clergymen or because both sides still wanted to salvage something. A technique was finally agreed on. Each side would talk not directly to the other but at each other through Rabbi Wax. It was cumbersome, but it allowed the talks to begin to move.

Sometime before midnight another man walked into the parish hall, rumpled gray hair, horn-rimmed glasses, one leg dragging slightly in a polio limp, gesticulating hands, the sharp clipped accent of New York. The international president of the union had come to Memphis.

"I came because I realized the situation was important and the reports I was getting were very distressing," admitted Jerry Wurf. Although he was more involved up and down the line in local situations than most international presidents, he had not intended to come to Memphis and certainly not within six days of the strike's beginning.

But nothing was going right. He had sent in Ciampa, his top field man. "You send in the top of the thing because in essence you're sending a signal for a boss—a signal which means our top guy is coming in because we're available for some wheeling and dealing, because we're not unaware that a strike in a city like that without preparation, without understanding our resources— we don't even know if the local labor movement is hostile or friendly. The whole thing calls for diplomacy, sensitivity. Maybe eventually we will have to holler and scream, but that should be last, not first."

Not only had Mayor Loeb missed the initial signal, but Ciampa, his best man, "screwed up beyond belief...played right into Loeb's hands...Bad judgment on my part, is what I'm really saying...I should have sent in somebody who was softer speaking, perhaps somebody who was southern and understood the mores and the cultural relationships...Maybe calling your boss four-letter words 'cause you're rallying your workers was the right thing to do, but that ain't the way we planned it....

"I got reports of these ridiculous negotiation sessions in front of television cameras. I got other reports." Even the optimistic reports were disquieting, and a call from John Blair, the union's public relations man, capped it. "The whole thing has gotten out of hand," Blair told Wurf. "Ciampa has gotten to the point where the mere sound of his name sends tremors not only through the white community but through responsible elements of the black community. They think he's bent on suicide rather than winning a strike. We need something strong in here."

Wurf understood the usual tactical and public relations value of his own presence. He was good at his job and he knew that, too. He had come out of college in New York to organize cafeteria workers, reveling in the rough and tumble of it all. Then a member of the Young People's Socialist League, "I was a sort of Norman Thomas Socialist...I used to stand on the street corners in a marvelous place in Brooklyn called Brighton Beach, which probably had more members of the American Labor Party when it was Communist-dominated than it had Republicans or Democrats. And I was fighting all these big mouth Stalinists with my own hot little hands and making them angry as hell. We had much more fun fighting them than fighting capitalists."

He went with AFSCME in 1947, and headed New York City's District Council 37. Its membership had jumped to forty thousand by the time he became president of the international. "In the district council I come from we practically pioneered the concept of the public employees' strike."

People around the district council 37 headquarters had been involved with early civil rights attempts, such as CORE, and Wurf himself, though he would have shrugged it off, retained much of his early idealism about unions, believing AFSCME in particular had an obligation to help the most exploited. "The need for a fellow who drives a sanitation truck in New York and earns ten thousand dollars a year is a serious need," he said. "He has a need for a union and he has a need for protection. But the fellow who drives the sanitation truck in some southern city and makes three or four thousand dollars a year, he has an even greater need and we were aware of this."

So in he came—Brooklyn-born; Jewish; soon to sit on labor's highest governing body, the national AFL-CIO executive council; renowned among his closest associates for his blunt speech and quick temper; given to long speeches; content at the symphony or ballet; a labor "agitator."

"I live in fear when I use that word," he once said. "Even with my own staff it is misunderstood. Good agitators are hard to come by. I consider myself a good agitator. This doesn't mean somebody lacking in responsibility. This means somebody who has the capacity for moving other men in a direction that makes sense, that's meaningful."

He came to Memphis determined to hold a reasonable posture and that night the mayor met him halfway. Loeb essentially had written off Ciampa. Wurf he would deal with. After a brief recess, all of the parties returned to the table and substantive talk began. It was 5:00 A.M., cold and dark in the winter morning, when they finally adjourned. Loeb earlier had again rejected exclusive union recognition, offered civil service and his "open door" policy for grievances, and refused to consider a union-dues deduction, stating, "The union would like for us to reach in the men's pockets." But after Wurf's arrival the union did lay on the table its first new proposed wage scale, which was somewhat lower than the original demands.

The talks continued at various hours for three days, First Methodist and St. Peter's Catholic churches offering their parish halls, the ministers desperately anxious that some movement occur.

And sometime during the course of those talks Wurf made what he thereafter considered a "serious tactical blunder from a trade union point of view." As a solution to the dues checkoff problem, he suggested that union dues be deducted from the men's paychecks through the offices of the independent employees' credit union, rather than directly by the city. It was a long-range solution. It could have been reached as a compro-

mise later on, but Wurf threw it on the table too early and when
Loeb immediately rejected it, there was no place to go. On that
issue they were stalemated. The dialogue became bitter, the
mayor holding that the city and the credit union should in no
way be involved in collecting union dues and Wurf protesting
that the credit union was not the "servant of the city...but of
those who are members of it." The credit union, he insisted,
could collect payment monies for dues off the top of the
paychecks in the same way it collected repayment monies for any
other kinds of loans for furniture or cars or whatever.

To make the suggestion about the credit union at that
meeting "was incredibly stupid," Wurf said. Yet from the
beginning in Memphis he was uneasy about possible violence.
"I was appalled by the hate mail Ciampa was getting...There is
always some hate mail, but never like this, and it was bitter and
vicious....He apparently had touched nerve endings...."

And Wurf was impressed by Rabbi Wax's call for a solution.
"Wax made a very eloquent speech and I, who am a speaker and
have listened to a million speeches, was impressed. And Wax
talked about us bringing peace to the situation or the rednecks
would come across the bridge and the town would burn....He
really carried on both in terms of the possibility of violence and
about the division that would take place between the races....

"This was a time which was sort of the beginning of a
realization among those of us who had been devoted to
integration that perhaps black leadership was no longer sold on
integration. Whites were no longer sold and polarization was
becoming a way of life. Black Power was frightening because
it, in effect, meant a complete end to all our efforts and dreams.
Wax dealt with that....and impressed me in a way that I'm almost
ashamed to confess. I think he was sincere...he struck me as an
honest man. Perhaps I was prejudiced by the fact I was pleased
to see a rabbi playing an important role. Who the hell knows?

"But I really was impressed by Wax and convinced that
Armageddon was twenty-four hours away, and made a cold
decision after conferring with my colleagues, to get down to the

nitty-gritty and give our ultimate position on dues checkoff....Because there was a way to get the dues deduction without the city giving it to us—the credit union...There were ways to get through these things so that these guys (the city) could preserve their posture, save face, deal with reality....I was convinced that we show our aces, give the mayor his way out. What we did was foolish. What he did was idiotic. Instead of taking it—if he had no desire right then to give—and tucking it away, he took it and threw it away and then it was gone....Loeb was not the least bit ready to deal...out of intransigence, stupidity, lack of experience, he took our position and threw it away."

These sessions, too, were beginning to deteriorate. By Wednesday, the fourth of the sessions and the tenth day of the strike, union leaders were expressing complete frustration and threatening to walk out, and Wurf was moving into a stance almost as tough as Ciampa had taken the week before. "We won't come on our knees and beg for mercy," he snapped once at the idea of Loeb's open house as a grievance channel, comparing it to feudal days when citizens appeared at court to ask favors.

Rabbi Wax left for his Florida vacation and was replaced as chairman by Dean Dimmick, who continued to be publicly optimistic. At least everyone was still talking. But to reporters and observers, it was apparent that the clergy-sponsored meetings were reaching the end of the line.

Wurf had brought a check for five thousand dollars and was cheered wildly when he presented it to the local. He began working with the men at the daily union meetings. "We must stick together and God will help us win," Jesse Epps intoned, and no one doubted it. A boycott was called on the Loeb chain of Bar-B-Ques, many attached to coin-operated laundry and dry-cleaning establishments, owned by the mayor's brother, William. The two brothers had reportedly been feuding for years, and the Mayor had divested himself of all interest in the chain, but the union was seeking pressure points on the city's leaders. The Loeb Bar-B-Ques in black neighborhoods would be hit by sporadic window breaking later in the strike. A boycott also was called against Pryor Oldsmobile, the car dealership of the city council chairman Downing Pryor.

The union now was estimating that it would take at least $15,000 a week for food, shelter, and emergency aid for the strikers and their families. The Memphis Light, Gas and Water Division had agreed to a two-month grace period on utility bills, a practice it had followed in several earlier emergencies. But the food supplies collected by the Concerned Citizens relief group were almost cleaned out.

One of the leaders of the relief group, O. W. Pickett, came now to tell the mayor that some of the strikers' youngsters were hungry. The situation was serious, he reported. A call was immediately put through to the state commissioner of public welfare, asking that he expedite methods for getting food stamps for the strikers and put the city on the line for ten thousand dollars to pay for them. "Food stamps came out of the general assistance commission budget, the welfare commission, which was an emergency operation in the city and county, jointly run," explained Loeb's administrative assistant Jerrold Moore. "There were some excess monies at that time, so it didn't require an appropriation above the established budget."

"We aren't fighting children," said the mayor.

One hundred fifty-four replacement workers had been hired. Some garbage was being picked up, though some sections of the city had had no collection for nine days. Garbage cans were becoming a hot sales item.

The NAACP turned out some eighty people for an all-night vigil around City Hall, including Wurf and other union representatives as well as Jerry Fanion, named just a few months before to the newly created position of community relations director for Shelby County, and Baxton Bryant from Nashville. Bryant was director of the Tennessee Council on Human Relations, a private human relations educational organization, foundation-funded, which had been working in the state for fifteen years. The Tennessee council had some two thousand members scattered in small chapters. Bryant had been in Memphis just the month before trying to set up meetings on police/community relations.

On Tuesday, February 20, the striking workers picked up the last paycheck for the period before the walkout.

A warm aura of civic pride and mutual esteem enveloped the banquet hall of the Holiday Inn-Rivermont, the expensive motel overlooking the river, the next night. Fourteen hundred people were gathered for the annual Brotherhood Award Banquet of the Memphis Roundtable, the local chapter of the National Conference of Christians and Jews. Frank Ahlgren, editor of Memphis' daily *Commercial Appeal*, was receiving the Brotherhood Award.

Ahlgren was considered by many to be the most powerful man in the city. He had fought the good fight for civic improvements, solid conservative government and culture. And if, in retrospect, he had not exactly laid his neck on the block on the racial question, at least he had been solid and respectable. The *Commercial Appeal* had never condoned actions of the Klan or the White Citizens Councils. It had not been enthused either with the tactics of Martin King or the civil rights movement. They were an affront to the slow and rational sort of racial progress in which Frank Ahlgren believed. He had worked long and hard with the quiet group of business and civic leaders who had brought most of the legal desegregation in Memphis.

The city's leaders gave him a long and loud ovation now, joined by political leaders from across the state and representatives of the far-flung Scripps-Howard enterprise.

Mayor Loeb arrived late to the banquet, bringing as his surprise guest Jerry Wurf, both straight from that day's collapsing clergy-sponsored talks. Wurf was not too enthused about dining with what he considered the religious establishment. " 'Let's take a Jew to lunch this week' never impressed me as a substantial effort to save the world," he remarked. He also was feeling alien to Memphis' southern Jewish community. Wurf usually took his Jewishness as a simple matter of self-definition.

But in Memphis he was acutely and wryly conscious of it, bemused that no liberal Jewish faction had come forth in support. And he had no great desire to face the correct but cool reception he suspected he would get on such a civic occasion.

But he and Loeb had been arguing again and the strike had to be settled. "At some point I said to him, 'Look, you silly son of a bitch, I'm not getting out of town....You know in the long run you can't win and in the long run you've got to live with us....I'm not going to leave Memphis. The union is not going to leave Memphis. You can beat us on Monday, Tuesday, Wednesday, Thursday; we'll come back on Friday....You got to understand that we cannot walk away from these men. Just can't. I can tell you it's a moral issue. I can tell you it's a pragmatic political issue. I'm just telling you that this is it.'

"And he began to give me this bull about if I was a Memphian, if I understood, and I told him that was a lot of shit. And he went on—but he was not in anger—and he said, 'Son of a bitch, you're getting to me. Why don't we go to this banquet tonight...perhaps we can get to talking to each other.' "

Mayor Loeb had been scheduled to sit on the dais. Instead the two men slipped quietly into seats at the back and into the air of general well-being that filled the room.

Except—there was Eddie Jenkins.

The Memphis State University ROTC Glee Club sang at the banquet. Jenkins was a member and at twenty-one already a married man with an infant son. He was also a member of the newly formed Black Students Association at Memphis State.

"After we sang, I happened to come out and I was looking for a place to sit. And all the guys sit down, you know. Already I was nervous. This was the first time I'd ever been to a thing like this, where people had on their formal bit and all, and I'm looking at all this different stuff on the table—forks and all this stuff— and I was halfway confused. I wanted to sit with some of the guys. Some of the white guys and some of the black guys, too, had waited tables and really knew what was going on and what to do, and I wanted to sort of pattern myself after them. So they all sit down, crammed around a table, and there wasn't any place for me. So I said, 'I'll sit over here.' I sit down and I looked around—and I looked at Henry Loeb.

"He was sitting by me. Jerry Wurf was across the table. Loeb turns around, you know, being a politician. 'My name is Henry Loeb.' I turned around and shook hands with the man. Just to show you how far you can progress in so little time, I turned around and shook hands with the man, and told him how proud I was to meet him and all this bit.

"And I even stood up and clapped for him—with all the contempt in my heart—lying to the white man again. I stood up and clapped for him when they introduced him over the mike and finally made him stand up."

The mayor had to rise twice before the ovation subsided.

"There was a bunch of us token niggers down there—all of us clapping and saying 'Yeah! Yeah!' All of us doing that. But I noticed Jerry Wurf didn't stand up. He didn't clap a lick.

"So I think, 'Well, here we are.' I saw this as an opportunity to really get the info right off the top. We were sitting there, you know. He asked me where I was from. He was very interested.

"So I said, 'Why are you holding out on the strikers?'

"And he said, 'I can't hear you with all this noise in here.' They were constantly introducing people and clapping.

"So I said, 'Why are you holding out?'

"Jerry Wurf said, 'You heard him. He asked you why you're holding out on the strikers.' He made some slight remark about Loeb and Loeb went 'Ha. Ha. Ha.'

"Loeb told me, 'We can't really talk in here. I can't hear you. I tell you what. I'll call you later tonight.' He pulled out this little pad and he took my number. He said he'd call."

Mayor Loeb did call that night, but Jenkins hadn't reached home yet. "I was very much surprised. I thought, gee whiz, maybe the guy ain't so bad after all. And then he wrote me a letter. I thought, maybe he is trying to be relatively fair. Maybe we just got him all wrong. And then I opened my letter and read it. And I thought, 'Oh well, I can just put this away and forget

about him being fair and square. It's the same old bag.'
Knowing what these people were going through, living with
these people, I couldn't accept this about being 'fair and firm.'

"Later I went down to talk to him at his Thursday open house.
He said, 'I respect your opinion.' Well, my opinion was the same
as thirteen hundred other people's. He didn't even consider it."

Several members of the city council had also been at the
banquet, seated together at a front table, as Councilman Fred
Davis explained that his public works committee was setting up
a meeting for the next morning. They wanted to question some
of the strikers directly about their problems. It would be helpful,
said council Chairman Downing Pryor, to have as many other
members present as possible. There was a need to listen to the
men themselves.

Councilman Bob James noted glumly, "The worst thing that
happened was when the council decided it would hear some of
the grievances."

Planted by the Waterside

4

"I'm planted by the waterside,
like a tree planted by the roots."
Ed Gillis

Councilman Fred Davis approached the February 22 hearing of his committee on public works confidently. Despite the mayor's disapproval, he was convinced the council had a duty to help end the strike and would if the strikers themselves could state their grievances without the union getting in the way.

Davis was acutely conscious also of his position as one of only three black members on a council of thirteen. He was in a unique position to draw attention to black problems. And it was vital that he show a face of moderation and responsibility.

His council position had not come easy. Even now he remembered the lazy flying of the buzzards as they dipped and glided above the cotton fields in those deep autumns when his mother took him out of school and across the river to pick. He came up through school delivering groceries, washing pots, working his way up to waiter in the skyway of The Peabody hotel. At Tennessee A & I State University he majored in accounting, mopped floors, served parties. From an Army hitch in France, he came back home and into insurance.

He was good at the insurance business. There was a stuttering sincerity about him. And he became good at something else—

politics. Aligned with the black Democratic wing, he organized his insurance area, Orange Mound, small, trim, into precinct clubs, initially composed of policy holders. He took part in the early sixties' civil rights campaigns in Memphis, was arrested in the move to open the fairgrounds, turned out his entire family, pregnant wife, baby in stroller, pre-school daughter, to protest double shifts in the schools.

His geographical council district was fifty-two percent white. His white support had come from various quarters—old liberals, friends of Sugarmon and Willis' integrated law firm, a couple of newspaper people. He campaigned with an integrated team. When the results came in from the first polling precinct, he knew he had won the council seat. "I had got me some white votes on that first box." So it was not without a sense of self-satisfaction that he looked out over the council chamber.

The meeting began smoothly enough. Councilmen Lewis Donelson and Rev. James Netters, who was substituting for the out-of-town Billy Hyman, sat with Davis at the long curved table on the dais. They faced the rosewood-paneled and scarlet-carpeted chamber. Below the dais and set off by a railing from the padded black leather spectator seats were several tables for city staff who might be needed for background information at council meetings. Citizens addressing the council stood at a microphone, directly facing the council members. A huge city seal of Memphis with steamboat, cotton boll, oak leaf for hardwood, and gear for industry hung on the front wall.

Other council members, Downing Pryor, Jerred Blanchard, Bob James, Wyeth Chandler, and Gwen Awsumb, were present off and on during the session, sitting sometimes up front with the committee and sometimes with the spectators.

Mayor Loeb was also an observer during part of the morning. In the afternoon he would go over to St. Peter's Catholic Church, wait vainly for Jerry Wurf to show up from the council chamber, and leave. The union, he declared, had broken off the clergy-sponsored talks.

Wurf and Loeb would not talk again for a very long time.

In the council chamber were a group of public works employees, union leaders, community supporters of the men, and a
number of black ministers, encouraged to attend the hearing by
strike sympathizers.[1]

"Now, who would like to speak?" asked Davis.

The first person to rise and make her way up front was Cornelia
Crenshaw, who had been working with food distribution for the
strikers. "What has she got to do with it?" murmured one of the
councilmen. Ms. Crenshaw felt she had a great deal to do with
it. The workers were being denied all of the things they deserved
because they were black, she informed the committee. Council
members watched her stolidly, but she had injected a jarring
note. The hearing quickly got back onto safer ground as several
of the union leaders moved to the podium to state why the men
needed raises and recognition of their union. There were some
amicable questions and answers.

"Now we would really like to hear from the men themselves,"
said Davis finally. "Do any of you want to speak?"

Several of the men raised their hands. Another strike supporter
headed for the microphone. T. O. Jones went to the workers
with raised hands and shepherded them outside. In a few
minutes, they all returned and sat back down. "Now I would like
to hear from those of you over here who raised your hands," said
Davis. Not a hand went up. "But you just raised your hands a
minute ago. Don't you want to speak?" They looked silently at
him.

"These men don't feel comfortable coming to such plush
surroundings," said union organizer Jesse Epps at the microphone. "They are not equipped to come in here and speak.
That's why they want to have some representatives to speak for
them and that's the union."

"We insist on hearing from the men themselves!"

Davis was beginning to lose his temper. The hearing was not
going as he had envisioned. Small groups were conferring.
Union officials, already burned by the charges of some city
officials and of newspaper editorials that they were duping the

rank and file, turned now on Davis.

"There has been an attempt here today," Jerry Wurf said, "to distinguish between the union and the men. If we are to have peace and tranquillity and to end this strike, you've got to understand that the men are the union and the union is the men."

Davis, supported by other council members, continued to insist on hearing directly from the men.

"Okay," said labor council president Tommy Powell. "If you want men, we'll get them here for you. They're at the union meeting right now. Give me a few minutes." Mayor Loeb retired upstairs to his office and the wrangling increased. Ms. Awsumb also decided to leave and a policeman escorted her out the side door.

Then the men came. By noon they were pouring into the chamber, filling empty seats, vaulting the railing by the city attorney's table, lining the walls and standing in the aisles and still they pushed in. The chamber seated 427. There were now some 700 men crowded in.

Davis vainly tried to gain order. "You wanted the men," someone shouted at him. "You didn't trust us. Here are the men!" The ministers stood, giving the workers their seats, and moved along the wall. One of the reporters suggested that some of the men stand in the press area. But as the first strikers started to move, Rev. Ezekiel Bell came down the aisle shouting, "You're not going to put us back in the balcony. We're out of the balcony. You've had us there for three hundred years and we're not going back!" Lt. Jerry Sanders, police sergeant-at-arms for the council, warned Davis of fire department regulations; the aisles would have to be cleared. "What about moving to the Auditorium?" someone suggested. Confusion was mounting. Jesse Epps was at the microphone. "I am the chairman of this meeting," Davis was shouting. "You will have to clear the aisles. We are not going to have any fire ordinances violated." "You wanted the men," retorted Epps. He turned to the men like a cheerleader. "Do you want the union?" he

shouted. "Yes," they roared. "I am up here...." Davis tried.
"You're up there because we put you up there," called Rev.
James Lawson, black pastor of Centenary United Methodist
Church. It was Lawson's first public appearance with the union
forces. "And we're going to get you down," came a yell. Epps
continued his cheerleading. "Did you walk out?" "Yes!" "What
do you want?" "The Union!" Davis tried again. "I have to walk
both sides of the street...." "You can't do it," shouted Rev.
Lawson. "You're with us or not." "You're not with us!" the
crowd picked up.

"They turned on him like wolves," said Councilman James.
"It got hotter and hotter."

"I felt as if I were in a nightmare," commented Rev. Netters,
second black councilman on the committee. "I had been in the
early sit-in movement and experienced a great many difficult
hours during that time, what we all went through...All of a
sudden I got the feeling that 'now I'm the object; I'm on the
other side.' It was the most weird feeling. I felt sick inside."

The meeting was noisy and confused and without council
leadership now. Word came back that they could move to the
larger Auditorium. Councilman Chandler stepped momentarily into the breach and suggested moving immediately. Councilman Pryor bolted out the side door and went around to the
lobby to urge movement outside. Inside Davis announced the
meeting would recess and resume at the Auditorium at 2:00
P.M. Some of the strikers stood up and started out.

"We ain't going nowhere," someone yelled. "We're staying
right here." "Stay," urged O. Z. Evers, an old political warhorse
who had worked for former-Mayor Ingram. "Stay until council
recognizes the union and recognizes they can overrule the
mayor. If they want to take someone to jail, they can take all of
us." The crowd cheered. "I call this meeting to order," shouted
Davis, "and I do not recognize Mr. Evers." "You will recognize
me," replied Evers. "I am a citizen." T. O. Jones came to the
microphone. "We are here and we are not moving till we get
some satisfaction," he told his men. Someone started clapping

and singing "We Shall Not Be Moved." "We should not leave,"
said Rev. Bell. "We were invited down here and we will not
leave." Wurf spoke, "We are uncomfortable. But I recommend
we stay here and see if we can't persuade the council to step into
this mess and clean it up once and for all."

"This meeting," said Fred Davis, "is adjourned." The councilmen rose and left.

"We threw Fred Davis like old Daniel into the lion's den and
they chewed him up pretty good," mused Councilman Blanchard. "We were so sure that it was purely and simply a matter
of labor and management. The blacks kept telling us different
and we wouldn't believe them, wouldn't listen to them....I saw
one of those black boys cutting on him. The maneuvering was
visible...They were calling up the shock troops. And I knew
Fred was in for trouble...."

"Up to that point," Davis said bitterly, "no one had questioned my integrity."

A combination union meeting, religious revival, picnic, and
sit-in began. In a small anteroom off the chamber, councilmen
conferred with strike leaders. In the mayor's office were other
meetings. Police were notified. Inspector Sam Evans, equipped
with a walkie-talkie radio, headed a small group of policemen in
the lobby, and outside 142 officers in some thirty squad cars
with motors running were parked within a block of City Hall,
but very few officers appeared within the council chamber itself.

State AFSCME representative Joe Paisley led the singing of
union songs. With great gusto they all sang "We're waiting for
the council...We shall not be moved" and "We're waiting for the
mayor...We shall not be moved." They sang "God Bless
America" and hymns.

No one had eaten lunch. Baxton Bryant, of the Tennessee
Council on Human Relations, sent out for a hundred loaves of
bread, twenty or thirty pounds of bologna, and fifteen pounds
of cheese, along with ham, mustard, and mayonnaise. Wives of
several of the strikers and Bryant changed the city attorney's
table into a space for making sandwiches, wrapping them in

paper towels and passing them out to the men who ate and carefully returned the paper towels to trash receptacles. "We cast our bread upon the waters," intoned Bill Lucy.

The meeting was putting new life into the strikers. City Hall was undergoing a psychological change in their eyes. No longer was it "theirs" and remote; now it was "ours" and they began to feel at home. "Amen," they called out and "Speak to the Lord" as ministers and other speakers came before them.

Wurf and Tommy Powell met privately with several of the councilmen. The whole ground of the meeting had shifted. The problem now faced by the council was how to end the sit-in before some incident flared. "End the strike," said the union men. "Give them what, in all justice, they deserve." "Be realistic," said the council. "You know our limitations." It was obvious to Councilman Donelson that Wurf was still seeing the strike solely as a labor matter. In fact, Wurf didn't know what he was getting into, thought Donelson. The council members went upstairs to talk to the mayor.

Loeb was getting full reports on what was happening in the council chambers. If he was thinking "I told you so," he was tactful enough not to say it. Donelson quickly sketched for him the things that Wurf would probably agree to, including a written letter of agreement rather than a signed contract. If someone, anyone, could sit down with Wurf for a few hours in private that afternoon, Donelson was sure the city could settle for a modest amount of money and limited union recognition. Wurf's losing the strike; he's just asking for a few bones, he told the mayor. And the racial thing is going to get worse before it gets better.

Loeb remained stubborn. "Look here," he said, waving a bunch of letters. "Five hundred letters supporting me and five letters against. The people don't want the union." "Henry," said Donelson, "I didn't think you were elected to count letters." "Well, I just thought you ought to know." "I do know," answered the councilman. "I do know how the white people feel. But you're mayor of the other forty percent, too."

Loeb stood firm. "After that," commented Donelson, "he didn't consult me very much more about it."

Talking, preaching, and singing continued in the chamber all afternoon. And winning forensic honors was the Rev. Zeke Bell. His words reported in the newspapers so disturbed many of the white readers that they forgot even their ire with Ciampa. Even many of his colleagues were surprised at his fire.

"When you have a meeting that could last all night, you've just got to have something to talk about," explained Rev. Bell. "So I looked at that city seal and its symbols, what the cotton and the steamboat represented. I went on to tell the story about black people in the South."

Black people, he told the men, had picked all of the cotton and many of them had been driven from their homes and many were still living on the farm but were starving and didn't have any wages to live on. Their daughters had stayed out of school to pick all the cotton, but never could a black girl be Queen of the Memphis Cotton Carnival. The steamboat had brought Negroes down the River where they were sold on the auction block right here in Memphis. This was no City of Good Abode as the city motto stated. The city fathers wouldn't listen to them. They had fought for the country and their sons were even now fighting for it in Vietnam and they had helped to make America what it was, laboring as they were now in the sanitation department. It was their responsibility to save the city and make sure it was a place where there was justice for everybody. They had as much right to this building as anybody else. So if they chose to stay all night, they could stay all night.

He pointed to the seal. "I'm not going to get up there and tear it down, but I wouldn't care if someone else tore it down...Black women have nursed white babies for hundreds of years. Now they say they don't have time for us...I wish to inform you that there are not enough rest rooms. I don't know what's going to happen."

The men roared, applauded, and laughed. Reporters covering the meeting watched incredulously. Council members, catching snatches of the speechmaking as they moved about, were appalled and angry. Outside the police held tense and waiting.

But the men were not primed to destroy City Hall. They wanted to get back on their jobs and get the whole struggle for their union over with. They would leave behind them in the chamber not massive destruction but a few scraps of paper, some sandwich crumbs.

"We had another private session and finally came up with a bright idea," reported Donelson. "The two Negro councilmen on the public works committee could vote to recognize the union and give them the checkoff and so on, and I could vote against it. And then they could all go home." The idea was tossed around. Modified and compromised, it boiled down to an agreement by the committee to vote for the pro-union resolution and then to recommend it to the full council for action.

Councilman Tom Todd, supporter of the mayor's position, came in at about 5:00 P.M. What he saw was what thousands of Memphians saw through their newspapers. "They had a milling mob of people in the lobby and in the room. Davis, Donelson, and Netters were up on the platform and more or less trapped in there. They didn't know whether they would get out alive or not. Those people had been talking that 'We're going to burn the city down, tear the council chamber apart, and if you don't give us what we want we're just going to make this place a shambles.' It was the union plus the 'purported' ministers. They were howling in there and I came in and was just dumbfounded to see all this going on."

It took a good hour to convince T. O. Jones and several others that the union had gotten the best it could from the council at that point. Strike settlement could be reached based on the resolution the public works committee would bring in. It was impossible to get all the council members together right then. Instead, the council would call a special meeting the next day at the Auditorium and vote on the committee's resolution.

The union leaders were willing to take a chance. At least they were forcing the full council into public action on the strike. They were doubtful they could accomplish anything more by continuing to sit in.

Davis read the decision at about 5:30 P.M. "Our committee has met for quite a few hours. The recommendation of our committee to the council will be that the city recognize the union as the collective bargaining agent and that there be some form of dues checkoff...."

The men were on their feet cheering. Jubilantly they thronged the aisles. Tomorrow they would win. The strike would be over. Victory rode their horizon.

Councilman Davis emerged from the meeting shaken and angry. Many of the people leading the attack on him and the council were friends of his, people with whom he had worked politically and in civil rights. He and Rev. Zeke Bell had been college classmates. "I could have been the glory boy...They tried to get me to do that—to tell Loeb off and make a grand statement...But I didn't want to be locked into this kind of image. This is not my style and I just refused to do it...This is what the Negro likes. Whether he gets what he wants or not, if he hears the white folks told off he is satisfied, even if he leaves empty-handed...I just couldn't get into a mess like that."

He would have been even more angry had he listened to Rev. James Lawson's assessment. "When thirteen hundred workers are demanding justice...a Negro politician can't sit in a council meeting and pretend that 'maybe you black people are not really representing the wishes of the workers'...Immediately he identifies himself with the power structure, the city council, and not with the workers...A whole part of what the black revolution and confrontation movement represents is that the old form of politics must go...A black politician must be identified with the people...His real strength is going to come when he sits there and that council knows that he's got thirteen hundred folks down there. That's when the council is going to respect his power."

Shelby County Human Relations Director Jerry Fanion was

acutely troubled all that night. What would happen if the council didn't vote the way the men expected the next day? At 3:00 A.M., sleepless, he got into his car and drove to the newspaper office to pick up an early-morning edition of the *Commercial Appeal* and check its coverage of the council meeting. The large editorial cartoon leaped out of the page and smacked him. The black silhouette of a hefty man with pronounced negroid lips and a battered hat pulled well down over his forehead, looking a great deal like a profile of T. O. Jones, was perched on top of a large garbage can labeled "City Hall Sit-in." On the ground were overturned garbage cans, trash, and garbage, and rising from the whole mess were lines representing fumes and spelling out "Threat of Anarchy." The cartoon was entitled "Beyond the Bounds of Tolerance." It was the most blatantly insulting drawing that Fanion could even imagine. As soon as the hour was reasonable, he put in calls to several county and state political consultants. To all of them his message was the same—"There's going to be trouble."

The city council emergency meeting the morning after the sit-in was closed and lasted four hours. Before the council lay the Davis committee pro-union recommendation drawn up as the result of the sit-in and a separate list of union demands. It was determined early that the Davis recommendation would be rejected. Instead the council drew up a substitute resolution of its own. There was the usual in-fighting about whether it should take any action at all, but the majority finally agreed to report to the strikers that it was suggesting to the mayor a compromise solution.

There were nine points in the resolution: 1) right of the employees to form and join a union be recognized, 2) right to elect union officials be recognized, 3) right to select representatives to negotiate for employees be recognized, 4) employees be included in civil service, 5) provision for fair promotions be adopted, 6) fair hospitalization be provided, 7) adequate life insurance coverage and uniform pension plan be established,

8) a meaningful grievance procedure with right of union representation at all steps be established, and 9) a wage increase be
provided at the earliest possible date. The council was sure that
the men were not aware of the concessions the city was already
willing to make and hoped to get these facts across to them.

Donelson tried to get into the resolution some mention of the
possibility of dues checkoff through the credit union, but the
council would have none of it. Actually, all of the council's
recommendations had already been approved by the mayor.
The resolution said nothing about a written union contract,
dues checkoff, or the specific date or amount of pay raises, the
three issues most hotly contested.

Councilman Todd pleaded at the meeting that no recommendations be made. The strike was the mayor's responsibility.
They were just opening a Pandora's box in getting the council
further involved. Loeb came into the meeting several times. He
okayed the council's resolution, but his disapproval of further
council action was plain. The council reconsidered and ended
the resolution by giving him the fullest possible support: "The
council recognizes that the mayor has the sole authority to act
in behalf of the city as its spokesman...." A final sentence
urged the men to return to their jobs while negotiations
were completed.

Mayor and council then went off to the Top of the Hundred
Club for a luncheon discussion with area congressmen on
getting more federal funds into Memphis.

It was quiet and orderly that afternoon as the men settled into
the auditorium hall to hear the council vote on the Davis
committee resolution. The confusion of the day before was
gone. The men talked quietly with each other, shifted in their
seats, watched expectantly as the council members moved onto
the stage. Council Chairman Downing Pryor, lean-faced,
something of the aristocratic liberal, spoke into the microphone. The council, he told them, had discussed a resolution
which would now be read and a vote would follow. They
watched him silently, the men, the union leaders, the support-

ing community people, the black ministers.

The resolution was read. The strike leaders listened closely. It took a moment for the import to sink in. No—this was not the resolution agreed to the day before. This was a substitute. Roll call began quickly. Awsumb-yes. Blanchard-yes. Chandler-yes. Donelson-yes. Fred Davis tried to say something about the pay raise. He was booed and hissed. He voted no. Hyman-yes. James-yes. McAdams-yes. Netters had intended to mention the credit union dues checkoff as a possibility for future discussion. Flustered by the rising tumult in the audience, he simply voted no. Patterson-no. Perel-yes. Pryor-yes. I am voting no, explained Tom Todd, because this resolution does not give unequivocal support to Mayor Loeb. No. The three blacks and Todd cast negative votes. The resolution passed. The agreement of the day before was not mentioned.

A roar went up. Men were on their feet now, shouting and shaking their fists toward the stage. The council, fearful of a repeat of the day before, had arranged for the microphones to be immediately cut off. Council members were met in the stage wings by a contingent of police who had been instructed to escort them in a body back to City Hall.

"But," said Ms. Awsumb, "where was Councilman Blanchard? And nobody could find Mr. Blanchard and we went back, and here's Mr. Blanchard over the rail down with the people."

As Jerry Blanchard had started for the wings, he could hear the voice of Rev. James Lawson calling, "Get us some mikes. Will you please listen to us? Will you please let us speak to you? Let us talk to our people. Please get us some microphones!" And Blanchard, like black Councilman J. O. Patterson, had turned back to the strikers.

Now, at Ms. Awsumb's urging, he joined the council group. He and Donelson realized that turning off the microphones had been a mistake, but it was too late. They headed toward the mayor's office. Blanchard was especially disturbed. For the second time in two days the council had been surrounded by protective police—and from their own constituents. And Jerry Blanchard was ashamed—not of the council's stand but of its performance.

"I take full blame for every bit of this because I had one...of the votes that said 'let's do it this way.' But in retrospect, God, it was terrible...We tell them what our pronouncement would be from Mr. Olympus...We went over there, dragged those three Negro councilmen with us, went out the back door...cut off the power...It's curious," he said, "but my whole review of the thing started from then on because I was sick of me going out the back door!"

It was Ms. Awsumb who later would put her foot down and refuse to be escorted out of any further meetings by the Memphis police. Since she was the only woman member, the rest of the council had little choice but to follow suit.

But that was to be another day. On this day the council left behind them a shattered idea of compromise and a roomful of angry men.

The leaders moved onto the empty and darkened stage. Doublecross! Betrayal! Without microphones, speakers were forced to shout. Without need of mikes, the men shouted back.

"Don't let them hoodwink you," cried Dr. Vasco Smith, waving the cartoon from the morning paper. "This is what they think of you. You are living in a racist town. They don't give a damn about you!"

Heavyset O. Z. Evers yelled that he was too mad to talk, but maybe they should get Stokely Carmichael and Rap Brown into Memphis.

State representative A. W. Willis, present for the first time, said he'd handle things over in Nashville and the strikers should keep on their course here. Jesse Turner called for the delivery of garbage to Main Street.

Labor council president Tommy Powell was almost beyond frustration. "We had promises from at least half of the councilmen that they would vote for you and they lied. They told us last night 'if you will get them to go home, we will vote for you!'

They lied. The union has tried to be on top of this thing and I have tried to keep it a union matter, but it is no longer a union matter."

T. O. Jones was on the stage. "We are ready to go to their damn jail," he yelled.[2]

"There was bitter, bitter anger in the room by the men and even more bitter anger by the leaders and by the preachers, accustomed to having a kind of phony courtesy which they treasure, that they had been treated contemptuously," said Jerry Wurf. "When we leaped on the platform, I leaped for peace because...several blacks were making the wildest speeches...The men were angry...men who for the most part were not red-hot radicals, which nobody seems to have understood. They were tired, beaten men, making a struggle that before they died they would stand up and be men. They were not bomb throwers. They were not young blacks. These were men whose choice was chopping cotton for three bucks a day or picking up garbage in Memphis for Loeb...men who scrounge and struggle and buy too many things on time and manipulate money lenders all their lives...scratching and scrawling and humbling themselves—not bomb throwers. But they were really worked up. And when that kind of guy gets worked up, he's worked up. And I was scared."

The idea of a march of the men from the Auditorium to Mason Temple Church of God in Christ, a little south of the downtown area, came out of spur-of-the-moment consultations on the platform. Some kind of protest had to be made. Some kind of further meeting with the men had to be held. Marching would help drain off the anger. It would cool everybody down. The men were directed to move out of the Auditorium and form ranks on the street outside. They would march.

Why are they going to Mason Temple? a reporter questioned Tommy Powell. "They're just going to plan the destruction of the city," despairingly replied Powell. "I tried and tried to tell people this was going to happen if some justice wasn't given these men. Now it's out of labor's hands."

The crowd poured into the street at the intersection of Main

and Poplar. Across the street, arms interlocked, stretched a
cordon of police, several ranks deep. The men were blocked.

"If we can't march, then we'll just stand here," one of the men
shouted. Several of the leaders roved among them, getting them
organized into a semblance of lines. Police were all around.
Striker Ed Gillis was somewhere near the front. "They was
blocking us, standing up against us pushing. We wasn't pushing.
We was just standing there and we was singing, 'I'm planted by
the waterside, like a tree planted by the roots.'...Wouldn't
nobody fight. I was just stopped, standing there looking."

Emergency squad cars were coming up now, spilling out
policemen who began putting on their green gas masks,
grotesque in the thin afternoon sunlight. Rev. James Lawson,
in his clerical collar, moved along the front line of police, talking
calmly, trying to allay the mounting tension. "It's not your
fight," he would say. "We're not opposing you. If we win, your
wages will increase. Don't let yourself be used."

Wurf, Epps, and other union leaders were huddled with
Assistant Police Chief U. T. Bartholomew. Bartholomew had
no instructions to let a march proceed. "Let us go," Wurf was
pleading. "We will be very orderly."

"I had never seen him beg like that," said one of his staff.

At this point a young white lawyer named David Caywood
walked up. He was president of the new West Tennessee
Chapter of the American Civil Liberties Union. Caywood had
no idea what had happened at the Auditorium, but he found the
intersection filled with men. He saw the gas masks, and stood
for a moment listening to the attempts to get permission for the
march.

Then he rushed the block to Mayor Loeb's office to warn that
they were fools for trying to stop the march. "We're not trying
to stop any march," Loeb told him in astonishment. "Well, the
police have their gas masks on," retorted Caywood. "Everybody
is getting pretty upset down in the street. They think they're
going to be gassed." Loeb put in a quick call to Police
Commissioner Frank Holloman. When Caywood got back to

the intersection, the gas masks were off. County Human Relations Director Jerry Fanion, still highly upset, had also gone to Loeb's office. The mayor suggested he stay with the march and act as an observer.

Jacques Wilmore, director of the southern field office of the U. S. Civil Rights Commission, which covered fourteen southern states and was headquartered in Memphis, was in his office in the Federal Building, next to City Hall, when one of his assistants, Bobby Doctor, rushed in. "You'd better come down," urged Doctor. "I think the police are going to kill a lot of black people." Wilmore followed him downstairs.

A few moments later came the order to let the march proceed through the center of downtown Memphis. The line of police officers fell back. Holloman's permission said the marchers must move in rows of eight down the west side of the street, their right hand side. They were to stay west of the white, center traffic line. Those instructions never got directly to the back of the march, and as the men started they covered the entire street. Rev. Lawson still moved along the sidelines toward the back where some of the officers were trying to press people inward. "Why get too close and provoke anything?" he kept saying. "We've got good control."

Tensions cooled as the march got underway. Something of a holiday spirit began to take hold. A few insults were tossed toward police but without heat. Marchers called to the few spectators on the sidewalks to join them. There was scattered singing. A few blocks south of the starting point, around Main and Jefferson, police squad cars came up from behind, funneling the march over into the west side of the street, and moved slowly along beside it. There were four or five men in each car. In the lead car were Assistant Chief Bartholomew and Inspector Sam Evans. Traffic going north on Main Street was diverted into other streets. In the empty half of the street other officers walked along with reporters, cameramen, several motorcycle police, and some uniformed deputies on loan from the county sheriff's office.

Rev. Zeke Bell and Rev. Dick Moon walked along together, talking to the policeman near them. "He was a friendly looking fellow," said Rev. Bell. "We were talking about how warm and nice the weather was and how we were really going to be tired when we got where we had to go." Dick Moon was one of the few whites present. He was the Presbyterian chaplain at Memphis State University and had come down to the auditorium meeting as much out of curiosity as for any other reason, though he and Bell had been friends for a couple of years. They walked along, chatting amiably.

Jacques Wilmore with Bobby Doctor and Ms. Rosetta Miller, another member of the civil rights commission staff, hiked along the sidewalk. "Man, I'm glad the police let the march go ahead or we were going to have a problem back there," said Doctor. Wilmore agreed. He could almost see the anger and tension on the part of the men lifting. "I think it's going to go all the way," he told Doctor.

Jerry Wurf pulled out of the front line of march about three blocks down the street, his limp curtailing any long walk. Labor council secretary Bill Ross also dropped out to drive him on over to Mason Temple. Lawyer David Caywood, walking along on the sidewalk and pleased that the march was in the right part of the street and that the police were being handled nicely, stopped them to meet Wurf for the first time. They talked for a few minutes before the labor men turned to their car and Caywood retraced his steps to complete his legal business at City Hall. It was about 3:30 P.M.

Baxton Bryant ambled along on the sidewalk with the civil rights commission group at first, but his friends out in the street kept taunting him with calls of "Chicken." He chuckled and waved at them a few times, then stepped down into the street and joined the front line of march.

Rev. Jim Lawson was moving up and back along the edge of the march. He had not noticed that squad cars had spread out along the line until one moved in next to him from the rear. He was about ten rows back from the front rank. He walked along beside the police car.

The police cars were edging further against the line of marchers, crowding those at the far ends of the lines up against the curb. One of the cars was now on the same side of the white line as the marchers. As a second car edged in, a group of men behind Rev. Lawson stopped short and said, "Get that car back and away from us." Rev. Lawson turned back to say "let's keep marching. They're trying to provoke us. Keep going."

Gladys Carpenter, a part-time employee of Councilman J. O. Patterson's office, also saw the car moving against the men. She was in the march because she had met Patterson at the Auditorium to pick up her paycheck. Now she moved from her place in line over to where the car was. "We did not want to have trouble, but to go about business in an orderly manner," explained Ms. Carpenter, who was no stranger to marching. She had gone from Selma to Montgomery and with the Meredith March in Mississippi. "I went over to keep them from running into the men. I thought they might not do it to a lady."

Then the squad car nudged against her side. The first lines of march were now a little beyond the intersection of Main and Gayoso, in front of Goldsmith's large downtown department store. They had come seven blocks.

Suddenly there was a loud yell from Ms. Carpenter. "Oh! He runned over my foot!" The men nearest her responded immediately. They swung to the squad car and began rocking it back and forth. Policemen inside leaped out. In their hands were aerosol spray cans. Police across the street ran over.

Rev. Lawson, hearing the commotion, was there in an instant, his hand on the car. "Stop!" he shouted. The first dose of the chemical spray Mace caught him along the side of the head. So did the second. All along the march police were suddenly moving in, spraying Mace, sometimes over the tops of their cars. "Mace," came the order from the front car that carried Assistant Chief Bartholomew and Inspector Evans. "Mace! Mace!"[3]

Rev. Lawson turned a few steps toward the curb, blinking rapidly. His eyes were partially protected by his glasses and he

knew enough not to rub and touch the spray. He turned back
again to the police car. That time he got a face full of Mace.
Police were hitting with night sticks and Macing and arresting
at the car. Confusion was everywhere. The march fell apart.
Women screamed. Husky sanitation men were cursing and
crying as the Mace got into their eyes. People were running.
There were scuffles. A few policemen and marchers were
knocked down in the street. Beyond the immediate area of the
second squad car no one even knew what had happened until
the Mace hit them.

"That gas was flying everywhere," said striker Gillis. "I pulled
my cap off and tried to keep it out of my eyes—put my cap on
my eyes—and they come around and shoot it up my nose…I
couldn't run cuz they was all around us. They kept us right up
against the wall and just started shooting that Mace on us. It
stung. I couldn't see cuz it was getting in my eyes."

Rev. Harold Middlebrook, assistant pastor to Judge Ben
Hooks at Middle Baptist Church, ran back toward Rev. Lawson.
He had been gassed once before—inside a church at Tus-
caloosa. His dark glasses blocked the first dose of Mace, but they
didn't help with the second. "It had been a very hectic day," said
Rev. Middlebrook without a trace of irony.

Rev. Zeke Bell and Rev. Dick Moon were Maced immediately—by the friendly policeman they had been talking with. "I
didn't know what he was doing," said Rev. Bell. "He just
wheeled and started putting Mace all over me. He was putting
it on everybody." Rev. Moon fled to the sidewalk. A number of
people rushed past him trying to get inside Goldsmith's department store, but Rev. Moon was, for some reason that he didn't
even try to explain to himself, afraid of being trapped inside.
"The police continued to Mace on the sidewalk, Macing and
screaming, 'Move. Move. Move.' It was all happening so fast.
There were so many of us pushed off that street onto the
sidewalk that we couldn't move. I got up against the building.
It kind of frightened me—the pressure of all those people on
me—and I thought I was going to go through the window. I

inched my way around the corner onto Gayoso Street with all the people. There was an old man next to me and I saw a club come right down on him and it broke the skin and blood spurted every which way—all over him…An old Negro woman was down on her knees. She'd been trapped. About five of us braced ourselves around her so she could get up on her feet and out of it…I had my clerical collar on and I must have gotten Mace directly in the face seven times…We kept saying to each other, 'Don't rub your eyes.' "

A police van arrived on the scene with gas masks and long riot sticks. Police grabbed them and turned back to the crowd.

Civil Rights Commission Director Jacques Wilmore, walking on the sidewalk, didn't realize anything was happening until the march stopped moving. Turning, he saw the crowd at the police car and the police starting to move. He stopped at the edge of the curb and watched with the eye of a practiced observer. The police were out of the cars, waving Mace cans, and pushing the strikers toward the sidewalk. He heard no verbal order given for the Mace. He noticed one black policeman who seemed to be hanging back, waving his Mace can ineffectually about.

As he stood there, a marcher in a green sweater bolted past. Wilmore heard the police say, "Get him. Get that man in the green sweater." Two police grabbed the man and other policemen came around. "He wasn't resisting arrest," said Wilmore. "He was kind of turning from side to side. I saw a policeman run up from behind him with his stick raised. At that point I pulled out my civil rights commission identification and said, 'Okay, now you've got him. You don't need to hit him.' The policeman gave the man's head a terrible crack and a policeman was coming from another angle with a Mace can pointed at my eyes. I turned toward him and held out my badge, and he reached around and gave me two or three squirts square in the face.

"I wasn't a very good observer then. People were piling in. The police pushed me up against Goldsmith's window and were pushing and herding people. The door at Goldsmith's was open and I was herded in with the crowd. I wiped my eyes and looked out. I still had my badge in my hand. In a few minutes the street was almost clear, just a few strikers still trying to get away…I came back out and talked to the strikers.

"If you are a black man, you can have all of the badges signed by the president of the United States yet particularly at times of crisis police officers just see the color of your skin." Jacques Wilmore's skin was black.

Jerry Fanion tried to tell the policeman who aimed the Mace can that he was the Shelby County human relations director. Then even with the Mace in his face, he stopped to pick up a lady who'd been knocked down by the curb, trying to get her into Goldsmith's whose doors were now being locked against the crowd. "Mace takes your breath away," he said. "If it hadn't been for the Mace, it would have looked like a game of cops and robbers. Everybody was running all over. But the men were just helpless." The men weren't the only ones. Police were catching whiffs of their own Mace. People waiting at the bus stop were also caught in the Macing. Ms. Carpenter, whose yell initially started the whole fracas, had been Maced and made it to the sidewalk in front of Goldsmith's, where a white teenager came up and asked if she wanted him to call an ambulance. No, she said, she thought she could make it. Was she sure? Ms. Carpenter had covered her head with her coat. By the time she got her coat down to get a look at her would-be rescuer, he, too, had been Maced. She never knew who he was.

Whittier Sengstacke, Jr., son of the editor of the Memphis *Tri-State Defender*, a black weekly, and his friend, Ed Harris, the paper's photographer, began covering the march at Court Square. They had moved south with it, along with reporters and cameramen from the dailies and television stations. When the Macing began, Harris ran back toward the police car with his camera. As Sengstacke stepped out in the street an officer aimed his Mace can and ordered, "Get back on the sidewalk." He was Maced before he could. Through blurred vision he saw Ms. Cornelia Crenshaw, also suffering from the gas. "Keep marching," cried Ms. Crenshaw. Harris fared little better as he tried to shoot pictures and dodge the Mace. "Don't take that picture. Give me that camera," an officer snapped as he advanced on Harris, nightstick in hand. Harris snapped the picture and ran. A few seconds later he was Maced. White newsmen covering the trouble were moving freely except for dodging the gusts of Mace in the air.

Harris found P. J. Ciampa lying on the curb. He snapped a picture of the union leader trying to get up. "Ciampa was in miserable shape. He was crying, couldn't walk. He looked like he was falling down."

"When all hell broke loose…I figured, 'Well, let me move here and talk to some of our troops,'" said Ciampa. "I'm talking to some of them and these three cops…'That's him!' they're saying. This one man had something. And I looked at him and said, 'Just a minute, mister.' Whoosh. The Mace hits me in the face and I start heading for the curb and I stumble and grovel and then I feel awful. I feel this stuff all over me. You can't breathe. You can't see…I was completely disoriented, don't know where, how to go. I was just groveling for something to hold on to. And the earth was the best thing I could find. And some hands started grabbing me and I thought, 'My God, they're going to—this is it. This must be the cops.' I was totally helpless. I thought, 'I've had it.' I thought they were going to tear me apart. And lo and behold, it was just a few courageous souls that just dove in amongst the Mace and everything else and drug me out of there."

Sanitation workers helped him into a bank whose workers helped him wash his face and eyes. "To go back out into the air felt so good in your lungs after that junk."

Baxton Bryant saw the Macing begin. But Bryant had never been arrested much less gassed. "It never entered my mind that any of that Mace was for *me*!…I turned and I still thought, Well, now, they're not after *me*! I was going away from Goldsmith's when someone touched me on the shoulder. I looked around. This little red-headed cop was at real close range. The Mace wasn't gas; it was liquid. He went right across my eyes with it…It does disorient you and you could run at a policeman and get killed just as easy as you could run from him."

In an alley he found Bobby Doctor of the civil rights commission chopping at a piece of ice frozen at the end of a drain pipe. He and Doctor wiped their eyes with the ice.

In the annals of Memphis civil rights history, the day would go down as "The Baptism of H. Ralph Jackson." Dr. Jackson was national director of the minimum salary division of the African Methodist Episcopal Church. The division's home office was in a new, modern three-story building dedicated only six weeks before. It was a block south of Beale on Hernando. Mayor Loeb had come to the dedication; so had a number of city councilmen who mingled with nine bishops of the AME Church and three hundred churchmen from all over the country. Memphis was proud of the type of leadership the Rev. H. Ralph Jackson was giving, leading his people, building such a fine building, planning a housing development for poor people, said the mayor.

To outsiders, Rev. Jackson was something of an Uncle Tom. He had never participated in the civil rights movement. Within the AME Church he had worked for years to set up a central division to subsidize the salaries of underpaid AME ministers whose congregations were unable to give them a minimum salary of three thousand dollars.

And Rev. Jackson was not particularly interested in helping the labor union. He figured the union could fight its own battles. But he was concerned about providing food for the men on strike. He had come down to the Auditorium because he had been invited by some of the strike supporters to speak to the council. "You can get a preacher to go anywhere to make a speech," chuckled Baxton Bryant, a former preacher himself. Rev. Jackson was angry at the Auditorium and irritated that he would not be able to speak to the council. He had never marched before, but he moved into the first line with some of the other leaders and he began feeling pretty good.

"I was born and reared in Birmingham. All my ministry and

work has been in the South so I have thirty years of discipline as a Christian minister. I have the natural discipline that comes to a black born in the South who has made any type of attainment in the South. In addition, I have been in the hierarchy of the church for nearly twenty years, which represents another type of discipline. I always prided myself, coming from Birmingham, living in the midst of racism, that the only encounter I had ever had with a policeman was over traffic tickets."

All of it was lost in a few seconds of Mace that swept across his face on Main Street. Thirty years of discipline. Gone. All lost.

"Because I was black," he said. "They would not have Maced white ministers…This happened to me because I was black. There was no other reason."

Portly, eloquent, fiery, an orator of the old southern preaching school, he was to tell the story again and again, at meeting after meeting. "Because I was black." And every time he told it he sputtered, became speechless, and got angry all over again.

As the march was decisively broken up, Ed Gillis summed it up, "They sure did treat us bad."

Attorney Caywood, leaving City Hall, had found squad cars going down the street and scattered groups of sanitation men coming back. Most of them were crying and holding their handkerchiefs. "We don't know what happened," they told him. "But we got gassed."

Wild rumors of mob violence, of window breaking and cars being overturned, by now had spread out from the downtown area. Jittery store managers were preparing to close early. Traffic was still blocked off Main Street and beginning to back up on the arterial streets. Jerry Fanion came up to City Hall, crying into his handkerchief. "I'm going to tell Mayor Loeb how disgusted I am with this whole city," he said.

On the sidewalk near the scene of the original confrontation several of the march leaders were trying to pull themselves and the remnants of the group back together. The march had to go on. There was symbolism riding on it now. Something of the march had to reach its destination.

"I didn't want to go on," said Rev. Henry Starks, pastor of St. James AME Church, who had been in the front line. "But I did it. I was sick in a way. I felt disgusted and broken. Here I had on my clergy garb and here I was hating on the inside because of what I had seen them do to a lot of my people."

There were about seventy people left from the original thousand. They went along the sidewalk a block to Beale Street where they turned east. Officers began to walk along beside them in the street. As they passed down the street from the *Tri-State Defender* office, where the two young reporter-photographers Sengstacke and Harris had already spread both their story and the fumes of Mace clinging to their clothes, editor Whittier Sengstacke, Sr., watched the procession somberly. "Damn it," he roared. "Get those cameras and get pictures of those nightsticks."

At Mason Temple the men began to trickle in. Mace fumes clung to those who had marched, to their clothing. It was almost impossible to stay in the room with them. Tempers were high as stories of the Macing were retold. Gradually union representative Jesse Epps and Rev. Lawson began to organize some kind of plan. Clearly the next steps should include a downtown boycott, daily marches, and the appointment of a strategy committee. Clearly also any kind of social, political, or church feuding in the black community must be forgotten in the face of what many considered a threat to the entire black community itself.

A march of the strikers scheduled for the next day would be replaced by a meeting of more leaders of the community. Getting them pulled together was urgent. Jesse Epps sent a telegram to every black pastor in town, inviting them all to the Saturday meeting. If they could call out the black preachers....

A temporary strategy committee was chosen with the understanding that it would be enlarged. Rev. Starks presided at the mass gathering in the church. Rev. Jackson came up to tell his story and T. O. Jones spoke. The audience sang "We Shall Overcome."

Mayor Loeb issued a statement that law and order would be preserved.

Charges including nightriding, assault and battery, and disorderly conduct were brought against the man in the green sweater and several others. Late that evening T. O. Jones surrendered to police and posted bond. Charges against him included incitement to riot based on his speech at the Auditorium and his presence at the car-rocking incident.[4]

Later that night Police Commissioner Holloman met with Rev. Lawson, Jacques Wilmore, Bobby Doctor, Jerry Fanion, and Jesse Turner in Baxton Bryant's Peabody hotel room. It was a quiet, almost exploratory meeting. It was obvious that the police commissioner's reports of the Main Street encounter differed from theirs, but he listened quietly. Mace, he told them, was far more humane than bullets. It had been in use in the department for two years as a method of subduing prisoners. The whole incident, he felt, resulted from a breakdown of communication. He was new in the department, but he could assure them that he wanted fairness, that there would be no discrimination in his police department.

Rev. Lawson talked. If they had been white ministers, they would not have been Maced. It was as simple as that. No more than seven or eight men had been involved in the car-rocking, yet instead of trying to isolate the incident, the police had indiscriminately moved against the whole march. Was Holloman aware of the reputation the police department already had in the black community? The Macing on Main Street was certainly not going to enhance that reputation.

Under the circumstances, however, the meeting went reasonably well and concluded with Holloman urging that they come to see him and keep in touch. He said keeping communications open was vitally important, and certainly no one present could disagree with that.

When Rev. Lawson reached home that night, he had a phone call. The strike strategy committee was asking him to act as chairman. He agreed.

His civil rights roots were deep. He had worked with the SCLC for a decade. He had been one of the founders of SNCC. Martin King had called Lawson the "leading theoretician of nonviolent social change in the country."

Over in Miami, Martin King had closed a five-day Ministers Leadership Training Conference that afternoon. He was due at New York's Carnegie Hall that night for a tribute to W. E. B. DuBois. He was tired and his doctor wanted him to get some rest in Miami. So he had tried—in-between planning for the Poor People's Campaign, meeting with Washington representatives of the community relations commission, holding a Miami fundraising luncheon, and attending the conference.

He spoke of the Poor People's Campaign, knowing that many even in that audience disagreed with it. But they must rouse the nation again—this time around the issues of poverty and hunger. "I'll tell you the truth," he said. "I'm tired of marching. And I'm tired of going to jail. I'm being honest about it. But it doesn't happen any other way." And his conscience pushed him now toward Washington.

We are Christian ministers, he said. If that meant anything, it meant taking up the cross with all of its "tension-packed agony and bearing the cross until it leaves the very marks of Jesus Christ on our bodies and our souls."

We are, he told them, God's sanitation workers, working to clear up the snow of despair and poverty and hatred. And if he could leave them with one thought, it would be to not give up on nonviolence. It hadn't really been tried yet on a massive scale in the North. It would work.

"For so many of us, this has been a mountaintop experience." But the valley calls us, he told them. "And we are called to minister to the valley."

Some half-dozen ministers from Memphis were at the Miami conference. They included S. B. (Billy) Kyles, who had just been appointed SCLC convener for Memphis, and Judge Ben Hooks, who was on SCLC's national board. Their wives were with them and the two couples were planning to fly down for a few days to the Bahamas.

But they were to return to the valley more quickly than they thought. When Ms. Hooks called her father in Memphis a little later, he repeated the distorted stories. "Oh, Lord, all hell's broke out here. They threw garbage in the streets. They broke out windows in Goldsmith's." Hooks and Kyles prepared to return to Memphis.

Nothing but the Strike

5

> *"God Almighty, man! Black people*
> *all over the city had nothing going*
> *on but the sanitation strike."*
> *Young black militant*

On the morning after the Macing, the city obtained its long-threatened injunction against the union leaders, charging they had induced and encouraged employees to mount an illegal strike.

Immediate impetus to go into chancery court was provided by the melee on Main Street, but the city had been ready to petition for an injunction for some days. Attorney Sam Weintraub, who had obtained the 1966 injunction against Local 1733, had been contacted by City Attorney Gianotti to draft the injunction petition. He was not to file, but to be ready when the time came. Weintraub drafted a supplemental and amended bill to the 1966 injunction. It briefly stated that an injunction against the same union under the same basic circumstances had been obtained previously and went on with the request for a new injunction citing the facts about the new strike.

After interviewing several city officials, Weintraub and his associates concluded that "the union international was aware of what was going to happen." Ciampa's trip into Memphis the first of February and the union meeting the night of February 11 convinced them the international was involved. "The Supreme Court has held," Weintraub explained, "that when the responsible representation (i.e., T. O. Jones) of a labor organization is acting for them such action must be construed to be the union operating with the union's blessing.... The second phase of responsibility is after the strike does start. If you then take over the strike, you're equally as responsible as if you had started it."

Mayor Loeb himself was not particularly in favor of obtaining the injunction and there was some division among his closest advisers on the timing, but the pressure to go into court had been steadily mounting. For days the newspapers had been calling for a legal vindication of the city's—and their own—stand on the illegality of the strike. And there was pressure from a number of businessmen, concerned that the entire strike situation was getting completely out of hand, and believing that if union leaders were held in contempt, fined, perhaps even sentenced to serve time in jail, this would be a restraining influence on the union.

Businessman E. W. (Ned) Cook reported from one meeting where the injunction route was discussed with some of Loeb's advisers. "The lawyers advised doing it. Loeb had already crossed the bridge in establishing the policy holding the line. The discussion was on how you hold the line, how you implement this policy. You give police protection to the garbage trucks. You control the union marches. And you cite the union for contempt...It was just a try to control the situation."

The court did its duty quickly. As in 1966, the court by-passed the usual procedure of taking the petition and setting a hearing date several days later. Chancellor Robert Hoffmann signed the injunction that morning; it aimed at stopping strike activity and giving the city the right to petition for contempt of court citations against the union leaders who actually were pushing the strike through speeches, marches, or other demonstrations. It specifically named Wurf, Ciampa, Lucy, Epps, Paisley, T. O. Jones and a number of other local men who had been listed in the 1966 injunction.[1] The injunction, said the chancellor when questioned, was binding only on the persons "specifically named as partied defendants."

"No principle of law is more firmly established than the principle that public employees do not have the right to strike," stated Hoffmann. "This is the law in Tennessee; it is the federal law, and it is the law in every state of the Union where the question has been adjudicated. The reason for this law is that public employees render services involving health, safety, and welfare of all citizens, and no individual or group has the legal right to interfere with the rendition of these vital services. Consequently, it is illegal for any person to authorize, induce or engage in a strike against the City of Memphis. Public employees, however, do have the right to quit their employment."

The injunction, while it did not stop Wurf and his staff from working with the strike, did effectively cut off any chance of direct negotiations with the city. It would be twenty-six long days before city and union officials would meet again face-to-face. In the meantime, attempts at strike negotiation would pass into other hands.

Nearly a hundred fifty black ministers came together at Mason Temple that same Saturday afternoon in response to Jesse Epps' telegram. They came from the large, established churches and from the small struggling congregations. They were Pentecostal and African Methodist Episcopal, Christian Methodist Episcopal and Church of God in Christ, and the various Baptists who represented more than half the city's black churchgoers. Roy Love, one of the first blacks to run for political office, came, and E. A. Campbell; S. A. Owen, for whom the junior college was named, and J. W. Williams; Rev. Cunningham, who had rallied the preachers to support the civil rights campaign in 1960; and Elder Blair T. Hunt, once principal of Booker T. Washington High School and Crump's chief black spokesman. There was Zeke Bell of the Presbyterians and Jim Lawson of the United Methodists, John Mickle of Second Congregational and Robert Atkins, the city's one black Episcopal priest. They ran the gamut of political and social action philosophies, in age from young to old.

Of all the leadership in the black community, other than that of the militant young, they were the most free, dependent financially only upon their own congregations, their own people.

The ministers had long played the traditional role of interpreting the needs of their people to white leaders. That role might be waning nationally, but in Memphis it was still strong. Many of their ministries were entangled daily in poverty, ignorance, violence, fear. Their spiritual authority made them natural leaders, so they tended to act as go-betweens, as buffers, between the black and white communities.

Much has been said about the adverse effects of the black Christian church on blacks in the South—how it taught them to accept the deplorable conditions in which they lived in exchange for a promise they would walk the golden streets; how it taught turning the other cheek when militancy was called for; how it taught the humility and suffering of Jesus as the inevitable lot of every person; how it was an emotional escape. But the black church also provided love, warmth, courage, and perhaps a touch of glory. It had brought a sense of community to a slave population cut loose from its tribal moorings and set adrift as freedmen and freedwomen in those floundering years after the Civil War. At its best it was a community of concern and security and a sanctuary, a rallying point for seeking justice in the wider world. Indigenous leadership developed there, and it was no accident that when the nonviolent civil rights movement in the South began the decade before, it was the men and women out of the black churches who were strong enough to carry it.

Still, the role of the black preacher as interpreter to the white community generally necessitated caution, compromise, tact, a little shuffling and Uncle Tom-ing. So it had come down through the years. Memphis was no exception except that the involvement of the black churches in the political machinery during the Crump span was deeper and the pattern of taking political handouts perhaps more common.

In the very early days of Memphis there were records of at least one black minister, a Methodist, preaching to mixed gatherings, but the segregation of Christians quickly followed. Slaves were brought to the white churches for services, but were separated either at different meetings in different rooms or relegated to the balconies. Several separate buildings for black worship were built, closely tied to the white mother congregations and presided over by black preachers. But in 1856 an ordinance was passed prohibiting teaching blacks how to read, as the First Presbyterian Church was doing, and banning blacks from preaching to their own congregations for fear that such practices gave blacks access to abolitionist writings and sentiments. The separate black churches were closed.

The great influx of freed slaves into the city during and after the Civil War brought with it a number of self-styled, former-slave preachers and also some dozen white ministers under the auspices of the American Missionary Association to set up schools and churches for blacks. It was the Baptists, often led by former-slave preachers, who gained the most members.[2]

The black ministers were generally not racial integrationists during Reconstruction, although they stood for equality in public life for their people. But during the quarter of a century when Republican Reconstruction power collapsed and the reestablishment of segregation was completed, most of the black ministers moved into accommodation with white policies, a stance they would hold up through the Crump period. It seemed the only way to make any progress. And a number of the ministers gained recognition as fine fellows to deal with in the eyes of the white community.

Even as the civil rights movement of the late fifties began, they put their reliance on voter registration, in which they labored mightily, and on the reasonableness of white community leaders rather than on direct confrontation. It was not until the Memphis desegregation campaign of 1960-61 that any sizable proportion of black clergy confronted civic authority by publicly supporting the demonstrators and collecting money for them in their churches, or, like Rev. Billy Kyles and Rev. James Netters, allowing themselves to be arrested sitting in the front of the bus. And when that campaign was over, most of them retreated with some relief back to their usual tasks.

"The Black Princes," someone named the preachers, and in the new days as in the old, much social and political power channeled through them. Lords of their own little congregations, their own little worlds, moving like ambassadors within the black community, making alliances here, breaking treaties there. Memphis in 1968 was no city of storefront churches. Many churches in the black community were red brick, frame, solid buildings, many sold off by whites in their slow, endless retreat from blackness. Religion was still respectable here. And from every black pulpit every Sunday, every Wednesday, the sure voices:

"The Lord will deliver His people Israel...from the rats, from the jails, from endless labor, from hunger and want, from sin, from sin....

"Even so, Lord, come quickly...."

To the white city administrations over the years they had been bespectacled men, calm men, humble men, friendly men, above all sensible men. They had gained concessions. It was hard to believe that they would call now not upon Sweet Jesus but Jehovah.

Indeed, it was not easy for the black ministers to come together. There were splits in the black community which ran deep. The political shambles of the preceding fall had left extreme bitterness that had not yet begun to heal. The early weeks of the strike had seen some attempt to re-establish power positions in the black community, and some friction among those who came forward to help the men.

But those first weeks had seen something else, too. Judge and minister Ben Hooks tried to explain. "When the sanitation men did strike, this struck a responsive chord. It was a sort of mystic thing. There was some movement around which we could

gather our energies, for certainly the response to the strike was
out of all proportion to the issues involved. Our response was
so overwhelmingly emotional and almost irrational that it can
only be explained in terms of a long feeling of frustration."

The ministers brought this feeling of frustration to the
meeting and, like the public works employees two weeks earlier,
they found a platform through which to express it. The strategy
committee had met earlier and drawn up a plan to present to the
ministers. The Macing was described, the plan to aid the strikers
discussed. There was some hesitation, some debate, and a great
deal of sermonizing. But they overwhelmingly endorsed the
plan presented by Rev. Jim Lawson and Jesse Epps who were
leading the meeting. They would go into their pulpits the next
morning and announce their support of the strike and of an
economic boycott of downtown. They would take up offerings
for the relief of the strikers.

They would open their churches for meetings. They would
come out, join the daily marches, and attend the mass meetings
when they could. They would speak at the union hall and at civic
clubs. They would rally their people.

Boycott....
Sustain....
Join with your brothers in the sanitation department.....
Is there no balm in Gilead?

So the union and the black community came together. It was
a merger of necessity that neither had originally intended. The
striking public works employees had become the symbol of the
black community and the union was their champion. In turn, as
long as the union championed the men, the black community
would champion the union.

What came into existence at that meeting and later that night
at a mass community meeting when additional segments of the
black neighborhoods rose to pledge support was not an organization but a viable movement.

Its aim was to get a favorable strike settlement for the men and to support them until that settlement was reached. Help was sought and welcomed from the entire community and the original strategy committee expanded. It was a movement that had begun when the first community people moved to support the strikers through encouraging words and food donations. Now it coalesced around a strategy committee and sought to unify the entire black community. At the center it was concretely concerned with the strike, but it was also inevitable that the issue of injustice to thirteen hundred city employees would spill over into the issues of injustice for all black people.

"We found," said Rev. Henry Starks, "that we were not only involved in a strike situation but that we had come face-to-face with an economic tradition, a racial tradition, a southern tradition."

In order to put pressure on the city to negotiate and settle the strike, the boycott which had been suggested and sporadically begun the preceding week was officially announced against downtown stores and their shopping center branches, against all businesses connected with members of the city council, and against any place bearing the name "Loeb."

"Buy no new clothes for Easter," chanted the leaders.

"Keep your money in your pocket."

"Boycott!"

Power to settle the strike, movement leaders believed, rested literally with Loeb. Their problem was to figure ways to force Loeb to move. They considered the white groupings, the churches, the old liberal coteries and the human rights organizations, the media, the politicians. But the media were hostile; the old liberals were turned off by the labor issue; the human relations groups were impotent, and the politicians were behaving as southern politicians had always behaved. They would momentarily hold judgment on the churches. In the end, they felt it was the business community that could influence the mayor, and business could be reached not through reason or justice or compassion but through economic pressure. They attempted to put on the pressure.

A possible alternative route lay through the city council, but to date that had resulted in nothing but division and confusion among the members. Nonetheless, they planned to continue besieging the council.

"We did not write off all help from the white community as such," explained union leader Lucy. "But we thought that we had to first of all just maintain our position, making sure that the black community understood the nature of the struggle."

The education and involvement of the black community began. "The sanitation workers must have union recognition, adequate salaries, decent benefits," said one speaker after another at the mass meetings. "There must be an end to police brutality and the indiscriminate, cruel use of force on peaceful people. We will escalate. Because the reporting is not honest, we are boycotting the *Press-Scimitar* and the *Commercial Appeal*. There must be fair treatment in all employment opportunities. There must be racial balance in all kinds of jobs, public and private."

Rev. Ralph Jackson at a mass meeting: "Loeb said that he wanted garbage to pile up as high as the apartments. Let's help him pile it up...we are on the march...and nothing will stop us."

Rev. Zeke Bell at a mass meeting: "Everybody work with us. We have so much to do....Please leave the sheet with your name on it at the door...Did they get the collection money up there in the balcony?...Now we're going to sing 'We Shall Over-come.' "

The black community stands alone.

We must unite now.

The crisis is upon us.

Unite!

Unite!

Records were kept of the amounts of money collected at the mass meetings and turned over to the union for food and services for the strikers. These amounts varied, but an average collection for a night ran about $800, most of it in small donations.[3]

By March 7, a total of $8,006.32 had been raised through-out the black community, and $7,000 of that total turned over to the union for the men. The rest was reserved for the ongoing work of the community organization.

Black people became involved at many different levels, march-ing, collecting money, distributing food, answering phones, running mimeograph machines. At rock-bottom level, they could boycott downtown.

It was a loosely knit movement "open at both ends," ex-plained Rev. Starks. People moved in and out of it, giving what support they could for a time, pulling out to return later in some other phase.

Daily marches through downtown were launched. The strik-ing men continued their daily noontime meetings with the union leaders. Some took part-time jobs during the strike, but every day many of them were free and they provided the bulk of the marchers. They worked at distributing the food and money that came in. They, their wives, and their children attended the mass meetings at different churches each night at which the black community roared its support.

"Sometimes I felt like we was going back to work shortly and then after a couple of weeks rolled around, sometimes I didn't feel like we was going back to work at all," said asphalt worker L. C. Reed. "But we all started participating in the meetings and that gave me a little more courage then. I knowed if we would stick together we would win."

A *Commercial Appeal* reporter talked to several strikers on an early march.[4] "We're staying with my sister now," said Willy White. "It's crowded all right, with my wife and eleven kids and me, but, man, the coins are gonna run out…Union dues have to come out because, man, you got to pay for somebody to protect and represent you. That's only fair. That's right."

"Dues won't be more than four dollars a month. I reckon I sure can pay that with a raise. I've been with the city fourteen years and this is the first time we really stood up for what we want," said Charles Justice.

James Randall was contemptuous of the cold weather. "You think it's cold marching today? Hell, it don't bother none of us. We work in any weather...I'm going to stick with the strike till the end."

The strategy committee—representing now both the union and the black community—was, like the movement itself, fairly loose,[5] but "It worked as a closely knit team of trust," said Rev. Lawson. "We took each other's word."

Trust among the leaders was essential for there had been no time to structure an organization, and all of the lines of operation seem to have been a little blurred. The strategy committee defined its function as it went along. Its members met each night after the mass meeting to evaluate what had happened that day and to plan for the next. Rev. Starks described it. "We worked this day and we hoped tomorrow would bring about something. We were active this day and we planned this night and early the next day we started working again." It was an exhausting business, for these same people were conducting and directing most of the daytime activities and carrying on their ordinary lives as well.

"Night after night after night at these meetings in all these churches," remembered Jerry Wurf, "I brought my fist down on so many Protestant Bibles I almost became converted...The only way we could win this thing was by mobilizing the black community to understand that what these men were going through is what the community was struggling for, and so we perceived it as that....It wasn't symbolic. It was the depth. It was the truth. It was the absolute. If these black workers with the power of the black community could win this beef, then the black community had achieved a measure of freedom that did not exist before. That is not merely symbolic!"

The tactics of boycotting, marching, and mass meetings were a natural. Most of the community people on the strategy committee had been involved in some phase of the southern civil rights movement. The NAACP had previously used those confrontation methods in Memphis. Picketing and mass meetings were an integral part of the labor movement. New techniques might have to be worked out for Memphis, but for the present they would go with some of the tactics that had worked in the past, starting somewhat low-key in order to allow for future escalation if it became necessary.

It was assumed in all quarters and a tenet of faith among ministers that the movement would be nonviolent in terms of Martin Luther King's nonviolence, and this point was stressed continually to all those who joined with them.

What was launched in terms of the entire community of Memphis was a new power bloc of great potential—organized labor combined with civil rights.

One of the young black militants watched the movement come together and marveled: "I think that this was the most beautiful time that I have ever seen—black people really united. We had one more time to come out on top—to really beat the white man. We had one more chance really. It was do or die. God Almighty, man! Black people all over the city had nothing going on but the sanitation strike. They didn't care if you were a black power militant or if you were an Uncle Tom. If you were behind the sanitation strike, you were a brother. It was really a beautiful thing."

Within a few days the community coalition that would work with the union had a name. It was called "COME," an acronym for "Community on the Move for Equality," based on the scriptural exhortation, "Come, let us reason together."

For the last time in that civil rights decade, a massive nonviolent protest was being raised in a major center of the South.

Drizzle and an occasional smattering of light snow hung over the city as February ended and March began. Over in the public works department director Charles Blackburn and his chief aides, Charles Woodall and Maynard Stiles, went onto a war games basis. After the logistics were worked out, it was to provide once-a-week garbage pickup for almost the entire city.

Blackburn put his big routing maps of the city up on the wall and borrowed every car in the department equipped with a radio. Small maps were printed daily in the newspapers showing the areas where the garbage trucks and their accompanying police escorts would be working the following day.

Everyone in the designated areas was to carry his garbage cans to the curb for pickup. And white Memphis rose to the occasion. There were large areas in the black community where garbage was not put out, and some areas where it was dumped into the street or in vacant lots. But in the white community getting the garbage out on the curb was at first something of a challenge, a cause. It was a show of solidarity with the city.

T. O. Jones had complained that no one took any notice of garbagemen. He was right. No one took much notice of garbage either. If it couldn't go down the garbage disposal in the sink, it went into a garbage can and the trucks and faceless men came and it went away.

Now, suddenly, everyone was involved with garbage on a very practical level. People checked their daily papers to see when the trucks would be at their homes. The cans had to be at the curb by 8:30 A.M. and little boys helped older people carry their cans and tagged after the men putting it in the trucks. Enterprising teen-agers got pickup trucks and collected garbage on week-ends to take to one of the four dumps that had been opened up and were staffed from 6:00 A.M.–6:00 P.M. by nonstriking workers and police. Many homeowners loaded up station wagons and delivered their own garbage to the dumps. Some Boy Scout troops took on garbage collection as a project. In one section, the Jaycees were collecting garbage.

"There was this community feeling that we were going to help each other, get the job done, live through it," said one East Memphis woman.

A Committee of Concerned Citizens announced that it was going to raise funds for bonuses for garbage workers still on the job. The committee had some well-known names on it—a lawyer for the school board, the president of a title and trust company, the chairman of a real estate firm. White Memphis was rallying round its garbage cans.

Mayor Loeb estimated the city could provide once-a-week curb pickup with sixty trucks and a six-day workweek. By March 2, there were fifty-two trucks in operation.

There was some minor harassment, some shouting at men as they went in to work, some circling of garbage trucks on the streets. There were also isolated incidents of taunting nonstrikers when they returned home—phone calls, rocks through windows, slit tires, broken windshields. And there were growing reports of small piles of garbage set afire in the streets. At Police Commissioner Holloman's request, the sanitation central headquarters had been moved to the Democrat Road installation in the south part of the city which was more remote and harder to reach.

Several hundred white trade unionists joined the strikers' walk downtown on the first Monday in March. Their signs proclaimed "Memphis AFL-CIO Labor Council Supports Sanitation Department Employees." And they were led by labor council president Tommy Powell and by Dan Powell, who lived in Memphis and was a director of COPE, the AFL-CIO Committee on Public Education.

In many places such support would have been routine, expected. In Memphis it was a breakthrough and bolstered at least momentarily attempts of union leaders to make the strikers feel they were in the mainstream of American labor rather than some ostracized little group fighting for its survival down in Tennessee. But the rank and file of the 110 locals affiliated with the labor council were torn throughout the sanitation strike. On the one hand, their leaders, the officers of the labor council and many of the officers of their locals, supported the strike. They might have been nervous about the increasing black civil rights involvement, but they saw the strike first and foremost, as Bill Ross said, "as nothing more than the revolt of the public employees, the same type of revolt we had in the early period of the building trades, railroads, coal mines."

But the average union member could not take that expansive a view. What he saw, for the most part, was what his friends and neighbors saw—a "nigger" union and a lot of potential trouble in the city. "Early in the strike," Bill Lucy commented, "we had people telling us that 'I'll help you all I can, but if the NAACP becomes involved, you can forget about me.' "

Organized labor was not very strong in Memphis under the best of conditions. What would happen if the animosity in the community expanded to include not only AFSCME but organized labor in general? It was not that the white union members did not wish the public employees well in their fight for recognition and higher wages. Had the struggle remained purely labor-management, even in the face of Local 1733's all-black membership, probably a majority of union men would have stood behind the fight for recognition. But the strike became overtly racial and at that point of decision on whether they were first off trade unionists or white southerners, most white union members backed off. While local union leaders, excepting those in the building trades, gave united public support to the aims of AFSCME, behind them their troops skittered in disarray.

Still, there was some support. AFSCME representatives were given a chance to speak at meetings of the locals. Some monies did come in, amounts from $25 to $100. During the first month of the strike, locals of textile workers; electrical, radio and machine workers; hotel and restaurant workers; typographers; maintenance of way workers; butchers; steel workers; and oil, chemical and atomic workers contributed. Local 988 of the auto workers came up with $600. Local 186 of the United Rubber Workers, which had opened its hall for the daily AFSCME meetings, made a donation of $835, the largest single collection ever taken at its gates, and promised more, although this support caused vociferous criticism among some rubber workers.

The executive committee of the Memphis Newspaper Guild took a position supporting the strike in spite of the boycott of their newspapers, only to have the membership respond by virtually censuring the executive committee. The opposition reportedly came from advertising and clerical rather than from editorial.

Within the Memphis Building and Construction Trades Council, independent from the labor council, there was no equivocation. "We got absolutely nothing from them, not even the time of day," said Bill Lucy flatly.

Taylor Blair, international representative of the International Brotherhood of Electrical Workers in Memphis, had personally gone to the building trades groups to elicit support for the strikers. Blair was convinced the city was sitting on a powder keg and in the first week of the strike he had held several meetings with the mayor in hopes of softening Loeb's stance. Now he arranged for Wurf to appear at a building trades council meeting.

"It was felt they had some influence on Loeb, so it was a very valuable meeting and Blair was doing what you do. He was trotting out a big gun, an international president," explained Wurf.

His appearance was a fiasco. "The president of an international union is sort of an honored person," said Blair. "But Wurf was just some Joe who had wandered in off the street as far as this group were concerned." The meeting carried on its routine business—reviewing building jobs, parceling out fair shares of the work. Wurf sat in the back of the hall.

When he was finally recognized and spoke, he noted that while the strike had been "wildcat—which we trade unionists don't approve of—in the sense that it was never properly brought on with a vote—still there it was. The workers were totally supporting it." He asked for their support.

"If you want to shake them off, you pass a resolution, vote 'em fifty bucks, or you set up a committee," Wurf explained. One of the first responses, related Blair, was that Wurf "could do the whole city a favor if he would order these people back to work and take a half-page ad in the newspaper apologizing to the people of Memphis for the inconvenience they had been caused." Wurf remained unusually restrained. "I uttered a few words about the tragedy of the situation and agreed it might be good to buy an ad and left."

Support was naturally coming in from AFSCME locals all over the country, but the first substantial assistance from another international body came when the field representative of the Seafarers Union presented a five thousand dollar check and promised an additional one thousand dollars each week.

Wurf tried to shrug off the lack of strong local labor support. "The trade union movement is an institution like any other institution…It is not a unilateral mechanism. It's got thirteen-and-a-half million people with hundreds of thousands of officials with all kinds of pulls and tugs."

Bill Lucy was even more sanguine in retrospect. "In the South with the attitudes not only of the general southerner but southern labor—that they could relate to this strike or struggle at all with all the factors involved was something…It was a step…It was a definite improvement. And the fact that they copped out in a lot of places was to be expected."

Ciampa candidly admitted some of the other problems the union was facing. In the food collection and distribution "this one bandit kept shifting the warehouse for the donations people were collecting…He was trading on it. Two cans to the workers and ten cans to the store…You can't make a public scandal out of it. You just box him out and move on….

"There were some phonies in the ranks. I remember another guy…You ended up saying, 'Don't touch me. Just tell me how much.' He'd never come for anything big. It was either five bucks for medicine, twelve bucks for vitamins, six bucks for shoes, four or five times a week. He was an absolute hustler…I think there were some attempts by some hustlers, but there were just too many honest, decent people to let that happen…."

That same first week of March, AFSCME leaders also came into court on the contempt of injunction citations brought against them by the city.[6] "In addition to their claim that we induced the walkout or encouraged it, we also were accused of encouraging them to stay out by attending these meetings," explained the union's attorney Anthony Sabella.

Testifying for the city were Blackburn and Stiles of public works, Mayor Loeb, four newspaper reporters who had been covering the strike, and Police Detective E. E. Redditt, assigned to attend union and community meetings. The city's last witness was Lyle Caldwell, a veteran of ten years with the sanitation department who had not left work until two weeks after the strike started. A brick had been thrown through his window wrapped in a message: "This is a warning. Stay away from work."

In the spectators' section John Spence, assistant in the Memphis Civil Rights Commission office, was seated directly behind Mayor Loeb. Loeb turned to speak and, seeing Spence's dour expression, asked, "What's the matter?" "I don't think things are going very well. I don't like what's happening," replied Spence, who had been a Memphis newsman for fourteen years.

"Nobody does," replied the mayor and reached back to shake hands.

Jerry Wurf was the final witness at the hearing, testifying that he had not known of the strike until the men were already out and readily admitting to trying to settle the strike at all sorts of meetings and to addressing the men.

Later he would say privately, "If our general counsel was here and heard me say this, I'd get busted, but...I have never been impressed with the injunction. If you got the power to win the strike, it's academic. If you ain't got the power, they're going to knock your head off anyway."

Attorney Sam Weintraub, who was acting for the city but who had cautioned against going ahead with the contempt citation, found himself facing Wurf in the hallway during one recess. "Wurf said, 'You know, I don't want to go to jail'...I said, 'Well, that's kind of an understatement.' 'No,' he said. 'I got a desk piled high...and, boy, this business down here is wrecking my business and I don't want to go to jail.' And I muttered something like, 'Well, I don't think anybody wants to put you in jail'...He said, 'Why'd you file the contempt citation?...I mumbled something which must have sounded awfully silly to him and hypocritical...And he said, '*Nu, Yoishou?*' That's a Jewish expression...Justice...It's the core of justice...It means open to justice from God...and he smiled when he said it."

Throughout the hearing Chancellor Robert Hoffmann had allowed testimony from witnesses explaining the union's previous grievance procedure, its demands, the city's stand, the proposed checkoff through the credit union. At one point he suggested, "Why don't we sit down and see how close together we are." He also sounded out both Wurf and Loeb about the possibility of advisory or nonbinding arbitration, but Wurf backed off saying he would have to confer with others about the idea and Loeb rejected it as interference with the city's business.

"That (trying to settle the strike) was what I was trying to do," admitted Judge Hoffmann. "I don't deny it."

Seven of the twenty-three original defendants were found in contempt of the injunction by Judge Hoffmann—Wurf, Ciampa, Lucy, Epps, Paisley, T. O. Jones, and steward Nelson Jones. The judge sentenced them to fifty dollar fines and ten days in jail, but added they could purge themselves by calling off the strike. They refused. Appeal bonds were immediately set, ranging from $1,000 for Wurf to $250 for T. O. Jones and Nelson Jones, and union lawyers prepared to appeal the ruling to the Tennessee Court of Appeals at Jackson.

Union leaders were not in jail, but they had been partially checked in their activities and the city was vindicated in its position that the strike had been illegal from the beginning.

De jure as well as de facto, the strike now held or failed through the efforts of the black community. Jerry Wurf was caught between the proverbial rock and a hard place.

River Is Chilly and River Is Wide

No Easy Riders Here

6

"Mister Crump don't 'low no easy riders here."
W. C. Handy

There was one direct meeting between Mayor Loeb and the black ministers moving to support the strike. "Some of the ministers had to know that the mayor would take no recourse before a total commitment could be made," said Rev. Starks. "They had to know that themselves."

Loeb came down to the AME Church Minimum Salary Building in response to their invitation. Leaving his escort outside in the cold with reporters, he went alone up to the dining room with Baxton Bryant of the Tennessee Council on Human Relations.

It was the kind of session Loeb liked. He fielded their questions easily. It was important they understand that he was not fighting them but the union, he explained. He refused to apologize for the Macing on Main Street and told them the police were doing an exemplary job. But he also commended the ministers for "helping contain extremist elements within the Negro community."

"The Negro ministers have had to do so much in order to survive," observed Bryant. "The minister's bag of tricks— courtesy and deference to the white man—has been one of his bags, and especially to public officials. And I'll be dadburned if some of them didn't like to 'Tom' enough that I thought that the meeting was going to be a farce."

Rev. Starks, leading the meeting, said, "There was only one thing that the mayor wanted to do—continue to talk....We were as far apart at this particular meeting as we'd ever been."

They did continue to talk at the mayor's office that night. Bishop B. Julian Smith of the Christian Methodist Episcopal Church and Rev. Ralph Jackson headed a delegation of eleven.

"We went down really to obey the wishes of the mayor as much as we could," said Rev. Starks, "to show him a semblance of hope through him by going. He has magnificent control. He can smile and he can extend his hand, but his position does not change."

Dr. Jackson felt the delegation of ministers was being talked down to. The mayor spoke of budget figures, but the group was not interested in budgets but in union recognition. "When they spoke of the dues checkoff," said Jackson, "it was not a matter of us putting money into the coffers of the union. It was not the mayor's prerogative to decide what the men wanted."

But Rev. Jackson also understood that since Loeb had publicly declared a checkoff was against his principles, there had to be some face-saving device for the mayor. "I said that I was Methodist and I'm accustomed to realizing that the bishops must come out in a good light and that he should come out in a good light, too."

But the meeting was futile. "Listening to him made us realize that there was no position that we could take that would be compatible with his thinking," concluded Rev. Starks.

Baxton Bryant, ever the optimist, reported to the waiting press outside that the black ministers had found Loeb an easy man to talk to and that Loeb had realized clerical support for the strike was coming from a solid phalanx of religious leaders in the black community rather than from some splinter group.

"There is no change in my position," the mayor told a reporter. "Be sure you put that in the story."

More black ministers threw their support to the strike.

The nerve center of the strike came to be an area on Hernando Street, just a block-and-a-half south of Beale. Here next to the modern AME salary headquarters was big old stone Clayborn Temple, built in 1891, which as Second Presbyterian Church had housed a white congregation until it was sold to the AME Church twenty years earlier. And now a white minister, Rev. Malcolm Blackburn, led a small congregation of blacks.

The Beale Street area encompassed much of the city's history and many of its cultural contradictions. It would pass from being the center of black Memphis to being the stuff of legends. The street had boasted schools, the Robert Church auditorium and park, theaters, banks, even the Beale Street Baptist Church, while its bars and clubs ran wide open. Sporting men, easy riders, sweet men and their women, fancy prostitutes, whores, snow pushers, conjure sellers, river men, cooks and housemaids, laborers and yard men, country people in to see the sights, musicians, gamblers, the famous and the unknown, Beale Street had them all. Controlled by whites, patronized by blacks, raided periodically by police usually just before elections, Beale Street habitués shrugged and sang the song bluesman W. C. Handy had composed reportedly at Peewee's bar for Crump's first election:

> Mister Crump don't 'low no easy riders here.
> Mister Crump don't 'low no easy riders here.
> We don't care what Mister Crump don't 'low,
> Gonna barrelhouse anyhow....

But the street had become more and more tawdry. By 1968 the glamour had long since departed. It had always been garish. Now it was only cheap, with pawn shops, cut-rate liquor stores, discount clothing stores.

Around Clayborn Temple was an area of rapid deterioration, broken gutters, decrepit houses with dirt yards and a few wilting trees, gas stations, liquor stores, little barbecue places serving the best barbecue in town. In back of Clayborn Temple was the large complex of St. Patrick's Church, once Irish, by 1968 practically empty. Up a block were the Memphis offices of the NAACP. Nearby were the Universal Life Insurance Company and Tri-State Bank, intermeshed with the whole structure of black finance in the city. South and around the corner was the Foote Homes housing project for the poor, low "garden" structures. A great deal of the immediate area, including parts of Beale Street itself, was slated for urban renewal, although little actual demolition had begun except at the corner of Main and Beale where the new Memphis Light, Gas and Water Division administration building was to be built.

Marchers, both strikers and community sympathizers, would move north from Clayborn Temple the fourteen blocks, or 1.3 miles, to City Hall. The pattern that evolved was to send two streams of marchers to City Hall each day, one early and one in late afternoon. The marchers would go in orderly single file, two car lengths apart, along the sidewalk, carrying signs and passing out literature, and return in the same order to the church.

The first day of organized marching, February 26, about 130 people marched on the sidewalks on either side of Main Street. One column was led by Rev. Lawson and Baxton Bryant and the other by Rev. Starks, who was cold and nervous. But John Spence, along as an observer, ducked into the Claridge Hotel to bring him a paper cupful of coffee and Rev. Starks cheered up. There were police all along the march route and a police helicopter circled overhead.

Once it seemed apparent that the daily marches would be internally controlled and peaceful, Police Commissioner Holloman, who had announced he would permit the marches if they were orderly and followed reasonable rules, pulled back many of his visible uniformed police. Holloman was trying to remain reasonably flexible.

The number of marchers varied with the weather. Participants also became more varied as different elements of the community joined in. The first Saturday afternoon march had somewhere around one thousand people, many of them students and among those a couple of whites.

Activities centered on the daily union meeting, the two marches to City Hall, and the nighttime community meeting, which moved from church to church.

"The area and economic power people in the black community turned over their power to the COME center," explained Jacques Wilmore, head of the civil rights commission. "The COME strategy committee exercised a great deal of control, but it was never the kind of control many thought. Lawson came the closest, but his power was with those who had power blocs and turned it over to him."

"The strategy committee was very open," thought John Spence, who sat in at many of the meetings. "All kinds of people would drop in to listen. Others would come in and speak....COME was mostly ministers. There were few businessmen. Maxine Smith of the NAACP was there frequently, and Ms. Crenshaw was in from the beginning, full of outspoken militancy....We sat at a long table in the Minimum Salary Building....Sometimes there was conversation—half in jest—about 'who's running this thing?'.... Lawson was chairman and would have an agenda....But there were resentments of Lawson's chairmanship. He was a strong chairman."

From the beginning the Memphis movement stood on a strong foundation because of the fusion of the black community and the public employees' union. Yet it also was forced to contend with problems that earlier civil rights campaigns had not. Perhaps only Montgomery had been so much a spur-of-the-moment exercise. The very size of the black community, more than two hundred thousand, made the very logistics of getting black folks together both philosophically and geographically a major tactical problem. The Main Street Macing of the ministers may have been Memphis' Pettus Bridge, but the police were careful not to overreact a second time. Loeb might be pictured in the black community from Pharaoh through son

of a bitch, but he never came on as a wild-eyed, out-and-out
ranting racist.

And outside help would be extremely slow in coming to
Memphis because the story was slow to be picked up by the
national news media, surfeited now by a decade of civil rights
confrontations and the rising mobilization against the Vietnam
War. In the face of Martin King's upcoming Poor People's
Campaign and the furor over release of the National Advisory
Committee on Civil Disorders report, a garbage strike in
Memphis hardly brought the national press rushing South.

One of the main problems of COME was how and how fast
to escalate strike activities, for such a movement gained momentum or it failed.

Relief for the strikers and their families was being dispersed
through the union, except for food stamps which were handled
by the city. The first allocation of ten thousand dollars had been
reached and some seven hundred union members with thirty-
six hundred dependents had gotten stamps. In the first week of
March, Loeb authorized a second five thousand dollars in food
stamps but he indicated this allotment would be the last.

Black churches were donating money on a regular basis, but
their contributions were not large. An all-day gospel and soul
sing at Clayborn Temple raised some money; small individual
donations continued and labor contributions were picking up
slightly, but it was apparent much more money was needed.
AFSCME's strike fund was reserved for extreme emergencies,
not for day-to-day operations.

That same week seventy-seven garbage trucks were operating.

The downtown boycott seemed to be taking effect—one high
estimate said sales were off as much as thirty-five percent—but
Main Street merchants denied they were hurting.

Rev. Lawson himself was critical of just picketing. "Picketing,
or poster walking, as such is not any good unless it can help
create the confrontation. That means that you can't have in a
downtown area a handful of people carrying posters. You either
have to have hundreds and thousands or you have to move from

that to sitting in or some other strategy. You have to mix your weapons, but you have to make sure that the weapon you use, in terms of non-violence, is appropriate to the kind of confrontation that will help you get your ends accomplished."

The strategy committee was not notably aggressive, although it had a number of militant members who were opting for a move into mass civil disobedience, mostly those close to the center of the NAACP. "Among the ministers," noted Rev. Starks, "we had ministers in the conservative groups....My problem was to keep support of them all." In keeping that support, militancy was blunted.

"Escalation was phenomenally slow," said one participant.

With rising animosity among both union and black leaders toward the two daily newspapers, the noon union meetings and the night community meetings were now closed to reporters and photographers of the *Commercial Appeal* and the *Memphis Press-Scimitar*. They were either barred from entering or asked to leave. Since neither newspaper had a working black reporter, there was little chance of sneaking anyone into the meetings incognito. Reporters hung around and picked up what they could second-hand and engaged in a contest among themselves to see who could stay longest in a meeting before being ejected.

It was not a complete communications breakdown. Black and union leaders would make statements and respond to questions from the press, but eventually there was no direct coverage of the mass meetings. Reporters did not catch the growing determination in the black community exhibiting itself in those meetings, and because they did not, white Memphis did not catch it either. None of the three commercial television stations scheduled a local special on what was happening, and television news coverage tended to focus on moments of high drama such as city council confrontations.

Editorials continued to insist that the worker's grievances could be handled if the illegal strike were ended and they viewed the injunction against union leaders as a step in that direction. After the Macing on Main Street, both papers acknowledged that racial feelings had, indeed, now surfaced, but they held steadily to the view that racial incitement was coming from an "organized group" of blacks who wanted to create problems. Now, the onus of their displeasure was directed not only at outside labor leaders, but also at the preachers and community leaders who became involved in the strike.[1]

And at the same time that editorial writers were calling for calm and a cooling off period, such words as "incitement"; "anarchy"; "ministers' sideshow"; "hot-heads, hankering for a racial clash"; and "politically immature" were being used to describe the actions of strike supporters. Letters to the editor reflected white citizens' disapproval of the entire affair.

When the newspaper boycott came into effect early in March and blacks were urged to cancel their subscriptions to the *Commercial Appeal* and *Press-Scimitar*, the communications cutoff became more serious. If the black citizen did, in fact, stop reading the daily newspaper, he was left with no source of news other than television or the weekly *Tri-State Defender* or *Memphis World*, both black weekly newspapers and both woefully inadequate in terms of resources to cover the type of story the Memphis strike had become.

To find out what the black community was thinking, one had to read the *Defender*. To find out what the city was doing, one had to read one of the daily papers. Few citizens bothered with both, and consequently the gap grew wider.

If newsmen were not welcome at the union and mass meetings, the infiltration of plainclothes policemen became an even greater irritant. The strike was cutting deeply into Police Commissioner Holloman's department. Schedules were continually reorganized; men were kept on extra duty. Officials considered it imperative to know what was happening within the strike meetings, forewarned being forearmed. So there was constant infiltration or attempted infiltration by black officers of the meetings and wide use of tape recorders. It was an open secret. Mayor Loeb heard tapes of the meetings in his office.

Frank Holloman was the new breed of police executive. A

graduate of the University of Mississippi, he had spent twenty-five years with the FBI as a special agent, and had been in charge of various field offices, including Memphis. From 1952-59, he had been an inspector in charge of J. Edgar Hoover's Washington office.

When he agreed to head up the Memphis Police and Fire Departments he replaced the politically powerful Claude Armour, who would go on to become public safety director for the state. Under Armour, Memphis had the reputation of a "law and order" town, and there were periodic outcries of "police brutality" from the black community when police, armed with billy clubs, guns, and a statute allowing "all necessary means to effect the arrest" of a resisting or fleeing felon, were somewhat casual in the use of all of these.

But Armour, who took over in 1950, also had the reputation as a tough but fair cop and a benevolent autocrat within the department. When racial integration did come, Armour saw that it came with little trouble. "He said he was going to maintain law and order," said one newspaperman, "and he didn't care whose ass, black or white, he had to run out of town in order to do it." Chief Inspector Henry Lux, in charge of the first school integration detail, agreed. "My orders were very simple. Black children were going to school and Armour had made up his mind to that. So I put fifty men on each campus—and they're going to school!" Throughout the early sixties' period of desegregation, the police had generally acquitted themselves with discipline and restraint and their loyalty to Armour held.

His successor Holloman did not come on as a tough cop. His favorite bit of philosophy, repeated in speech after speech as he tried to build better police/community relations, was "We must learn to walk in the other fellow's moccasins." He took over a police department of around 850 officers, understaffed for a city the size of Memphis. It was top heavy with brass and he would soon freeze all promotions. Once ad hoc and on-the-street, training now consisted of a twelve-week course, and the

Memphis Police Department also was channeling men into training sessions at the FBI Academy. Many of its top officers had been there.

Salaries were low. Starting salary was around five hundred dollars a month and a lieutenant with twelve years' service would earn between $800 and $900. There was unlimited sick leave and three weeks' vacation after ten years, and the department paid ninety percent on life and hospitalization policies.

Like other police departments, the Memphis force was clannish. "Let an officer get shot and you have to get in line to get into his room and see him," said one officer. It was a "clean" department. Police payoffs were rare and petty when they did occur. There was no organized crime in Memphis, but general crime, as across the rest of the country, was on a serious upswing. The 1967 figures for Memphis showed an increase of 18 per cent in serious crimes over 1966. Holloman continually sought authorization for a larger force.

There were some tensions within the department and there was uncertainty about Holloman. There was resentment among some of the older men over the trend toward requiring college education for police officers, a trend Holloman pushed. Some regarded the embryonic attempts at police/community relations as "fluff," and the department stood together as a solid wall whenever charges of police brutality arose. Certainly there was racial prejudice within the ranks. But, on the whole, the Memphis Police Department at the time of the strike was neither a shining example of progress nor a wretched center of politicized prejudice.

Holloman entered the strike period with no prior rapport with black leaders. His chief aides in the strike were Police Chief J. C. Macdonald, a hard-headed Scotsman, and a coterie of seven assistant chiefs, from whose ranks the calm, soft-spoken Henry Lux would rise to become the next chief of police. He would handle field operations of those men assigned to various activities of the strike and so be very visible, as would Inspector Sam Evans in his dark glasses, barking orders to the emergency squad through his walkie-talkie.

Although he had no real experience with routine city policing, Holloman was prepared to run a police department. He was not prepared for a garbage strike. Routine crime continued but in addition to their regular duties, police were now detailed to escort the garbage trucks and to patrol the substations. They were deployed on Main Street for the daily marches, at city council meetings, and, undercover, at all of the mass meetings. By the first week of the strike, ward car men were on 12-hour shifts and days off were canceled. Patrolmen were compensated for overtime on their regular salary scale, and top officers accumulated time off.

Holloman was playing the situation by ear and he was inclined toward overcaution and oversaturation. The internal security division was expanded to gather intelligence about the strike. Police were getting tired and after the Main Street Macing more tense. All sorts of rumors of threatened trouble came into police headquarters. "There are numerous police informers," explained one officer. "They are not paid except maybe with a half pint of whiskey or an overlooked dice game. And they're going to tell us just enough to keep us off their neck....But all they had to do was tell one officer the Scott Street sanitation substation was going to be blown up, and the jungle drums started beating."

Prevailing police opinion was swinging around to "Why in hell does this bunch have to go out and strike and disrupt this city? We want raises just like they do."

It was department policy to use black officers in the visible forefront because this was a black strike and it was hoped the use of black policemen would help keep down hostility. But every time a black plainclothesman was identified and evicted from a closed meeting, the level of tension on both sides rose. The lot of the black policeman throughout the entire strike was hardly a happy one. And gradually the information received by police about the movement's plans and strategies began to dry up, and any cooperation between police and the COME leadership was closing off.

The COME strategy committee was also increasingly concerned at the increase of garbage pickup. Picketing of the
Democrat Road installation, from which all of the trucks now
moved out into the city, had begun routinely the first of March.
On the first morning some thirty pickets arrived early. They sat
across the entrance, but on police orders moved out onto
Democrat Road, where they marched back and forth carrying
signs and shouting at arriving workers. None of the trucks
pulling out of the station and swinging into the road were
blocked, nor was there any attempt to do so during the first
week.

Rev. Malcolm Blackburn, of Clayborn Temple, joined the
pickets each morning. He had been somewhat careful of
picketing because he held Canadian citizenship and was unclear
just what some grounds for deportation might be. "But the
picketing was becoming increasingly ineffective," he said. "The
scab laborers were paying less and less attention once they knew
they were safe, that no one was going to hurt them out
there....And there was a little too much fraternization going on.
One morning when it was wet and rainy and I was complaining
of the cold, Director Charles Blackburn was willing to invite me
over to the barn for a cup of coffee.

"I remember one day we were down there, some of the young
people and Zeke Bell sat down on the road. Rev. Starks came
along and said, 'Now, look. I'm as ready to do this as anybody,
but this is not the time. This is not what we agreed on.' And they
were persuaded to get up."

But a few days later Rev. Blackburn took matters into his own
hands and with six sanitation workers refused to move from the
center of the road, blocking the trucks. They were rather
promptly arrested.

A regular arrest procedure had been worked out by COME.
The integrated law firm of Ratner, Thompson, Sugarmon,
Lucas and Willis was usually called. They would arrange bond,

usually assuming responsibility for it, since the lawyers were not paid in full until after the strike was over. Rev. Blackburn and his fellow pickets were out of court on bond in time to appear at the noon union meeting and tell their story.

Actually the most visible early signal that the strike was escalating came from the increasing involvement of young blacks. At first teen-agers began coming down to Clayborn Temple after school and marching. "But the young people felt they weren't being terribly effective or useful, just doing the same as adults," said Rev. Blackburn, who worked closely with the students. "So we had to dream up things. We used to sit down in the dining room at the AME building—Middlebrook, Bill Smith and I and some of the young people's leadership—and say, 'Now what are we going to do this afternoon?' You had to continually draw the line with the young people that would keep them involved effectively or you were going to lose them."

Rev. Harold Middlebrook, 26, of the strategy committee, was in charge of youth activities. Although the program was un-structured, there were kids who acted as contacts to get the word around in the black high schools. A graduate of Morehouse College, the Atlanta student activities, youth work at Ebenezer Baptist Church with the Rev. M. L. King, Sr., and SCLC's Selma campaign, Rev. Middlebrook was an assistant at Judge Ben Hooks' Middle Baptist Church and worked as a clerk at the Memphis post office.

And he was opposed to using students for daily marches. "That was the silliest thing I ever heard of....I decided it was time for us to do something different." So the youth group borrowed a casket from R. S. Lewis funeral home. "We could have had a hearse," said Middlebrook, "but we took just a cheap wooden casket covered with velvet so if it got damaged it would be easier to pay for."

The students were off to bury Freedom at City Hall. About two hundred strong, they marched up Main to City Hall Plaza where a mock funeral service was held.

JUSTICE IS DEAD AND LOEB KILLED IT read one sign.

"Oh, Freedom…before I'll be a slave, I'll be buried in my grave…." sang the jumping, clapping circle of kids.

"This kind of startled everyone," said Rev. Grant Harvey, another young minister. "Even the garbage workers already marching downtown didn't know we were coming."

"I kind of wish I had gotten somebody and put him in the casket and then opened it," Rev. Middlebrook mused.

Some sixty policemen accompanied the procession back to the church, moving in closer when several garbage cans were overturned on Beale, but there were no arrests.

The idea of burying Freedom had not been checked through the strategy committee. If it had, Middlebrook contended, there would have been no burial. The strategy committee would have held back.

Youth marchers began changing tactics. "Usually they lined up in the street and went the same way," explained Rev. Middlebrook. "Then one day they lined up inside the church so that when they busted out the door they were moving…against the pattern of traffic. The police couldn't follow." March leaders would suddenly switch and move the student march over onto Second Street against the one-way traffic. Police covering the march were forced to leave their squad cars and motorcycles and work on foot. The object was to keep the police guessing, to catch them off guard. The marches were still on the sidewalk; they were still controlled by their leaders. But the unwritten agreement with the police had been breached.

One day some thirty kids were outside several major department stores on Main, following any blacks who made purchases. On Monday, March 11, nearly a hundred students walked out of Northside High School, seventy-seven percent black in enrollment. In a pouring rain they clapped and chanted "Black Power" and "Down with Loeb" as they passed through downtown on their way to Clayborn Temple. Few had raincoats or umbrellas. There some of them joined the late afternoon youth march, and for the first time several groups of kids broke away from the main march and raced down alleys, pursued by police.

"Some of the kids got suspended and this dampened a lot of spirits," admitted Rev. Middlebrook.

There were no more mass walkouts from school then, but the Northside students' march had set up a psychological chain reaction in the high schools. Only small groups of individual students might slip out during school hours and join the downtown activities, but many of those who stayed at their desks kept track of the strike, ready to act if anything came up.

Several days later thirty young people, including ten girls, led by Rev. Middlebrook and another young minister, Rev. Roosevelt Joyner, were arrested on charges of blocking traffic and creating a disturbance at Third and Pontotoc during school hours. "We were standing in front of garbage trucks," said Rev. Middlebrook. City court Judge Bernie Weinman released the adults on their own recognizance and sent the students over to Juvenile Court where they were kept until their parents came.

A day later at dusk some 125 young people picketed one of the parking lots on Front Street for an hour, and on Saturday, March 16, a large group carrying signs walked the perimeter of Poplar Plaza Shopping Center in white East Memphis.

The schools were drawn into the strike through the increasing activity of students. Any student truant for the fifth time received an automatic school board suspension and his parents had to go through board channels to have him reinstated, although local principals could suspend for fewer truancies. Explained School Superintendent E. C. Stimbert, "We never did suspend any child for marching, for demonstrating....We wouldn't suspend them for that any more than we would for attending a Baptist convention...or stealing watermelon or whatever.... They were suspended for not being in school...."

On Friday, March 15, Juvenile Court Judge Kenneth Turner issued an order directing the police to pick up all students younger than sixteen found on the streets during regular school hours, regardless of what they were doing. The state law on truancy permitted this as well as fining parents from two dollars to ten dollars each day of the child's truancy. Within hours police had picked up a small group of thirteen- and fourteen-year-olds in the downtown area.

There was also an upsurge of juvenile vandalism. Garbage cans set out on curbs for pickup in black neighborhoods were kicked over. Loeb's Bar-B-Ques had windows broken. Police and firemen answered something like seventy calls on the nights of March 7 and 8 for trash fires, vandalism, and false alarms. Squad cars were hit by rocks and bottles at two separate locations on two separate nights. A Molotov cocktail was thrown into a grocery store near Clayborn Temple. A sort of rally was held one night outside the Food Circus on South Lauderdale and ended with youths surging into the store, knocking things off shelves. The night manager grabbed one of them, held a pistol to his back and refused to release him unless the others left. They left and the group outside broke his window. A firebomb exploded in front of the home of a sanitation worker who had returned to work, and a few bricks crashed through windows.

"These young people go to meetings, are inflamed by fiery speeches, then disperse in small groups and are able to create havoc," said Holloman. "How their (the COME ministers) consciences condone it is beyond me."

In fact, much of the vandalism was carried out by young blacks who had little or no contact with COME. Because public attention was centered on the strike, the willy-nilly vandalism tended to focus there also.

The strike also accelerated black organizing at Memphis State University. By 1968, 7.2 percent—1,152 out of 15,914 students—were black, one of the highest percentages of any of the formerly all-white colleges and universities of the South.

"You have to get over being awed, you know, having never gone to school with white people," commented Eddie Jenkins, Mayor Loeb's dinner companion at the NCCJ banquet. He had come to Memphis State in 1964. "You have to get used to going to school with white people. You feel like a fly in the buttermilk

when you go into class. You feel set apart....The students
generally reflect the attitudes of the community and we know
what these attitudes are. They generally don't associate with
Negroes. Lots of kids' attitudes were, 'Man, I really must be
getting somewhere cuz here I am out at the white folks'
school.' "

Blacks from all social and economic classes were enrolling at
Memphis State. Like white students, many of them were
working to put themselves through school. Eighty percent of
the students were commuters. The student body was essentially
conservative; student government was controlled by the frater-
nities and sororities.

The blacks were a quiescent bunch, sitting together in classes
and in the student union, leaving the campus as soon as classes
were over. There was a black fraternity and a black sorority, but
no blacks had ever been pledged to any of the other Greek
groups. All other university organizations were, of course, open
to them, but few black students, for whatever reasons, moved
into them.

The football team was glaringly white in a city where tough
black high school players were courted by colleges in other parts
of the country. The first black, unrecruited, had won a place for
himself on the freshman team the preceding fall, but as yet the
crowds at Memorial Stadium had seen no black in the uniform
of the Memphis State varsity racing down the field. "We would
like to recruit Negro players in Memphis, if they can play," said
Coach Billy J. (Spook) Murphy. "There's no problem or hazard
now in having Negro athletes, as there was several years ago."

The most notable breakdown of the barriers between black
and white students had come in the informal atmosphere of the
Speech and Drama Department. There in the spring of 1967 a
play "High John de Conqueror," written by white student
Dalton Eddleman from Arkansas, had been produced. "High
John" centered on the affection of a white boy and a black girl
in a rural southern setting with the symbolic figure of High
John, the old, blind blues singer of black folklore, moving

through the plot. It was the first time the theme of interracial love had seen the light at Memphis State, a time when an interracial couple on campus was almost unheard of. In the spring of 1968 an integrated cast was in rehearsal for "The Death of Bessie Smith."

Ron Ivy, later to be the leader of the Black Students Association, had played High John. Later he recalled his wonder at even becoming involved. "I just sing the blues....I always liked them....I went over to tryouts. And this guy said, 'Why didn't you come before? Didn't you see the sign outside saying 'Tryouts for High John?' I said, 'Yes, I saw the sign.' I just never looked at it. I look at the bulletin board but I never think about what's on it. It doesn't relate to me."

In the fall of 1967 Ivy was spokesman for several young blacks convinced that some changes had to be made in the status of black students at Memphis State. "I saw something lacking," he explained. "I would go to parties...and Memphis State students always seemed so backward. They knew what was in the books but the culturizing process a college is supposed to give its students, the Negro students here were missing it. They disassociated themselves from local events....They were just like high school students....I saw the need for at least some awareness on their part of the fact that they had to play a larger role than just saying, 'I go to Memphis State.' "

Eddie Jenkins was among the students who went along with him. They tried first the route of joining with the white students on campus who were mildly New Left, but their aims were divergent, and the blacks went their own way into a Black Students Association.

Ron Ivy would muse for a long time over his own particular feelings about the black/white situation.

"The white kids in the neighborhood—we'd play ball in the daytime and fight at night....It got to be almost a ritual...When it'd start getting dark the white boys would start calling us 'niggers' and we'd start calling them 'crackers' and then we'd fight...fists and sticks and bottles....And the next day we'd come back and play another game of baseball....I often wondered why in the world we would play ball all day and then at night fight....

"I started working at sixteen at The Peabody hotel as a busboy. My father was a waiter there....And all of a sudden my father—who I always respected because he was the person who came in at night from work—he was always the person that if anybody was gonna be called 'Mister' it was him—I leaned that he was a 'boy,' 'my boy,' somebody else's 'boy.' I remember a white man and he said, 'Who are you?' And I said 'My name is Ron Ivy.' He was a regular customer and he said, 'Oh, you're Ben's son.' And I said, 'Ben who? I'm Mister Ivy's son.' And he said, 'Well, you won't never be the man that your father is because he's a good boy.' And this was killing me....And after that I did everything I could while I was working at The Peabody to stay as far away from my father as possible so I couldn't hear this kind of stuff....I understood. After all, he was working. He knew he had to work if we were going to eat. I always understood....

"I learned a lot of things, about what was supposed to be a Negro's proper place. I learned about smiling. If you wanted to keep your job, if you wanted to make money, you always smile and you never look at a person straight, because if you looked at him straight and if you talked to him like you talked to anybody else, then you were being arrogant. And you wouldn't get any money....

"I found myself in a very difficult situation when I came to Memphis State. I was talking to white kids out here. I had white instructors and even if they didn't mean it, I think they tried to make me feel as comfortable as possible. And they did talk to me as a person and I talked to them just like I talk to anybody else. And then I'd leave Memphis State and go to work and I'd be a different person for the next four hours. I found myself talking to people when I was working like I would talk to people on campus, and finally found myself getting 50 cents instead of $1.50, getting evil looks or insulting remarks from people.

"Like a man called me 'boy' once. I never will forget. I was eighteen and he called me 'boy.' I turned around and asked him who in the hell he was talking to. I thought, 'Listen at you; you've lost your mind.' But I just felt like asking him who the hell was he talking to, hollering 'boy' across the room. And I had heard people call me worse things than 'boy' and I hadn't said anything all those years....

"I hated to go to work...hated to play this role, just hated it so, hated it to my bones. It looked like I'd rather be broke than to have a cent doing this type of work....I knew that I couldn't stand this. I knew that I wasn't gonna stand it. I knew that as soon as I got out of school and got me something else to do, I would run. I would leave these kinds of jobs alone for the rest of my life...."

Throughout the fall semester of 1967, the blacks on campus organized. Their regular meetings were called the Black Forum, attracting thirty to fifty students. Black awareness was the main theme and the weekly meetings brought about a sharing of all sorts of problems on campus. A paper called the *Black Thesis*, heavy on polemics, poetry, and opinion, made its appearance, printed on borrowed paper on a church mimeograph. The university dean was working to facilitate the BSA becoming a recognized campus organization.

But militancy was a far piece down the pike. When the sanitation strike first started, only individual BSA members who had neighbors or members of their families working for the city responded. But with the Main Street Macing and the formation of COME, the number of Memphis State students attending the mass community meetings steadily increased and reports were brought back to the campus group.

It was the white members of the Liberal Club, however, who forced the hand of the black students because on Friday, March 1, whites held a campus march to support the striking workers. The blacks joined them.

"Wednesday, March 6, was the second march," said Eddie Jenkins. "We even had some faculty members. When I got there about noon we had thirty or forty white people standing around waiting to march. I went into the student union and said, 'Black people, we're going to march!' They were sitting there playing cards and eating and talking, listening to radios....I said, 'Are you gonna get hung up on what whitey thinks of you? Isn't the issue greater than what they think? If not, then we may as well forget any struggle at all.' People were still talking, eating, and playing cards. I was standing up on a chair then. A few started getting up, but they really hadn't started to move. So I got a little angry. I said, 'I'll tell you what—you house niggers! If you want to sit here and be house niggers the rest of your lives, you sit here. Cuz us yard niggers is tired and us yard niggers is gonna get us up and we gonna go out there and we gonna march. White folks waiting to march with us and we're gonna march. You house niggers sit here!' And cards started falling. And hamburgers started being gobbled. Some just put them down and started getting up." The second march was bigger than the first.

The following week Mayor Loeb appeared on campus, and when word got out that he was there, black students ran to the student union, gathered other students and signs, and marched out to meet him. The mayor, about to get into his car, walked back to them, and a babble of noise erupted punctuated with words like "my open house....a bunch of racists....no!....no!" In this milling crowd, the mayor triumphed. "There are many, many things we agree on. There's one we're not going to agree on, I'm afraid, and that's the union-dues checkoff." He invited them all to his open house.

But there was also another group of blacks, college age and older, militant, organized, somewhat unclear about their ultimate strategy, moving into the strike. These were members of the Black Organizing Project, commonly called the Invaders, who had first come into public view the summer before when several of their members got into a dispute with War on Poverty officials. They had caught more attention in the black community throughout the fall and winter, working at one point in the Willis campaign for mayor. Now the BOP surfaced again.

A young black man with "Invaders" stenciled across the back of his jacket came to the microphone at one mass meeting. "I'm a radical," he began. "I'll tell you just like that. I'm a radical....Before Henry Loeb will listen, the garbage has to be in the street...not in your back yard. As long as those trucks are allowed to roll, they can keep it picked up wherever they want it picked up....Preaching and money raising are fine. Somebody has to do it. But there are some *men* out there. We've got to do some *fighting*. Not marching—fighting! And when you talk about fighting a city with as many cops as this city's got, you better have some guns! You're gonna need 'em before it's over!"

The presiding minister granted the young man his right to talk, but he reminded the audience that nonviolence had been chosen as the weapon of this campaign. Outside the church some of the older men discussed this new factor. "We may be in trouble this way (letting the militant philosophy be made public)," said Rev. Blackburn. "But if we did not recognize this mood as part of the picture, we most certainly would be in trouble."[2]

Behind the incident lay a year of young blacks trying to organize at the grass-roots level. Bobby Doctor, of the civil rights commission, had watched the attempts from the beginning, for he himself had been a militant student not many years before over at Orangeburg. "They were the young, aggressive-minded black people in the city...developing a certain amount of dignity and pride, black consciousness and awareness....And they were influenced by the national awareness of these things....They recognized that the black community must develop a new image, a new self-image, an image of strength, dignity, pride. Certain types of power and control must be developed within this black community if it is to make certain demands of the total community, demands which would speak to the needs.

"No other group in Memphis was beginning to speak for the disadvantaged, poverty-stricken, ill-educated mothers with 'illegitimate' children, young kids, drop outs, guys who hung around the pool halls, pimps, winos, prostitutes, persons who heretofore had not in any way been a piece of the action, persons sort of altogether out of the mainstream."

One of the BOP organizers related their history. "In 1967 Coby Smith and Charles Cabbage hit the streets with what is known as this Black Power bit." Coby Smith was already something of a celebrity—an honor graduate from Manassas High School, student president, one of the first two black students to attend Southwestern at Memphis College, intelligent, articulate. Charles Cabbage was a political science graduate from Morehouse College, and had worked with SNCC just when the influence of Stokely Carmichael was at its highest point. "Cabbage had graduated from Carver High School. He knew everyone in Memphis. He had the contacts. Organizing would be easy..." continued the organizer.

"We started walking the streets trying to get this thing going. All of us talked about it. Whenever we met one brother we always tried to convince him that he ought to come and join the organization....We started meeting wherever we could...printing our sheets...having publicity gimmicks to let people know the Black Power people were here and ready to burn Memphis if Memphis didn't deal with black and white problems."

What was developing in Memphis was an indigenous independent youth organization—heavy in rhetoric and nebulous on solutions—of the same type that had sprung up in other southern black college centers seven and eight years before. Here Memphis was late, and because it was late, the emphasis had shifted from nonviolence to violence or at least the threat of it and from an attempt to gain individual civil liberties to the emancipation, economically and socially, of the entire black community. It was organized in the streets partially because philosophically the street group was now the center of revolution, but partially also because there was no one organized college group in Memphis around which it could coalesce.

LeMoyne College was a private, liberal arts commuter college with an all-black student body, founded and still supported in part by the American Missionary Association (an arm of the United Churches of Christ). The students had a reputation for being conservative and the college president Dr. Hollis Price, dignified, highly educated, active in civic endeavors and more militant than most in comparable positions but still careful, frowned upon student activists.

"There are a great many young people here who want to go to college," said history professor Dr. Peter Cooper, who had taught there for twenty-seven years. "That they have sort of middle-class aspirations is not strange. They want to have that car and a nicer home and have their children get the advantages that they didn't have."

Owen Junior College, a small black school operated by the Baptists and struggling on a small budget to help poorly prepared high school graduates, was little more than a glorified high school. There were a few blacks at Southwestern at Memphis, but they were hard to find in a ninety-eight percent white enrollment. Memphis State blacks were just organizing themselves.

Still, a few students from all of these campuses—from the NAACP youth chapter at LeMoyne, the Afro-American Brotherhood at Owen, recruited by Coby Smith at Southwestern and by Ron Ivy at Memphis State—were part of the new organization.

And a smaller group was created within the Black Organizing Project—the Invaders.

"The Invaders were the fire-power hand of BOP," said the guy who was there. "The Invaders were responsible for security, for putting out sheets on guerilla warfare, training people in liberation tactics. They were the military end of BOP. John Smith became sort of the unofficial head of the Invaders. He'd had military training and the tactical know-how in the Army and was great at organizing young guys. Since a black boy when he's fourteen isn't really a boy, he's a man—he knows what the world is all about—we decided to get people in high school and freshmen and sophomores in college to make up the Invader group...."

They named the group "Invaders" after the currently popular television show in which alien beings filtered in among earth people. "See, we looked, talked, acted in the form of everyday ordinary people. So if you saw me downtown, I'd look like any other shopper and you wouldn't know if I was really a black man getting ready to bomb your place or just a black man in the city. Tactics were to get people in legitimate positions....When we got people like John going to jail every day during the strike it was because he is in charge of the Invaders and it's their position to take these sorts of stands."

When black candidate Willis entered the 1967 race for mayor, BOP moved toward him as a rallying point. In return they wanted his commitment to a population-based percentage of blacks in all city positions. And they wanted money and administrative help for their organization. They worked for Willis, but Willis lost the election. "Now this is when we found out that we hadn't done as great a job of convincing the community that we were there for their good as we thought we had. We didn't have the middle-class areas....The black people in the city were not ready for a black mayor, but for a white mayor liberal. As far as we are concerned, there is no such thing as a white liberal. If a cat is liberal he is useless...the white society won't accept him and won't have him and there is not a damn thing he can do for us, because we are getting tired of all this help from the outside.

"We believe in self-help. We don't want white people sitting in and saying, 'O.K., let me show you how to do this.' We don't need that. We would rather fall down fifty million times and have learned and have done it ourselves."

With the Willis defeat, "We were getting a backlash from everybody. People felt if Willis hadn't run, Ingram would have won and they would have had themselves a mayor....Willis cut us loose." Split over the recriminations and explanations of the Willis defeat as well as over Willis' public rejection of Black

Power, BOP was further cut up by its own internal leadership struggles.

Then came the sanitation strike. It put everything back together. "The feeling was to get Loeb and take the whole white community with him, every last one of them....They didn't give a doggone what white person it was....Coby came in with his group from North Memphis...And Cabbage came in with the group from South Memphis....Then we brought in the threat element...the Invaders....the militant army to make people just a wee bit afraid so that we could sort of push things....The Invaders never intended to burn the city down—they live here, too—but to keep people hopping and to keep them afraid....We were representing the threats that Lawson and them would need in order to sort of make the white man afraid....

"The fellows felt about Lawson like he was just another black brother who had his thing to do. We understood and respected it, but if he ever got in the way, he could go, too. He wasn't really one of us...." the BOP organizer concluded.

Rev. Lawson, though, seeking representation from all segments of the community, had added Cabbage to the COME strategy committee the first weekend it was formed. Relations were not smooth.

"They came in with ideological, rhetorical displays," recalled Rev. Lawson. "They had no recommendations of how we could systematically organize, effect the boycott, the marches, and the kinds of changes we wanted for these men, deal with the problems of food, clothing and money....Eventually I simply said, 'You've got a better scheme? Go ahead. No one is stopping you. You're free. But don't obstruct.' "

"We didn't participate in the picketing," said one BOP member. "But the boycott was fine with Cabbage because it hurt the white man's pocket."

So the Invaders did their own thing. March 5: three arrested on reckless driving and disorderly conduct as they left City Hall. March 11: two arrested in the cafeteria at Carver High School trying to persuade students to leave school. When police arrived they lay on the floor resisting arrest. March 13: nine arrested at Main and McCall downtown for shouting, acting boisterously, and threatening people. March 14: two arrested in a group of thirty blocking traffic; they continued their noisy demonstration in jail, stopping up the drain in the shower stall to flood the room.

"We had these goddamn crazy kids with their five-dollar pistols coming into the situation," said Jerry Wurf. "Men like Lawson were invaluable in their understanding that you didn't treat the Invaders like the anti-Christ but you didn't let them take over either."

Still the Invaders were now a factor in the strike. Mild in comparison to militant groups in other cities, they nonetheless waved the Black Power banner across Memphis. They overestimated, of course, their impact on the white community. Most whites didn't comprehend and didn't fear what they simply considered a bunch of hoodlums, although their actions did strengthen the white belief that the whole strike alliance was an unsavory bunch. Probably their greatest effect was on the black high schools where more and more jackets appeared with "Invaders" across the back.

They were acting independently of COME when it suited them, joining in actions with which they agreed. COME leadership, while it continually eschewed violence, never did publicly disavow them in this period.

The COME strategy committee was in full agreement about bringing in outside speakers. The purpose was dual—to hearten local forces and to garner national publicity, still in short supply although the national news magazine stringers were beginning to cover and Norman Pearlstine of the *Wall Street Journal* had written the most comprehensive articles on the early strike.

Names of various speakers were bandied about, but COME was aiming seriously at three—Bayard Rustin, Roy Wilkins, and, after them, Martin King. Rustin would come through the union, Wilkins through the NAACP, and Rev. Lawson had already been in touch with Dr. King.

The difficulties of convincing Roy Wilkins, national NAACP president, to come showed that the Memphis strike was still not assigned any top priority by national civil rights leaders. Local president Jesse Turner had invited him earlier but Wilkins begged off. He had just finished work with the President's Commission on Civil Disorders. But COME was pressing now for an appearance by the national NAACP executive so Turner, in New York for a meeting, went over to invite him personally.

"I told him we just had to have him and get this thing on a national level," said Turner. "This was a fight that we could not lose. He had his secretary find a day that he could squeeze it in and we took it. It was March 14."

At the same time, union officials were contacting Rustin, of the A. Phillip Randolph Institute, who somehow managed to wear the hats of labor, civil rights, and pacifism all at the same time. Rustin also picked March 14 as a good day for Memphis.

"Welcome to Our Civil Rights Visitors," hailed the *Press-Scimitar*. "Look First at City's Record." The newspaper hoped that Wilkins and Rustin would examine the strike from all sides and give "some constructive ideas as to how community relations can be restored to their former level" and help get the strike back into negotiations, which could be done when the men went back to work. Nor, it was hoped, would the visitors forget "that they are visiting the city with the best race relations record in the nation," the highlights of which the editorial then recalled. "Oh, God," murmured one of the black leaders as he read on.

The rally brought some ten thousand out to Mason Temple, one of the few auditoriums anywhere that could take such a crowd. Wilkins responded in his speech that night that there had been racial progress in Memphis and that whites deserved a lot of credit, but "things just haven't moved fast enough....We can have peace and harmony in our cities this summer, but they can't expect us to do all the sacrificing." It was, he thought, "deplorable" that full-time workers could still qualify for food stamps.

Rustin called Memphis "one of the great struggles for emancipation of black people" and compared its impact to Montgomery. In New York's recent sanitation strike, workers had gotten a $425 a year raise. "No one expects Memphis to come up to New York's standards, but they do expect more than eight cents an hour" (one of the city's early offers). Rustin also turned a jaundiced eye on the newly released Kerner Report (the National Advisory Committee Report on Civil Disorders). "As if we need another report on how Negroes act...Where there is justice, order is maintained; where there is injustice, disorder is inevitable." He urged the audience to take the downtown boycott seriously.

Both speakers counseled continued nonviolence. Be firm but peaceful. In one of his less inspiring metaphors Wilkins urged, "Don't foul your nest. Don't go out and tear up the town. Just don't give an inch in your demands." Rustin, bathed in sweat and arms high above his head, led in the singing of "This Little Light of Mine."

It was a thoroughly satisfying rally. The strikers stood up in a body to wild cheers. Garbage cans were passed for the collection. There were hymns, freedom songs, and Black Power signs. Whites, conspicuous in their small numbers, were impressed.

Rustin met with COME leaders into the early morning. He offered whatever future support he could and went back to New York to talk about Memphis. A thousand dollars came in from the national NAACP.

Attempts to bring in Dr. King continued. "My first conversations with Martin, he was at a point of exhaustion and had been ordered by the doctor to rest absolutely," said Rev. Lawson. "He said that he simply had to take the doctor's advice, particularly since he already had the Poor People's Campaign ahead of him, that he'd been told he would drop if he did not rest. He went to Mexico, as I recall, for five or six days in the sun to relax and rest....I kept in contact with Andy Young, Bernard Lee, and his secretary Dora McDonald.

"I gave Martin some indications of what had gone on...the

extent to which it was nonviolent, and that we were keeping it within the context of the work that we in the past had done….Having worked closely with these men over the years I knew something of the type of questioning and conversations and concerns that would be important for them as they came into the situation….

"Martin definitely said he would try to come because he was deeply interested in what was going on."

Rev. Lawson announced publicly that Dr. King had been invited to speak in Memphis and the date was being arranged.

Jim Lawson was himself already a controversial figure, and would become more so as the strike progressed. His speech was precise, thrusting, words punching, and there was no soft black cadence in it—neither in appealing to whites nor in exhorting blacks. He never used his voice like the best of the black preachers—to wrap around the listener and lift him or carry him on down. When he spoke he not only looked other men in the eye, he evaluated them, watching not with suspicion but with interest or, more disconcerting, with amusement. When he laughed, even in irony, the laughter was deep and compelling, pulling listeners into it or leaving them with an uneasy feeling that he saw nuances in situations or in themselves that they had somehow missed.

Several years before, said one of the city councilmen, "My wife came home from a church-wide, city-wide meeting, and she said, 'Boy, we've got something on our hands.' And then she told me about Jim Lawson. She said then that she wondered who sent him here, because he just didn't fit…she decided that he was a dangerous person. Later we found out that he was arrested for draft dodging…for advocating and inciting riots. He was advocating the burning of draft cards. He was supposed to be a delegate for (the Christian Peace Assembly in) Prague and he was involved with the North Vietnamese in some way. This really bore out what she suspected."

Son of a Methodist pastor, Lawson had grown up in Massillon, Ohio, in integrated neighborhoods and schools. There were nine children in the family and they were a close-knit bunch. They liked to sing; they were proud of a great-great-grandfather who had escaped from slavery through Maryland.

Eventually all four boys would declare themselves conscientious objectors. But it was not until Jim was facing prison for that stand that it became a family crisis. "My brothers and I said to my mother, 'If you did not expect us to take this to heart, why did you teach us then that love was the law of God the the law of man?' I can remember my brothers and I between the living and dining rooms with my mother there, running back and forth, and our saying this to her. And her suddenly stopping and pausing for a very long time, and never again did she ever question or say anything about these positions....In those days we called it love, not nonviolence."

He was a secure, athletic, and active kid, into drama, debate, and band, working in his father's church and in national Methodist youth organizations. At Baldwin-Wallace College, outside of Cleveland, he was elected president of his very visibly white freshman class.

Despite the white friends and the integrated situations, the black definitions began to close in on him as he grew older. The northern version. The term "nigger" on the street. A refusal of service at a restaurant. Some trouble in barber shops. On the college campus a furor over mixed dating. His first reactions had been highly emotional, "a sense of real isolation and alienation and rejection." But he struggled through to a position—"that I would absolutely refuse to act abnormal when I'm a normal person....I'm not going to be disciplined or contorted into some form that I'm not."

In college he was reading Gandhi, A. J. Muste, Niebuhr, Tolstoy, and doing all his outside class work in the areas of race and of war and peace. He and a few companions had already tried out the sit-in technique, pioneered by CORE. He was moving toward the Methodist ministry and was preaching at a small rural church weekends of his senior year. But he had also

taken a non-cooperative stance against the post-World War II
military conscription act.

"It was a saying that the life and ministry of Jesus was a kind
of life that I wanted to shape for myself...that I could not go into
the army, no matter whose army it was...that the law of love as
Jesus tried to live it and teach it permitted a man to lay down his
life for another life, but it did not permit him to make the choice
that the other man's life should be laid down instead of his
own....The just war/unjust war is really not as issue....Back
then I said that I would never obey a segregation law, and
conscription laws were similar in that they were a complete
denial of the meaning of freedom. Therefore, I would not
cooperate with them."

The Korean War began. He was called up. He did not attempt
to claim ministerial exception, but simply refused to accept his
induction notice. In April 1951, he was sentenced to three years
in federal prison. Prison was a decisive experience. He read
voraciously, tried to integrate the cell blocks and was transferred
to a maximum security facility, and found, if he had not already
known, that even hardened criminals were "still genuinely
human with the same fears and doubts that other people have."

He got into long discussions with the first Black Muslim he
had ever known. "He tried to convert me and I tried to convert
him." And, he grinned, "another guy I came to trust explicitly
was a hard-nosed, rough, hard-as-nails thief from
Washington....His thesis was that his profession was as honorable as my intended one....They'd all say to me, 'Well, you're
a nut. If you'd talked to me I could have told you how to stay
out of the army and not pull any time for it.' "

Thirteen months later he was paroled for the Methodist
mission in India, to work as a coach and minister to the student
Christian movement out of Hislop College in Nagpur. Already
intrigued by the possibility of applying nonviolent forms to
black protest, he observed intently the Gandhian-influenced
and post-Gandhian social and political arena. Again, his base was
simple. "In this vast revolutionary age, the human race either has

to learn to deal with injustice and conflict in essentially pacifist, soul-force ways or the human race is going to commit suicide."

Gandhi had called his nonviolent technique for Indian freedom *satyagraha*, Sanskrit for love or truth or God-power. The British had called it "passive resistance" when they faced it in the women's suffrage movement. America would call it "nonviolence," but Lawson would continue to protest that designation as too passive sounding. For him, nonviolence was a life style, an active and aggressive engagement to bring change.

Martin Luther King's Montgomery boycott in 1955 reached the newspapers even half a world away. Lawson, reading the story in India, "was so elated by this that, all alone in my office, I started clapping my hands and jumping and shouting." Someone was actually trying what he had been hoping for. Before that, he had never heard of King; now he tried to follow the boycott in whatever news stories he could get.

He came back to the United States by way of a summer trip across Africa, then seething in the vision of revolt against colonialism. In 1956 he was enrolled at the Oberlin College graduate school of theology in Ohio. It was there he met Dr. King, still in the midst of the Montgomery campaign, and they explored their common concerns. Lawson had intended to finish up his degree, but 1957 brought black movements in Little Rock, Nashville, Clinton, and in some places there was violence. But it was a news picture of a black minister in Nashville waving a gun in the middle of a threatening white mob that sent him South.

"I said to myself, 'It's all well and good for you to be in this protected climate talking about "that's not the way," but the only way you can really say is if you're in the midst of it.' " He took a job with the Fellowship of Reconciliation as southern secretary, working out of Nashville. FOR had worked with King in Montgomery, and Lawson was to continue its close co-operation with the newly formed Southern Christian Leadership Conference, appearing at its conventions, workshops, and retreats. "Essentially, we were calling people to the movement."

Montgomery was the nonviolent experiment. "We're talking about men putting their wits, their minds, and their spirits to work developing superior ways of overcoming enmity and the enemy...you have to be committed to nonviolence...you have to try....You have successes and failures, frustrations, but by persistent experimentation you begin to see some possibilities."

Crisscrossing the South, he refused in principle to use segregated facilities, so he often faced direct opposition. "I'm not opposed to self-defense at all, developing the form that best preserves one's life....My own way has been to try to face the opponent. Cowering eggs it on....It's much more difficult for the average human being to do evil against you if he's looking at you, in your face and eyes...."

He enrolled in the Vanderbilt University divinity school and then was one of the leaders in the Nashville mass student demonstrations in the spring of 1960.[3] Reaction was swift. The Vanderbilt trustees voted to expel him. Protesting that action, the divinity school faculty resigned and other resignations were threatened across the university. By summer, downtown Nashville was partially desegregated and Lawson was reinstated at Vanderbilt. But he finished up his academic work at Boston University.

That Easter he had been one of the chief organizers of the Student Non-Violent Co-Ordinating Committee in North Carolina.[4] When the first Freedom Riders were attacked in Alabama, he headed a contingent of Nashville students who went down to continue the ride, and he was involved in varying degrees in the SCLC campaigns of Albany and Birmingham, in the Mississippi Freedom Summer, and in the Meredith March into Mississippi.

In 1962 he came to Memphis to pastor Centenary Methodist Church, an urban, black congregation that ran from poor to well-off and which generally supported his wider concerns. He immediately became part of the desegregation efforts and was soon embroiled in the controversy over getting War on Poverty control out of the hands of city politicians. He was chairman of the WOP advisory committee and worked with the Shelby County Democratic Club. In the 1967 election, with his parishioner Willis going for mayor, he ran for the city-wide school board and was soundly defeated.

Through the years in the South he kept up his contacts with international and U.S. peace groups. In 1961 he served as an advisor to the World Council of Churches assembly at New Delhi, a role he would repeat later in 1968 at the World Council assembly in Uppsala, Sweden. He substituted for Martin King at a Montevideo workshop on nonviolence and the Latin American revolution. He belonged to the ecumenical Christian Peace Assembly which had members from Iron Curtain countries.

During most of the summer of 1965, he was in South Vietnam as part of an international and interfaith team sponsored by the Fellowship of Reconciliation. Its purpose was "to go over and look for ourselves and try to talk to all kinds of people, particularly religious and Buddhist leaders....Our concern was peace but we also went to see what the situation would teach us." They also talked extensively to newsmen, mostly centered in Saigon, many of whom were already saying that it would take a massive commitment of American troops simply to reach a stalemate in the war. The team tried but were unable to get into North Vietnam.[5] Lawson was also scheduled to attend the Christian Peace Assembly at Prague early in April 1968. In the face of the mounting Memphis crisis, he canceled his trip.

Lawson lived with his wife and three small sons in a modest home close to his church. He drove a small car. His reputation as an original thinker was found not in Memphis but in church and peace circles beyond. He sought no actual political power base, although he was not adverse to the role of Warwick the Kingmaker, and much of his influence was behind the scenes. He publicly eschewed "meaningless dialogue" for confrontation, yet no one appeared on as many podiums or carried on such persistent talk with so many people on all sorts of levels and topics ranging from race and religion to Third World politics.

Unlike many other black leaders, he had no personal, emotional following; people respected him but they did not swarm over him. He hardly appeared humble. He demanded too much too matter of factly—that those who cared for their fellows live totally or ultimately die in that service. As before with Jesus, it was a hard saying and Lawson did not soften it. There was great compassion in him, and understanding and love, but few whites saw it that spring in Memphis.

"Lawson's a rough, tough, intelligent, capable adversary," said one of the city's leaders. "He eats morality for breakfast," said a reluctant admirer.

Union president Jerry Wurf looked at him. "Lawson is an eternal optimist. In some areas he's very realistic and in other areas....He is not a hateful man. He is the kind of guy who when he found I didn't hold his position at that time on Vietnam, well, he spent hours with me....This is a man who'd reason with a policeman, with a labor leader about Vietnam....

"What Lawson never understood was the degree to which he was hated in Memphis—far out of proportion....They feared Lawson for the most interesting of all reasons—and I am indulging in psychiatry—they feared him because he was a totally moral man, and totally moral men you can't manipulate and you can't buy and you can't hustle...and that's why they hung the label of super radical on him."

The councilman's wife was correct, of course. Jim Lawson was a dangerous person. But she had sensed danger in the wrong context.

Martin King was now deep into the intricacies and planning logistics of the Poor People's Campaign. He returned to the old places he had made household words even for those who had never been South. He had been in Birmingham, Selma, and Montgomery during the early days of the Memphis strike. In Albany, Georgia, he would say, "We are going to build a shanty town in Washington....And we're going to let the whole world know what it means to be poverty-stricken."

Never had his personal presence seemed so crucial to raise enthusiasm and to bring forth the funds that would be required to sustain the effort in Washington. By March he was swinging around the country for meetings—New York, Michigan, California. Yet never had he seemed so tired. His aides and friends remarked on it, worried. King brushed them off and kept on.

Down Where We Are

7

> *"If you don't settle it here...*
> *you may have to settle it down where we are."*
> S. B. (Billy) Kyles

The city council as a whole remained in a fluid state over the strike. This was not a tactical decision. It was a result of the membership being so badly split that the council found itself moving forward on one foot and backward on the other, with the ever-present danger of one of its members cutting loose from the body politic altogether and marching to yet a different drum.

The council's initial statement of what it considered a fair settlement had attempted to please everyone, had pleased no one, and had culminated in the Macing on Main Street. But if settlement was not in the immediate offing, council Chairman Downing Pryor was at least determined that the council should provide an open forum, so he courteously responded to Jerry Wurf's request to address the council again at their regular meeting on February 27, just four days after the Macing.

Wanting another show of strength for the council, strikers came directly from their noon union meeting at Firestone Hall to City Hall and the daily march up Main from Clayborn Temple was timed to meet them.[1] The council was also ready.

Signs were up restricting the number of people to be allowed in. There was to be no standing in the aisles. Loudspeakers had been arranged to broadcast to those in the lobby who could not get into the chamber.

White college chaplain Rev. Dick Moon came up with the marchers from Clayborn Temple. He was tense and frightened that Mace would again be used on them, and sight of numerous policemen in and around City Hall did little to initially reassure him.

"We filled up the council chamber," he said, "and we waited and waited and waited, while the city took care of their most important business—all these zoning things and whether we are going to let (William) Loeb put in another Bar-B-Que on the corner of such and such." The council was following its routine agenda.

Pryor had agreed to hold the council in session till Wurf could speak to them, but Wurf was tied up at chancery court over the strike injunction. There was an hour's milling recess waiting for him. Finally Pryor was persuaded to recall the council and let some of the COME leaders speak for five minutes each. Police moved along the side walls and stood there, one with a two-way radio and another with a bullhorn.

"We aim to talk to you on our own terms," Rev. Billy Kyles rose to say. "If you don't settle it here, it is going to be settled anyway. You may have to settle it down where we are."

"Negroes are still the victims of two sticks," said Jim Lawson. "If you don't beat us over the head with a night stick, you hit us over the head with an agenda."

Rev. Moon observed of the council, "They all listened very quietly. I remember seeing Gwen Awsumb sitting and knitting through the whole meeting...I could see all of these black people sitting there and thinking—what is she doing?"

"I could tell by the attitude of the council things weren't looking too good," observed Rev. Harold Middlebrook. "Ms. Awsumb sat there knitting...She ought to have more sweaters and scarves than anybody in town." In fact, Ms. Awsumb knitted to replace smoking.

Wurf finally arrived. He again outlined the union position. "The mayor has made much of the fact that he will not sign a contract. It has become a posture which is more important to him than the substance of the issue." He urged the council not to abdicate its responsibility, not to turn that responsibility over to the mayor.

"It was a very polished speech…and the council was very solicitous of him also," said attorney and ACLU president David Caywood, who was observing from the back. "And then Wurf said, 'All right. That's it.' …Wurf turned and several preachers tried to stop him and said 'Let's stay.' Wurf was shaking his head…They left."

The council was left to face its responsibility. But just what was that responsibility? What was the legal function of the council as marchers paraded the streets, police guarded garbage trucks, and the mayor sat unmoved in his office? There was agreement that the handling of city employees was an executive function of the mayor. But did the council, which approved the city budget, also approve departmental wage settlements? Was union recognition a public policy decision to be determined by the council or a routine administrative matter? Where did the lines cross? What was the council's responsibility? The new form of government struggled for slippery footing.

Yet that council of 1968 was remarkable in a number of ways. It was made up of twelve men and one woman who had stepped forward to run for the most part out of a sense of civic responsibility rather than for any individual personal or political gain. Payment for the position was six thousand dollars a year. Under the new Program of Progress charter, it was the first purely legislative council elected in the city in more than half a century. More than half of its members had worked to bring about the new form of city government and they were firmly and ideologically committed to it. The POP campaign had been politically non-partisan, a crusade for better government.

Partisan politics were cloudy that year. It was obvious that the
Republicans were on the way up and the Democrats on the way
down, but nobody knew how far up or how far down. And in
the electing of a city council, most citizens paid little attention.
They voted for the person and in the process cut off the ballot
a number of old political hacks who had been around for a while
in favor of new faces.

Not that the council was apolitical. At the time of the election
Downing Pryor sat as a squire on the county court and J. O.
Patterson was a state senator. Tom Todd was a former state
senator. Lewis Donelson and Gwen Awsumb were instrumen-
tal in building the moderate wing of the Republican party.
Wyeth Chandler's father had been mayor of Memphis during
the Crump period. Bob James had been an unsuccessful
Republican candidate for the U. S. Congress. And Fred Davis
had long been active in the Shelby County Democratic Club.
But the council did not square off along political lines.

It was a business-oriented group. Aside from four attorneys,
Baptist minister Netters and Ms. Awsumb, who had held
numerous civic and church administrative positions, its members included a car agency owner, two insurance men, a jewelry
store executive, a lumber supply business owner, a real estate
dealer and hotel owner, and the owner of a housekeeping service
agency. In general, council members were moderately wealthy
and middle class. Many of them had known each other socially
and in civic activities for years.

Despite this basic rapport, by the first of March the council was
in chaos over the strike. That day reporters hovering outside a
closed, special council meeting reported a loud, angry session.
"It was a regular donnybrook," admitted council Chairman
Pryor, advocate of permitting everyone to let off steam. At the
end of two stormy hours, the council had reached no decision
on the strike.

There were four groupings within the council: those who
thought the council might be able to maneuver and aid in the
settlement; those who advocated a strictly hands-off policy;

those in the middle who might move in either direction; and the blacks.

At the outset the blacks stood alone. Motions to take some kind of action in the strike were defeated on a 10 to 3 vote again and again. Fred Davis, though hurt and angered by the attacks of black strike leaders and very conscious of the racially split district he represented, would continue to try to convince the council that it should act to help the workers before the city was split beyond repair.

Rev. James L. Netters, pastor of Mt. Vernon Baptist Church in the inner city, was a soft-spoken man. Pushing the POP charter was the extent of his political activity, but he had worked quietly in civil rights and anti-poverty religious groups.

Ironically, early in the strike he was awarded a ten-week Ford Foundation scholarship to the Urban Training Center in Chicago to study the problems of poverty and the national welfare structure. The course was designed to help ministers orient themselves to the economic problems of their communities. Netters had been delighted for he felt it would be of immense value to his work on the council. As originally planned, he would have been in Chicago for most of each week and back in Memphis for weekends, but as the strike situation got worse, he found himself flying back and forth to Chicago several times a week. What was being discussed in Chicago was being enacted in Memphis. He did not finish the course.

Of the three council blacks, J. O. (James Oglethorpe) Patterson, Jr., 33, staked out most clearly the role of the new black politician. And some of his fellow members sensed insolence. Patterson was already something of a wheeler-dealer power broker in the black community. His father was Bishop J. O. Patterson, of the powerful Church of God in Christ. Patterson held a law degree from DePaul University in Chicago and had entered politics within a year after opening his Memphis law office. He was elected to the state legislature in 1966 and to the council the following year. There had been little strong opposition.

On the council he took an independent—some viewed it as uncooperative—stance early by refusing to attend the Tuesday morning executive sessions, which were closed to the general public. In principle, he was protesting any council operation that was not completely open to all citizens, although newsmen were allowed into the executive sessions. In practice, the result was that Patterson arrived at the Tuesday afternoon council sessions almost as unprepared as any citizen who might drop in. He was also commuting back and forth between Memphis and the legislature at Nashville, by then in session.

Patterson did not attempt to cajole his fellow council members. He laid his cards on the table. Yet fellow members sensed an insincerity about him, a carelessness that belied his expensive suits and carefully worded phrases, a carelessness about what they thought. Patterson was possessed neither of Rev. Netter's charity nor of Fred Davis' eagerness to learn. He was a loner and the council, despite its differences, was already a group. He was a politician and they considered themselves, in some way, on a different level. They were concerned about the opinions of their constituents; he seemed assured of his. Council members grew in this period to know each other's weaknesses, but he never shared his. Perhaps that was the worst of all.

Of the ten white council members, three of them, Downing Pryor, Lewis Donelson, and Jerred Blanchard, maintained early in the strike a certain openness toward the labor issue and certainly a desire to keep communications open with both blacks and union leaders.

Had it been seventy years earlier, Pryor and Donelson would have fallen into the old Bourbon aristocracy grouping. Council Chairman Pryor traced his family back to Memphis of the 1820s. "The 1819 population of Shelby County was proportionately just like it is now," he mused. "It was just over 300, 200 whites and 103 slaves." His own great-grandfather had sat on the county court; he himself was elected to the court in 1966.

Pryor had spent ten years in the U. S. Air Force, commanding a B-24 squadron in World War II, and was owner of Pryor

Oldsmobile Company. His political opponents charged him with being a member of the "Jet Set." And, indeed, Pryor was wealthy, well-educated, widely traveled, interested in art. He had also, for all his drawl and folksy demeanor, a wide theoretical grasp of the social changes happening in the country. And he believed that what was happening in Memphis was part of a much larger social change.

Pryor was sympathetic to the strikers' grievances, though not necessarily to unionization, but after the council's first suggested solution fell apart, he was not sure which way to go. He was disgusted with the mayor's handling of the problem, yet, as elected chairman of the council, he did not want to see the council at loggerheads with the executive nor the council chairman publicly feuding with the mayor. There was inherent political power in the council chairmanship; he did not choose to exercise it. One of the aims of the POP crusade, in which he had worked tirelessly, was a smoother operating city government. So Pryor was loath to roughhouse.

Instead he continued to quietly attempt behind the scenes to mediate and communicate between council members themselves, between council and mayor and council and COME, hoping always that something would break the deadlock. Outwardly he remained conciliatory toward everyone.

Lewis Donelson was a lawyer specializing in tax work. He would become the council's acknowledged expert on budgetary matters. His forebears stretched back to John Donelson, who had founded the city of Nashville, and to Andrew Jackson Donelson, ward and later secretary of Andrew Jackson, who came to Memphis in 1854, ran for vice-president on the 1856 Know-Nothing ticket of Millard Fillmore, and arranged for the annexation of Texas. Donelson's great-great-grandfather was A. O. P. Nicholson who walked out of the U. S. Senate when the Southern states seceded and was later chief justice of the Tennessee Supreme Court.

A small man with large glasses, a graduate of Georgetown University's law school, Donelson had become the leader of

the Republican "New Guard" and locked horns with black Lt.
George W. Lee, titular head of the Memphis black Republicans
since the 1930s. Donelson won, and would be plagued thereafter with an anti-black reputation, for the black Republican
remnant would become politically impotent.

But in fact, Donelson stood in the anomalous position of
southern political moderate. Within the structure where he
moved, he was a man of solid integrity. No amount of wailing
from the citizenry would shake his conviction that Memphis had
to get more tax revenue. No race-baiting from either side shook
his belief that the city must move toward accommodation with
its black citizens. He had been a member of the Community
Relations Committee, and one of the things which bothered
him most during the strike was the inability to get any hard
commitments from black leaders. It had not been like that
before. "You made an agreement with Jesse Turner of the
NAACP, and it was carried out. This time there was no
assurance no matter who you dealt with."

Donelson was not awed by Henry Loeb. More than any of the
other white council members, he was willing to stand up against
the man and the office, and to refuse to allow the council to be
used as a rubber stamp for Loeb's positions.

The third member of the council whom blacks looked to
with some hope was Jerred Blanchard, although until Blanchard reached the council his image was that of a fairly
conservative Republican. Upon graduating from Yale, where
he had an athletic scholarship, and from the University of
Missouri law school, he had intended to practice law in
southwest Missouri when World War II interfered. Commis-
sioned in the Signal Corps, he served again during the Korean
War in a supply squadron out of Memphis, retiring as a colonel
in the reserves. He was a big, bald-headed hulk of a man, a
practicing attorney who listened carefully and spoke slowly.
Indeed, to blacks, he appeared to be one of the few council
members listening carefully during the early days of the strike.

At the other end of the council spectrum were Wyeth

Chandler, Robert James, and Tom Todd, all opposed to unionization, to a dues checkoff, to negotiation under pressure, and all in solid support of the mayor. Chandler was the youngest, 38, a practicing attorney, deep-eyed and dark-haired, handsome in a heavy way, authoritative. He had lived in the same midtown neighborhood all his life and had literally grown up in Memphis politics. Under the Crump dispensation his adoptive father, Walter Chandler, had served in the U. S. Congress and as mayor of Memphis.[2] The family home had been full of political comings and goings.

There was only one political ticket in those days and that was it, his son Wyeth would say. Everybody was Democratic. "It was not really the thing to be—a Republican." He would pinpoint the change as having occurred when the Democrats turned to the liberal Estes Kefauver and Albert Gore, Sr. The old yellow-dog Democrats who'd come up with conservative leaders found they were more conservative than Democratic and slipped out of party activity. Crump, thought Wyeth Chandler as had his father before him, had understood the people and kept the city moving at the pace it wanted to go.

Wyeth Chandler was disenchanted with the Democratic Party although he hesitated to become a Republican, so deep were the Democratic roots in his past. He was opposed to the new form of city government, as was his father who died at age 79 in the midst of his son's city council campaign, on the grounds that the council would be a part-time job. In the old days, political office was a full-time thing, no dilettantes those men.

Wyeth Chandler's view of the strike was hard and clear. Unions in city government were wrong and the city certainly had no obligation to do anything for a union. The council had no power to do anything in the situation but had led blacks to believe it did. The council should never have gotten involved in any way. Once it did, the confusion was compounded.

"All clear thinking will go out of the window sometimes under the type of attacks, threats, and statements that were made by these people," he said. "I became almost unreasonable about it.

I won't pretend that I was acting as a reasonable man or as I would ordinarily."

Tom Todd was the most closely aligned with Mayor Loeb. Todd came out of Virginia and a family that traced its origins back to colonial days. After serving in World War II as a naval aviator, he joined the textile industry and was sent to Memphis to learn the cotton trade. He stayed, branching out into real estate and farming. He owned twelve hundred acres just over the state line in Mississippi, much of it rented out for cotton and soybean allotments and the rest used for cattle. When he could get away from Memphis he liked dove and quail shooting on the farm. He had married into the Snowden family, whose fortunes had been built on cotton, and through the family owned the Chisca Plaza Hotel in downtown Memphis. He lived in a great, century-old showplace of a home named Annesdale near downtown in a partially deteriorating area that Todd philosophically believed had no place to go but eventually back up.

His entrance into politics showed something of the demise into which that occupation had fallen in the years just after Crump. "I fussed and fumed and criticized and condemned the lousy politicians for years...One day back in '61 or '62, there was an editorial in one of the newspapers saying there just weren't enough candidates running...and why don't people step forward and offer their services....That gave me the impetus."

He won and in Nashville in the state senate for two terms continued an independent conservative course. "I had been opposed to things these minority groups, labor and Negroes, wanted. For example, I was told if I didn't vote to repeal capital punishment the Negroes were going to vote against me. I voted for it. I said, 'I don't give a damn what you people say you're going to do to me.' On minimum wage I said, 'I'm not going to vote for a minimum wage, and a state minimum wage and the bureaucracy that goes along with this is utterly ridiculous.' " He also switched party affiliation to Republican, lost in the next election, and in 1966 was defeated for a post on the county commission.

"You always hear of the politicians—their friends want them to run," he laughed. "I don't have any friends, I guess. Nobody has ever said, 'Tom Todd, why don't you get up there and run for something!' Nobody has ever told me that. I just get up and run on my own."

On the council, Todd took his position at the outset of the strike and never budged. "It would have made it a lot easier if these creatures (union leaders) had come down here and acted as men and not...as gangsters. You can attract a lot more flies with honey than you can with vinegar." But even had they been "as sweet as pie, we would have been very reluctant to have had a union because we feel—I feel, I'll put it—I think the mayor feels—that there really isn't much a union can do for these people that the city can't do for them....They [union leaders] didn't care about the workers. And this is what's so damn addling about these people. They weren't interested in the workers. Hell's bells, forget them. All they wanted was a checkoff."

Todd had had some experience with unions. There had been an attempt to organize the employees of his Chisca Plaza Hotel. "We had a strike here and we had this same type of thing come down...out of Chicago to give us a checkoff and leave town. And we fought them for two years and we beat them. But it's the same rotten characters."

Councilman Bob James was a transplanted northerner, sent south in the mid-thirties by the petroleum sales division of Firestone to cover the Arkansas farm section. He thought it pretty scrubby after the lush, rich, fertile efficiency of Iowa where he had grown up. But he liked southerners, found them socially more relaxed, less efficient, and he liked it. In 1938 he formed the Memphis House Cleaning Company, an agency which sent out teams of maids, janitors, and scrub women to clean buildings, and he gave up the $150,000 three-year City Hall cleaning contract at the time of his council election.

He was a man of strong opinions. In his early years he considered himself idealistic and something of a liberal. He remembered sending home to his family a snapshot showing slash pines and cut-over land on the back of which he wrote, "This is a result of the rugged individual government that your friend Herbert Hoover advocated." He was also fascinated by cooperatives. "I didn't know at the time they were a tax shelter," he explained.

At the beginning of World War II when John L. Lewis took out his United Mine Workers, James was so angry that he had a thousand cards printed attacking Lewis' action and sent them to all his friends and customers suggesting that they write letters to the editors. He served in the Navy during part of the war, and first became involved in politics when he worked house to house in five precincts for Eisenhower in 1952. By 1960 he was campaigning for Nixon.

In the next four years he made two unsuccessful runs for the U. S. Congress. James was ready by then to expand his interests. His business was running smoothly. "And I'm kind of skittish about growing old and giving in to old age. ...The mother who knows nothing but home and she is bored and she has no outside interests and her husband down at that old miserable, dull office, self-satisfied and smug and in a rut and he probably doesn't even know it...I decided I wasn't going to get in that trap."

He was giving his time to more than Republican politics. In 1961 he had seen a film called "Communism on the Map" at the local Lions Club and was so impressed that he went immediately to the American Legion and signed up to show it to other groups. As chairman of a committee, he showed the film "at least three hundred times all across the Mid-South" and even to the Oklahoma state legislators.

Like Pryor, James saw the Memphis crisis in more than local terms, but to him it was part of the world-wide Communist conspiracy and he associated it with the revolutions of the peasants in Cuba and China and the miners in Bolivia. Everyone knew that the Communists picked the weakest groups and exploited their problems to divide and conquer a country.

He also understood the crux of the black problem as economic. Blacks, he believed, "became economic slaves after they
were political slaves...They can't compete. They're not trained
and there's prejudice. The government tries to intervene and
does it clumsily and ineffectively. ...There is no solution except
a slow assimilation—a slow improvement of their qualifications
and eventually the opportunity to get jobs on merit." He had
been successfully employing blacks for years in his company—
though not yet on the supervisory level.

The other four members of the council, Gwen Awsumb,
W. T. McAdams, Billy Z. Hyman, and Philip Perel, filled in the
middle ground. They sided with the hard-line, hands-off councilmen, but they were not rabid nor did they make the same kind
of fiery and scornful speeches, although when time came to vote
they consistently stood with Chandler, Todd, and James. If the
three black councilmen could get any action on the strike, they
had to convince not only the more open-minded Blanchard,
Pryor, and Donelson, but also one of these four in the middle.
Only then was there a chance for a 7 to 6 vote.

Gwen Awsumb in the early days seemed most approachable.
Wife of Wells Awsumb, an architect, and the mother of three
grown children, one of whom was serving in the Peace Corps
at the time, she was a close political ally of Donelson and shared
his moderate views. As a young woman she had taken her
children out in strollers door-to-door to talk to voters about the
embryonic Republican Party. In 1956 she had run unsuccess-
fully for the state legislature, but that was too early. There had
been no Republican from Shelby County since Reconstruction.

Coming out of work with the City Beautiful Commission, the
Episcopal home for dependent girls, and the YWCA, she was the
first woman to hold high elective office in city government. She
was equally comfortable behind a silver tea service or in council
chambers, her white hair elegantly simple, her suits and dresses
stylishly understated. And while Gwen Aswumb might enjoy
the southern chivalry of her male counterparts on the council,
she did not cater to it or depend on it. As intelligent as any man

on the council—and more so than many—she was as competent through her volunteer service posts as they through their business experience. She knew it. They knew it, too.

The district she represented was East Memphis, the wealthiest area of the city and certainly the one most remote geographically and mentally from the problems of poverty and the sanitation workers. Gwen Awsumb was far ahead of most of her constituents in her awareness of the city's need to come to grips with poverty and racism, but she balked on the idea of unionization of city employees. A friend, with her weekly during the strike at a private prayer group, reported her deep concern with the growing polarization within the city coupled with her adamant refusal to encourage the union. She thought the city had bungled badly at the beginning. She knew that unions in general were an integral part of the economic system, but she felt strongly they should not exist among city employees and that recognition in sanitation could lead to strikes at the city hospital complex or the utilities division. She believed the city "could not settle with a sword hanging over its head," and that nothing should be done until the men cut off the strike and went back to work.

"The ultimate destruction of the country could come through municipal unions," she would say. "It was time somebody dug their heels in and said this has gone far enough. If we could make this contribution to the whole aspect of this question across the country, we would have made a great contribution. ...If the whole country goes in this direction (public employees unionization) ultimately, at least Memphis can be known for stopping it or delaying it or pointing out the dangers. I desperately fear a paralysis of the entire country when this is a *fait accompli*."

On a gray March day, over cups of tea in the beautiful modern home designed by her husband, she reassured two women who lived in her district. They had turned to her, deeply distraught by what they saw as the pulling back of the black community into itself and the strain put on the tenuous lines of friendship between blacks and whites. "We felt kind of hysterical sitting there," said one of them. "Gwen looked so cool and competent." The union could be beaten, she assured them, and then the city could get about its business of becoming a good place for everyone to live. She was as concerned as they, but everything was under control.

They were convinced that she would not change her mind. She would fight for the things she saw as right on a ground of her own choosing. She would not admit that this battlefield was already prepared and the firing begun.

Strife and confusion were the last things that W. T. McAdams had expected during his tenure on the city council. He had come onto the council committed to civic economy and to a program of improving the sidewalks, curbs, and gutters in his district of North Memphis and Frayser. Frayser was predominantly an area of middle-class and blue-collar working people, site of the International Harvester plant. Rightly or wrongly, it had the reputation of being the heartland of what was left of the Ku Klux Klan and Citizens Councils. McAdams' North Memphis area was almost entirely black, one of the oldest sections of town. Racially his district divided into about eighteen thousand white voters and about twelve thousand black.

McAdams, if truth be told, was a lot more content with the world when he was out on a tractor on his fifty-acre farm north of the city than he was with any of the various jobs in sales and insurance he had held. "I've been out on the tractor today," he would say. "Cutting bushes and getting some beans planted." He had grown up on a farm down at Oakland, Mississippi, and came to Memphis in the late thirties, where he bought a farm on whose northeast corner he developed a small shopping center, no mean achievement since he had to borrow the money to pump 265,000 yards of sand from the Wolf River bottom land to develop it.

"I was actually looking forward to serving on the council," he said. "I was just very, very proud to be elected." He and his wife had campaigned for his council seat "as hard a work as any two ever did." Initially he had believed the council job would probably take up Mondays and Tuesdays, but the strike quickly disabused him of that idea. "Actually," he was to say rather wistfully in the summer of 1968, "if I could get out clean—without someone getting sore at me—I'd give a year's salary to get out of the council."

His principal stated opposition to the strikers' demands was based on finances, for he was not opposed to unionization per se. "Maybe they were not making as much as they should have been, but they were making what they had been promised and concessions had been made. ...I was disappointed that a group of citizens would do a thing like that in the city of Memphis. ...It's all right for them to be unionized, but they ought to go along with the city's ability to pay."

McAdams had begun work with a twenty-five-dollar-a-week salary and twenty-five-dollar-a-week hotel expenses and an old yellow company car to take him through Mississippi, Arkansas, Alabama and Tennessee. "And when my Daddy told me we couldn't afford something, I believed that, and we didn't keep on hounding him." In a way, it was as simple as that.

Philip A. Perel was the most intimately concerned with the economic health of downtown Memphis where the main Perel Jewelers was located. Member of an old Memphis family, Perel had helped found the Retail Merchants Association, and the Better Business Bureau. He also put a lot of time and effort into the Cotton Carnival and the Main Street Christmas Parade, and had been one of the organizers of the Arthritis Foundation. His downtown store was one of the first to be integrated in terms of employees' lounges, working conditions, and advancement opportunities, a move which had aroused white criticism at the time.

Perel was a quiet man, quietest on the council, content to let the others do the arguing—no dearth of applicants for that—and held his opinions so close to his vest that while part of the council classed him as a supporter of the mayor, others thought he leaned towards a more liberal interpretation of events and might swing over to vote with the minority.

The thirteenth member of the council was Billy Z. Hyman, whose business interests were tied very closely to the black community, for Hyman Builders Supply's central lumber office was located in the heart of black South Memphis. However, the district which elected Hyman was the primarily white Southeast. Growing up on a small farm in central Mississippi during the Depression and then in Memphis, Hyman had worked during high school at a filling station on Florida Street across from the present lumber yard. He was very familiar with black areas of the city, for he had gone into the lumber business in the 1954-56 period when ordinances were passed requiring people to get their houses up to standard and he worked all over black Memphis. His company had replaced a firm called Jordan Lumber which in past years had been the only building supply firm that would finance black churches with long-term arrangements. The neighborhood trusted Jordan, and Hyman builders got the carry-over of good will. Hyman, with one foot among his white neighbor constituents and one foot among his black business neighbors, was also to remain rather quiet during the strike.

But pressure on the council was unremitting.

On the same day, March 5, that Rev. Lawson announced that Dr. King had been invited to Memphis, there were rumors that COME was planning a sit-in at the regular afternoon council meeting. Two hundred policemen entered City Hall by the side door before the meeting began, reported the *Press-Scimitar*. Police going off duty at 3:00 P.M. were ordered to remain on till 7:00 P.M. An estimated hundred sheriff's deputies ringed the building.

The council had been briefed that if a sit-in happened they were to avoid moving through the crowd. "The whole basement was teeming with police," said Ms. Awsumb. "I've never seen so many police in my life. They had a paddy wagon down there."

As before, the council chamber filled with strikers and COME supporters and those who could not get seats filled the lobby. And as before, Chairman Pryor was willing to let grievances be aired.[3]

"Dick Moon…read to us from the Bible," said Ms. Awsumb. "The passage was from Jeremiah where the people tried to get their leaders to do something—whatever it was at that time. And the end of the long passage had something to do with the leaders being deaf and they could not hear the people say 'We will burn this city down.' And he clamped the Bible closed, turned on his heel and went away. …I was just horrified…for him to participate to this extent was appalling to me."

Donelson, who agreed with the chairman on the need to listen to citizens' grievances, nonetheless noted, "but I had the view, too, …that we should not put up with any real disorderly conduct or abuse."

The council did not put up with much of it that day, for Rev. Zeke Bell again forced an angry verbal confrontation. The *Commercial Appeal* reporter recorded his words to the council.

"I say you men don't have any backbone and you are all going to hell…I don't like rats. I don't like black rats. I don't like white rats.…

"We're not going to leave this building until we get what we came for. We will be gassed or killed. We are going to stay till Shiloh comes…

"The white preachers are too damn scared to tell you what you need to hear. You are not reasonable people…

"All these men are asking for is dignity and respect…If these men were white, you would have already done something. …"

Rev. Bell would protest later that his words were misinterpreted, pulled out of context. But at the threat of hellfire, the *Commercial Appeal* reported, Donelson "shaking with rage, his face flushed and his hair flopping…jumped to his feet, yanked the microphone upward and began shouting, 'Mr. Bell, Mr. Bell. We have listened to you patiently. Either you speak to us in respect or I will move for adjournment.' "

Rev. Bell responded with his reference to black and white rats, and Donelson and Bob James were both shouting "Mr. Chairman. Mr. Chairman," and calling for adjournment. The council immediately voted to adjourn, with Netters and Patterson opposed.

But no one left the audience, and several of the ministers rose to urge the crowd to stay in their seats until another session of the council was called. "Let us pray before they gas us down," said one minister. The three black councilmen and Jerred Blanchard stayed with them. "I stayed because they were staying and going to be arrested," said Blanchard. "I wanted to find out about how the police handled them and how they handled themselves."

"The strategy was that we were going to stay," said Rev. Moon. "And we were going to get some people into jail. We wanted martyrs, not dead ones but live ones in jail. ...We had decided the day before what leaders of COME would be in jail...Of course, the labor people were not going to jail because they were already in enough trouble."

ACLU president David Caywood heard on the radio that the crowd was prepared to stay in council chambers and that City Hall had been closed. He rushed over to Mayor Loeb's office and found there was no communication going on with the sit-in leaders. "For God's sake," he said to Loeb. "Let me go down and talk to them if you're gonna arrest them and maybe we can do it peaceably."

And Loeb, related Caywood, "in his own inimitable way, thinking he was gonna help me out, said, 'Well, I'll send six policemen down there with you.' And I told him that I frankly didn't want a single g-d policeman with me." Speeches and singing were going on in the chamber. Caywood found Rev. Lawson. The problem, he told him, " 'is how are you gonna get arrested? You gonna tell them they got to carry you or what?' And Jim says, 'Well, I've been arrested a good many times and nobody has ever had to carry me yet. We'll walk over there.' "

Caywood reported back to Loeb that arrangements could be made to handle the arrests peacefully, and he returned to council chambers with Assistant Police Chief Henry Lux. "I got Lux and Lawson together and they worked it out. I went and sat on the podium…I don't know what the conversation was, but Lux was down there shaking hands with all the preachers and talking to them, and all the other policemen were in the back."

"My mission, of course, was to get the people out of City Hall," said Chief Lux. "My plan was to lock the doors…which we did…because we didn't need any more from the outside. We had enough to contend with…We had initially about four hundred sitting in…I walked down…and shook hands with the leaders and we laughed and talked a few minutes…and I said, 'From the looks of this audience, boy, there's some big ones in there if we have to carry them out. You don't want me to have a hernia.' And we kind of lightened the air a little bit."

It was after 5:30 P.M. when Chief Lux made the announcement that the group had thirty minutes to leave City Hall. "We don't want any trouble and we don't anticipate any trouble. If you choose to stay, you will be in violation of a city ordinance and a state law."

"I'm here," said Rev. Lawson to the crowd. "I'm going to stay. You have to do what is in your own conscience. No one can make the decision for you. It is not dishonorable to go to jail for the right reason."

A number of the men had been moving out of council chambers for the past hour and more left now. Those left were singing. "But we didn't sing very happily," said Rev. Moon. "I remember we were just kind of sitting there singing, looking around. There were police all around. And we thought this was the time then for a Macing, but it didn't happen."

"Eventually the crowd got down to 116," said Chief Lux. "I'd suggested just fifteen or twenty leaders walk out arrested, but they all wanted to go."

Outside City Hall a crowd of black students who had come up on the late March from Clayborn Temple milled about excitedly. Lux was worried. "They're out there; their arms are linked and they won't open up." Rev. Malcolm Blackburn went out to talk to them. "They're going to holler and they're going to jeer, but they're not going to do anything else," he reported back to Lux. "Man, just let them holler," replied Lux. "Sticks and stones is the only thing I'm worried about."

One of the commanding officers came up to check. "What are we going to do when we get outside and they (those being arrested) start to run?" Lux replied, "Let them go. We don't hold them. They're not going to run anyway, but if they do run, let them go, for God's sake. We don't want them." Lux was musing over a piece of wisdom he'd come across. "You don't necessarily have to solve a problem. A lot of time you can de-exist a problem."

Inside, with occasional chants of "We want arrest," the workers and their supporters were lining up two-by-two for the walk over to the city jail. As they left, a policeman stepped in behind each pair. Those arrested were singing "Leaning on the Everlasting Arms," weird and echoing as they crossed the lobby and out into the early dark.

Beyond the policemen, "All of a sudden we had a cheering section on either side," recalled Rev. Blackburn. "The young people were very loud, shouting and singing, and some of them crying as we went through the line."

"The police were mostly courteous," thought Rev. Moon who was walking with Jim Lawson. "We had a very friendly conversation with ours. I think we won him over...But Rev. Starks was behind me, and I heard the officer saying, 'Get along, boy. Go on, boy. Move it, boy.' And I remember Rev. Starks saying, 'I'm not a boy. I am the Reverend Mr. Henry Starks and if you call me "boy" just one more time you are going to arrest me for assault.' "

Caywood continued making calls to see what could be worked out legally on the disorderly conduct charges, both city and state, which would be filed against all those arrested. The final result was that Judge Ray Churchill in city court the next day continued for sixty days the cases of all those arrested. If there were no further violations within the sixty days, the cases would be automatically dismissed. No one was required to post bond. Attorneys Walter Bailey and Otis W. Higgs, two of the city's dozen black lawyers, worked with the case.

At the jail that night photographing, fingerprinting, booking, and then releasing those arrested was a drawn-out process that found groups of people standing and sitting in the corridors and in various anterooms. It was after midnight when the jail was finally cleared of demonstrators. A few frictions developed. Ms. Maxine Smith, executive secretary of the NAACP and one of the few women among those arrested, was led into the men's cooler with its open urinal and line-up of men to use it. Protest got her moved quickly.

If she stood out in the march to the jail that night it was not only because of the red dress or the carefully nurtured "natural" hair style. It was because she was an articulate, demanding, criticizing, exhorting woman whose name had been a byword in the city's racial history for a decade.

"Maxine Smith from the NAACP! She's a tartar!"

But she is invited in the middle of the strike to a meeting on combating prejudice in children. The night before she has been in jail with the demonstrators. At the meeting she is black gloves, *haute couture*, out-suburbaning the young suburban mothers. Her voice is quiet. Only when someone uses "nigra," does she flare up. The white women are embarrassed. They are wary of her but they like her—wife, mother, believer in the fundamental dignity of man. She will not allow identification. She is more wary than they. She is more than wife, mother, believer. She is black. If they forget it, she reminds them. She will not play at being their bridge to blackness.

Which is an arbitrary decision. She is what she would not be.

Memphis in the thirties. Neighborhoods are more mixed-up then. White and black children throw stones at each other with impunity and forget. In the afternoons the three children leave school and walk to the old veterans hospital. Their father is a postman and he is sick. Maxine is the youngest but she talks for them. "I want to see Mister Joseph Atkins." And the clerk, "We don't refer to niggers as Mister around white folks." She asks for Mister Joseph Atkins every time. It is her first confrontation. Her father died when she was nine.

At nineteen, she had already graduated from Spelman in Atlanta with a B.A. in Biology. Behind her lay the black schooling, the all-enveloping society of the Baptist church where her mother was a secretary, the lean years when her mother did without to get the children through school. Martin Luther King, Jr., was at Morehouse College. She knew him as the younger brother of a friend—a quiet boy who walked the campus carrying his umbrella—son of one of the biggest Baptist preachers in Atlanta.

She went up to Middlebury College in Vermont for graduate studies in French. It was a white world but it never struck her as fundamentally different. She had not particularly wanted to go to Middlebury, but the University of Tennessee was not admitting blacks. It paid for her tuition elsewhere.

The calm. The New England village surrounded by the mountains. "Of all the beauty I have seen, I would choose the quiet beauty of Vermont." The calm...the calm...

She taught a couple of years in Texas and Florida, and married Dr. Vasco Smith, a dentist from Memphis. They spent two years at air force posts. And they came home to Memphis.

Now the South was stirring, the long low rumblings of black people cracking the surface. In Montgomery black people were walking. Rosa Parks had refused to move to the back of the bus and the quiet boy from Morehouse with the umbrella had begun to speak.

When Laurie Sugarmon, then wife of attorney Russell Sugarmon, suggested that they enroll in graduate school at Memphis State University, Maxine Atkins Smith said, "But what if they accept me?" She had already taken all the French that Memphis State was offering. But it was a lark, a bit of derring-do. It was the spring of the movement. So she and Laurie deposited their six-month-old infants with family and went off to break the color barrier at the local university. It was hot that summer of 1957, and she got more angry as the heat mounted. Day after day they went from office to office; they made appointments that were not kept. They sat. Their qualifications were not sufficient for entrance into graduate school. Laurie Sugarmon had graduated Phi Beta Kappa from Wellesley; Maxine already had an M.A. In the end they lost. A year later, Memphis State began admitting black students. By then Laurie Sugarmon was working on her Ph.D. at Johns Hopkins. She would return to become the first black faculty member at Memphis State.

And by then Maxine Smith was involved in the NAACP. Black students were on the move now. Everywhere across the South was the salt-scent of freedom—a sit-in at a Nashville lunch counter, a demonstration in an Atlanta bus station. She was membership chairman of the local NAACP. Membership rose from hundreds to three thousand in two years. Boycotts and marches began in Memphis. She was coordinator. After the libraries were desegregated under court order the NAACP had to move back into court to get the "colored" and "white" signs off the library toilets. Students sat in at the art museum and it opened up. So did the fairgrounds. The parks were opened by court order, but their swimming pools closed by order of Henry Loeb, then mayor.

There were arrests, some four hundred of them. She was never arrested and felt somewhat cheated. "It was fashionable in those days." Now the NAACP membership and program had expanded to the point where a full-time staff worker was needed. She became executive secretary of the Memphis chapter of the NAACP.

There was great wild hope in those days. Although three men were killed on the campus of Ole Miss, eighty miles to the south, James Meredith stayed. Meredith was frequently at the Smith home in Memphis.

It was June 1963 in Jackson, Mississippi. The boycotts and demonstrations begun in Jackson and led by Medgar Evers, NAACP field secretary, followed the Memphis pattern.

Dr. Smith went down from Memphis to speak at a mass meeting on the night of June 8. His wife and Rev. Billy Kyles went along. "It was a great meeting, a rabble-rousin' freedom meeting," she said. "I've never seen spirit that high. Maybe it was because it was in Mississippi and the policemen were sitting there and black Mississippians were totally unafraid.

Afterwards there was a relaxed gathering around Medgar Evers at the home of a friend. "Keep your determination," Maxine told him. "Don't let anything stop you." She put her arms around his neck and kissed him. Shortly afterwards, Medgar Evers left for home.

Twenty minutes later he was dead, shot in ambush on his own doorstep. When the call came, they wanted to go to his wife but they were advised to stay inside. As far as they knew, there was no police protection for any of them. "In the nightmare after Medgar was dead, just waiting for morning, I must have dozed and the words from the meeting kept coming back...Medgar's face...He was thirty-seven years old."

Five months later when John F. Kennedy was killed, she closed herself in her inner office and beat her head against the wall. "Medgar is dead. Medgar is dead," she said over and over.

And for her the high green spring of the movement settled into dry, dusty summer.

Over in Nashville, the state legislature had been in session for several weeks, the general concern of the country over riots and the specific concern of Memphis over the strike surfacing in a series of "law and order" bills to control civil disturbances and anti-strike or mandatory settlement bills that were thrown into the legislative hopper. But the Shelby County delegation itself was split over what it thought should be done on the state level and much of the legislation was being hotly debated. There was no reason to look to Nashville for help for either side.

In Memphis, Councilmen Donelson and Patterson had both placed strike-related resolutions on the city council agenda. Patterson's was quite clear-cut. It allowed union-dues deduction for city employees through the credit union, applicable to any organized groups of municipal employees. One Donelson resolution concerned minority employment in private industry, setting up a commission to match jobs and the job hungry and encouraging job training. The other ensured the hiring of blacks at all levels of city employment, in essence making Memphis a fair employment practices city. Donelson had been pushing for this fair employment practices idea since before the council took office.

It was the fifth regular Tuesday afternoon council meeting since the strike began. Donelson's resolution on an employment commission for private industry sailed through unanimously. But aware that he would run into strong opposition on the fair employment practices ordinance, he deferred it, saying, "I do not believe it can be considered properly in the atmosphere growing out of the sanitation workers' strike."

Patterson was blocked. His resolution on dues checkoff through the credit union was doomed, as the council and the several hundred strikers and supporters in the audience knew. But Patterson pushed on to the cheers and applause of blacks. As the council voted to table, the strikers walked out of the meeting in mass protest.

But this time the vote was not 10 to 3, whites against blacks. It was 9 to 4. Councilman Jerred Blanchard had changed his vote.

"I became the fourth 'nigger' on the council," Blanchard commented dryly. "That was the night the phone started ringing."

He had been at the University of Missouri law school when a young black newspaper reporter brought suit to enter the university's journalism school and lost in the courts. In 1943 he was an officer with the Signal Corps on the Burma Road.

"When you saw a British Gurkha, you knew you were looking at a black man…We kicked two or three American officers out of our club just because they were black. But we let all these British Negro officers from South Africa come in because they were British. And the Indians—we let all of them in...This was the army and war...no time for a social conscience, but you wonder what in hell's going on? ...That man's blacker than this man. But this man can't come in because he's one of *our* blacks." In the Korean War his supply squadron in the 516th Troop Carrier Wing, operating out of Memphis, was integrated.

Blanchard practiced law, kept in touch with old undergraduate friends from Yale, worked in the rising Republican party, won his seat on the council, and was enormously pleased when Loeb was inaugurated, for he saw great progress ahead under the new form of government and an end to the political shenanigans of the past.

A big, homely, visceral man, Blanchard. Saw too much. Cared too much. And cared about Henry Loeb in the way that big gutsy decent men care about one another in that no-holds-barred world of war and poker and politics.

"One of Mayor Loeb's great strengths is his appointments. He has been just tremendous in all of his appointments...Henry's a very decent guy. Decency is essence to him. He's been stubborn and opinionated, but he's essentially decent...They call it the plantation kind of thing, but this is just decency as Henry Loeb understands decency and he tried...During that early period I thought he was magnificent. He never quailed. He didn't quibble. He said, 'I'm not going to give you the checkoff; I'm not going to give you a written contract.' But he never cut off utilities; he increased contributions for food stamps and got waivers on insurance policies. And he just couldn't have been better. Every time I'd look at him I was so proud of him I just wanted to bust."

But Blanchard continued to watch and listen, not only to Henry but also to the blacks. When does a person cross a line? Was Blanchard changed after the tumultuous Fred Davis committee hearing? He was mad as hell at the union. "There are many, many people around who don't think the unions are the be-all and end-all of existence!"

Was he changed at the meeting at the Auditorium when the

council cut off the microphones and went out the back door under police escort? "I was sick of me going out the back door and cutting off the power so these guys can't even talk. …Cowardice is cowardice and surely there is no room for it today."

What changes a man? A black preacher pleading for microphones no one will turn on? A mayor sitting now behind bodyguards? A Macing? Because the issues of the strike are still the same. And who is to say that right is enthroned in either the city or the union hall? Or, for that matter, decency? Or courage?

Yet "When you take the oath of office to represent 600,000 citizens of the city, you either believe it or you don't. And from time to time I would ask what I was doing for these 240,000 black citizens, and the answer always came back: 'Not much!'"

"You've got to try to see through black eyes. Otherwise you never will see the problems, have no way to resolve the problems. This is really where the mayor had so much trouble. He's looking at this thing from the top of a white shiny horse…And when finally late in February this began to seep through my unconscious—that's when the thing really began to shift in my view…"

Becoming "fourth nigger" on the council was an untenable role. It wasn't Blanchard's style. He tried to balance, pivot. He went to private meetings, set up meetings, tried to get people in touch with one another to find a way out of the strike. But the tightrope he walked swayed and the audience watched open-mouthed—Gurkhas, slant-eyed blacks, his golf partners at the country club, Yale '39, the conservatives who voted for him.

By mid-March Blanchard was picking up hints from some conservative businessmen that they could live with the dues checkoff to get the strike over with. And he was convinced that Loeb was "painted into a corner…hoist on his own petard…upped…And sooner or later he was gonna have his throat cut, and it was so plain." But to his suggestion that Loeb turn him loose to try to get a resolution favorable to the union through council, everyone understanding that Loeb would publicly oppose it, the mayor's response was, "I just don't understand you. This thing is wrong."

And Jerred Blanchard changed his vote.

Loeb was by now transformed into the larger-than-life symbolic defender of *laissez-faire*, the "law," and a racial status quo. Yet "I never, ever heard Loeb treat a black person with anything but respect," commented *Commercial Appeal* reporter Joe Sweat who covered him daily. "I never heard him make a derogatory statement about Negroes in general. He couldn't say 'Negro' correctly, poor bastard, but he just couldn't say it. He wouldn't enter into any jokes on that subject...One day a young black guy came up to the office looking for a job, and Loeb spent almost an hour with him, showing him how to answer want ads in the paper. He was very bound up in helping individuals with their personal problems. But he was just not progressive."

Because he was not in personal contact with current black or even liberal thinking, because he did not read much, it seems he never made the connection that blatant racism and genteel structural racism could produce the same lack of results for blacks.

"He's a classic example of the Christian ethic in the Calvinist philosophy," explained a close friend. "He believes you should get up early in the morning, work hard, stick to your last, do what's right, and go home and go to bed, and do the same thing day in and day out. He doesn't just talk this ethic or think it; he actually lives it....If you or I take a stamp from our company for a private letter, that's stealing, but it's of no consequence and it doesn't make any difference. Loeb is the kind of guy that buys his own stamps and puts them on his own letters down at City Hall because he doesn't want to steal....You won't ever find Loeb trying to alibi anything. He is just going to do what he thinks is right. He doesn't give a damn whether you like it or not. As long as he can look in the mirror the next morning, why it doesn't bother him....I think this creates in him a certain rigidity. He's not a racist....He's not mean. He's anything but devious...His motives are not unkind. He's not trying to build a political machine. If he's had one beer, he won't drive an automobile....His household budget is always balanced. Everything is in order. Everything is in place. He answers all letters. When he tells you he's going to do something he makes a note so he'll be damn sure he doesn't forget it. He does it...He's probably done more for people than ninety-nine percent of the bleeding hearts that wear their actions on their sleeves. He's tough. He's tough-minded. And he believes in certain things and nobody's going to run him off them."

Stories of his frugality were legion. So were stories of his honesty. His wife Mary would jokingly complain that he would not allow her to use his city car to run to the grocery store or go to church. Ned Cook recalled a pop stand they had run together as teen-agers. "I could leave him alone with the stand and he wouldn't drink the pop. He could never leave me."

He was wealthy, but the Loeb family had worked its way into wealth. His great-grandfather had run a tailoring shop patronized by the men who traveled and worked the river. His grandfather went into business in shirts and men's furnishings and launched into the laundry business in 1889, the old man would joke, when no one else could do up the shirts he sold. His father, William Loeb, Sr., ran the first successful Community Fund drive in 1930 and was involved in all kinds of charitable work. At his death in 1942 the newspaper obituary would praise his devotion to the people who worked in his laundry business as well as say, "He abhorred the slightest tinge of dishonesty, and to him there was no degree between right and wrong." By 1968 the laundry business was being run by Bill Loeb, Henry's younger brother, who as a boy suffered the results of a crippling bout with polio contracted at a summer camp. The family continued to take philanthropy seriously.

Henry Loeb was fanatic about privacy both in his philanthropic and family life. His wife Mary, in fact, disliked political life intensely and it was common gossip that she was far less conservative than her husband. Although coming as she did out of Memphis' cotton society, she appeared smiling at his side on required occasions. But she was far happier out of the limelight, and Loeb respected that, just as he demanded that others respect his "no comment" when, shortly after the election, he left behind his Jewish religion and joined the Episcopal church in which his wife and children had been brought up.

"He was not a dapper mayor, by any means," said Joe Sweat. "He would come into the office quite often with an old pair of pants on...not dirty or threadbare, but they would not be the stylish thing. He had a raincoat he kept in the office and I bet the damn thing must have been twenty-five years old. It was scruffy....He was a big man and he liked the outdoors, especially duck hunting...But his greatest day-in day-out recreation was swimming in his backyard pool, and he was full of stories about this dog of his that would swim in the pool, too....He used salty language, full of 'God damn" and "son of a bitch,' and he enjoyed a good bawdy story—among men. But he had this gallant thing about women. If a lady was coming into his office, he'd put on his coat."

Loeb was a political animal, no mistaking that, liking crowds, handshaking, meeting new people, but he could also be bluntly rude and arrogant if he had judged a man's character and found it wanting in the traits he demanded. "Essentially he's developed boorishness into a fine art," said one wit.

Labor mediator Frank Miles, who first met Loeb when he was running for commander of the local American Legion in 1952, called him "the politickingest son of a gun that ever came down the pike."

He worked publicly for the handicapped in many ways, setting up a sheltered workshop, staffing vending stands with the blind. As public works commissioner he had given jobs to the handicapped as well as to those with minor prison records to help in rehabilitation.

Jerrold Moore, who would serve for four years as his administrative assistant, delineated the mayor's administrative strengths. "We had every opportunity to propose, argue, debate, try to persuade him before the decision was made. But once that decision was made, there was no question in anybody's mind about what was going to be done…He delegated responsibility. One of his favorite expressions was 'When you get a good man on the job to do it, let him do it.' " His greatest problem, thought Moore, was his image.

His relationships with the local press who covered him that spring were amiable, though they had not been particularly warm his first term in office four years before and they would deteriorate again. He would occasionally ask the reporters' advice about a course of action. "I thought that was partially a tactic, but partially that he might really want it," said Sweat. But the mayor was leery of "outside" or out-of-town reporters even from the beginning of the strike and by the end was outright hostile, refusing often to see them. But even early on Sweat could remember one northern reporter calling and Loeb making fun of his accent for others in the room.

After Dr. King's entrance into Memphis attracted out-of-town reporters in large numbers, it was Loeb's feeling that they had nothing to lose by tearing him to pieces. With eastern reporters he would make a point of his degree from Brown University, noting that he "was not completely ignorant of Eastern Establishment ways." The national press was later to pillory him, but even before that he had dismissed with contempt most of their attitudes toward Memphis and its ways. They did not know what they were writing about, and he would not bother to defend himself.

"One of the vilest reports was that I didn't want to sign a 'nigger' contract," he said once. "I was brought up by a father and mother who wouldn't have permitted me to use that expression. My father would have worn me out. It was never used in our house. Nobody has ever heard me use it." His comment was beside the point, but it was how he thought, and for the type of letters that were to come in, like one from New York which read "Well, big buddy, ain't it about time you spit the grits out, wipe the fatback off'n you jowls and the black-eyed peas out of your ears, and start listening and talking," he had nothing but anger and disgust.

But it was not reaction to national press reports that pushed him into any of the positions he took, for these had been staked out early in February and never changed. Why should they? He had the support of almost all the letter-writing citizens, representing, it was assumed, the bulk of ordinary people, and he had the support of the media, of the business establishment, and of his close advisers, "splendid men who could tell him all about bond issues and finance and things of that sort, the usual business of a city," grumbled one critic, who added, "When he's right, Loeb is just real real right, and when he's wrong, he's just abysmally wrong."

Mats and Spittoons

8

*"One man's estimate may not be the
same as another's. That's why they
have mats under spittoons."*
E. W. (Ned) Cook

Outside of the city government/union/COME axis, assorted individuals and groups tried to break the strike impasse.

And some Memphis leaders still believe that the strike came
within a hairsbreadth of being settled during the few days just
after the February Macing of the ministers and the obtaining of
the injunction against the union. John Spence launched that
attempt, which centered on a letter that Mayor Loeb would
write and which Jerry Wurf could accept in lieu of a union
contract. The problem was in working out a letter that would
be acceptable to both sides.

Spence, in the Memphis Civil Rights Commission office, was
a great believer in the type of power structure group that the
Memphis Committee on Community Relations had once been,
a group where everyone was on a first name basis and the
problems of the city could be discussed rationally and pragmatically.

The initial group Spence now brought together included
Jacques Wilmore, head of the civil rights commission; three

councilmen, Pryor, Donelson, and Chandler; Carl Carson, who
headed a large trucking firm; Bert Ferguson, white president of
the leading black radio station WDIA; LeMoyne College
President Dr. Hollis Price; Jesse Turner of the NAACP; Rev.
Lawson; and attorney David Caywood.

The meeting was friendly, and they began to work over the
union's demands and try to combine them with the city's stated
position. Caywood brought the report from people close to
Wurf that the union would not insist on a written contract per
se. A letter might work. They also decided to call for help from
Loeb's lifelong friend, E. W. (Ned) Cook.

Cook was a millionaire, a tough businessman who had helped
expand the family business enterprises from cotton and land into
grain and lumber. He was widely traveled, as likely to be found
skimming around South America in his private plane as at the
Hunt and Polo Club, a big, shrewd, likable man. His financial
contacts within the country and in cotton centers throughout
the world gave him a perspective on Memphis that many local
businessmen simply did not have, and there was hope he might
encourage Loeb to be a little more flexible. As Cook had once
said, when faced by a controversy within the airport authority
which Loeb had named him to head, "One man's estimate may
not be the same as another's. That's why they have mats under
spittoons."

But the group's plans got off to a rocky start. When Pryor and
Caywood arrived at the hotel suite to talk to Wurf about the
proposed document, he was furious about the injunction, and
during a three-hour meeting they were treated to the union
leader's opinions of the strike and the mayor. "Wurf said there
was going to be serious trouble and it was because Loeb was
both stupid and honest," recalled Caywood.

But they had heard correctly. Wurf would not insist on a
written contract as long as there was some kind of agreement in
writing. He would settle for a ten-cent-an-hour raise immediately and five additional cents on July 1; dues checkoff through
the credit union; union or legal representation at all levels of the

grievance procedure; and some fringe benefits. He was also willing to give the city a no-strike clause.

Cook delivered a Wurf-approved document to Loeb. Loeb reworked it, inserted his own terms, and sent it back again to the union with Cook. Cook and Caywood now met with Ciampa and Jesse Epps and they all had a drink while comparing the mayor's and Wurf's documents.

"There was a difference in wording and a difference in emphasis and there may have been a nickel's difference in money, but if you had these two documents side-by-side, you wouldn't know why the strike lasted," said Caywood. "But in the middle of one of these things, everyone gets a little inflamed and they start cutting the bologna pretty thin. 'The' means something other than 'the.' "

Ciampa and Epps turned down the mayor's draft. What made it unacceptable was the exclusion of any mention of a union-dues checkoff. Cook was irritated. "You know, we've got Loeb a little less rigid and you ought to be a little less rigid. …Otherwise, you're going to burn the town down." Ciampa's response, Cook recalled, was that the union was determined to win the strike even if they had to escalate it into a race issue.

Cook's anger was further reinforced the next morning. He had dropped over to a nearby pancake house for breakfast and was quietly reading his newspaper when Jerry Wurf and several union people sat down near him. They were discussing the strike and did not notice Cook, who buried his head further into his paper "and drank eight cups of coffee and read 'Orphan Annie' eighteen times." Cook observed, "It was pretty obvious how you could settle from listening to Wurf…About a dime less than they got as long as they got the checkoff through the credit union and some grievance procedure, with emphasis on the language that a union existed. …And they were talking about how they were going to use the black preachers and get them involved in this and, if they had to, they were perfectly willing to escalate it into a race issue using the preachers." Cook reported the conversation back to Loeb.

David Caywood, meanwhile, sought the advice of Councilman Jerred Blanchard. They worked through another rewrite of
the document, one copy for Cook to give the mayor and one for
Caywood to take to Jerry Wurf for approval. But Wurf was
indignant. He threw down the rewrite of Loeb's suggested
document and announced he was tired of dealing with the
mayor. The Loeb draft was not acceptable.

Complicating settlement attempts even more was a story in
the morning *Commercial Appeal*, reporting that Loeb was
considering the possibility of handling union-dues collection
through loans from the credit union. "Such a suggestion, if
made, would represent the first offer by the mayor regarding any
method of dues collection other than those made in person by
union agents."

But the headline announced in large black type:

LOEB MAY OFFER
COMPROMISE PLAN
TO COLLECT DUES

Loeb was furious. He had no intention of "compromising," and
he promptly denied the story.

"That was when we lost it right down the drain," said
Councilwoman Gwen Awsumb. "We could have ended it that
day if they had not used that word 'compromise' because this
is a word that to our mayor is as bad as 'nigger' to the Negro.
It's like waving a red flag. And he backed off...and you could
never get him back to that middle ground again."

Still the would-be peacemakers persisted. By Wednesday,
February 28, the whole document was worked around again in
the form of a letter which Loeb could send out to the workers
and which the union could accept in place of a written contract.
Loeb again refused. He had readied a letter of his own.

This time attorney Lucius Burch and Blanchard made a last-
ditch attempt to get Loeb to take their negotiated letter. No,
said the mayor. But he handed them a copy of the one he was

planning to send out to the men that afternoon. Burch scanned it quickly. There was still a possibility of settlement. "Let me take one more crack at Wurf," he urged the mayor. "One more crack." Loeb finally agreed they could show his letter to Wurf in secrecy and see if with only minor changes it might satisfy him.

"You couldn't tell which side had drawn the letter, because both sides had used that blasted credit union as the gimmick," Blanchard said. "But there was a difference, and each one of them knew it...maybe because when you're going for his jugular vein, you know he's going for yours, too."

Joined unofficially by James Manire of the city legal staff, Blanchard and Burch returned to Burch's office. "It was raining to beat the devil and Wurf drags that bad foot in, and we sit down and talk with very, very little preliminary." Caywood found them when he returned from court. It was dreary now and dusk outside and they drank a little whiskey. Blanchard and Caywood were convinced the strike was almost over.

Manire was less sanguine. They weren't talking about the same thing with the credit union, he explained. What the mayor had in mind was the worker's right to borrow a lump sum or even monthly amounts from the credit union, turn the sum over to the union, and have the money deducted from his paycheck to repay the credit union. What Wurf was seeking was a direct deduction of dues off the top of a worker's check by the credit union which in turn would forward it to the union if the worker authorized such individual deduction to be made.

But on that rainy afternoon Burch telephoned back to Loeb, "The only thing that's standing between you and settling this strike is your word that you will not tamper with the credit union." The gist of Loeb's reply was that any city paymaster who honored the credit union's request to pay monies over to the union would be fired and that Loeb would see that the credit union was not on the list of authorized city payroll deduction agencies. "No one knew where such power came from," said Caywood. "Loeb said he was gonna do it and the hell with it."

Everyone finished his drink, and went on home. "That was the

end of the letter writing," said Caywood. "Everybody was tired
of writing letters. Loeb sent his on out."

Loeb's letter to the strikers was a reiteration of what he had
already offered. There was no reply.

After the failure of the talks begun at St. Mary's Cathedral,
leaders of the Memphis Ministers Association were also not sure
which way to move. At their meeting of March 4, Rev. John
William (Bill) Aldridge, assistant at Idlewild Presbyterian Church,
sat somewhat unbelieving through routine reports of the social
action committee and of the race relations committee. Suddenly
he stood up. Memphis, he told his fellow ministers, was facing
its worst crisis since the last Yellow Fever epidemic. What could
the ministers association do now?

A motion was passed that their president, Rabbi James Wax,
contact Rev. Starks, head of the black Ministerial Alliance, and
set up a joint meeting on the strike and race relations.

Rabbi Wax had worked tirelessly to further Jewish-Christian
relations, fought for better government, and served on the
Memphis Committee on Human Relations and innumerable
other civic boards. In 1956 alone he had been honored for
promoting better race relations by the black *Tri-State Defender*,
as a distinguished citizen by the Memphis Newspaper Guild,
and as an outstanding citizen by the Veterans of Foreign Wars.

Now Rabbi Wax hesitated. Neither he nor the majority of
members of the ministers association wanted to openly oppose
the mayor. He knew there was a small group calling for a much
stronger stand by the ministers association, but he felt to move
much further would identify the ministers too closely with the
cause of the strikers and hurt the attempt at objectivity. To him,
the best chance in ameliorating the strike still lay through the
time-honored methods of behind-the-scene attempts to change
minds rather than in some public posture that would antagonize
many of the ministers' churchgoers.

So he did not push hard for the joint meeting with the black
ministers but instead opted for a *via media*. Several teams of
ministers talked to individual members of the city council.

Response was cordial but nonproductive.

"Why was there a delay in this joint meeting with the black ministers?" Rev. Aldridge was to ask later again and again. "Why didn't we meet? Didn't the Negro ministers have time to talk any more? Or was the issue so hot that nobody called the meeting?"

The meeting just didn't materialize, said Rev. Starks. "Besides," he added, "we had decided that maybe we (blacks)could work in one area and they (whites) could work effectively in another....I realized that the rabbi identified with the power structure, that the white ministers' relationship with the power structure is different from mine."

Rev. Starks, in truth, had expected far more support from the white churches. But as the strike dragged on, he realized that any support would be found in "scattered concerns in the various white churches, but not in any unified approach."

One of those "scattered concerns" had already raised controversy among Memphis Catholics, for on the weekend of the February Macing, members of the small and unofficial Catholic Human Relations Council realized they would have to move immediately to support the strike or not bother to move at all. Telephone calls went back and forth among members, and by that Sunday evening a night letter supporting the demand for union recognition and warning against deterioration of race relations in the city went out to the mayor, the city council, and the newspapers.

Other integrated groups, the Young Democrats, Baxton Bryant's Tennessee Council on Human Relations, and the women's small Saturday Luncheon Group, had shown support for the strike. But among predominantly white churches only the Catholic council, the tiny Unitarian-Universalist Fellowship, and the Presbytery Committee on Social Justice of the Presbyterian Church had taken a public stand, and the Presbyterian statement was to receive no public exposure for yet another week.[1]

Now telephone calls poured into Catholic parish rectories

and to the newspapers denouncing the Catholic Human
Relations Council. "The council does not represent the Catholic church," said these calls. "It does not represent me." Pastors
were irritated, laymen irate.

And Monsignor Joseph Leppert, dean of the Memphis
Catholic clergy and founder of the human relations council, was
not pleased. He had counseled waiting, discussing, informing
the Bishop in Nashville. There were only about ninety-five
thousand Catholics in the entire state of Tennessee, less than
three percent of the population. Shelby County had about forty-
five thousand of these Catholics, and those who were black
made up an infinitesimally small number. There was no black
priest in the state. Over in the hill country in eastern Tennessee
not many years before Catholics themselves had understood
what it meant to be looked at with fear and prejudice. Half of
the counties in the state were still considered mission territory.
In Memphis, although all churches were open for worship, the
Catholic clergy had decided not to integrate their parish schools
until public school integration. The last separate black parish
had been closed in 1966.

Monsignor Leppert was a small dry reed of a man, nearing
seventy, ascetic, reared up in Greenwood, Mississippi, and forty-
two years a priest in Tennessee. There was no bombast in him;
he stood in the back of crowds. Yet he was there, always there.
His dialectic was the prayer of St. Francis of Assisi. To fight
him—and there had been many Catholics who had fought his
views on racism—was to tilt at windmills, for he was not where
they were at and he moved steadily toward whatever vision of
God it was that called him forward. Pastor of St. Therese of the
Little Flower Church, his parish school enrollment was about a
third black, making it probably the most racially balanced school
in the city, public or parochial.

But that Friday night, the first of March, at the first regular
human relations council board meeting after the sending of the
union support letter, Monsignor Leppert was unhappy.

The board carried on its routine business. The group's annual

Mayor Henry Loeb addressing striking Sanitation workers at City Hall on February 14 and warning that they must return to work or lose their jobs.
The Commercial Appeal

One of the "CIAMPA GO HOME" bumper stickers directed at AFSCME field services director P. J. Ciampa and used across the city during the early weeks of the strike.

Ernest C. Withers, *Withers Photography,* Memphis

Police breaking up the February 23 march up Main Street. This macing of both strikers and shoppers was the forerunner of tragedy.

Bob Williams, *The Commercial Appeal*

National Guard patrols on Main Street following the riots of March 29/30.
The Commercial Appeal

Many march participants were sympathizers drawn from the surrounding area.

Courtesy of AFSCME

The looting on Beale Street (March 28) which leads to police decision to turn marchers back.

National Guard outside City Hall on April 9. Note continued presence of "I AM A MAN" signs by strikers.

Poor People's Campaign Rally on May 2, three weeks after settlement of the Strike and almost a month after Dr. King's assassination. The site is the Lorraine Motel, the podium standing directly in front of the railing where Dr. King was shot.

All photographs, except for that on page 229, are used courtesy of
The Mississippi Valley Collection, Memphis State University Libraries.

Brotherhood Banquet and Mass were only a month away. How were ticket sales going? The nuns at Siena College would make crepe-paper flowers for the center of each table. The liquor store owner was sure he could provide bottles to hold them. The bishop was scheduled to be out of state. Would he be back in time?

By 9:00 P.M. board members were shifting in their seats. If they were going to have to fight with Monsignor over their public support of the union, why not get to it? Some of them were ready to fight if there were any clerical attempts to put restrictions on their right to write letters or take stands. They would not seek prior approval from the bishop. This was the Vatican II church.

The monsignor did get to it. His voice was mild. "I think we must reach an understanding. Neither the bishop nor I want to restrict you, but we must avoid precipitous actions…"

Bill Ross began to talk, his cavernous face gray with fatigue, his speech deceptively slow and easy. Ever since he had been secretary of the local AFL-CIO labor council, he said, he had known Thomas Oliver Jones. It was he who had convinced the national AFSCME to put Jones on their payroll as an organizer. For eight years Thomas Oliver had devoted his life to one thing—changing the conditions of garbagemen in Memphis. Now Ross' voice was hard. Did Monsignor, did any of them, have any idea what it was like to be a garbage collector in this city? No place to wash, no place to urinate, moving always in the city's filth for a wage that wouldn't even support a family? Hard work, heavy work, back injuries. No workmen's compensation. The union had used every bit of reasoning at its command. But the mayor would not yield. Now he would not even listen. Labor leaders, national labor leaders, had been Maced—MACED—on the main street of Memphis, Tennessee! And Henry Loeb would not even listen.

We are, said Bill Ross, beyond a labor dispute now. He put his face in his hands.

"I understand that," the monsignor said gently. "We want to

help the men. The question is—how we do it without antago-
nizing those parts of the white community who can best help
them? I was at the city council meeting last week and I was
greatly disturbed. Racial overtones developed. They were openly
stated. Harsh things were said. That meeting did not help the
situation. It hurt it. We must not become involved in racial
hatreds, in obscenities…"

"Obscenities!" Allegra Turner's voice rose wildly. She was
Louisiana Catholic-born, wife of the president of the NAACP.
"I'll tell you what obscenity is. It's answering the phone at two
o'clock in the morning and hearing someone say, 'Your husband will be dead by tomorrow night.' It's having people write
letters saying 'Get out of town, you goddamn niggers.' It's
watching your children go off to school and not knowing if
they'll come home again because they've been threatened, too.
That's obscenity!"

There is silence now. When talk resumes, it is quiet. I was not
trying to stop you, says Monsignor Leppert. I just want us to stay
in close communication with each other. This bishop belongs
in on the communication, too, they say. The bishop is a good
man.

When Martin King marches in Memphis, white Catholics
from the human relations council will march with him. After all,
obscenity is obscenity.

Early in March another Catholic clergyman, Father William
Greenspun, a big, mutton-faced, Paulist priest, came into
Memphis and with a clunk into the strike. Greenspun was
advance man for a team of Paulists who were to set up an
exploratory, experimental urban ministry at old St. Patrick's
Church whose property bordered that of Clayborn Temple.
"St. Patrick's," he said, "was a parish run down so badly that it
had no place to go but up." Within the parish boundaries lay a
large black area designated for urban renewal, a welfare population. Greenspun's dream was to bring forth a new Christian
community centered on social services and liturgy, with the cooperation of ministers of all denominations in the area.

Before entering the Paulists, he had served in the Air Corps, worked in a factory and belonged to a union, and earned a sociology degree. As a priest he worked in ghetto parishes in New York and Baltimore and for six years sat behind a desk at the National Catholic Welfare Conference. He had worked closely with the National Council of Churches in setting up ecumenical "living room dialogues" and had coauthored the program's first discussion guide. He was also concerned with restructuring the Paulist order itself. "We tended to put apostolic deadwood in places like St. Pat's," he explained, but now young priests were being invested in urban ghetto work.

Father Greenspun had come into Memphis the previous December to look it over with an eye to sending in some younger men. He got interested in Memphis and returned himself. "I was a national guy coming to the local level. The national bureaucracy is finished. It's a new ball game, and we've got to develop models in specific geographic areas...In many cities white ministers can't go into the black community anymore. I thought, I'm starting this work when all the white priests are leaving it. I'm coming in with my suitcase when they're going out with theirs."

He was to characterize the strike period as a "social system in revolution...not a Memphis problem...not racial. It was a cultural problem. The parochialism of a city was being shaken."

But first he had to decide what to do about his own garbage in the old rectory. Initially he had hoped to remain neutral in the strike, but he walked around the corner to one of the mass meetings at Clayborn Temple and then he went to a union meeting and then he was hooked on the union cause.

"Firestone Hall should have been on film. You'll not see it anywhere else in the world. It was...worth coming to Memphis for. Here were a thousand workers and a minister who'd stand up and begin a liturgy in which the secular and existential were so united with Scripture and hymns you felt you were on a mountainside listening to Moses or with the Israelites marching around Jericho's walls waiting for them to crumble...Negro

Christianity is rapidly going. The strike itself hastened the death of this beautiful thing because it does have its negative aspect of pie in the sky, and the young militants have none of this in them. But there is this reawakening sense of personhood. The most phenomenal movement in the world is the passion for personhood. You find it in the Church, in teen-agers, in Negroes, in the poor, world-wide. People in Memphis are so hung up on communism. But communism is finished as well as capitalism. People don't realize what revolution they're facing."

He made one effort to get the distribution of food to the workers into neutral hands such as a Catholic welfare group, on the theory that much more help from whites would come into it then, but he was curtly rebuffed by the COME leadership, and he learned his lesson quickly. White aid was welcome. Any sort of white takeover was not. So he joined with the small group of white Catholics trying to set up meetings with both priests and laity to get the other side of the strike story across.

A few other small groups were making moves. At Buntyn Presbyterian Church arrangements were being made for several of the member families to become a worshipping, active part of Rev. Zeke Bell's black Parkway Gardens Church for several months, although the strike controversy was hurting that effort at race relations at both churches.

At Southwestern at Memphis College, the editors of the weekly campus newspaper, the *Sou'wester,* were calling on students to support the strike. Southwestern, of Presbyterian origin, small, expensive, and strong academically, had just come through a furor over the Greek system on the heels of the pledging of the first black to a fraternity, and the editors now cast a journalistic eye on the strike. A few students began collecting supplies for the strikers and joining the daily marches.

On Sunday, March 10, Southwestern students also appeared at sixteen white churches to pass out sheets explaining the strikers' cause. "I wore a suit," said *Sou'wester* associate editor Bill Casey, "but a few of the kids did look like beatniks, and people were shocked and scared...I had several sheets wadded up and thrown at me." The tactic was not too successful although several churches invited students back to talk.

Just before the mayor's Thursday open house began on March 7, nineteen women, stylishly dressed and sporting white gloves, trooped up to Loeb's office. They made a bright semicircle around his desk. "Well, Mayor Loeb," their spokeswoman said, "we have come to tell you we think the strikers should be given what they ask for. The city is being torn apart and no principles about labor unions are worth that." The two reporters covering Loeb looked up with quick interest. It was the first wide-open indication that the mayor's white out-East support did have a few cracks in it.

This was a minor crack. The women were then attending a five-week workshop on ways of raising children without prejudice in a prejudiced society. Sponsored by the Memphis Chapter of the National Conference of Christians and Jews and endorsed by the Catholic Human Relations Council, B'nai B'rith, and Church Women United, the workshop was the first attempt of its kind in the city. It had begun the middle of February and had leveled off at about sixty women, most of them young mothers, some fifteen of them black. And it was the fear of increasing racial polarization that sent them now to Loeb.

"Sure, we were trying to create an impression," said Kay Portman, one of the workshop organizers. "We looked as if we were all out for a spring luncheon. Our husbands did represent a pretty good cross section, lawyers, professors, business, and we were loaded with out-East addresses...The mayor was most cordial...We told him what we thought in a sort of unorganized way...and he took out of his billfold a piece of paper with all his responses to the union's demands on it, showing how many concessions he was already making. We kept saying that we were concerned about black/white relations, but he sort of by-passed that concern....

"Then he really caught us off guard. He leaned forward and said, 'I'm just fascinated with accents. Can you all tell me where you're from?' And he picked out some of us who'd done the talking. It was pretty shrewd. He picked women who'd moved here from California, Missouri, and Indiana before he made a slip and pointed to someone from Dyersburg, not too far away, and before one of us had sense enough to say, 'But we're all Memphians now.' He'd illustrated, of course, that a number of us weren't originally from Memphis or even from the South. I think the implication was that therefore we couldn't possibly know what we were talking about. We were outsiders. But he never came out and said that, and he shook everyone's hand, and invited us all to come back anytime....I don't know what good going to see him did. He wasn't moved by us."

The newspaper story listed the names of all nineteen women, and those at the top of the list got a few harassing phone calls, but each recruited a friend to attend the next week's open house with the same message for Loeb. There they ran into a counter-group of some forty women come to congratulate the mayor on his "firmness and fairness."

"One of them was passing out a pamphlet about 'Return to Your Church Home,'" said Kay Portman. "Our people did talk to Loeb, but we dropped the idea after that. ....It was getting too late for that sort of thing...We went on with the workshop."

Three days later another group gathered at Westminster House, Rev. Dick Moon's bailiwick by the Memphis State campus, to see what moves might be open to white strike sympathizers. The meeting managed to sort itself into what its backers called a "non-organization," called Save Our City (SOC). Save Our City saw itself as a sort of ad hoc information conduit, channeling those interested in helping the strikers into areas where they could be useful.

A three-column newspaper ad was taken out to announce strike support and to invite others to join the thirty-three signers. "One response was that the only way to Save Our City is for people like you to keep your nose out of other people's business," said Rev. Moon.

Still, Save Our City, calling for a white presence in the black community's strike efforts, did serve as a rallying point for isolated liberals, and its chairman, Presbyterian minister Darrell Doughty, sat in on COME strategy meetings as a liaison to the white community.

In general, it was a few young Presbyterian ministers who were the most outspoken in insisting that Christian principles were entangled in the strike.

Rev. Bill Aldridge laid the most on the line for he was assistant at Idlewild Presbyterian Church to the highly respected Dr. Paul Tudor Jones, and while the older minister made no attempt to stop him, it was clear that neither he nor the majority of the church, actively concerned about many civic issues, were in sympathy with Aldridge's actions.

Mississippi Delta-raised, Rev. Aldridge had come to the ministry late—after graduation from Ole Miss, service in the infantry, and four years of managing a cotton plantation. He studied theology in Switzerland and was already publishing scholarly articles on hermeneutics when he returned to the South, where he would also teach at the Cumberland Presbyterian Memphis Theological Seminary. "I think Bonhoeffer said patriotism is a hollow thing from the other side of the border," Aldridge would comment.

He had preached on the urgency of greater racial rapprochement that preceding summer, but the first week of the strike he was aloof, critical of both Ciampa and Loeb. What began pulling him into the strike situation was the immediate condemnation by his parishioners of Ciampa and the union and a chance conversation he had with Rev. Jim Lawson. Then prodded by Presbyterian layman Taylor Blair, who was international representative of the International Brotherhood of Electrical Workers, he called together a week after the strike started the Christian Social Relations Committee of the Memphis Presbytery which got off a letter to the mayor calling on him to formally recognize Local 1733 as the designated bargaining agent for the public works men. Letters went to Loeb's office saying "John William Aldridge does not represent the majority of people at Idlewild Church." The writers often forwarded carbon copies to Aldridge.

By mid-March the session of his church had officially raised the question of the committee letter with the Presbytery.

Rev. Aldridge was one of a handful of whites at the first mass meeting in the black community after the February Macing. "Goodness knows why I was there," he said. "I came home and was going to sit down and relax and take my shoes off when I saw the meeting in the paper and I just went on down there." That night he was asked to read the Scripture and say a few words of support. But he was gravely concerned about the lack of white presence, so he began contacting white ministers and students at the seminary and at Southwestern. Soon there were enough whites to be noticeable. "It would be bad enough to draw your lines at Christian versus non-Christian...but this was black against white. White took precedence over Christian. And this is what I just didn't want."

So he ducked out on church meetings to attend meetings on the strike, all the while becoming more controversial.

As a chaplain at Memphis State, Rev. Dick Moon was much freer. Like Aldridge he had come to the seminary late—after four years in Air Force intelligence. In Memphis in 1964 as minister of a church on the edge of the changing Lamar and Bellevue neighborhood, he tried to familiarize himself with the economic and welfare situations and with the black leadership, and he had served as interim pastor for Parkway Gardens Church before Rev. Zeke Bell came to Memphis. In the summer of 1967 he found himself the only white person among blacks protesting the selling off of a small city park in the black area, and he worked for Willis in the mayoral campaign. By the time he began marching with the strikers, he no longer found it unusual to be a token white.

Rev. Moon took the brunt of white displeasure over their "own"—and especially a minister—supporting the strike. He was the first white Memphian, outside of labor, to march publicly, and in the early days of the strike his presence was always conscientiously reported on by the press.

Rev. Darrell Doughty was an assistant professor of religion at

Southwestern college, a slender, good-looking young man. He had majored in engineering physics at the University of Southern California at a time "when everyone who did well in math and science was funnelled into engineering." He took a year's graduate work, but his curiosity about physics subsided and "suddenly I wanted to do something different." He entered San Francisco Theological School, and from 1962–65 was in Germany getting his doctorate in New Testament interpretation. He taught one year at Princeton Theological Seminary before coming to Southwestern.

He and his wife Mary liked Memphis. "Though generally we recognized that the church at least played a different role in the culture here, a different role than I had ever envisioned."

They gradually made contact with a few Memphians whose liberal concerns matched their own, and through Vasco and Maxine Smith of the NAACP were welcomed to Zeke Bell's church where Doughty began to move into an unofficial role of assistant pastor and his wife Mary became the church's only official white member. Drawn then into the orbit of the black community, Doughty began attending meetings of the Shelby County Democratic Club and when Willis announced for mayor he agreed to act as liaison to the white community. At this point he came in contact with the scattered whites throughout the city who were ready to seriously consider the idea of a black mayor. It was this small group that the three Presbyterian ministers called on again during the strike.

Doughty had neither Bill Aldridge's sense of mission nor Dick Moon's warmth. Unlike most whites concerned with the strike, his heart did not bleed. The strike for him was not some great socio-economic passion play, but a chess game of principles and power, the winning or the losing depending on the proper application of pressure on the right square. He was part of a communications network of church people throughout the country set up to channel information on local black unrest as the anticipated long, hot summer of 1968 approached, and he acted as a contact with the National Council of Churches during

the Memphis strike. So he saw the strike as national in its
implications. On that basis, he was critical of what he considered
the very southern slant of it, the leadership of the black
ministers, the inclination to distrust outside advice, the slowness
of escalation. Yet, as in the Willis campaign for mayor where he
was also extremely critical of its operation, he looked around to
begin garnering white support.

 The problem these men faced as white clergy in a racial
contretemps was to apply the social gospel when its tenets ran
counter to the established civic, religious, and congregational
patterns. With the exception of Bill Aldridge and only a few
others, white ministers who publicly allied themselves with the
strikers early were not dependent on a local congregation for
livelihood. They were in special services of the church and were
free from congregational pressure in a way that most members
of the Memphis Ministers Association were not.

Since many of them were not originally from Memphis, they
were also free from the pressure of their sisters and cousins and
aunts bewailing their lack of respect for certain Memphis
orthodoxies.

By appearing publicly at the side of the strikers, they moved
a giant step beyond the majority of members of the ministers
association who were still trying to work through private,
individual contact with white community leaders. But in practical results their public witness through much of the strike was
negligible because they swung behind them no local power
groupings.

"And we thought we were in the middle of it," ironically
remarked another active Presbyterian, Rev. Dick Wells.

Perhaps only to the strikers themselves did they matter as
continuous proof that there were concerned whites.

For in mid-March the white community and its business
leaders still remained almost solidly behind Mayor Loeb. It was
costing the city from $4,000 to $5,000 a day in overtime for
police, but about $195,000 had been saved in February in

salaries in the public works department. Sales were rising in the suburban shopping center branches, somewhat offsetting the downtown boycott, and while merchants on Main Street were more and more inconvenienced and irritated, they were not ready to cave in to economic pressures, and they were joined in this determination by other less directly affected segments of Memphis' financial and business structure. The business community was active that spring in launching a $4 million program to revitalize the local chamber of commerce, moving it from a local booster club to what they hoped would be a decision-making force in the city.

Power in Memphis fluctuated and depended to some extent on who held political office, but there was also a group of men controlling the city's financial, commercial, and industrial life who continued in power regardless of who was elected or who was brought into the city to run the branches of national business operations. This local group included the officers of the banks and lending institutions, real estate developers, insurance executives, and men from older families who headed the Memphis-originated businesses in such commodities as cotton and hardwood.

Ned Cook pooh-poohed the idea of a powerful monolithic city Establishment. "Well, I've been to a number of luncheons with the so-called Establishment and I can't remember anything ever being decided....I think one of the things that's held Memphis back is, frankly, not the existence of an Establishment as such but the lack thereof. Nobody could ever agree in Memphis on anything."

Yet if the city's leaders did not agree on specific programs for the city's progress, they did hear the same speakers at the same Rotary luncheons, dine together at the same Memphis Country Club, work for the same symphony league and arts council, send their children to the same private schools, provide royalty for the same Cotton Carnival. They shared the same attitudes.

They were opposed to municipal unions. "When you say 'recognize' to a businessman that means 'to recognize-as-the-

exclusive-bargaining-agent.' These words run together. Now
every businessman that you run into, the last thing he wants is
an exclusive bargaining agent agreement with a checkoff," said
lawyer Lucius Burch. James Cherry, business manager for both
Scripps-Howard newspapers and in close touch with the larger
advertisers, said the business community felt that the strikers had
to give in, that they were simply wrong and had to see the light
of day.

Take any leading member of the chamber of commerce, said
one close observer. In all likelihood he went to some place like
Ole Miss. He's grown up here, heard the folklore from his
parents. He believes blacks are different, a sub-order. He's got
a leftover slavery rationale. He doesn't read the the *Saturday
Review* or *Harper's*. He reads the local papers. He's influenced
by his tennis group or his golf group, and what they talk about
is economics, getting more jobs, bigger factories, bigger ex-
pressways. He doesn't know what a young black militant is
thinking. He doesn't know him and would never even get a
chance to see him. And even the more open businessman, the
one whose enlightened self-interest had led to the racial progress that had been made in the past decade, lined up now behind
Loeb.

Adamantly anti-union, casually anti-black, many business
leaders were also convinced that the mass of the black community did not want to be involved in the strike situation but that
representatives of this opinion were now afraid to speak out.
Councilman Hyman explained, "The real, true leaders like
Hollis Price (of LeMoyne College) and Maceo Walker (of
Universal Life Insurance) couldn't afford to speak up. We talked
to a number of this type. They weren't in favor of the strike or
violence, but they couldn't come forward...because they would
get criticized for taking up for the white community."

"For so long the white community made the mistake of
choosing what they call safe, sound, conservative Negroes to
leadership positions, and most of these people had no standing
at all with their own people and they just made a mockery out

of both sides. When something came up the so-called Negro leader could not address himself to it because he had no forum. He was the white man's leader, not the Negroes' leader," countered Judge Ben Hooks.

In this crisis there were none of the old leaders to deal with behind the scenes anyway. The union and COME had moved too rapidly and by-passed them. And the businessmen would not attempt to deal with men like Ciampa or Rev. Lawson, whom they characterized as immoderate and irrational as well as wrong. Additionally, there were the continuing stories that Lawson was a Communist or a Communist dupe.

Here or there a leader of industry might mutter in the privacy of someone's den or over a drink on the nineteenth hole, "Why the hell can't Henry get this thing stopped? Can't we give 'em something to shut them up?" But when John T. Fisher, thirty-four-year-old head of the city's important Plymouth-Chrysler dealership, Fisher Motors, took himself and several friends out to meet Rev. Lawson and to talk about the black community's grievances, he found that they were the first ones who had even bothered to initiate such a meeting.

Fisher was already open to some problems of blacks. His older sister was married to Oscar Carr, one of the leaders of the integrated Mississippi Freedom Democratic Party, and Fisher was on the board of the Memphis Boys Clubs, now integrated, and on the vestry of St. Mary's Episcopal Cathedral where he worked closely with Dean Dimmick of the Memphis Ministers Association. Married to a former Maid of Cotton, he was also a trustee and chairman of the board-elect of St. Mary's School, a private girls' school which that spring was preparing to welcome its first black student.

By early March Fisher was extremely concerned about approaching violence in the strike. It was not his social or business friends but those centered on the church who were raising the alarm. And he found it difficult to explain to his four-year-old son why there were policemen with the garbage truck that came to their house.

So Fisher and several equally concerned friends went to see Mayor Loeb, although Fisher had been hesitant. He had grown up next door to the Loeb home and although Henry was some years older, Fisher had known him all his life and was afraid it might seem he was taking advantage. And he was "very fearful of being meddlesome," he said. "No one had appointed me to go out and solve the sanitation strike." His group found the mayor happy to see them and inflexible on the strike.

The following week the same group set up a meeting with Rev. Lawson at his church office. It was a quiet, easy-going discussion that lasted three hours, and it was the first of several such meetings Fisher would set up.

But the meetings were of little consequence that March. At one of the mayor's Wednesday morning breakfasts there was much discussion about how the strike had evolved into a racial issue. Would it now get out of hand with somebody really getting hurt? Or could it be brought back to an economic problem? Could the city get what was referred to at that meeting as "the more responsible element of the Negro community" to dampen the fires? Could the Negro community be split into strikers and the more responsible types? Could these more responsible types get the strike back on an economic basis?

"At that point a calculated decision, a risk was taken…that this could be done," said Ned Cook. "It almost succeeded."

Still one group that did have power continued trying to break the strike deadlock. They were an expansion of the group that John Spence had brought together and that got bogged down in Loeb's "letter in lieu of contract." At the core now were Councilmen Blanchard, Pryor, and Donelson, former-Mayor Edmund Orgill, Spence, and attorneys Lucius Burch and David Caywood. They had direct access to Loeb personally, to the media, and to black community leaders and they all knew Rev. Lawson, now considered a direct channel to the top union leadership.

Into this group now came Frank Miles, director of industrial relations for the E. L. Bruce lumber concern which was part of the Cook family conglomerate. Miles had arrived in management via the unlikely and abrasive path of unionizing for the Teamsters. He had been a Dixie Greyhound bus driver in Memphis when the Teamsters local went out on a wildcat strike, and when both of the local's top officers became ill, Miles found himself leading the unsuccessful strike. Later as the Teamsters' representative, he helped organize the Memphis Labor Council and moved politically with the liberally oriented group which broke Crump's political power. In 1952 he took a job with the Federal Mediation Service, and four years later moved into labor relations for private corporations.

So it was with a certain amount of professional detachment that Miles watched the beginning of the sanitation strike. Along with Taylor Blair, of the IBEW, he had talked with Loeb early in the strike, but he had then pulled back, believing at that point that neither Loeb nor the union were willing to listen to outside assessments. His years of being a mediator, of seeing both sides, had left their mark both professionally and philosophically, and although he considered himself "management," there was probably no man in Memphis that spring who attempted to be more fair-minded than Frank Miles.

Just after the union leaders were convicted of contempt and effectively boxed in, Miles had a rather casual conversation with council Chairman Downing Pryor about the leadership vacuum that would now exist within the union forces, "whether that leadership had been good, bad, or indifferent."

The council chairman agreed with him. Pryor was already worried about violence. He was to attend one meeting on strike alternatives where the chairman would say that if violence came "when the boys from the north end of the city or the ones from the south come, they carry those deer guns in the back windows of their pickup trucks. You see them every day. ...When they start up with those pump guns around here. ..." Pryor had been hunting in Montana a month or so before, firing at four or five hundred yards. A gun with a 4-inch scope that could kill two blocks away hung on his own gun rack. The possibilities stretched away horribly in front of him.

He was also worried about the lack of labor relations know-how at City Hall. Miles' experience would make him invaluable in helping to settle the strike, yet there seemed no way to get him officially involved. The mayor scented victory; he was not about to appoint a strike mediator and even if he were, any appointment by Loeb would have made a mediator unacceptable to the union, their antagonism to the mayor was now so deep.

Miles also thought the union was on its way to losing the strike, and in that context he told Pryor that there should be discussions with the union, the black ministers, and everybody else "having any real concern for these people, to try to first of all get them to go back to work, and then start (to organize) the other way around. They would then be on the inside."

The city, of course, had been calling for a return to work from the beginning, but Miles saw this not as capitulation but as a holding tactic for the union that might in six months, in a year, lead to victory. In the meantime, tension would be eased.

Pryor liked that approach. Around Friday, March 8, a meeting was held at Tri-State Bank to see if black leaders might like it well enough to urge the union to follow that course. These and subsequent meetings were supposedly secret, but too many people were involved to keep the reports down.

Miles had little time to work out the fine points, but he placed before the group, which included Rev. Lawson, Jesse Turner, and Maxine Smith, the option that the best thing the workers could do at that point was to get back and cover the jobs and continue pressuring from the inside. "The whites kept putting it up to Rev. Lawson as to whether or not this idea might have some merit and whether or not they should try to convince the union of it." But the blacks present were noncommittal, simply agreeing to talk to the union about it.

The union turned the idea down flat. "They said, 'We're not ready to give up,'" said Miles. "And we could expect this. It was just something to try....Sometimes the union went on and lost,

and other times they went on and won. I could appreciate Jerry
Wurf's position. He would have had to stand before the men
and say, 'Look, we have lost this thing...so we're recommend-
ing that you go back to work.' This is a hard thing to do and
often a union representative is not ready for it till the strike has
gone on for some months....And Wurf knew that if he lost here,
it would hurt him in other places, although there hadn't been
much national publicity yet."

Nothing ventured, nothing gained, so the planners went back
to planning and the blacks to organizing the community. Then
on Monday night, March 10, Councilman Blanchard called
Miles with another idea. Why couldn't all the parties agree to
submit the idea of a union-dues checkoff to a referendum of all
the people of the city in, say, August? "Fine idea," Miles told
him, "but the union is not ready for that any more than they
were ready for last week's idea..."

"I told Blanchard that I thought that the idea might at some
time be good, but not now. The union would turn it
down....I'd never heard of any place that ever had a referendum
of its citizens on union recognition. What such an idea could
have been used for is when the situation got so bad that no one
knew how to back out of it, a backing out point. ...My advice
to Blanchard was not to put it out now, but to hang on to it
because in a few weeks it might be a way...."

But it was too late. The idea was already being circulated. "It
was all good intentions," said Miles. "Some of them just got so
hopped up with the idea, it got around. This is what we should
do. Go-go-go...We'll talk to the union, the whole problem will
be solved, everyone back to work, strike over with."

Even Loeb knew of the idea and approved. "It was the kind
of idea the mayor would grab and hang on to," said Miles. "And
he wouldn't want to let go of it either."

Now there was to be a meeting in Councilman Donelson's
office on Saturday morning, March 16. "We were going to try
to convince Lawson and the ministers and Jesse Turner to
exhort the union to go back to work immediately and then

submit the question to a referendum in August. If a majority of the people voted the men should have the checkoff, then the city would give it to them." It was to be the great compromise. Both city government and the union would follow the will of the people. What could be more democratic?

Exactly what the would-be mediators were basing their optimism on is difficult to fathom, unless they believed the union had hit rock bottom. There was not the slightest indication that a referendum of Memphians, even in the calmer days of August, would support a dues checkoff. In fact, everything pointed to the fact that they would not. To the union the plan offered a postponed defeat, better perhaps than immediate defeat, but defeat all the same. If it offered face-saving in March, there was a built-in kick in August. Additionally, if citizens voted on the dues checkoff issue for the first group of city workers to organize, would they then be entitled to vote on portions of all subsequent labor contracts between the city and any other employees who might organize? If not, why not, once the precedent had been set?

"The frame of mind at that time was very bad," commented Ned Cook who had come to the meeting bearing the word that Mayor Loeb would not oppose the referendum plan.

The meeting was confused. "Everyone was in a big rush to get going, get the show on the road, get Lawson and the ministers in touch with the union with the idea," commented Miles, who thought the group was "spinning their wheels" and that the idea was going to fall flat on its face. The blacks said there would have to be guarantees that Loeb would not campaign against the dues checkoff in August. Cook recalls that Rev. Lawson agreed to try to sell the idea to the union, and as they left he gave Lawson his home telephone number to get in touch, along with repeated assurances that Loeb would accept the plan. Lawson remembers being concerned about passing the right of workers to organize over to a vote of the city and being personally against the whole idea, although he did agree to take it back to union leaders. The one point of agreement was that something had to be done about the strike—and soon.

It would not be done that day. Journalistic enterprise blew the whole thing out of the water. For as Cook, Caywood, Miles, and black state senator Russell Sugarmon left the meeting shortly after noon, the early edition of that evening's *Press-Scimitar* was on the newsstands. Caywood casually picked one up. On the front page was the headline:

CITY VOTE LOOMS
ON DUES CHECKOFF

A story explained the referendum idea. "I like the sound of it," the mayor was quoted. Ciampa had told the reporter he didn't believe a referendum would "solve the immediate problem."

"Well, that's the end of this," said Sugarmon. "That just cuts the ground out from under Lawson." "The newspaper just couldn't keep their mouth shut," agreed Cook. "I felt damn sure if that story hadn't been printed, the strike would have been over that day."

Miles was the most angry and disgusted. "I looked at Ned and looked at Caywood. I said, 'You mean to tell me that when we were sitting up there talking, when we have asked that man to go over and talk to that union committee, that somebody had already given the story to the paper this morning?'...Of all the stupid things I ever heard of in my life, that was the most stupid."

Angrily pacing his office, he finally put in a call to Rev. Lawson to ask if he had known the story was in the paper when he went to the union. He hadn't, replied Lawson, but when he started to talk about the proposal, union officials had picked up the newspaper in front of them and said, "Oh, you mean this in the afternoon *Press-Scimitar*?"

"I said I could imagine how he felt," said Miles. "I had no real part in it, but whatever part I had played, I wanted to apologize for. ...It's a funny thing, but I think Lawson realized I was sincere."

That referendum move lost more than it gained. The conciliators had unintentionally tripped up Rev. Lawson, whom they regarded as the key to the union. And they had handed another weapon to Loeb—*vox populi*, let the people decide. Miles had been right; Loeb was to hang on to that idea.

That night Rev. Lawson made the announcement everyone had been expecting. Martin Luther King would speak in Memphis two days later.

Here Comes Dr. King

9

"Now here comes Dr. King!"
Frank Miles

The urgent invitation to come into Memphis issued by Rev. Lawson and pushed by other COME leaders caught Dr. King at the height of now hectic preparations for the Poor People's Campaign (PPC). He had been receiving continuing reports about the Memphis strike, and the more closely he looked at them, the more he could see the pattern. The attempt of public employees in Memphis to organize and deal with their own problems and the economic issues facing them was an example that could be understood by poor people in other places. The plight of the underemployed often was almost as bad as that of the unemployed.

That the Memphis strike had become a civil rights movement, under the aegis of his own nonviolent tenets, provided an even more dramatic illustration of how the old movement techniques could be tied in with current economic demands. If Memphis could help the PPC by concretely dramatizing the economic demands he was talking about, he felt he could help the workers in Memphis by bring national attention to their struggle.

Yet there was the time problem. He simply could not be everywhere. Despite a few recent days of rest, he was continually warned of overwork by his doctor.

Finally it was worked out that he would come to Memphis for one rally, a move achieved by transferring an already-scheduled Southern Christian Leadership Conference staff meeting in Clarksdale, Mississippi, on March 18 to the Lorraine Motel in Memphis.

Spring was in Memphis now, the warmer winds circling and sweeping up from the south. No longer did marchers come daily up Main Street shivering against the cold and damp. The rains that fell now were more gentle, kind, and frequently the sky was blue. Leaves were still tight, tiny swirls of yellow-green against the bare branches, but the grass had turned pale green, sporting in the yards of the careless the dark shoots of wild onion. Forsythia had burst, wild waterfalls of bright yellow in unexpected corners, and the more subtle flowering quince. The crocus was already gone, but daffodils ran the lawns and gardens, their white and golden heads and long leaves bending and trailing in the winds. The dogwood and azalea, the crabapple and redbud and tulip tree, waited, tight-budded, patient, while the daffodils rioted at will. At little Handy Park on Beale Street, birds sang.

In the beauty was the ugliness. Rev. Dick Moon's wife Glenda got phone calls describing in vivid terms her intercourse with black men and the parts of her anatomy that must be black. Councilman Downing Pryor had garbage dumped on his front lawn. Stories came to the white community through their maids of threats being made against workers who had returned or who wanted to return to work and of how black families were sneaking their garbage out into the country in the dead of night. Councilman James Netters' three children were threatened on the phone and teased at school by black children who knew only that their father was not out marching. Councilman Donelson reported obscene calls—"one, that there was a plot to kill me came to my mother."

Union leaders were threatened by calls and letters. "They'd

say, 'You black son of a bitch, we're gonna get you,' " said
T. O. Jones. Bill Lucy was convinced their phones at the hotel
were bugged and their rooms searched. Councilman Hyman's
lumber yard was picketed by a group of youths yelling "Down
with whitey" and "Kill whitey." Rev. Starks and his family were
bothered throughout the strike at 2:00 and 3:00 A.M. by callers
who would hang up as soon as the phone was picked up.

The harassing calls and mail were nondiscriminatory. They
were aimed at almost everyone whose name was prominently
mentioned in strike activity on the side of city, COME, or union.
Most people got only a few calls, but someone like Rev. Moon,
a white who had "gone over" to the blacks' side, was constantly
bothered. And the crackpot threats made against Mayor Loeb
and Rev. Lawson throughout the entire period confounded
sanity. It was as if a whole host of people with twisted minds were
thrown to the surface by the tension boiling in the city.

Maxine Smith of the NAACP was an old hand at receiving
threats. "Whenever there is any activity, the mail and crank calls
pick up. You just don't have time to think of that type of thing.
Not that it might not happen, but if you go around putting all
your energies on that, you can't function, really."

But many Memphians caught up in the strike were not old
pros at either civil rights or union battles, and the calls and mail
did make them uneasy and sometimes frightened.

The great majority of the city were not aware of this sort of
harassment, nor were they consciously aware of the polarization's most physical and telling sign—the presence or absence
of garbage cans at the curbs. Most whites did not travel the
residential streets of black Memphis, and blacks did not cruise
the side streets in white areas. If, like the maids, they had moved
back and forth, they would have known what Memphis State
student Ron Ivy noted.

"In my neighborhood there were no garbage cans out on the
curb…But coming to Memphis State every day and passing
through the white neighborhoods, I saw them lined with
garbage cans. I saw polarization going on. I saw white people

getting together behind Mayor Loeb."

Garbage cans! Those supporting the city put them on the curb for pickup. Those protesting did not. The outward and visible sign. There were never any figures on how many black families let their garbage pile up or managed to get rid of it some way other than placing their garbage cans out on the street, but the signs of noncooperation were there. The polarization, the pulling back of each community, white and black, from the other was there. And the depth of ill will, the intensity of the hostility, were both shocking and frightening to those who had really believed that Memphis was well on the road to good race relations.

It was as if the bitterness had always lain somewhere close to the surface and when the thin veneer of dialogue and hand-shakes and politeness and kindly interest were stripped away by the strike, true feelings emerged on both sides, contempt, resentment, anger, fear, despair. And they were not pretty.

His entrance at a side door of the strike rally swept the overflowing crowd, sitting on steps, standing in aisles and doorways, spilling outside Mason Temple that night of March 18.

A wedge was formed to get him to the podium. The applause rose to a cheering crescendo. The crowd was on its feet, applauding, shouting, arms raised in the clenched fist salute with so many interpretations and one basic meaning—power.

Martin Luther King stood before them.

The resonant voice, as familiar to all of them as that of a close friend, began, and the crowd settled back, the preachers to move him on throughout the talk with their exhortations of "Tell it" and "Go on. Go on," working with him as jazzmen push each other, forcing always toward the breaking through of words into the emotional climax.

He was slow, ponderous. "As I came in tonight, I…said to Ralph Abernathy, 'They really have a great movement here in Memphis.' For you are demonstrating here something that needs to be demonstrated all over our society…that we can stick together."

The strikers and their supporters cheered back at him, proud of their struggle and proud he could see it.

"One day our society will come to respect the sanitation worker if it is to survive, for the person who picks up our garbage is…just as significant as the physician. For if he doesn't do his job, disease is rampant.…

"And you are reminding not only Memphis…but the nation that it is a crime for people to live in this rich nation and receive starvation wages."

They held each other now, he and the crowd. If they did not understand the whys and wherefores of America's paradox of poverty and plenty, many of them were nonetheless the fleshing out of that paradox. Integration without economic equality was not enough. Economic equality was what Memphis was all about.

"So we assemble here tonight…to say we are tired. We are tired of being at the bottom…We are tired!"

Up, up he went, the words that had eased the tired feet of Montgomery so long ago now splintered and nearly drowned out by the roars of Memphis.

"And so in Memphis we have begun. We are saying that now is the time. Get the word across to everybody in power in this town.

That now is the time.

To make real the promises of democracy…

To make an adequate income a reality for all of God's children…

For City Hall to take a position for that which is just and honest.

Now is the time!"

He was no longer the outside speaker come in to buoy them up. His words and their response were fusing them together. "You know what?" he continued almost conversationally. "You may have to escalate the struggle a bit. If they keep refusing and they will not recognize the union and will not agree for a checkoff of the collection of dues, I tell you what you ought to demand and you're together here enough to do it. In a few days you ought to get together and just have a general work stoppage in the city of Memphis."

Mason Temple was pandemonium now, the frustrations of thirty-six days of controlled and seemingly fruitless action caught in the vision of this one giant moment of defiance, one giant moment to demonstrate their solidarity and power, the great moment that would end the strike.

"And you let that day come and not a Negro in this city will go to any job downtown, not a Negro in domestic service will go to anybody else's kitchen, black students will not go to anybody's school..."

Behind the podium the Memphis strike leaders were talking quickly with Dr. King's aides, Andrew Young, Bernard Lee, and James Bevel. Could Dr. King come back into Memphis and lead a march on the day of the work stoppage? He had caught the immediate mood of the Memphis struggle, its importance to his national work, thought Rev. Lawson, and Memphis needed him. Agreeing, Andy Young scribbled a note on the yellow page of Lawson's scratch pad suggesting that the Southern Christian Leadership Conference return and lead a march. Ralph Abernathy added his initials and the note was slipped in front of Dr. King as he spoke. But he ignored it and, with the crowd still roaring, he sat down.

In the confusion of people starting to leave, Rev. Abernathy came to the microphone. Surrounding King were a number of his aides and Memphis people. Would he come back? At the podium Abernathy was saying that since the people of Memphis were so enthusiastic, perhaps SCLC should lead them down to City Hall. People moving out stopped still and waited. It could be squeezed into his schedule, King's aides thought. There was more conferring around the podium.

Then Dr. King spoke again. He was in the midst of the Poor People's Campaign, he told them, and they could make Memphis "the beginning of the Washington movement."

If they wanted him to, he would come back and lead a march to City Hall.

If they wanted him! The milling crowd was jubilant, jumping, shouting. Some wanted him to start off for City Hall that very moment, some in the morning. But four days later was set as the date.

So Martin King committed himself to Memphis, an involvement he had originally neither envisioned nor desired.

That night there were no second thoughts, only excitement. Eighty-two trucks were out picking up garbage that day. Strike money was running low. But Dr. King would lead their march, and the walls of Jericho would fall before them.

Dr. King was caught up in the warmth and spirit of that rally and the Memphis movement. After the disappointments and frustrations of the past two years, the sullenness of northern ghettos and the complexities of trying to squeeze any kind of economic concessions out of convoluted power structures, after the attacks on his stand against the Vietnam War, in the midst of the bone-tiring effort to garner support for the Poor People's Campaign, that night in Memphis was like coming home.

Here was the unity he preached. Here were the people who believed in him and in the nonviolence that was his essence. He had been told time and again that the old movement was gone, useless, no longer effective. Yet here he was surrounded by just such a movement.

For a moment, time turned back and his faith in the rightness and righteousness of his way surged up, as simple as in the early days.

Still, some of his SCLC staff were not convinced. The same arguments held that had caused their apprehension about his coming into Memphis in the first place. The main thrust was the PPC; there was no time for anything else. But the idea that Memphis could be used as a prelude to Washington prevailed at the staff meeting that night after the rally. Later at the Lorraine

Motel where they were all staying, food was brought up. Members of a Texas college choir, also staying in the motel, heard Dr. King was there and came by in their pajamas and bathrobes to sing a "Hallelujah" motif for him. It was past midnight when the Memphis visitors left and the SCLC staff was able to concentrate again on the logistics for Washington, being reworked now because of the surety of support from other minority groups.

In the morning, King drove south into the Mississippi Delta, Marks, Batesville, Clarksdale, Greenwood, Grenada, and later swung across Alabama and Georgia, to meeting after meeting for the Poor People's Campaign.

COME and union leaders began getting the word out that Dr. King would lead a march from Clayborn Temple to City Hall on Friday, March 22. Rev. Lawson stated he expected ten thousand marchers, school children among them.

White extremist groups cranked their mimeograph machines up to a faster pitch. Memphis had long passed the point where propaganda on the mongrelization of the white race was publicly tolerated, but the suspicion that the civil rights movement and its leaders were tied in with communism and anarchy was still a socially acceptable point of view. A goodly number of flyers attacking Rev. Lawson and also Bayard Rustin, who had come in to speak, were already circulating along with reprints of the anti-King sheets that had been around for years. These flyers would turn up tucked under car windshields in a church parking lot, distributed outside of various meetings, sent through the mails. Their letterheads read "Counter-Revolution" or "Enlightened People on Communism" or "Special Edition of the 'Voice of the Ridge,'" the publication of an extremist group in Forrest City, Arkansas. The "dossiers" on specific people, such as King, contained the usual innuendos, half-truths and misplaced emphases. The Lawson "dossier," for example, had been circulated under the signature of the United Klans of America, Inc., the preceding fall when he was running for the school board. The conclusion of the new anti-Lawson/Rustin sheets was, "Communism believes that out of conflict comes progress. It appears that Rustin and Lawson agree. If it is a 'long, hot' summer, then look for the boys who get instruction from Moscow, Hanoi, or even Prague. It's time we call a spade a spade."

King himself had never been directly in conflict with Memphis before. He had come in to make speeches in the city, but he had never headed any civil rights activity there. No one was quite sure what to expect, but his promise to lead a march was just one more brick on top of the tottering pile of civic dismay. There was, on the whole, a sort of tired anger against an outsider meddling in "our strike," but there were no anguished cries to stop him from entering nor was there any mass demand to settle the strike so he would not come. "Let him come," was the general response, "and see what good it does him or the strikers." Responsible citizens would stand with Henry Loeb.

The day after the King rally, the council's regular meeting ran until 8:00 P.M. with two recesses for members to meet behind closed doors while several hundred strikers and supporters who were again monitoring the meeting sang hymns. "The council is going to have to break the stalemate, that's all," Councilman Patterson announced, although he admitted not having enough votes to get his dues-deduction resolution passed. Finally Chairman Pryor recessed the council until Thursday afternoon, March 21, eve of the King march, when the council would again consider Patterson's plan, as well as a Loeb ordinance restating his position against the dues checkoff, drawn up, said the mayor, "at the request of five councilmen who came to my office."

That next evening after the King rally, union representative Bill Lucy stepped before the microphone in the youth building of wealthy St. Louis Catholic parish in East Memphis. Two evening discussions on the strike had finally been set up by Baxton Bryant and the Tennessee Council on Human Relations. Lucy spoke on Tuesday night and the mayor on Wednesday. The meetings were something of a breakthrough. Though the crowd obviously supported the city's position, Lucy, stressing the union's effort to improve the lot of the workers and calling the checkoff "necessary for the stability of the union," not only sounded reasonable but also got several rounds of applause along with the expected hostile questions. "I think people found out that the union fellows didn't carry machine guns...and that there were legitimate problems that had to be solved," commented Lucy afterwards, as surprised as anyone by his courteous reception. Both speakers stated their positions and for more than an hour each fielded questions. Equally surprising, the mayor also came under attack for his adamant stance.

Frank Miles, a member of the parish, was in the audience both nights, and as Mayor Loeb finished up on the second night, Miles and one of the city's labor leaders who had also known the mayor for a long time stood talking together, both concerned not only about the strike but about Dr. King's pending march. "This fellow had gotten up in the meeting and given Henry hell," said Miles. "He was asking some real pointed questions because he had told me, 'I'll let my garbage stack up in back of my garage till it's a mile high before I'll ever haul it away.' " As the mayor walked toward them, the union leader turned to him and said, "Frank and I were just saying how absolutely silly this whole darn thing is and how dangerous it is." "You know," said Loeb, "I haven't had anything to eat and here it is about eleven o'clock and Mary is going to be mad at me besides. Why don't you two guys come over to the house while I get a bite to eat?"

In the den of his home, they kicked around the strike problem. "By this time," said Miles, "I'm sensing Henry is beginning to see some of the things that I had talked to him about and other people had. He's as bullheaded and stubborn as a mule. As far as his ideas and opinions and principles are concerned, it takes him a long time to give up on one, but I could see that he's beginning to see the real dangers ahead. First there was the vacuum, then the ministers, and now here comes Dr. King. It's getting bigger and bigger."

Was there a chance Loeb was open to some new approach?

The union leader came in. "Why, in God's name, don't you let Frank here act as mediator in this situation and call your people together with the union, and sit down and try to work this thing out?"

The question was flat out now, and Loeb moved warily around it, asking and answering his own questions. The results of "mediation," as opposed to "arbitration," were not binding but subject to approval of both group participants? Right. No one was committed to any concessions in advance? Right. The city was winning the strike. The union was running out of money. Enthusiasm was falling away. Perhaps, but now Dr. King was coming in. For all the wishful thinking, who really knew what that meant in terms of black support? The black community was bound to split over the strike issue. Perhaps, but it had not split yet. If he were in something of a bind—and Loeb never, ever admitted that he was—the way out was in throwing approval of the dues checkoff onto the voters in a referendum. But if the union refused point-blank to go along with that idea? He had made concessions. Sure, but that was past and the strike continued. Maybe...just maybe...it would be a good idea to hold sessions with Miles as mediator. Miles had the experience. Nothing else seemed to be working.

Miles had conditions of his own. In the first place, the request for his services as mediator couldn't come from this meeting with Loeb. It would have to come from a more neutral quarter such as the city council or Miles "would be dead before he started" as far as the union was concerned. And if he sat in as mediator he would have to have a guarantee that no legal questions over the injunction against the union leaders would be raised by the city and that meetings would be closed to the press. Miles would be the public spokesman. There were to be no more reporters in the balcony or any negotiating in the fishbowl. The attempt to reach agreement must be given the greatest possible chance for success. All right. It would be hard to swallow, but Loeb would check with city aides. He would get back to Miles.

Miles also contacted the assistant manager of the Claridge
Hotel to find out about reserving several conference rooms
because experience had shown him that even the site of such
meetings could become an issue. And as he sat later in Dr.
Jackson's office at the AME Minimum Salary Building talking
with several of the union people, it did become one. Wurf was
willing to meet with the city. He would name his committee,
and they would like to hold the meetings in the Minimum Salary
Building.

"It was a kind of delicate question," said Miles. "But I could
see that the AME building would be no good. Suppose there
was a big crowd when the city representatives came out. So I told
them I had taken the liberty to reserve rooms at the Claridge,
which was close to City Hall but away from it, too. And I said
the rooms won't cost us a thing. If we go anywhere else, we'll
have to pay for it....Rev. Jackson was sitting back there doling
out money for some poor soul who'd come along. I think he had
money on his mind....And he said, 'Well, if you've got it for
nothing, go ahead.' So I went over to the hotel and told the
assistant manager, 'I've stuck your neck out. I've said you
offered a couple of conference rooms for free.' " In the spirit of
public service, the Claridge executive agreed. Go-ahead for the
mediation proposal now rested on the approval of the city
council.

There were no prior agreements that any activity or attempts
to break the strike would be held in abeyance while mediation
proceeded. Dr. King's march would go forward; so would the
city's use of newly hired workers and whatever other pressures
were available. It was far too late for either side to trust solely to
mediation. Yet the city's agreement to even talk again with
union representatives was the first major breakthrough since the
abortive Memphis Ministers Association sessions a month
earlier.

And there was another breakthrough, this time in the news
media. The preceding Friday night, March 15, Norman Brewer,

news director for WMC-TV, the local NBC affiliate, on his
nightly editorial commentary had called for an end to the strike
through resumption of talks between the city and union,
regardless of where legalities lay. It was a public stance unusual
enough at that point to cause a great deal of comment among
his faithful viewers. On the day after Dr. King's speech, the
evening *Press-Scimitar* printed a lengthy letter from county
squire and NAACP president Jesse Turner attacking the newspaper's refusal "to comprehend the depth of the Negro's fight
against racial discrimination."

The next evening, just before Loeb spoke at St. Louis Church,
the *Press-Scimitar* dropped its editorial bomb and moved from
the position it had held for a month. A letter from Dave Yellin,
head of television/radio broadcasting studies at Memphis State,
and his wife, writer/editor Carol Lynn Yellin, was printed. "We
voted for Henry Loeb…his actions have not fulfilled our hope."
They urgently urged the mayor to set up round-the-clock
discussions with the union.

Far more crucial,

IT'S TIME, RIGHT NOW,
TO SETTLE SANITATION WORKERS' STRIKE

said an eight-column headline, running the entire width of the
editorial page and followed by an eight-column editorial. "The
sanitation strike is now in its sixth week, and the time has come
for a real, all-out, day-and-night effort to bring it to an end." The
paper was preparing its readers for strike mediation.

The next day reporter Charles A. Brown explained to *Press-
Scimitar* readers the city's relationship to some of its employees.
There were several hundred card-carrying craft and trade union
members, such as carpenters, plumbers, painters, mechanics,
and brick masons, scattered around in various departments,
divisions, and under separate boards. Their wages and benefits
varied, depending on what kind of agreement had been made.

There were, for example, unionized bus drivers, working

directly for the Memphis Transit Company, who had the dues
checkoff, a no-strike clause, and a binding arbitration agreement. On the other hand, men in the fire and police departments, not unionized, had a no-strike clause in their work rules
and were forbidden to take part in any action in sympathy with
blocking work in those departments. The city school teachers,
direct employees of the Memphis Board of Education, had
checkoff of their National Education Association dues.

The city also had contracts for specific jobs with firms using
union labor. In these cases, the contractor handled the union
problems, presumably including wages.

In short, the city's labor policy was a patchwork of compro-
mises and exceptions, and Brown's story did little to enhance the
mayor's contention that the city could handle the problems of
its workers in the same orderly way it always had.

The printing of that information and the shift in editorial
emphasis presaged a change in the handling of strike news by the
two daily papers, but Judge Ben Hooks was to say, "It came too
late. Many white men of good will never really found out what
the thing was all about until the strike had been going on for
some two, three or four weeks, and by that time the pendulum
of public opinion had swung so far in the white community
against this thing that it was almost impossible to change it."

But the main failure of both daily newspapers, the *Memphis
Press-Scimitar* and the admittedly more conservative *Commercial Appeal*, during the strike did not lie with their initial editorial
positions. Opinionated editorials are to be expected; editorials
are opinions, irritants though they may be to those who disagree
with the opinions expressed. Nor was it a result of both papers
being philosophically and pragmatically aligned too closely with
the business and civic interests of the city which opted for a slow
and orderly transition of the black population into a responsible
middle class.

It was not because neither paper had black reporters, hurtful
as that fact was in a forty percent black city and facing a black
strike.

The chief failure was not even the appearance of Hambone day after day, first page, second section, of the *Commercial Appeal*. "Hambone's Mediations" was a small cartoon, drawn by *Commercial Appeal* artist Cal Alley and syndicated to other newspapers.

Hambone was a little old Negro man, bright-eyed, wide-mouthed, clad in overalls or baggy pants, vest and shirt sleeves. Often he wore a battered hat and carried a pipe. He always stood alone, usually against a background of the farmyard where he labored for "boss man" and "missuz," and dispensed homely philosophy in dialect on the nature of people and life in general.

"Trouble 'bout givin' ev'body ev'thing dey wants, purty soon dey won' be nothin' lef' fur nobody!!!"

"Dey says dat 'expert' man whut gits fi' dollars a hour sho' is slow—huh! I don't see nothin' cu'ious 'bout dat!"

Hambone was mild, humble, helpful, kind, humorously wry in his comments. White readers loved him. Perhaps so did some blacks. He was the old nigra, the real nigra. He was grateful for small favors. He kept in his place. He wasn't about to go marching or pushing. Yet he was imbued with a certain gentle dignity, despite the degradation of the name, the appearance, the dialect, the accommodation.

But the time for Hambone—if it had ever existed—had passed. And to blacks involved in the strike, Hambone was the stereotype that must go. Insofar as whites would prefer to deal with Hambone, they were unable to deal with T. O. Jones.[1]

The real failure of both papers lay in the lack of news coverage of the black community in this crisis and of general background news stories which could have put the strike into some kind of context. Brown's story of the city's relations with some of its unionized workers was five weeks in appearing. There was no tracing of the public works employees' six years of attempting to organize. There were no in-depth interviews with union leaders such as Ciampa or Jerry Wurf, who was already well on his way to becoming extremely powerful in American labor. No religion writer attempted to explain how the black ministers equated strike support with their Christian calling. There were no human interest stories about striking garbagemen and their families.

And the *Press-Scimitar*, having waded into the waters of controversy with its mediation editorial, now retreated back toward shore with an editorial on the eve of Dr. King's arrival. "Tomorrow Dr. King may taunt Memphis with a cry of 'Shame!' in an effort to bring about massive and overnight changes. We're not ashamed, Dr. King. We have not done all we have wanted to do, nor even what we should have done. But we're not ashamed. And if you don't watch out, Dr. King, you, and some of your fellow ministers here in Memphis just might undo what already has been accomplished."

The *Commercial Appeal* would remain silent a little longer, standing on the rock of editorial disapproval of illegal strikes and senseless agitation. It was going to take more than hints of mediation and an impending march by Dr. King to put the *Commercial Appeal* in a flap.

It was cold and raining intermittently—an inch and a half in the past twenty-four hours—when School Superintendent E. C. Stimbert parked his car by the Minimum Salary Building the afternoon before the march. He had been asked to meet with some of the march leaders on the subject of school children participating. It was a *pro forma* meeting. March leaders explained they considered school children an integral part of their movement. Stimbert responded that, nonetheless, he could not close the schools nor give students permission to stay out of school and march. He was neutral about teachers working with the strike as long as they did not bring it into the classroom.

The rain began changing to desultory snowflakes as they talked. "We looked at it with some curiosity," related Rev. Lawson. "I said, 'It won't last. It's too wet.'" Certainly the snow wouldn't continue here at the end of March. The city's yearly average snowfall was only 5.6 inches, most of which never stuck. There had been only two white Christmases since the weather bureau started keeping records.

But the snow was coming down harder. As they talked, they kept a weather eye on the window. The discussion was academic; if a child who had his parents' approval really wanted to march with Dr. King, he would do so regardless of Stimbert's position and they all knew that.

The snow was thickening now. "I've experienced a good many blizzards in Nebraska," mused Stimbert, "but I had never seen such large flakes. They were as large as dollar pancakes."

Rev. Jackson had the last wry word as, the meeting finally ending about 6:00 P.M., he stared into the whitening street. "Well, the Lord has done it again. It's a white world." They all laughed, but Stimbert stepped through snow that now seemed to be several inches deep to reach his car.

At City Hall council members had been meeting informally in closed session throughout late afternoon as Pryor and the moderates pushed for unanimous support of a resolution calling for strike mediation and tried to find a way of wording it that would affront none of the principals. It was 6:30 P.M. when they finally convened in public session with Pryor distributing small slips of paper that read "Where no counsel is, the people fall; but in the multitude of counsellors, there is safety." (Proverbs 11:14). The snow—it must be rather widespread, some remarked—had prevented Rev. Netters from getting back from Chicago and Councilman Patterson was late from Nashville.

The resolution calling for representatives of the city and union to sit down to continuous discussions to end the strike and for Frank Miles to act as "conciliator" was passed.

Pryor—who was to say afterwards, "Those early weeks were the worst period I have ever been through in my life....I have never worried about anything as much"—was immeasurably relieved. Pressure for settling the strike was now off the council's—and off Pryor's—shoulders. The mediation session would begin on Saturday noon. Only the massive march Dr. King would lead in the morning stood in the way.

But Dr. King was not to march that morning. All night long

the snow came down, sometimes in languorous flakes, sometimes in quick, hard flurries, piling higher and higher now as the temperature settled below freezing. It was not a blizzard; no violent winds howled over the city. It was just an inexorable dumping of 16.1 inches of snow, the second largest snowfall ever recorded in Memphis. The storm stretched from Mississippi up to Michigan, but Tennessee, Arkansas and northern Mississippi were the hardest hit. In Memphis snow was to continue until shortly after noon on Friday.

The city stopped dead in its tracks. School was called off. Businesses theoretically open were missing employees and retail stores, customers. Gardeners rushed to cover the budded azaleas, but there was little to be done about the magnolia trees, many of their buds stripped by the heavy snow. The daffodils bent with the inevitable, but trees and tree limbs came down. Power lines were down; Southern Bell Telephone recorded ten thousand problems with telephone service. Abandoned cars dotted the streets and highways, and the scattering of cinders on bridges and viaducts was useless until the snow stopped. With air and bus traffic behind schedule or stopped completely, the terminals were full of stranded travelers. The public works department optimistically sent out three garbage trucks to begin pickup, but when all three got stuck, collections were called off.

The outlanders, the kids from the North who had moved to Memphis, dug out and paraded their unused sleds. Their fathers, after trying to dig out their cars or ascertaining that the buses weren't going anywhere, came huffing, puffing, and stomping back into the house.

Rev. Lawson got up at 6:00 A.M., looked outside, and turned on the radio for the weather report. Then he called Martin King in Atlanta where the airport was fogged in. Chances are we'll cancel the march, he told King. I'll call you back. Within the hour he talked to King again. "We'll postpone it. We've got a perfect work stoppage though!" Another date would be decided on. The snow had postponed the march, not stopped it.

At the Minimum Salary Building a few marchers came in, to

sit around throughout the morning drinking coffee and ruefully joking about the snow. L. C. Reed, in the sewers and drains division, was especially disappointed. His football hero son Oscar was in Memphis, en route back to Colorado from talks with the Minnesota Vikings for whom he would play, and both Reeds were up early and ready to march. L. C. Reed would have liked to have his boy march with him.

One lone figure did picket City Hall that morning—a round-faced white man, his eyes slits against the whirling snow and his ears, unprotected by his cap, slowly turning red. His gloved hands clutched a sign reading "Do Right Mr. Mayor." And Thomas Moore, Local 988 of the UAW at Harvester, reported that he would march till his sign, already sodden, fell apart. "I'm a labor man. I've been opposing this mayor a long time," he told a reporter. The mayor, whom no snow was going to stop from reaching his City Hall office, stomped out through the snow to bring Moore a cup of hot coffee and invite him inside to warm up and chat.

That afternoon the sun came out and the long icicles began dripping into puddles, driveways were cleared and a few cars made forays over the snow, and Memphis began to shake the snow off its back and look with amazement and admiration at its glittering white image—a day afterwards referred to simply as "The Day of the Big Snow" with the same awe that old-timers spoke of the "Blizzard of '98." The tension hanging over the city lifted a little.

Frank Miles opened the first session of mediation the next afternoon, Saturday, March 23, at the Claridge, planning it as an organizational meeting with actual discussions to begin the next day, Sunday. All signs were hopeful. Dr. King had not marched, so whatever that might entail had been avoided.

Representing the city were legal staff member Myron Halle; Director of Finance, Institutions and Public Service Harry Woodbury; attorney Tom Prewitt who was called at the last minute to substitute for ailing City Attorney Frank Gianotti; and Tom Todd of the city council. For the union were P. J.

Ciampa, Bill Lucy, T. O. Jones, and Rev. H. Ralph Jackson representing COME.

As Miles started to read his suggested plan for the meetings, attorney Halle interrupted to question the presence of Ciampa, Lucy, and Jones. The city, he said, felt they could not sit at that table and negotiate with members of a union committee under a contempt citation and conviction in chancery court. They wanted legal clarification on the chancery court limitations.

"This caught me flat-footed," admitted Miles. "This had been number one on my list of understandings with Loeb." The union committee was furious. In good faith, they protested, they had come to the meeting, only to be met with the same objections that had held up negotiating for a month. What, they asked, was the city trying to do? Sabotage the mediation before it even got underway? The city obviously did not want to settle anything.

Only the diplomacy of Miles held the group together until they agreed that the city would go into court on Monday morning and get clarification of the injunction. But while Miles could keep the mediation from falling apart at the outset, there was little he could do about the psychological effect of the city's move on the union representatives. They had distrusted Loeb and expected little from mediation; now they distrusted him even more and expected even less.

Judge Hoffmann did clarify for the city in court on Monday morning, March 25. The three union men, he ruled, could take part in the talks without violating the court injunction because the key word of the injunction was "coerce" and there was no element of coercion in mediation. That Monday afternoon the union and the city began meeting again.

That Monday night an unlikely company of some 450 Memphians trooped into the gym of Holy Rosary Catholic Church to honor Monsignor Joseph Leppert with the annual

Brotherhood Award of the Catholic Human Relations Council and to eat $2.50 barbecue on paper plates. Present were the bishops of Tennessee and Mississippi, two city judges, officials of the NAACP, city council members, black and white ministers, COME activists, supporters and opponents of the strike, Catholic, Protestant and Jewish, from across the city.

"It was a lovely affair," the honoree Monsignor Leppert was to say dryly a few months later.

"It was evident that everything was going to be resolved in the city because everyone loved his brother and even his enemy. We had representatives from both groups there that night. It was the last time such a group was even together in the same room."

Bishop Joseph Durick, apostolic administrator of the diocese of Tennessee, beamed from the head table. The bishop was a lover of humanity, good Scotch and banal poetry, but also of peace. Five years earlier he had been in Birmingham, one of the religious leaders calling on Dr. King to stop the demonstrations. King had responded with his famous "Letter from Birmingham Jail." Now Bishop Durick was on his own way toward becoming a cause célèbre. Two days before he had given one thousand dollars from his discretionary funds to the Memphis strikers. "For the poor among you," he had said simply. It was the first gift of money from other than black religious denominations, and already some white Catholics were protesting his actions, as well as those of several nuns who had turned up among the marchers.

The next morning, Tuesday, it was announced that Martin Luther King would return to lead the postponed march two days later, on Thursday, March 28. Again march preparations began.

Late Wednesday afternoon union representatives walked out

of the mediation sessions, charging the city negotiators had their hands tied by Mayor Loeb. The city countercharged that the union refused to discuss anything until the issue of union recognition was first resolved. There were accusations of news leaks, of union grandstanding to focus publicity on King's march. Frank Miles calmly took the official position that the talks were merely recessed. He began laying plans to bring both sides back together.

Through the Deep Waters

Situation out of Control

10

"The situation is now out of hand...
request permission to break it up...
request permission."
Henry Lux

Moving through Harlem, Queens, and Newark on more Poor People's Campaign recruiting, Martin King was, he told a reporter, "very tired....I've been getting two hours of sleep a night for the past ten days." Over and over he repeated that the nonviolent pressure he would bring on Washington was the only viable alternative to rioting or "timid supplication." The meetings, though small, were enthusiastic and, on balance, the New York foray had gone well. He would lead the march in Memphis. Then the final push toward Washington would begin. On March 27 he flew back to Atlanta and early on the morning of the Memphis march, March 28, he boarded a flight for Memphis. The plane was a little late.

At 8:00 A.M. in Memphis the day was gray and overcast with the sixty-one-degree temperature beginning to push upward. First indications of trouble came at mostly black Hamilton High School on the south central side. Arriving students were met at the bus stop and along the campus by several COME represen-

tatives and by a few students from other schools urging them to
cut classes and join the march. For many students no urging was
necessary. The thought of marching with Dr. King as well as
defying Mayor Loeb beckoned.

It was spring and there was a cause.

Students were trying to enter or leave the school, milling in
front, standing in the street. A few desultory bricks were hefted
at a laundry truck passing; the back door opened and clothes fell
out. The driver scrambled to reload the truck and get out of the
way. A white woman unwarily drove her car onto the block,
honking her horn to clear the way. Her car also was bricked
before the space opened. At 8:30 A.M., a message to headquarters from police helicopter 201 reported that students were
massing at Hamilton.

Then majestically along the street came a garbage convoy—
the trucks and police escort. Missiles began to fly. Police radioed
for aid. Hovering overhead was the police helicopter. Police cars
zoomed in, and police began sealing off the school area to traffic.
"Students attacking officers on scene with bricks and bottles"
went out the police report. Additional cars were ordered in.

"The policemen jumped out of their cars and made a straight
line in front of the school," related a student. "They wore tear
gas masks and were armed with billy clubs and tear gas." More
sticks, bottles, rocks and bricks arched toward the police line,
along with taunts. "Move the police back from the crowd,"
came the order from headquarters. There was a momentary lull.
Some of the students moved back, then surged forward again.

"I was very afraid because someone had locked the side door
(of the school)," said one girl outside. In fact, the school
administration, with the exception of one or two male faculty
members, had virtually withdrawn from the confusion outside
the building, leaving the police to manage.

Outside, kids were running back and forth, darting toward the
police, back, along the width of the campus. Officers were
dodging missiles. "It was a game of cat and mouse," said one
boy. Then police moved onto the campus, running, swinging

their nightsticks in an attempt to break up the crowd. The kids fled in all directions, some playing a game, others badly frightened, police running after them.

"I fell and hit my head against a wall and the police hit me," said a girl. "They fell themselves and they picked themselves up....The officer said I was probably hit by the swinging of his elbow, not his stick...I really don't know what it was. I saw stars...."

In a few minutes the melee was over, the students scattered. Pull back, ordered headquarters. Don't charge the crowd. An ambulance was called. Another girl had been hit in the head with what was variously described as a bottle, nightstick, or brick. She was taken to the hospital for twenty-three stitches. Police pulled back from the campus.

At first in twos and threes, then in larger groups, the Hamilton students began moving toward Clayborn Temple, several miles away. There was no attempt to stop them.

Reports were also coming in to the police of groups of students leaving Carver, Northside, Southside, Lester high schools. "Through the window at Lester," one eyewitness said.

By the time the Hamilton school story reached the march assembly point, it was "reliably" reported that the police had killed a girl.

Marchers began filtering into the streets by Clayborn Temple and the AME Minimum Salary Building, starting point of the march, as early as 8:00 A.M.[1] By 9:30, they were massed in the Hernando and Pontotoc intersection, the main body stretching two blocks south on Hernando and scattered groups along the intersecting arms of Vance, Pontotoc, Linden. Like the river several blocks to the west, the crowd was in constant movement. Hernando itself was blocked to traffic from south of the Temple up to Beale and the march route further cleared to City Hall. The casual onlooker, not knowing the purpose, might have described the scene as a sort of giant street carnival.

"It was a real homecoming sort of business for a lot of us," said

John Spence, again present as an observer. "We would see people we knew...see somebody we hadn't expected to see and be pleased. ...Here would be a fellow from Atlanta or Washington that we hadn't known would be there and we were surprised and we'd shake hands...."

There was a scattering of small children. One mother pushed a baby in a stroller, and skinny little boys from the neighborhood, in jeans and T-shirts, darted in and out of the crowd. There were ministers and strikers and their families, young businessmen in horn-rimmed glasses and white shirts and ties, the civil rights leaders, smartly dressed young women in stiletto high heels, and older heavier women, gray old men in tattered jackets, shuffling as they moved. And more and more teen-agers came in, groups shouting the names of their high schools, some in Invader jackets, moving along the edges of the crowd, clowning, showing off, cheering, chanting their opposition to Mayor Loeb, greeted with grins and chuckles by their elders.

There were teachers. "I spotted about twenty other teachers," said one. "They laughed and talked about what if they should lose their jobs. We turned our signs over and on the clean side wrote in lipstick:

MEMPHIS CITY SCHOOL TEACHERS.

People began to shout and cheer."

A few whites were visible, the usual union people, students, clergy. Most of the clergy were clustered near the front. There were a few men from the communications network of the National Council of Churches, and Ed Stanfield of the Southern Regional Council in Atlanta, which was already compiling its first report on the Memphis strike. Catholic priests who marched did so with the blessing of their bishop, Durick, in decided contrast to other denominational men. There were a few white high school students with black friends and students from Southwestern, one group from the *Sou'wester*, there specifically to cover the demonstration for their campus paper. Farther back in the crowd were several white women from the Rearing Children of Good Will workshop. "White presence wasn't exactly overwhelming," said one of them. "From where we were, the only other white people we even saw the whole time were a couple of Southwestern students."

They missed seeing Joyce Palmer, a young white mother of three small children, who with her husband had moved to Memphis only three months before from Minneapolis. "I had been reading the papers...and I noticed that there'd been a Catholic nun marching in these little small marches. I'm a Catholic but it wasn't that she was Catholic but that she was a white woman. The night before it said in the paper the negotiations had broken down, and I just felt I had to go down there and at least have one white face in the crowd. I didn't know if there were any white people ever marching." But she didn't know anyone, and she was apprehensive. "I also have never known any Negroes except for one couple I just met a couple of times in Minneapolis....So I wasn't sure what their attitude was toward white people and that's the main reason I worried about going...

"I parked the car on Linden and started walking up the street. There were people all over—all black. I felt like everybody was looking at me and I felt really strange. Then I saw a group of white and Negro women together and I went up to this white woman and I said, 'Can I march with you?' I told her I was all alone. I forget what her name was. After that I began to feel entirely at ease. But I did have to find this white person. I don't know why. The march was delayed, and at first everybody was having fun and talking and laughing. Eventually people got pretty restless and wondering what was taking so long.

"I have a big purse with a clasp on top and a Negro woman said to keep my purse in front under my sign. So I held it like that and pretty soon I forgot about it....Somebody said, 'Your purse is open.' And somebody said, 'I think somebody took your billfold.' He had a red shirt on, they told me. My billfold was gone. It was embarrassing because I started to bawl. I don't

know why...Ten dollars was all I had and my driver's license
and credit cards. It wasn't the money...Especially the Negro
women around felt just so bad....It was just such a letdown to
have somebody steal there in this great cause and all goodness
and justice and right."

Police were pulled back from the immediate area of Clayborn
Temple, although a few stood in nearby intersections for traffic
control. As early as 9:00 A.M. Rev. Blackburn and Rev. Jackson
walked a block east to the corner of Vance and Fourth to see
how the crowd was. They found large numbers of people
heading toward the Temple. At the corner they also found a
squad car with several officers standing outside. Had they
continued to make a circle several blocks out from the Temple,
they would have found many more squad units. For the city
police department was completely mobilized that morning,
many officers pulled off their normal assignments or shifts and
sent into units in the march vicinity. Some three hundred
officers were committed to the general march area, supple-
mented by fifty men from the sheriff's department who had
been on call to city police since late in February. Officers were
being held back from the march to minimize possible friction.
The emergency squad, or TAC squad, was also standing by.
Each TAC unit consisted of three cars, usually with four men
each, and a commanding officer. The TAC squad was one of
those innovations that resulted from rioting in other cities. Each
unit acted as a flying wedge; it could be moved rapidly from one
area to another and theoretically provided enough immediate
force to break up any disorder before it got out of control. The
TAC squad had been formed to handle several of the early City
Hall demonstrations, but did not come into full use until the
King march. In addition to TAC units, regular patrol cars were
working along with officers on foot.
But the police were undermanned for any kind of an extraordinary situation and there was also a shortage of equipment. A
number of officers carried their own private weapons, a practice

that had been going on for about twenty-five years. With so many extra men pressed into service for the march, there were not enough shotguns to go around. Nor were there enough protective riot helmets, and none of the helmets had the plastic shields which protect the face from flying objects.

There were not enough portable radios either, said Assistant Chief Lux, "and this was a vital factor, not only in direction but in control, too…We had tried to get some equipment, but they just wouldn't provide the money and it wasn't until you had the problem that we really got a blank check." There were not enough gas masks. There were some of the longer batons for crowd control but most police relied on their usual night stick or billy club, which they had personally purchased just as they bought their own regulation .38 pistols. The pistols were to be carried at all times on duty.

Police were allowed a certain amount of leeway and personal judgment. Although they were supplied with small canisters of Mace, a number already had decided that Mace was not effective for general crowd control. If it were necessary to resort to firearms, many policemen preferred shotguns to the regulation pistols.

In some ways Memphis police officials had profited by mistakes in other cities. For instance, night sticks generally were to be kept out of sight, in the squad car or under the coat, to avoid unnecessary confrontation, and some officers did not carry them at all.

There had been some riot training in Memphis, but in a crisis situation, officers in other cities had found breaks in any training pattern. Experience showed that police first on the scene and facing hordes of demonstrators tended to respond rather chaotically until a field commander arrived and they got into formation. In the case of sniping or of missiles hitting nearby, police seemed for a few seconds to revert to individual response, for deeper than any patterned behavior lies the instinct for self-preservation. Other cities had also seen a follow-the-leader effect among police. If one officer started hitting, others would hit also.

In general, apprehensive Memphis policemen that bright spring morning were operating under the same set of orders they always followed. Enforce the law. And they were, said Lux, under the same restrictions whether they were enforcing that law for two people or for a thousand. "You hope it will be a peaceful march...you try to be prepared for any eventuality."

As the police helicopter swung back and forth over the area, it evoked different responses from the crowd, fascinating the younger children but upsetting those older. "It seemed as though we were in a cage with guardsmen flying over us to keep watch," said a LeMoyne College student.

To police officials it was extremely naive that anyone could think a march of thousands routed down Main Street and to be led by Martin Luther King would not be closely watched. That they opted to rely on helicopter reports and perimeter squad cars rather than saturating the immediate area with visible police presence was a tribute to the cooler heads among them. For the rumors coming into police headquarters presaged nothing but doom and disaster. Top police leadership was pretty sure no outside militant groups, black or white, right or left, had come into Memphis that day. Still the rumors persisted. Dr. King would not live through the march. Stokely Carmichael was in town and the motel where he was staying would be bombed. Militants were going to make trouble on the march. By this time key police officers always slept with phones by their bedsides in case of emergency. It seemed to police as if the sanitation crisis would never end.

Now reports were coming in that groups of kids from the black high schools were heading for the march area and arming themselves with bricks and bottles along the way. "It does not look good," said Police Chief J. C. Macdonald.

At 10:15, said attorney David Caywood who was in the area, "some kids were trying to bust into a liquor store right around the corner from the church." He watched as Rev. Lawson "elbowed, shoved…put his back to the door and faced those fellows…yelled at them…pushed them back away. He broke it up."

"When I got my sign reading:

MACE WON'T STOP TRUTH

I joined the marchers already waiting," explained a girl from LeMoyne College. "By about 10 A.M., the marchers began to get very restless. The teen-agers began to sit in the middle of the street and some of the adults went into the church to sit down…and the tension was mounting higher and higher….I could see what appeared to be a large branch with a sign hanging from it and a noose. With the wind blowing, I first could not read the sign….Suddenly the boy holding the branch was above the crowd and saying ironically and sarcastically that this would be a peaceful march and that there would be no violence. Everyone that heard him laughed….When the writing on his sign came into view, it read:

LOEB'S HANGING TREE.

A sudden chill ran through me…."[2]

By 10:30 A.M. the cloud cover had completely dissolved and the sky was pale blue and warm. The temperature was still rising and marchers began shedding their coats and jackets. The game plan of the march was simple. Dr. King would lead, immediately followed by COME leaders and the ministers. Next would come striking workers, "all dressed up in their best clothes like a Palm Sunday procession," observed Father Greenspun of St. Patrick's. They would be followed by the general community.

Hundreds of signs had been printed and stapled onto flat sticks about three feet long. Some read:

JOBS JOBS JOBS

and:

JUSTICE AND EQUALITY FOR ALL MEN

and:

UNIONIZATION FOR THE SANITATION WORKERS.

But most of them gave the stark message now a rallying cry for the movement,

I AM A MAN.

Marshals, identified by yellow arm bands, would keep the march in lines, keep the sidewalks clear, keep general order. They would all march to City Hall, mass on the plaza for speeches by Dr. King and others, and reform to march back to the Temple.

The mayor and other city officials would look out of their windows and count the political cost. Businessmen would look from their offices and shopkeepers from their shops as the thousands of marchers came past, and mentally compute the fiscal cost of continued boycott. Out-of-town reporters following Dr. King would spread the word that the black community of Memphis was united and on the move, and more outside support would come in.

But the game plan was missing some tactical data.

First was the delay. Dr. King was late in arriving, and the vast crowd, increasing by the minute, grew more and more restless and impatient. Communication between the front of the crowd, where the leaders gathered, and the back was practically nonexistent. Rumors, like the Hamilton High one, spread; the helicopter crisscrossed overhead. And still the march did not move out. A little after 10:30, word from the airport that Dr. King's plane was in and he was on his way spread through the crowd.

Rev. Billy Kyles was a marshal. Only that morning it had been announced that he, along with Catholic Bishop Durick, was among the new members of the state advisory committee to the U. S. Commission on Civil Rights. "I was trying to get Jim Lawson to let us move that march. I said, 'We've got to go. We'll let Dr. King join it wherever it is when he comes'...But Jim insisted on waiting."

Lawson, trying as much as possible to stick to plans, was also uptight. He and Rev. Jackson had just stopped one man from haranguing the crowd as he stood on the shoulders of several others. "Look, this is a nonviolent march," Lawson and Jackson kept repeating. "If you cannot follow instructions, we urge you to go home. Don't stay here." But nobody went home. Each simply melted into the crowd.

More serious was the marshals' inability to control the crowd, and here the leadership in its agonizing reappraisal later shouldered full responsibility. "We didn't work hard enough at disciplining and training marshals," admitted Lawson.

Few of the marshals, who included a number of the young men working with COME, were experienced in mass marching and many were unable to handle the crowds. Nothing in the daily single-file marches, tightly controlled, had prepared them for trying to move groups of teen-agers, for example, who paid no attention to them. And the marshals tended to stay near the front. "We never even saw a marshal," commented one woman "until the march was actually moving and we were funnelled into it." "There weren't enough of them at the back, so I stayed back," said Rev. Kyles. Rev. Zeke Bell, with some members of his congregation marching under a banner of Parkway Gardens Presbyterian Church, also stayed near the rear.

The sidewalks around the Temple were never cleared and it was impossible to separate the marchers from the onlookers. A sweep of marshals down the sidewalks might have accomplished it, but there was no such sweep. The marshals also faced the problem of the signs passed out to marchers. Younger blacks were hand-lettering their own messages on the backs and raising them high. On the back of

JOBS JOBS JOBS

could be read:

LOEB'S BLACK DAY,

or more to the point,

LOEB EAT SHIT,

or

FUCK YOU MAYOR LOEB.

The kids loved it; it was vulgar, sassy. Their elders were uncomfortable but no one stopped them.

More ominous was the stripping of signs from the sticks, leaving the younger people with three-foot-long weapons. No one ever admitted whose idea it had been to attach the signs to sticks, and never again in a mass march in Memphis were such sticks used. On March 28, they were. Discarding signs in the street, groups of boys swooshed and swished their sticks about, and although marshals did move to confiscate them as the march began to move, a number of kids filtered through with sticks at their sides.

But the greatest weakness of the COME planning was the lack of rapport of older black leaders with the more militant young and the almost total lack of communication with the small group of peripheral petty wheelers and dealers on whose home territory around Beale Street the march was being staged, the guys who hung out at the pool halls, the guys with the flashy suits and conked hair, pickpockets, pimps, the younger guys learning to live hand-to-mouth on the edges of crime.

"A man I will call Mr. K. said there were fellows sitting around drinking wine and beer while waiting for the march to begin," reported a LeMoyne student who marched. "They began to talk about looting stores and most of all how they would be dressed and how much money could be made if they hit certain stores like Lansky Brothers (clothing), various pawn shops and liquor stores."

Southwestern student Marty Frisch was on Hernando with other campus reporters. "We started out with the adults, talking to them....The adults stressed it was to be nonviolent. But we moved gradually on back because the youth were near the back and kids with Invader jackets were way back. There were young people going all along the sidewalk...some yelling 'Black Power!' "

The Invader leaders were not around, thought Lawson.

Actually, the Invaders were leery of the mass march, reported one of their spokesmen. They were lying low, but people not really familiar with their group tended to identify anyone wearing a tiki and talking Black Power as an Invader and any cat wearing an Invader jacket as a leader.

"It wasn't as easy as just having King in to lead a march," the spokesman continued. "The tension in the city was such that if twenty thousand people marched down Main, all the police would have to do is look the wrong way and the place would have blown up....There were some youngsters in high schools who had been led to believe that this could be the day, man, that we could really tear the city up....So the talk began to go around—about knocking out so and so—or getting this whitey, you know. It was as hot as hell....People were drinking early that morning, drinking anything they could get their hands on. Behind the Minimum Salary Building and the Temple they were drinking wine....It was sort of like a festive holiday, but just a wee bit different. They were all really ready for some excitement."

John Spence ducked into Clayborn Temple and found there a handful of young militants talking to some students, but back on the street he was "firm in my impression that the crowd was an orderly crowd that wanted an orderly march."

Councilman Fred Davis stood talking to NAACP president Jesse Turner and looking at the cats with the sticks walking up and down the street. "There was an element in the crowd that we couldn't get rid of at that time. Nobody could do anything with them. I said, 'Mr. Turner, do you believe that we can conduct this march and go all the way around and come back to this place without anything happening?' No chance! He didn't believe we could do it...but at that point the march was so locked in. If they had tried to call it off, it would have blown up right there."

"When we knew King was in the city and on his way, we brought the front line up to about the intersection," said Rev. Lawson. The car bringing Dr. King, a white Continental driven by Jesse Epps, had difficulty maneuvering through to the head of the march. It was a few minutes before 11:00 A.M.

"When the car got there, pandemonium broke out. Everyone was excited....My initial response was to tell Dr. King to get to a certain point until we got the march moving properly and then I would tell him to come and join us. I said I felt we shouldn't get going until the people on the sidewalk either moved back or got out of the way or until we were certain things would go along smoothly...He initially agreed, but then after consulting with people in the car and with one or two of our folk from Memphis, a couple of the SCLC staff people came out and said, 'We've been in this kind of situation before. There's a lot of excitement in the beginning, but if we hold on and go on, the march will get itself straightened out and everything will be all right.'

"Ralph and Martin got out of the car, and a large group of fellows charged from where they were in back and got immediately behind him, forcing the ministers and some of the workers out of the way...But they followed the march." They were, Lawson decided, a group that wanted to be close to the leader.

"When Dr. King comes, cameras and people and even preachers are going to surge around him and want to shake hands with him even in the middle of a march," explained Rev. Kyles. "It makes mass confusion."

"When Dr. King arrived," recounted yet another LeMoyne student, "some of the students crammed and jostled him a bit, and I managed to squeeze and squirm a way through them to shake his hand....Everything got off so well. People began to wave their signs and students broke out with soul sounds. Then seconds later, I saw a group of about thirty high school students start to tear up an abandoned bedstead that was in front of a house until they all had an iron pipe."

"At the back, we didn't even know Dr. King had arrived until the march began to move," said another participant.

The march moved out. Later, spot checks would show that a massive work stoppage of blacks had not occurred. Yet many individuals did take off and come to march. The crowd was somewhat vaguely estimated somewhere between ten and fifteen thousand.

In the block between Linden and Beale, Lawson and the other chief marshals cleared people out of the streets to get the march through. By the Minimum Salary Building, where Shelby County Human Relations Director, and now COME activist, Jerry Fanion stood on a flat-bed truck with several newspaper reporters and walkie-talkie radio equipment, other marshals tried with no great success to funnel the crowd into some sort of lines. Directly in front of Dr. King walked Lux, chief ranking police officer on the scene. Lux was extremely uneasy about the march for he, too, had caught the feelings of unrest, but he had rejected the idea of checking with Commissioner Holloman or Chief Macdonald on whether it should be stopped before it got started. Perhaps when it strung out it would settle down. Besides, how could it be stopped now without precipitating the very confrontation everyone was trying to avoid? Farther along, the march would pick up an escort of five motorcycles which moved half a block ahead of the main body.

Linked arm-in-arm with Dr. King and Abernathy in the front row were some of the local ministers, including C. M. E. Bishop B. Julian Smith. Immediately behind them came the young men who had crowded in, then strike leaders, clergy, strikers, and the community in one large undifferentiated mass followed. Hundreds of signs bobbed up and down, and there was some ragged chanting of "We Shall Overcome" and "Down with Mayor Loeb." The sun was beaming down now, and most of the marchers were talking, joking, and waving to onlookers, all pretense of lines forgotten as they strolled along. As the head of the march swung west around the corner onto Beale Street by Handy Park, two blocks back hundreds of others were just beginning to move.

At Handy Park, the tiny patch of green grass and trees with the statue of bluesman W. C. Handy, himself ten years dead that very day, several old men detached themselves from sunning and came to the curb to cheer the march on. "Come on," yelled the marchers, "join us."

Councilman Fred Davis and Dr. Vasco Smith left the march at Handy Park, cutting across the grass, planning to swing over and meet the march at Main and Gayoso. Baxton Bryant, walking immediately behind Dr. King, detached himself and began to walk along the sidewalk, next to the windows of the small stores that lined Beale.

"We sanitation workers were all together, but after we got past Handy Park, well, we got mixed up some kind of way, and they had a lot of youngsters in there and they were going through the crowd hollering, 'Let me get by'…They come up through the line. So we kinda mixed up from Third on to Main Street," explained L. C. Reed.

And ahead, out toward the front of the march, small groups of teen-age boys and younger adults moved along the sidewalks, outriders, pushing through the spectators, parallel with the march but not in it, some with sticks swinging at their sides.

The head of the march was crossing Second Street now, moving toward Mulberry and Main. From a scaffold *Press-Scimitar* reporter Wayne Chastain and a television cameraman watched it come forward a block away. Suddenly six teen-agers "clad in a gaudy array of bright yellows, blues and purples" moving ahead of the march were at the base of the scaffold, shaking it, reported Chastain. "Shake those whiteys off of there…knock them down." Several police cars pulled toward them from beyond Main, and the kids ducked back into the oncoming crowd. The police cars moved back.

LeMoyne student Ronald Hooks, with a camera borrowed from his uncle's photography studio, was in front of the march taking pictures. "People were trying to walk much too fast for a crowd of that size," he observed. "Dr. King was being pushed and people were walking on each other's heels." "The escort truck leading the march, the head of the police escort, didn't move nearly fast enough," said Bill Ross of the labor council. "Consequently King and the truck right in front of him soon became engulfed in young people."

Suddenly there was a resounding crack and the smashing of glass. The first window had been hit.

"It broke right by me," said Ross. "I didn't see who broke it. It was a shoe store."

"The first kid I saw trying to break a window was only twelve or thirteen years old," said Baxton Bryant who was on the sidewalk. "And the first two or three windows didn't break. One cracked."

"We had started up that block between Main and Second when things started to happen," related Rev. Dick Moon. "I remember first of all seeing glass broken out of Pape's clothing store, and when it happened everyone in the march just sort of moved away from that area. And people were yelling, 'No! No!' And then all of a sudden another window broke on the other side of the street and then everything seemed to calm down."

At the head of the march Rev. Lawson heard the first windows bursting in back of him. He sent some marshals back. "See if you can keep them from the windows." He then asked Chief Lux for a bullhorn, which Lux got right away. Lawson had the bullhorn as the march reached Main.

John Spence was almost a block behind. He couldn't locate the crashing sound, but it chilled him. "Oh, Lord! What's happening? Who's doing this? Somebody in the crowd said, 'This ought not to happen.' "

There was no real looting at that point, said Ross. The kids would reach in, grab something, and throw it down. "It was just the idea of hearing a window crack....These were light sticks for these big windows. Just throwing a stick from fifteen or twenty feet wouldn't break a big window. It took two or three of these kids with these sticks pounding on them. And then they would pop."

"At Second and Beale, they had broke out that glass there and a violin was laying out there in the street all tore up," said sanitation worker Ed Gillis.

Attorney Walter Bailey, who had already represented a number of those arrested previously in the strike, was with Spence, keeping one eye on his wife and on Rev. Kyles' wife who walked in the street with their small children. "I saw a group of young punks with sticks hitting a pawn shop window, and I said to myself, 'Good heavens! What the hell are they trying to do to us? Get us all shot?'...I was terribly frightened because I lost track of my wife and little boy. I didn't want them to get trampled in the process of people panicking...."

Two blocks farther back marchers just passing Handy Park stopped irresolute as the confused sounds of shouting reached them. "What happened? What happened?" A crashing of glass was heard and more shouting. "Windows! They're breaking windows!" "Damn it!" cried one man, "they're ruining the march!" Around him other marchers looked at each other. Then silence. "Keep going," suggested another marcher. "They've stopped. It's all right now." That section of the march moved forward again, gingerly, ears straining for noise up ahead. For some moments it was quiet. The march again seemed under control.

At City Hall a few blocks farther north, city council members Blanchard, Hyman, and Awsumb had just emerged from a meeting on plans for sewage disposal facilities that the city was being required to build to prevent the throw-off of sewage into the Mississippi River. A speaker's platform and loud-speakers had been set up in front of City Hall for the march rally. The march, police told them, was still on Beale Street.

"I was watching, fascinated...the national television set up their cameras on the top of the roof across the street," remembered Ms. Awsumb. "And I thought, gee, we are really getting big time. I will have to watch that at 6:00 P.M. tonight (on the newscast)." She and Billy Hyman decided to get a sandwich in the building and stay for Dr. King's speech. Blanchard headed toward his law office.

"I eased down Main Street...checked with the peace officers from corner to corner, and you could hear it coming in. You hear these voices coming in on that police radio...walkie-talkie...I was listening to Chief Henry Lux from corner to corner....Now I was about at Court Square...Lux said there were people breaking glass out of the windows—very calm dispatch—clinical really."

The march swung around onto Main Street, a solid phalanx stretching from curb to curb, King, Abernathy, and the Memphis leaders with arms interlocked, Lawson and other marshals out in front. Suddenly a large group of kids came around the corner just after them on the sidewalk, smashing store windows as they ran.

"They just flaked out of the sides of the march," observed Chief Lux. Like falling dominoes the window breaking rippled back from them and began all down the five blocks of Beale where marchers still came forward, wrote reporter Chastain. Clubs sailed through the air on Beale. There were yells of "Smash glass" and "Burn it down, baby!" Chastain ran to where a cordon of police were standing, but they were cut off by the main body of marchers from the glass breaking and looting that had now started and from another small group of police who had moved into the Beale and Second area. The lead window-smashers were now slightly ahead of the march at McCall and Main.

At this point Rev. Lawson stopped the march. It had come seven blocks and lasted about twenty-five minutes.

His first concern was to get the marchers turned back. The front line stopped and turned around. His second concern was Dr. King's safety. He moved directly toward him. "Take Dr. King down McCall and out of the way," he ordered.

"And Martin balked," Lawson said, "so I said directly to Ralph Abernathy something about 'I understand Martin not wanting to, but I think he should go on.' And Henry Starks backed me up immediately...A handful of people surrounded Abernathy and King and they moved down McCall over toward Front Street and out of the way."

The King group flagged down a passing motorist and were

driven some blocks south to the Holiday Inn-Rivermont on the river front, the nearest hotel anyone could think of in that direction. Dr. King was by then escorted by three motorcycle policemen dispatched by Police Chief Macdonald with orders to stay with him and protect him.

Rev. Lawson took the bullhorn and moved down the middle of the street. "This is Rev. Lawson speaking. I want everyone who's in the march, in the movement, to turn around and go back to the church."

As march leaders moved calmly into the middle of the crowd saying "Turn around! Go back! Go back to the church!" thousands of people turned and started back the way they had come. Around them windows continued to break.

A few seconds later, at 11:18 A.M., Police Chief Macdonald, at the request of officers on the scene, ordered the march dispersed. A line of police which had stretched across Main a block ahead of the march began adjusting their gas masks and coming south. Another group began moving from the south to meet them. Police around the route perimeter closed in toward Beale. In a final orgy of excitement the kids on Main threw their sticks across to the west side of the street—one bruising Lux on the leg—and a few boys ran over to break windows before darting back onto Beale.

School Superintendent E. C. Stimbert and the schools business manager John Freeman had watched the march start up Main "in a rather orderly fashion and all of a sudden this chaos and confusion and tires screeching and the police moving in....We just continued to stand. It was like watching a battle a block and a half away. We didn't stay very long because we were not sure how quickly this would all spread....We were sick...Why does this have to happen?...It's not only a different ballgame, but somebody blew up the ballpark and tore up the rulebook."

Councilman Davis also saw the breakup of the march on Main. "I was watching the police who were directly in front of me and...the crowd coming from the other end...The first time they (police) just put on their gas masks and started in. They didn't shoot Mace at that point. They came back and they called for help and then motorcycle policemen started down with them...and at that point they started firing rounds of Mace."

Farther up Main, Councilman Blanchard reached the next policeman with a walkie-talkie in time to hear Lux saying, " 'The situation is now out of hand. They're breaking windows on either side of the street. I request permission to break it up.' You know, you just don't believe it! At that point I really took off down Main Street toward Beale....I had my raincoat. It was too hot to wear it and I had it tied around me and it was flying." What was the smoke in the air? he asked a reporter. "Tear gas." "Oh, God," groaned Blanchard and kept on going.

Those first few minutes after the march turned were wild confusion. Lawson and other march leaders moved steadily down the middle of the street, urging everyone back to Clayborn Temple. Their problem was acute. In the march were families, children whose parents had brought them along so some day they could say "I marched with Martin Luther King," and older people, none of whom could run fast or far enough. Lawson's wife and five-year-old son were somewhere in the march. He knew the police were moving in behind him on Main; he did not know what was being done on Beale. If the crowd completely panicked and some ten thousand people started to run, children, old folks, women would be knocked down, trampled, injured. Somehow the peaceful demonstrators had to be led out of the area to safety. "Do not run" went out the shouts. "Walk to the church. Do not run." At Beale, Lawson and most of the march turned east, back the way they had come. But smaller groups tried going south on Main and others tried to leave the area by heading west toward Front Street and the river.

Rev. Dick Wells and several other white and black ministers, including Charles Dinkins, head of Owen College, stopped irresolute in the middle of Main. "We'd almost been knocked down by some of the people (looters) coming out of the stores," said Wells. "We better get out of the middle of the street," someone said. "Why?" asked another minister. Things didn't look much better at the side. "Just then a gas canister hit and rolled past us," said Wells, "and he didn't ask any more questions. We jumped into a doorway...and the first line of police rushed past us." Slipping out, they went north up Main, one of the few groups to get through in that direction.

As the move back started, union leader Bill Lucy held Dan Powell, of COPE, against a building on Beale to avoid the crush before they worked their way to Main to find out what had happened. "Lucy was very upset because he thought this was the end of a powerful push we could have made," related Powell. "Then we ran into this black woman. She was crying. She apparently wasn't hurt...but she was crying. And Bill...tried to comfort her and get her out of the way...back into the doorway of a building." Now blocked by police lines from getting back to the church, they moved over to Front Street and then back toward The Peabody hotel.

Local union president T. O. Jones cut loose from the front of the march and ran for cover. "It was every man for himself." But most of the sanitation workers themselves who had marched off from the church in a body, turned and marched back the same way. "We never had any problem with what we call the 'tub-toter'—the actual sanitation men," said Chief Lux.

Councilman Netters had flown back from Chicago that morning. He had caught up with the march at Main and Beale. Now he retreated south on Main. On the east side of the street was an open lot where an old building was being razed to make room for the new six-million-dollar Memphis Light, Gas and Water headquarters. There were piles of bricks and kids were hefting them back toward police. Police responded with tear gas. "A canister almost struck my foot...I thought it was a brick, and when it exploded I was almost overcome by tear gas." He retreated north but was blocked there by police.

A number of marchers did get down Main to Linden, a block south. There a line of police were channeling people through the lot where a gas station was being torn down. There was a fence half down, but possible to scramble over. Several ministers held there, trying to calm the people and helping them, a couple of them nuns in habits, over the fence, which got more and more flattened.

AFSCME field director P. J. Ciampa cursed the bum knee that prevented him from running as the tear gas canisters began falling. Two of the strikers were helping him. As they caught up with the hired COME sound truck, his friends hoisted Ciampa on the back of the truck. "Man," they said, "you can't run." "So I sit up on the back of the truck and—ah, that feels good!" said Ciampa. "I look around...and, my God, I'm the perfect sitting duck....By this time somebody sensed the same thing in the cab of the truck and says, 'Come on in!' He told me to announce over the loud speaker to return to the church, to turn around, and avoid the policemen. Don't bother the policemen." Steering carefully through the crowds, loudspeaker blaring, the truck made it back to Clayborn Temple.

The main action was now on Beale where minutes before a quick surge of window-breaking, looting, and panicky crowd reaction was as visible as a large wave swelling down the five blocks to Fourth. Marchers toward the back were not even sure what was happening. They had, as yet, seen no police, and the rumbling and shouting were in front of them. Then the march seemed to head backward amid shouts of "Go back! Turn around!" The word passed quickly. "It's over! Go back!"

The looting in all this confusion was remarkably quick and efficient. The kids did most of the window-breaking and some of the looting, but there were older, more experienced hands working after them, a swift entry into stores, a quick rifling of goods, and then retreat into the anonymity of the crowd. Store owners, stunned and frightened, did little to try to stop them. One store proprietor related how she and her daughter locked themselves in the bathroom while their place was ransacked. "By the time the police got to Beale, the looters were already halfway home," commented one observer.

The list of establishments caught with some loss in this hit-and-run exercise ran down a half block on Main and all along Beale. Hardy's Shoes. York Arms. Federal Clothiers. Main Liquor. Adams Hats. Uncle Sam's Pawn Shop. Paul's Tailoring. Lansky Brothers clothing. Schwab's department store. American Loan Co. pawnshop. Pape's Men's Store. Quality Liquors. Most owners were long-time residents of the street, almost all white with black employees. The loot was merchandise, hats, shoes, clothes, cameras, radios, musical instruments. Few took time to go for the cash drawers.

Robert Orr and several other Southwestern students were just west of Handy Park. "I saw one store get hit rapidly. They smashed both windows almost simultaneously and started pulling out musical instruments. We just stood there shocked from the sheer stupidity of the thing. Every marcher around me was saying, 'This is stupid'...Then it broke into chaos. The marchers panicked and started to run, partially because there were stores being looted and partially because people were running from Main. It looked like just a big steamroller of people, converging very rapidly. People started to panic, running into Handy Park. I was swept along with the crowd....I wasn't really frightened....But then I saw a big Negro boy almost within arm's reach of me throw an empty whiskey bottle, with no apparent emotion, with no apparent hate or anything, into the midst of the crowd. It hit a Negro woman in the back of the head and just shattered...I heard the woman next to her say, 'Oh, my God!' It cut the back of her head...I was very frightened then...at that kind of undirected hatred. I felt there was absolutely no security for anybody. I ran out of the park...and down a side street....I was stopped by three looters, one carrying an electric guitar and a saxophone. They asked me if I had seen any police and I said no. They asked, 'Are you friendly to the police?' I uttered a rather emphatic, 'No, sir!' They said, "Well he's all right,' and went on."

"At the corner of Handy Park was a big, black guy swinging a stick," said Joan Beifuss, there with the Rearing Children of

Good Will workshop segment. "He was saying, 'You white folks get on out of here. We're gonna burn down this mother-fuckin' city!' I wanted to just burrow in the ground and cover my head up with my raincoat! People were running all through the park. This one teen-age girl was sitting on the grass and sobbing and sobbing....We headed toward the church. Every so often a bottle would pop in the street. What was frightening was the senselessness of the whole thing, the careless way people were throwing things and running around and yelling. We thought at Clayborn Temple everything would be all right, but there was a guy standing on the front steps draped in a bolt of material that must have just come from some store on Beale. We decided we'd keep going....

"Our car was parked a couple of blocks farther by a housing project and in the streets around were kids, some of them little, running around with material or other funny things in their hands. We saw our first policeman there. He was just standing all by himself on the curb, not trying to stop anybody....As we drove out of the area we could hear the sirens of more police cars heading in."

At City Hall Mayor Loeb and Police Commissioner Holloman had, by 11:32 A.M.—several minutes after police received orders to break up the march—begun the first moves for calling in the Tennessee National Guard, and the mayor put in a call to Governor Buford Ellington. Twenty minutes later Holloman received a call that the National Guard had been alerted. By noon Gov. Ellington had announced that forces of the Tennessee Highway Patrol were on their way to Memphis and that the first members of the National Guard would be assembling shortly. From Nashville, the Governor's private plane flew west toward Memphis, bringing former-Police Commissioner Claude Armour and representatives of the Air National Guard and the Tennessee Bureau of Investigation.

Subdued panic was spreading through the downtown area as news of the melee spread. Commissioner Holloman was asking that citizens stay away from downtown and the area immediately to the south. Garbage pick-up for the day was abruptly terminated.

Facing police coming onto Beale by foot, motorcycle, and squad car was a vast array of blacks moving every which way. Most were aiming toward the Temple and they hurried along in groups, bunches, individually, straggling, hurrying to catch up with others. Kids still moved diagonally back and forth, a few belligerently ready to face the police.

First concern of the police had been to get the march off Main Street and prevent further damage there. Second was to get the bulk of the marchers contained in the Beale-Clayborn Temple area, but already scattered incidents were reported on side streets and spreading. The third objective was to clear Beale and arrest the troublemakers. But police were having difficulty differentiating between the troublemakers and the other blacks milling around.

Ron Ivy had managed to hold some of the Memphis State Black Students Association group together near Main. "When the policemen started chasing people, everybody else started running except the people that had looted," he noted. "And the looters had picked up whatever they had stolen and gone home." Be still, he told the students with him. Don't run. They started walking in a body back to the church and "a lot of policemen with a lot of sticks and clubs ran by us without looking at us....They were concerned with the people fighting and running."

Baxton Bryant was still near Main and Beale, though that intersection was now fairly clear. "Glass, man, was just crashing your ear for half a mile." He watched a white deputy sheriff work over a young black man and then turn toward a television cameraman who'd caught the picture. "He never broke stride," said Bryant. "Didn't look like he even glanced about him, just took his club, backhanded, right across the camera and head of this photographer." The blow knocked the cameraman back through a broken window. Blood flew, and Bryant and two city policemen rushed over to pull him out. "The line officers had no use for local television men," commented a police lieutenant privately.

Joyce Palmer, who'd had her billfold heisted, was by herself again. The women she was with had fled. With some detachment she watched the chaos all around her. And she was confused about how to get back to the Temple. "So I saw this policeman standing there and I asked him how to get back. I knew they all disapproved of my being there, but I knew he wouldn't want me to get lost or hurt and he'd tell me where to go. He just growled." She made her way back on her own.

Harold Whalum, the elegantly dressed president of Union Protective Life Insurance, was knocked down and hit when he protested police calling several women he was trying to protect "black bitches."

Lawson was now back at Hernando, bringing the bulk of the march with him. The first line of marshals had remained several blocks behind to cover the rear. "The people actually in the march essentially followed our instructions," said Lawson. "Some of the marshals were magnificent. I stood at the intersection in the middle of the street with the bullhorn telling people to move on back....

"I could smell tear gas by this time. I could hear the shots of the tear gas guns. I could hear windows breaking and shouts. I saw a couple of skirmishes between young cats...there to do the junk. They chased a policeman up the street on Third. He came down on a motorcycle...but they started attacking him and chased him up the street...I was concerned that the police might fire, especially when I saw this—and the looting."

Lawson was operating automatically. He still did not know that Dr. King was safely away nor that his wife and little boy had walked over to St. Patrick's Church with Father Greenspun. Nor was there time to consider the wider implications of the disorder. His singleminded responsibility was to get those peaceful demonstrators off those streets.

Tear gas was welling up from the street, thick now on some parts of Beale. Sporadic violence continued. Police Lt. D. W.

Williams was struck on the head with a demonstrator's sign, and as he grappled with his attacker, both fell through a plate-glass window. NAACP president Jesse Turner and Rev. Harold Middlebrook, both trying to get the marchers back to the church, were Maced. Councilman Fred Davis was poked in the side with a night stick and ordered to move on.

Hundreds of people cut loose from the march individually or in pairs and unobtrusively worked their way out of the area on side streets, but fear persisted even as they fled. Mattie Sengstacke, wife of the *Tri-State Defender* editor, and COPE director Dan Powell's wife, Rachel, ducked off Beale Street into a cul-de-sac. Panicked, they rested and then retraced their steps and tried another way. At Second and Union, said Ms. Sengstacke, a policeman with a can of Mace "held it to my face and I just looked him in the face and kept going. He didn't spray it." A portly, dignified woman, she and Rachel Powell then cut back south to the *Defender* office where the Sengstacke's teen-age daughter Ethel and several friends met them with red, streaming eyes. "We got the car and I said, 'Let's get out of here as fast as we can!'"

Marty Frisch linked up with several other Southwestern students and they got to their car. "They wanted all white cars out of the area....All of a sudden there were six black boys and they opened the doors and got in and I think there were twelve of us in the car. We didn't even know the boys and they were just as scared as we were and were just trying to get away." Marty felt safer with the friendly black youths in the car.

Another LeMoyne student was in a portion of the crowd chased down Third. He and his friends got off the street and ran through yards and alleys. "We jumped off a six-foot-high fence, something which I couldn't have done unless I was scared to death—which I was."

Other marchers ended up over at St. Patrick's rectory, a comparatively calm oasis where cuts could be treated and heads cleared.

Councilman Blanchard met up with David Caywood at Main

and Beale and they somberly watched police laying tear gas all along the street. Blanchard related, "Dave said to me, 'Well, if you've got any guts, you'll go down there with me.' Caywood's a Democrat and I'm a Republican. So if I turn tail and go back to the Commerce Building and practice law, then forever he says, 'Republicans got no guts.' " They walked into the tear-gassed area.

Over at the Big M restaurant, on the corner of Linden and Danny Thomas, "A couple of police officers...told the manager to close up," said Whittier Sengstacke, who was on the scene with his two young *Defender* photographers, his own son Whittier, Jr., and Ed Harris. The Big M was a gathering place for black businessmen in the area. "One of the employees said, 'Let him show you his badge.' That's the thing that made the police angry....The patrons began to come out peacefully. But the officers began to hit them over the head." Protesting and throwing out angry words, the Big M customers moved to their cars, but officers also moved about in the parking area. "Some guys got into their cars and were ready to leave and police pulled them out and beat them," said Sengstacke. Twelve cars on the parking lot were damaged.

The final clearing of Beale Street took place as police formed a wedge and worked their way east, ordering everyone off the street and emptying the stores, cafes, pool halls, and lounges. Most patrons left voluntarily if sullenly when ordered, but some police avoided the niceties altogether, barging in and shoving them out. By order of Inspector Sam Evans, all business places in the disorder area were closed.

It was now a few minutes after noon, a short half-hour since the march had broken up. Except for police, Beale Street stood deserted in its rubble of broken glass, bottles, bricks, articles of clothing, trampled signs, wisps of tear gas. But down Hernando and at Clayborn Temple the trouble was just getting started and there police and angry young blacks would harry each other for the next several hours.

Sanctuary. Clayborn Temple. They came to it terrified, angry, stunned, some hurt, forgotten now the high moment of the cause and Martin Luther King, conscious now only of the need to protect their own bodies and to get safely home out of this nightmare. The church could hold fifteen hundred persons and when its pastor Rev. Malcolm Blackburn got back, every seat on the main floor was taken and groups thronged the aisles. To the pulpit came the ministers and union leaders to make what order they could. The names of lost children were read; instructions were given on how to treat tear gas in the eyes. They would all stay in the church until it was safe to leave. As new marchers arrived, they reported on activities outside, but several attempts by young militants to stir up the quasi-congregation fell flat. As far as anyone knew, the area was cordoned off "so there was a kind of waiting period, trying to find out when and whether it would be safe for people to leave," said Rev. Blackburn. There seemed to be a lull outside. "Gradually we told people that they should begin to leave and go quietly and go directly home." Some did and walked calmly out of the area. Under the circumstances Clayborn Temple was at first comparatively safe.

But outside the momentum grew. Police would move in a wedge down Hernando and before them the groups would toss missiles and flee, for this was their home territory in a way that the commercial Beale was not. As soon as the street was cleared and police started away, young blacks would regroup and start to follow them, yelling and taunting, and the police would come back in. Police cars screeched and officers would leap out with shotguns in one hand and riot sticks in the other, secure an area, jump back in their cars and screech away to answer another call, for sporadic looting was now breaking out south and east of the immediate Temple area.

Baxton Bryant stayed on Hernando for several hours watching, ducking occasionally into a nearby house when the street got really rough. "When the police would leave, then out from under the houses, from behind houses, from in houses, the chunkers would come out and retrieve their missiles, brickbats, bottles, clubs, anything else they could get. And when the police started coming, they'd get back around the buildings, and, man, just as quick as one got out of the car they'd start whamming away.

"The police showed a lot of restraint as long as they were under direct command," said Bryant. "I saw them stand there and take a lot...But once the command was given and they moved out on their own, they were a totally different breed."

A newspaper story told of a thrown bottle and a deputy sheriff, running and screaming "Shoot the son of a bitch." "You better cool down," advised a city policeman who stopped him.

John Spence watched a line of police advance along Pontotoc, ordering people off the street into the houses. "The police would say, 'Get in your houses! Off the porch! Inside!' I tried to say, 'Take it easy. Take it easy. You don't have to be so rough.'...I was showing my credentials to one officer who kept saying, 'Who are you? Why are you saying anything? Are you with these people? Have you been here all along?' I didn't know why that was relevant, but I said yes, I'd been there all along. He said, 'Well, you oughta be with them. Go on. Get with them.' I was shoved very forcibly, and then he pulled out his Mace and squirted me....This was after seeing my credentials. It was a repeat of what happened to Jacques Wilmore on February 23."

At some point Spence made his way on foot the dozen blocks back to his own office to call Washington and say "hell had broken loose in Memphis." Then he went to the police commissioner's office to check the situation and offer the help of the civil rights commission staff. "Holloman was pretty agitated at that point....He was saying, 'Nobody's telling me anything. I don't know...they didn't give me a line of march. I haven't had any communication with these people. I've had to play this by ear and do the best I could.' "

Heading back to Clayborn Temple with attorney Mike Cody, Spence found police all over the Hernando-Pontotoc intersection. "David Caywood was standing in the street and I remember thinking, 'I wish I had your nerve.' I was hanging to the side of the building because things were being thrown from the porch of the Minimum Salary Building and the police in both directions had tear gas or shotguns."

Breaking into liquor stores in the area continued and spread. Rev. Kyles and Jesse Turner had prevented one such entry at Beale, and Spence now watched a "group of young men in their twenties—the thug and drifter element in there—breaking into one liquor store, taking the liquor, passing it out and drinking, all on the spot and very fast."

Down on Linden, Baxton Bryant watched guys coming along with loads of liquor in their arms. "There's one guy that had bottles literally stacked all the way across his arms. Just the most free fellow I've ever seen. He gave every one of those bottles away except one, and he put that one in his pocket...and took off as fast as he could."

Councilman Blanchard and David Caywood, reaching one corner, had held up to stand guard over a liquor store already partially ransacked. "We knew that if they got enough booze out of there that the problem would be intensified," said Blanchard bluntly.

But there were not enough police to stand guard at every liquor and sundry store, and owners made out the best they could, some guarding their own stock and at least one man hurriedly loading supplies into his car to get them away.

Many of the injured had been brought by friends into Clayborn Temple and the Minimum Salary Building, and COME leaders were frantically trying to get ambulances in as more and more calls over their shortwave radio detailed the need for medical help at such and such a corner. Reporter Kay Black observed, among others, a man with a mangled bloody arm, a child with a bloody head, and a woman whose forehead looked like bloody pulp as she crouched on the floor moaning and crying. There were reports that other injured had run into the private houses along Hernando. At one point at the Temple, Rev. Blackburn found one man beaten by police, semi-conscious; another who had fallen off a car; an asthmatic girl suffering from tear gas; and on the trunk of a car in the alley a semiconscious man whose back might be broken, onlookers feared. And there were countless others cut by glass, hit by police, or sick with gas.

Ambulances were refusing to come into the area, so David Caywood got on the phone to Commissioner Holloman, promising that if city fire department ambulances were sent in, march leaders would guarantee their safety. Ambulances did come in and take out several of the injured with no trouble.

As the skirmishing continued outside, large numbers of people, including women and children, were still caught inside the church. There were few interludes in which people could get away. Reporter Black described Lawson "ashen and with hands shaking" on the phone to Commissioner Holloman asking for police aid to get the women and children out, but they could coordinate nothing.

Additionally, the trouble makers were using the church itself as a refuge. "Kids would come out of Clayborn with sticks and bottles and bricks and throw them at police across the street," said Caywood. "The police would just sort of charge them and they'd go back into the church. The police didn't go in the church." The church was filled, said Lawson, and the cats using it as a cover would throw bottles from the front or side and then charge back in. The ministers tried to stop them.

Before they could, police threw tear gas on the steps of Clayborn Temple. Acrid fumes sifted into the packed sanctuary. Some people panicked again, frightened that the police were coming in and hysterical as the tear gas began to work. Others raced for the back exits. Old striker Ed Gillis was inside. "They (police) was out there. We knowed they was all out there cause folks done come in with their eyes and heads full of gas...Then it was burning my eyes and face in there...It was burning me awful bad—my eyes." Some people began jumping out of the windows at the back of the church.

Councilman Netters came in shortly after. He could tell he was in a new mass of gas. He recognized one of his constituents who'd been badly beaten and made sure two friends would get him home. He made announcements about lost children over the microphone. He talked to some of the younger kids who were "threatening to burn and wreck buildings...I asked them to leave....Some did leave. Others just listened...Everyone was either hurt or mad or scared, emotional in every way...By then I had reached a point of numbness."

A number of unidentified persons around Clayborn Temple that day tried to help in small ways. A Southwestern student scrounged up a bucket of water somewhere and returned to the Temple to bathe people's eyes. A man named Seward stayed with the loud speaker on a truck right in front of the church, yelling at both sides, trying to make peace. There were people who helped lost children, aided the injured, calmed others. Without them the situation would have been far worse.

Next door in the Minimum Salary Building an equal amount of confusion had built up. People fleeing from gas had flooded the hallways and offices, but there were also the kids dashing in and out to confront the police. On the upper floors kids hung out of windows to watch the street and cheer until Rev. Jackson shepherded them all down to the cafeteria.

On the first floor, in an office loaned to them as a meeting place for the various religious representatives expected for the march, ministers Darrell Doughty, Dick Moon, Zeke Bell, and Sam Allen, the National Council of Churches' observer, were taking turns on the phone reporting on the march to the NCC headquarters in New York.

Then a tear gas canister was lobbed into the small lobby of the building. "We heard the crash," said Rev. Doughty. They also heard the frightened rush of people in the hallway. "The back door was glass and we heard that break," said Dick Moon. "People were forcing their way out of the building."

When they opened their office door, the gas poured in. "It was horrible," said Dick Moon. "We lay down on the floor to get decent air and we were all just lying there on the floor crying. Then the telephone rang and we picked it up. Of all people it was

Police Director Holloman and he says 'What's going on down there? Who am I talking to?'"

"He wanted to talk to Jackson or Lawson," explained Doughty. "But he couldn't get through to them. He said he wanted to make a point. He said, 'Your people are picking up rocks and taking them through the church and throwing them at our men.' I said, 'I don't know. I can't see the church.' And he said, 'Our men have not been in the church.' And I don't know that either because I can't see the church. And then I said, 'I'm sorry, Mr. Holloman, the tear gas is too thick here and we have got to leave.' And he said, 'Well, do the best you can,' and hung up. I had the feeling he was out of communication." The churchmen evacuated their office through the window.

"We are leaving for posterity, I guess, the spot on the wall where they fired the tear gas canister into the Minimum Salary Building," union leader Bill Lucy grimaced.

As reports and rumors spread throughout the black community, unrest mounted. By 1:30 P.M. all transit authority buses had been pulled off the streets for the first time in history, stranding thousands of riders. The move was made after three bus drivers were attacked and five buses damaged.

Most of the first police calls were coming in from South Memphis; it would take a few hours before young blacks to the north would really get going. Police power was stretched thin as officers in the squad cars hurtled from place to place during the sunny afternoon in response to calls for help, most of them minor but with the potential for bigger trouble if large crowds began to gather.

Schools throughout the heart of the black area had been emptying steadily since midmorning. An estimated twenty-two thousand students, most of them black, had early been reported absent, and later it was almost impossible to estimate how many children were then out. One thing was clear; wherever trouble developed in the black community, there were young children there to watch.

A LeMoyne student described the effect of mounting rumors in the neighborhood of Ford Road School, just southwest of the city in Shelby County. A neighbor woman ran crying from house to house. "Get your children from school. Get them quick before they are killed. The white folks is murdering them in their classes. Oh, Lord, what are we gonna do? A white man just walked into Ford Road School and stabbed two little girls. Oh, Lord, have mercy!" Parents, understandably, headed toward area schools.

It was impossible to control the rumors and that they were so widely believed was one of the most frightening aspects of that whole day. "Honey," one old grandmother said, "anything you can name, the white folks is evil enough to do it."

Many of the schools, however, remained calm, the control of the teachers communicating itself to both children and parents, although these schools also closed early.

One school, Booker T. Washington High School, a good twenty-minute walk from downtown on South Lauderdale, had expected confusion and had laid plans to cope with it. Booker T. Washington had an enrollment of twenty-two hundred students, all black, some seventy-five percent living in housing projects and many of them children of public works employees. The sanitation strike had now been a part of their lives for six weeks.

On the day of the march, assistant principal Mose Walker was in charge of some fifty male teachers stationed around the perimeter of the high school grounds. There were not many children in school that day. Women teachers were handling classes inside the building. Outside, the men, easily identifiable in shirts and ties, were to stay on the campus and keep an eye on things. No one without a legitimate reason was to be allowed on the school grounds. Right next to the school property was a Harlem House restaurant and immediately beyond that a cleaners.

Throughout the morning, with small groups of people moving north toward the march area and others getting their children from the school, as well as with the usual morning activity of the neighborhood, the streets around the school were never empty. Toward noon the glass window at the cleaners was suddenly broken out, the automatic burglar alarm began its incessant ringing, and several people ran off with articles of clothing. But with the line of teachers watching, no further looting occurred, and the Harlem House window was not touched. Now a trickle of people were coming back from the march spreading the news of trouble. The trickle became a stream of both adults and children. A few carried various pieces of merchandise.

It was an hour and a half after the burglar alarm began ringing when police TAC units augmented by a sheriff's patrol car arrived in the area. The teachers estimated seven or eight cars. The officers were in shirt sleeves, with gas masks, and were armed with the long riot sticks.

Walker recalled, "No attempt was made...to identify any looters. They began swinging at people's legs and just knocking them out from under them on the street....They were clearing the area of the sidewalk, and running and ordering people off. They were jumping out of the cars and swinging and grabbing people....Several kids and older people were bloodied, but I still just told my teachers, 'Stay on the school grounds'...As those who had looted ran in front of the school grounds, suddenly one of the police officers jumped out of a squad car...and shot a gas grenade right in the middle of this group of teachers, almost hitting one seventy-year-old man who's retiring this year." As other teachers ran over to see what had happened, "suddenly the police rushed the school grounds where there's nothing but some fifty teachers, standing there in ties and shirts, keeping the peace. They rushed the school grounds threatening us with arrest....They even ordered us off the school sidewalk, back into the building....

"Why—why would they shoot tear gas? ...There's not a child, not a running person, not an obvious looter, no hedges or anything blocking the view....Every teacher there was crying with their handkerchiefs....I stepped between the police and my group of men teachers who were very incensed, just moved them back. They responded right quickly....

"Why?" Walker asked the officers as he identified himself. " 'We got to do our job,' one policeman answered. 'We got a job to do.'...Not one officer had on a name plate, a badge. Not one."

That afternoon the teachers talked about what they should do, of how they could bring charges against the police. In the end they did nothing. "We had no proof, no badge numbers, no officers' bars, no names. A day later the tears had dried up."[3]

Gradually violence in the Clayborn Temple area began to taper off, partially with the sheer weariness of everyone involved. The church was emptying, exhausted marchers getting home as best they could.

There was much witnessing to the march, much agony. But the kaleidoscopic memories, told to a LeMoyne student, of a twelve-year-old boy whose father took him and his brother to march with Martin Luther King perhaps catches it all. The boy was fascinated with the helicopters and marched along hearing people sing:

> I don't like bread and butter,
> I don't like toast and jam.
> I don't like Henry Loeb
> Cuz he ain't worth a damn.

He never got to Main Street, but he saw the window-breaking and looting on Beale. His father took him and his brother back to the church "to keep us from getting hurt." Everybody was saying there shouldn't be looting. People came into the church beaten and Maced. "Some children were lost...it was very noisy." The tear gas fumes came into the church and burned his eyes. "My brother was crying. He is ten." On their way to catch a bus home, they saw two bus drivers attacked. His father reported it to a man directing traffic. Then their bus came and they went home.

"I only wanted to march down Main Street to the City Hall and hear Dr. King speak," he said at last.

Rev. Lawson went home for a few moments before heading to the Rivermont to confer with Dr. King. The phone call caught him there. Did he know that the police had shot and killed a sixteen-year-old boy?

Larry Payne cut classes that day. A high school junior, he worked nights and weekends as a hospital page and lived with his father in a four-room house just south of the city limits. By midmorning, he and a bunch of boys he knew and some he didn't were around Beale and Hernando, talking, wisecracking, watching a game of cards in progress. The march crowd eddied about them. By 11:30 A.M., he had carried his placard in the march and was on Main Street. A United Press International photographer caught a picture there, which was sent out nationwide with the march news story. It showed a motorcycle division officer, helmeted and booted, pulling a guy out of the smashed display window of an already stripped tailor's shop. To the side was poised a youth, identified later as Larry Payne, a stick in his hand.

Shortly after noon Larry was at the apartment of his mother, ten blocks south of Beale, in the Fowler Homes, several blocks of two- and three-story public housing units. He had with him several new pieces of suiting material and was planning to have two pairs of pants made. Later he wandered outside to join a group of guys talking about the march and about how maybe they should go over to the Sears store, two blocks away. There was disagreement; the group split up, some of them heading toward Sears.

At 12:45 P.M. Patrolman L. D. Jones and his partner Charles F. Williams, in squad car #2, were dispatched to answer a looting call at 903 S. Third, Sears. The officers had been pulled off their regular cruising area in North Memphis to stand by and when trouble broke out on the march they had been in the chaotic Main/Beale/Clayborn Temple area both in their car and on foot. Jones had his own weapon, a 12-gauge, single-barrel, sawed-off shotgun.

At Sears they found a broken show window and other officers interviewing the manager. They drove east where a group of "male coloreds" reportedly carrying portable televisions and stereos, were heading toward Fowler Homes. At the project perimeter they met another officer on foot. Suspects carrying televisions had run into the project yard, he reported, but he had already been verbally threatened by residents and was loath to move into the project without a car and radio. Williams drove on in and pulled into a parking lot.

A boy was running about thirty yards from them. He carried a portable television set. "There he is," said Williams. "Catch him." Williams turned to notify dispatch, and Jones jumped from the car with his shotgun and began running. The boy was headed toward what looked like a basement door. When he reached it, he darted inside and shut the door, opened it again to look out at the approaching officer and closed it. About fifteen feet from the door Jones slowed down and began to approach more warily.

He was being watched by a number of project residents, a group of teen-agers, a small boy sitting on the curb playing marbles, a high school senior hanging out clothes on the line. But until Jones began to call, "Come out with your hands up," there was no great alarm within the project area. Jones moved toward the door. "Come out with your hands up," he kept repeating. He wanted to get the suspect and the television set out of there. He wanted to get out of that project. "Come out with your hands up."

The door began to open slowly. Only the boy's right side and arm were now hidden by the door. He said nothing. Jones stepped forward. He was now just an arm's length away. "Get both hands up." He reached out his left arm to grab the boy by the collar.

Then, said Jones, he saw the knife moving up in the boy's right hand. In that split second he raised his shotgun and fired. The shot sounded muffled; the barrel of the gun had been against the boy's lower chest. He slid slowly down the door jamb to the ground. A rusted but sharply honed butcher knife was later reported found just inside the doorway. No fingerprints could be raised from it.

Within minutes police reinforcements had arrived. Project residents, screaming, cursing "white mother fuckers," crying, were being pushed back by police. The boy's mother was hysterical. "He had his hands up," murmured the boy at the clothesline. "I saw the white palms."[4]

Larry Payne was pronounced dead at John Gaston Hospital.

Mission Accomplished

11

"Mission accomplished. He's coming back!"
Jesse Epps

That night under curfew in Memphis blended into a striated view of dark almost deserted streets layered with streetlights for James McGinnis, of A Battery, 3rd Battalion, 115th Artillery Division, Tennessee National Guard.

McGinnis was a young philosophy instructor at Christian Brothers College. Three weekends before, the National Guard across the state had held a full practice alert, but there was no sense of urgency about it. McGinnis had been playing a leisurely game of tennis as the King march downtown was broken up and not till early afternoon did he learn that the Guard had been called out. He left his wife a note saying he probably wouldn't be home for dinner, but to expect him later. McGinnis would not get home for six days.

At the armory he was assigned to call in members of his unit. It was 6:00 in the evening before some fifty-five of his sixty-five-man complement were assembled and early morning before the last ones came in. "We weren't prepared to react instantaneously. This whole thing sort of took everyone by surprise."

Guardsmen were coming into the city from all over West Tennessee—Dyersburg, Trenton, Paris, Martin, Savannah, Lexington, Jackson, Camden. With them came about eight

armored personnel carriers, looking like huge lumbering tanks
with rubber-cleated tracks, used to transport troops under fire.
One convoy, moving into the city at about 7:00 P.M., was
strung out for five miles along Interstate 240, the east-west
route across the state.

"It was a novelty. We all wanted to go downtown and see what
was happening," said McGinnis. "You read about it in other
cities, but we hadn't seen it personally. And most of the fellows
were kind of curious."

His particular battery was divided into three patrols or squads
of some twenty men each and rotated onto the streets. The
Guard was meshed into the police command and deployment
of Guard patrols came out of police headquarters; the Guard
was used to augment police activity, to protect various buildings and major shopping centers, and as roving patrols. They
were equipped with rifles and bayonets, and the patrols were
supplied with tear gas grenades, although McGinnis noted
that he had never been trained to use tear gas.

Most Memphis Guard units slept at the armory, other state
units at the fairgrounds or the Armour Police Center, rolled up
in blankets, their heads on gunbelts and canteens for pillows.
Between patrols they killed time playing cards, watching television, sitting around talking. No one seemed to know how long
they would remain on duty, and at the armory they began to
gauge their future by the amount of food that was brought in.

McGinnis' patrol primarily worked at keeping people off the
streets and "it seemed like it was very quiet. And it was more like
a game than anything, and it was pretty soon a nuisance....We
never encountered anything. Maybe I was just in quiet areas...and
maybe the fact that we were riding around in the streets was the
reason, but it just seemed like we were playing games for a while
and the people who were involved were few."

However, reports of firebombings, vandalism, and looting
came in, though their numbers decreased as the weekend wore
on. At the height of the disorders on Thursday, police switch-
boards recorded 1,115 calls for assistance; on Friday, 984; on

Saturday, 862; and on Sunday, 672. Arrested for riot-related violations were 226 persons on Thursday; 53 on Friday; and 71 on Saturday. Fire Chief Eddie Hamilton reported 517 fire calls answered from Thursday through Monday noon, nearly three times as many as would normally be expected. Most of the fires were set in trash or garbage, although small sundry stores and liquor stores were favorite targets for crude homemade fire-bombs and subsequent looting. Five or six blazes the first night were termed very serious, the worst at a milling company.

There were scattered reports of sniping, but officers were never pinned down by sniper fire and no one was arrested for sniping. Officers dealt chiefly with looting, firebombing, curfew violations, and with groups that tended to gather whenever police or firemen appeared.

Two hundred eighty-two persons, including some who had been in the march, had been arrested and held without bond by Friday morning. Many of them young, some wearing bloody clothing and bandaged, they appeared in city court in a marathon session for arraignment. They faced charges ranging from curfew violation and looting to both city and state charges of disorderly conduct and breach of the peace.

Sixty-four persons would be treated for injuries by midnight Thursday, but the bulk of these had flooded hospital emergency rooms in the immediate aftermath of the march. Many of the injured were suffering from cuts on their heads, shoulders, and hands. To the emergency room at John Gaston, the city hospital, came two of the injured bus drivers, four of nine injured policemen whose wounds ranged from head cuts to body bruises, and the body of Larry Payne. But the exact number of injuries that day was never certain because a number of blacks either sought no treatment or went to their own doctors. By the end of the weekend, ten more persons had been treated at hospitals for injuries due to the disorders, bringing the total to 74.

Despite the mayor's statement that the curfew was "share and share alike," complaints about its enforcement came out of the black community where a number of people, stopped by police, highway patrol, and sheriff's deputies, accused them of swearing and calling "nigger," of pulling people out of cars, of barging into homes, of roughing up blacks unnecessarily. And another layer of bitterness was added to the already strained police/black relations.

But on the balance, the trouble in Memphis, while serious, was not catastrophic as it had been in other large cities. And to assess the Guard presence as overreaction and the troubles as a "mini-riot," as was later done, is to judge in retrospect, with some sense of balance that was not present at the moment. The fear early that pleasant spring evening was real. So was the breaking, looting, and firebombing. No matter that only a few troublemakers were operating in the shadow of the black community.

Assistant Police Chief Lux estimated that no more than 700 to 800 "asked for the whole thing....You don't have any more nuts in the black community than you do in the white....Heaven forbid all 250,000 of them getting involved. I'd have run. What else could you do? I don't care what you've got in the amount of firepower....You'd have had to bring in, my God, how much army?"

But Detroit reinforced Newark which reinforced Watts, and the specter lay across any city with a large black population. For whites a suppressed vision of black retaliation for God-only-knew what real or half-remembered crimes, explained now in socio-political terms of family structure or poverty level or lack of access through the political structure but lying deep, deeper, in the Middle Passage and the loam of the Delta, the running and the rats and the rickety children. For blacks the ever-present consciousness of police with night sticks or rifles, shock troops of the white community, and the fear that their own embittered children could set off the conflagration that could lead only to more destruction.

But the incendiary point had already passed, even if no one realized it. It had passed when most of the blacks in that march turned around, responding not so much to police force as to their own leaders, their own sense that rioting was still not the last option left open to them. What occurred Thursday night and decreasingly on Friday and Saturday were small spin-offs, and they were effectively contained. There was an organized movement which still offered hope.

But even a mini-riot was a riot, and that Thursday night the Panama Limited train, Chicago to New Orleans on the Illinois Central tracks running the river edge of downtown Memphis by-passed the city. It did not stop.

The sun came up next morning, and despite dire forecasts, the city still stood, light glinting off its tall buildings, off the water at the foot of the bluff. It was warm. Storekeepers hit the day before by vandalism were out sweeping glass and nailing up plywood window covers and preparing to reopen. National Guardsmen were out and about, and Beale Street was sealed off, but the trouble had subsided.

First very rough estimates by the Insurance Council of Memphis figured about two hundred buildings had windows knocked out, chiefly in the Beale Street section but stretching into other areas in North and South Memphis and at some shopping centers south on U. S. 61. Goods in windows were looted in about thirty-five percent of these stores; looters actually entered only about five percent of the places. Glass firms were unable to fill all the orders pouring in. The loss to merchants, excluding fire damage, was believed to stand around $400,000.

Schools were open, although attendance was off by a third and schools in the rioting area were still unsettled. Reporters on the south side found school-age kids playing marbles and football in the streets. Buses rolled along, but service would be curtailed again in the less severe curfew that evening. Garbage crews began picking up where they had left off. No liquor or beer was being sold.

Law enforcement officials might look gloomily toward nightfall, but most citizens began to relax. If the worst had not happened on Thursday, surely it would not happen at all.

In all quarters the assessment began. Civic leaders, reported the *Commercial Appeal* in a survey of leadership response, were at a loss to explain why the disturbances had started or to suggest solutions. Some refused to discuss the matter at all, and others blamed the media for the "national black eye the city has received." There was widespread support for the prompt police action. The head of the Downtown Association was distressed about bad publicity, but the head of Future Memphis, Inc., thought the city's image would be improved by the "careful handling of it (disturbance) by our law enforcement officers." The executive vice president of one of the banks thought "everything will be just fine and the more people who say it will, the quicker things will straighten out."

The president of the chamber of commerce was quoted locally as deploring violence and Martin King's entry into the city and saying frankly he didn't know how to get the community together again. In a *New York Times* telephone interview he assessed the situation. "It's not bad at all....If the Negro ministers would tend to their ministering instead of trying to stir things up, we wouldn't have this trouble. Nothing can be done about this situation. It's going to take maybe forty years before we can make any real progress. You can't take these Negro people and make the kind of citizens out of them you'd like...." Many Negroes, he continued, had no background and often couldn't work.

For the next three days in their editorial columns, the *Commercial Appeal* and the *Memphis Press-Scimitar* would create a framework in which the disruption could be judged. The riot was called tragic, senseless, "a damn shame." From all accounts, it was a lawless, senseless, reckless rumble by Negro youths of high school and college age, bent on inflicting pain and humiliation on the Memphis community, and motivated by the heady anticipation of trouble in the streets.

Both papers credited the quick and firm action of law enforcement officials with nipping a riot in the bud, although police overreaction was reported along with black provocation. The *Commercial Appeal* found "overall good performance" on the part of police and congratulated the ministers who had tried to restore order.

What should be done now? asked the press. Preserve law and order. Restore a sense of calm and thoughtfulness. Bring Negroes into broader participation in the city. Return to fellowship. Rebuild understanding. "Only this can remove the blemish on our good name left by yesterday's mad outbreak."

And end the strike! How? Get back to the conference table. Mediate. Give and take. Ministers, get the men back to work.

Despite the *Press-Scimitar*'s statement that "at this point, it would not be wise to accuse any individual group...," blame for what had happened piled up in editorial columns all weekend. "We know who is agitating for more trouble and who is trying to restore calm," announced the *Commercial Appeal* rather ominously.

Young Negro "rowdies" were excoriated; so was the strike leadership that couldn't control its own demonstrations. But the greatest ire was turned on Martin Luther King himself, here again the *Press-Scimitar* relatively more moderate than the *Commercial Appeal*.

King was labeled an outside agitator. He was unappreciative of progress already made in Memphis, although he himself stayed in one of the city's best hotels, the Rivermont, "nothing unusual" about that since all such accommodations were open. King was irresponsible in calling for a work stoppage and for students to play truant. "He got what he asked—to an embarrassing degree" and later tried to disassociate himself from the trouble. "Who, Me?" asks King in astonishment as he stands surrounded by debris in one editorial cartoon.

King was a coward. He had fled the melee instead of trying to stop it. One story reported "his efforts to climb aboard a meat truck were rebuffed," and was headlined: CHICKEN A LA KING.

King was "using" Memphis as a testing ground for the Poor People's Campaign. And he was no longer an effective leader. There were grave doubts the PPC could be peaceful.

There were also several sharp digs at organized labor. In the wake of the disturbances, George Meany, international president of the AFL-CIO, had publicly offered the "good offices" of his organization to help reach a strike agreement. Mayor Loeb's refusal had been quick, and the *Commercial Appeal* backed him up. "Memphis has had enough of Dr. King's help. It can do without George Meany's intrusion on a wing of fancy wafted upon the mistaken idea that there is a 'rudimentary right' to strike against the people's government."

The focus of disapproval shifted to higher echelons, to trade unionism and to Dr. King. Yet AFSCME could not be separated from trade unionism, nor King from the Memphis movement in which he was now both symbol and participant.

The editorial stance of the black weekly *Tri-State Defender* was equally if less immediately provocative, since it would not appear for another few days. In a bitter attack on police action the editorial used the terms Nazi cops, storm troopers, genocide of black people, trigger happy cowboys "waving their shotguns out the window and rudely spitting tobacco on streets where Negro women are standing." An editorial cartoon showed Loeb's "vigilantes" wearing KKK hoods. A more somber editorial took a long-range view. "A disturbance was bound to occur sooner or later. And Memphis authorities knew it. They made the fatal choice. Between settling the strike and clubbing the marchers into submission, they chose the latter."

There was confused political activity. An offer of federal assistance by President Lyndon Johnson in the event that local law enforcement was unable to handle the disturbances was politely rejected by Mayor Loeb. In the U. S. Congress one speaker after another rose to demand that, with the evidence of Memphis before them, the Poor People's Campaign in Washington be called off.

Memphis' three area Congressmen, Dan Kuykendall (R-9th), Robert (Fats) Everett (D-8th), and Ray Blanton (D-7th) joined in the chorus.

Kuykendall, on April 1, rose to say that Memphis had exposed King's fraudulent methods and the "evil of his activities." Everett, more folksy, said King "joined the 'bird gang,' which we call it in West Tennessee...he ran like a scared rabbit." Blanton called for cancellation of the Poor People's Campaign.

Governor Buford Ellington had alerted another 8,000 Guardsmen, the remainder of Tennessee's 11,500-man contingent, in case they were needed in Memphis, and Loeb was assured that if there were much trouble enforcing the curfew, the governor would declare a state of emergency with its extended enforcement powers. Ellington was being pressured both to intervene in the strike and to keep hands off. In the end he kept hands off.

Those few clergymen involved in human rights work with various denominational headquarters or with the National Council of Churches and its spinoff Communications Network who had come in for the march, remained, and national news of the rioting brought in a few more.

Much of the analysis that first night, as police and Guardsmen patrolled the streets, was based on the experience of these men in other rioting cities. "We expected Memphis to respond like all of the other cities," reported Rev. Dick Moon. "We saw Thursday as the first day of rioting, Friday about twice as bad, and by Saturday all hell would break loose."

There was also a feeling among some of these observers that Dr. King's next march would bring a showdown with the Black Power people, whether that march took place in Memphis or Washington. A few thought King was trying to get that confrontation out of the way in Memphis before he got to Washington. Dick Moon didn't exactly agree with that interpretation, but he confessed he didn't have much hope for the next march, wherever it was held, being nonviolent.

On a more immediate, practical level, they tried reaching influential white ministers and convincing them to prepare for

possible increased rioting, by opening up their churches in order
to feed people, by putting families in touch with each other, by
housing families. These were the sort of emergency operations
that had been desperately needed and slow to emerge in other
rioting cities in the past few years and would, in fact, be needed
again in many cities in fewer days than even the most pessimistic
imagined.

Some forty ministers came to a meeting that Friday afternoon
at Westminster House by the Memphis State campus. "There
were differences," said Rev. Darrell Doughty. "Some local men
were less impressed than others, and some men took them
(warnings and suggestions) very seriously." Most of them
rejected the dire predictions that widespread rioting was yet to
come, but they felt strongly that the churches needed at least to
plead for understanding in the city.

Other clergy in the city began working in the same direction.
One group, including Monsignor Joseph Leppert, Episcopal
Dean William Dimmick, and Methodist District Superintendent Frank McRae, moved to get a joint public statement from
the Methodist, Catholic and Episcopal bishops of Tennessee,
H. Ellis Finger, Jr., Joseph Durick, and John VanderHorst.
Their statement saw an "essential difference between a labor
dispute and racial injustice," and called for immediate settlement of the strike so that work on social reform and racial
relations could begin.

But the bishops felt in no position to make specific suggestions. All they felt they could do was encourage mediation and
"mutual respect." And because the statement was so general, it
was used to support varying points of view. "Wise advice" and
"wisdom from three churchmen" the two daily papers labeled
it, the *Press-Scimitar* using it as a basis to call upon Dr. King
to give up his next proposed march and the black ministers
to call off their daily marches, and the *Commercial Appeal*
emphasizing the "vast difference" between the bishops' advice
and the "minister-led marches of racial protest."

The statement was misinterpreted, said Rev. Frank McRae. "I

don't think this is what the three leaders had in mind."

But also bolstered by their own interpretation of the bishops' words were a number of ministers association members who felt that at last their efforts to help settle the strike had received public approbation from their religious superiors. Throughout the weekend there was talk among these ministers about calling a "summit" meeting of civic, business and religious leaders to "demand" a strike solution.

Members of the city council moved early that Friday morning into a series of meetings, and Lewis Donelson labored mightily again to pass some kind of statement that would commit the council to union recognition and end the strike. "That was the very last battle," said Councilman Blanchard. "All morning we were at it...all day long."

Donelson was angry. Quite early that day several council members had conferred with a small group of civic leaders and the remark had been made that "yesterday was a great day for Memphis," implying that the status quo had been reasserted, and Donelson was appalled.

There was no groundswell of pressure for the council to take a stronger stand in favor of union goals. Still Donelson fought. Shortly after the "belly-busting count" several of the council-men went again to check with Mayor Loeb, said Blanchard. "God Almighty! We got it again. Right across the board about decency and justice, when you're right about a thing you're right, and these men are wrong. And that the council was afraid. The council was afraid!

"And I thought of Fred Davis standing down there with all those damn bricks flying around. And Jim Netters getting those people off the streets. Afraid! And the mayor sitting there behind three sets of locked doors with bodyguards, telling us we were afraid!

"We went...back to the council chamber and Lewis really turned it on. He was so magnificent....He said, 'I just had to try one more time.'" But he couldn't swing it. They were still a vote short, the three blacks, Donelson, Pryor, and Blanchard against the others.

Once their hope had been that Gwen Awsumb would join them, but she could not in all conscience vote for the dues checkoff, and they would not let her fool herself into believing that the vote they sought was anything but the checkoff no matter in what terms it was couched to be more palatable. That was one of the most discouraging days of my life, Donelson was to muse later.

Burden for settlement still rested where it had two days before—on the mediation efforts of Frank Miles. Miles was playing a waiting game. He did not immediately attempt to get the city and union spokesmen back to the bargaining table. He wanted to let things cool a little, giving both sides a little more time to think out their positions, now with the warning of the Thursday disturbances and the further sundering of race relations as an added consideration.

By Saturday, eighty-nine garbage trucks were back on the street.

Radio reports and television films of rock-throwing, looting, and beatings, of Dr. King's "followers" turning to violence, had been on their way to the national networks almost before the march had been broken up. When Memphis leaders arrived at his hotel bedroom shortly afterwards, they found Dr. King calm, though internally he was badly shaken. If he felt betrayed by the organization in Memphis, he did not reveal it.

"He didn't really have any idea of what had happened because he hadn't worked with us," said Rev. Kyles. "He had just come to lead the march and he was very disturbed. I sat on the bed and we talked."

Several of his staff, continued Kyles, were angry "that we would bring them into a situation like this without really telling them that the possibility (of violence) was there—especially on the heels of the criticism that the mass march days were over."

A press conference was quickly called and by 5:00 P.M. a confusion of reporters, cameras, and onlookers had assembled. From a chaotic mix of initial statements and specific questions, certain basic strategies emerged. A just settlement of the strike was still uppermost in all plans on the local level and the success of the Poor People's Campaign on the national, but Dr. King would take time to return to Memphis again, and a giant, nonviolent march *would* be held. No date was yet set, but SCLC would help plan it. Nonviolence was viable; it was still the only real tactic to achieve justice. Meanwhile the regular daily meetings, marches, and boycott would continue.

Dr. King had not run away from the march; local leaders had moved him out for his own safety. The mass march had been peaceful and had been turned around by its leaders, not the police. It could not be compared to an event like Watts, and did not presage a summer of violence. The young people who had broken it up had been on the sidelines, not part of the march. These young people could, and would, be brought into the movement, and the movement, both locally and nationally, was going on.

That was the public facade. Behind it both Dr. King and the Memphis leaders struggled to shore it up.

Rev. Lawson certainly believed that violence did not yet endanger the Memphis movement, that there was no reason to stop or pull back. Yet he also knew that while COME once might have been able to proceed on its way leaving the young militants to their own devices—though that had always been a questionable policy—they would now have to be brought in. By not doing so before, by not allowing the time required for the dialogue and rhetoric that would have followed, he had miscalculated.

For Dr. King, a long agony now began. What, in truth, did Memphis now mean to his leadership, his commitment to nonviolence, his dream of the Poor People's Campaign? For if the city two weeks before had been a byway, an excursion, on the way to Washington, it now loomed squarely in front of him. The road to Washington now lay directly through Memphis. Did that mean that he personally must march nonviolently through Memphis or he would not reach Washington at all?

Early in the morning after the abortive march, Dr. King met for the first time with members of the Invaders. Word was out that he wanted to talk with them, but they initiated the move, angry that they were being publicly blamed "for an already tense situation that just happened and exploded," as one of them put it.

As Charles Cabbage, Calvin Taylor, and Lorenzo Childress approached the door of Dr. King's room at the Rivermont, they found a *Commercial Appeal* reporter waiting outside. The reporter might well have been startled. Calvin Taylor was at that time the one black journalism intern on the paper's staff. Cabbage, a Morehouse graduate, had originally intended to work for SCLC in Baltimore, but there was a mix-up about money and Cabbage had returned to Memphis.

"Dr. Abernathy opened the door," said Taylor. "He said Dr. King would be out shortly....We said okay and sat down in the room....I took a seat close to the balcony. I wanted some fresh air and they had the door open....It was a white room with blue furniture, the carpet blue, very cool. I looked at the river....

"Then Abernathy started questioning us...Cab and me, we got mad because he was accusing us of having caused the riot....Just about this time Dr. King came in. He had gotten out of the shower. He had on an aqua-looking green sort of shiny silk suit. For a man he had very soft-looking skin. He wasn't black. He was brown. I guess he was about my color...I noticed his hands, you know. His hands were very soft....When he saw that it was Cabbage, he couldn't believe it....

"Everyone sort of shifted around so that Dr. King could sit in and hear what was going on. He wasn't bitter. In fact, because I say that we were partly to blame, I felt partly responsible for the mood that he was in. You have heard of people talking of men of violence. But this man actually lived and believed nonviolence. This is one of the reasons he looked so soft to me. Because you talk about depressed! He looked as if he was about to cry every time he mentioned it. Not so much 'Why did you have a riot with me leading it?' but 'Why would you resort to violence anyway?' As if to say 'You know that violence hasn't worked for white people. Why would you do that?' The man actually believed in that kind of philosophy....

"I have never seen a man that looked like peace, and that man looked like peace. You know what I mean? I swear he did. I was kind of shocked.

"Dr. King wasn't raising his voice. There was no shouting. The only time Cab shouted was when Abernathy accused the Invaders of being responsible. Then Dr. King said, 'Well, it doesn't matter who was responsible. Lawson and them should have told us. We should have sat down and talked before we had this march. When I come back to the city that's what we're gonna do—sit down and talk. You fellows who have been out here working in this area, you will be in on it. You will not be left out.' ...

"It was unbelievable....Dr. King didn't raise his voice and yet, when he spoke, Cab just didn't have no comebacks for him....I have never seen Cab like he was that day in my life. You can see him talking to a policeman and you say, 'Well, he'll be quiet because that cat will bust him in the head.' But Cab will knock the hell out of him. You know, it just doesn't make any difference to him. But with this man, violence just wouldn't get it. That strong-force approach—you just didn't use it. If you did, you knew where you were going—no place....

"Dr. King just asked, 'What can I do...to have a peaceful march, because you know that I have got to lead one? There is no other way.' Cabbage told him that he didn't know what he had to do, but he said, 'If you're blaming us for it, we won't even participate in your next one. Then see what you get.' But Dr. King wasn't eating that mess up...I felt a little bit ashamed, because if you had known Dr. King before, there was no way in the world you could have made trouble....

"That man, like I said, he was just strange. Nobody can be as peaceful as that man....When he came into the room it seemed like all of a sudden there was a real rush of wind and everything just went out and peace and calm settled over everything....You could feel peace around that man. It was one of the few times in my life when I wasn't actually fighting something....Although we were sitting there talking about the previous day and its events, it was like it never happened. Somebody just woke up and we were talking about it like a psychotherapy session...."

They agreed, said Taylor, that the Invaders would help plan strategy for the next march, and that SCLC would give "financial administrative assistance to help us in our program...because we were working with the poor people." Memphis would also provide some people for the Poor People's Campaign.

"When the meeting broke up, the feeling was great....Dr. King was supposed to call Lawson later that afternoon and tell him that we had a meeting and where they were going to hold another meeting...But King had to leave town...and when he didn't set up the meeting, Cab felt like he ran out on us."

But Dr. King felt that the opening had been made with the young militants, and he was scrupulously careful at a press conference later of local and out-of-town reporters to express his confidence in them.

He left for Atlanta, arriving about suppertime Friday night. Coretta King described him as "sorrowful and disturbed." He was sleepless, wrestling not with the specific Memphis problem but with what he now saw as a massive threat against his whole concept of nonviolence.

He was tired, worn down. National leaders tend to be somewhat protected by their office, presidents and politicians by batteries of aides, others by organization structures. SCLC was not that sort of tight organization, nor were his aides able to cut him off from the masses of people who wanted to reach him. The simple pressure of people had been part of King's life for a decade. Even for an unemotional man—and King was not that—the constant exposure to other people's emotions, their love, hope, fear, hate, despair—their requests and demands— must eventually wear away some inner protection, leaving the momentary feeling of giving so much of oneself that there is nothing left to give. As Christians long have preached, love replenishes love, but that is perceived only by faith and discipline in the darker moments. Dr. King understood this; his own life was not bereft of its dark nights.

Even at home in Atlanta it was hard for him to be alone for any length of time. There were long discussions with Dr. Abernathy that Friday night and early Saturday morning.

There are stories that he disappeared that Saturday, that for a while no one knew where he was, that he sought his own Gethsemane. For if nonviolence failed now, did that mean it had never been the right way and his life an ultimate farce? And what of the people he had led? Did he lead them now into the escalating violence that he abhorred, that was none of his making?

But his Gethsemane, if such it was, was necessarily brief. The SCLC staff and some board members from other cities began meeting that morning at Ebenezer Baptist Church. Before them was placed the question: what should be done about continuing in Memphis in the face of the Poor People's Campaign?

Jesse Epps went over to the meeting from Memphis as a sort of dual representative of the union and COME. He found the SCLC staff "very bewildered and very confused and wasn't sure what it ought to do." They were into Memphis now; they would see it through one more march. The beginning of the Poor People's Campaign could be delayed two weeks to accommodate Memphis. But many staff members thought that Dr. King himself should not go back. "Let some of our staff folk go back in and we can handle it." "Dr. King, you can't go back to Memphis. You know we don't want to get bogged down in a little private fight with a little mayor in Memphis." They also talked about how labor hadn't kept its word in many instances where the civil rights movement was concerned, Epps added.

He did his part. "Dr. King was getting all kinds of bad press, and, like the devil's advocate, I had collected all the newspapers I could which said 'King had run.' ...We knew he didn't run.

But I said to him, 'You're as much stuck in Memphis as we are, and you can't leave Memphis no more than we (in the union) can. And if you do, you're doing in a sense what the press says. You're running.'

"It bothers me even now…because he was a man of courage…I say to myself, 'Maybe if I hadn't of gone, he wouldn't have come back to Memphis.'…But I guess somehow we all sort of chart our own destiny and Dr. King would not have come back if he did not want to come back….But somehow, for ill or for good, I feel that we did have something to do with influencing him to come back to Memphis."

Epps did not. At some point Dr. King had already determined that he personally should return. But he would not do so without the consent and support of SCLC's executive group. Over the day-long discussion, support swung behind him. "The staff finally gave in and said, 'All right. For this one time,' " said Epps. "Dr. King got up and said he was glad the staff had finally agreed…And there was a little prayer meeting in that office.

"And everybody emerged from that meeting in a sort of jubilant way. And I came away saying, 'Mission accomplished. He's coming back!' "

Like King, AFSCME saw beyond Memphis. If King had to come out of Memphis with proof that nonviolence was still valid, AFSCME had to come out with proof that the thousands of low-paid state and municipal workers throughout the South could organize, even under the most recalcitrant of city administrations.

"Either Memphis was the dam or the gate," commented Epps. "And to lose it was not losing it for State-County, but losing it for the whole AFL-CIO in the South. It was going to be difficult for anybody to win any kind of union elections hereafter because Loeb would set the pattern for what ought to be done."

The national publicity now had ended forever any chance that the union could fold its tents and slip quietly away without injuring its efforts elsewhere. Not that Jerry Wurf had any intention of folding his tents. But Memphis officials had been reckoning for some days that the strike was beaten because the drain on the black community both in enthusiasm and economics was just too great to sustain much longer. They were correct about the economic drain. The strike was now costing somewhere around $50,000 a week, an astronomical figure in a low-income black community like Memphis which could raise so little of that amount itself. Ultimately the strike would cost AFSCME about $300,000 in benefits and assistance to the men alone.

"We never knew for sure from one week to the next whether we would be able to sustain these men," admitted P. J. Ciampa. "The mistake we made is that instead of giving a stipend, we started out by saying, 'We will take care of your needs…your basic needs.' Nice and high sounding. 'We'll see that none of your family is hungry. We'll see that you have a roof over your head, that nobody suffers from lack of prescription money or medicine.' And then there started to be evictions and repossessions. Only at the very end of the strike was each man given a weekly forty dollar check."

The striking families, many beset with financial woes before the strike even started, had managed as best they could and had brought their problems to the union. And the ministers associated with COME found themselves functioning almost as social workers. Many of the men were caught between the union and money pressure to return to work or find another job.

One letter received by the union in mid-March showed the struggle:

> Dear Sir:
>
> I am sorry that I cant come to the meeting Because I have to try to get my Rent Paid if I can. I am trying to Borry the money BY Sunday so Monday I can go and Pay My Rent and if I cant get it I will try to Fine me a Job so I can Pay it. I cant give up to wate on the union to help

me…Because I aint working (for the city) and aint gont to
work out untell the strick is over. So will close this letter But
not my love to all and may God Bless All.

Not until the latter part of March did Jerry Wurf, faced with
estimates of more than a quarter of a million dollars if the strike
continued another few weeks, officially turn to other AFSCME
locals for help. "Considerable funds came in from that,"
explains Ciampa. "But we hustled money wherever we could."

Wurf was also getting conflicting advice from his own staff on
the wisdom of continuing the strike. "We're dead. Let's give it
up. People are paying too big a price."

"My position was that we had to go on; there was no way
back," Wurf would say. "Perhaps we should have treated it as
one more wildcat strike and tried to ease our way out of it, but
we hadn't done that…the obligation, in spite of all the suffering
or even because of all the suffering, was such that we couldn't
walk away from it. And I thought we would ultimately reach
some point where we could have an existing union."

But Wurf knew also that he needed additional massive
financial help from outside Memphis and outside of the international union. In Washington on March 28 (where he had
been when the march broke up), he found it in George Meany,
head of the international AFL-CIO. Meany would be met with
Memphis everywhere those few days. But first Meany would talk
to Wurf. They were unlike, these two. If the old plumber
Meany represented the massive establishment of organized
labor, Wurf still represented, as he had done in the AFSCME
takeover, the Young Turks. Meany, old now, conservative
within the union grouping, hawkish on Vietnam, was already
moving away from the strike as a weapon, and Wurf was
strongly advocating it and this was the least of their disagree-
ments over the aims and tactics of unionism.

"Nevertheless," said Wurf, "the thing is that Meany understood the nature of this beef, made a donation of twenty
thousand dollars or something like that—and did this very

important thing—sent out a letter over his signature to every union in America to give us money."

Such letters go out infrequently, perhaps two or three times a year, from the top AFL-CIO leadership endorsing strikes the AFL-CIO considers legitimate and worthy of and needing aid from all organized labor, and unions across the country respond.

Funds would not reach Memphis immediately, but at last there was a potential financial backup upon which Local 1733 could depend. With it, Wurf, despite the march disaster, was prepared to go on indefinitely.

While meetings went on in all sorts of high places, down at the union hall and at Clayborn Temple the strikers gathered again for their daily meeting and marches. Rev. Dick Wells and several other white ministers joined with them, following the pledge Wells had made the day before in the middle of the march breakup. "The one thing we do, we go back to the union hall tomorrow."

As they moved up the side aisle in Firestone Hall, the "garbagemen saw us. They began to stand in silence…By the time we got to the platform everyone was standing in silence. We had come back in the midst of their defeat, or our defeat….Sure, there was something of paternalism—here's the great white man who's come down. No doubt about that. It was difficult to try and overcome that…All you could do was to be with them and shake hands."

Police allowed the community march that day only on condition that it was restricted to four hundred public works employees and their adult supporters. Young people were weeded out. As the marchers walked quietly up to City Hall and back, led by Chief Lux, Baxton Bryant, and Rev. Ralph Jackson, four armored personnel carriers with mounted machine guns and two truckloads of riflemen with bayonets fixed flanked them along Pontotoc and up Main. Beale Street was blocked by a line of Guardsmen with rifles at ready. Behind them on Beale prints of the rubber-cleated tracks of the personnel carriers were visible in the warm asphalt. During the next day's march, the personnel carriers were left behind and Guardsmen at Beale held their bayonet rifles down at port arms, a sign that tension was easing.

It was raining that Sunday, March 31, Passion Sunday, as Guardsmen patrolled the streets and ministers stood in their pulpits and spoke to their people.

All denounced violence. Some affixed blame one place or another. And the prayers went up for reconciliation, as if God would do what his people could or would not. Dean William Dimmick, with candles burning on the high altar of St. Mary's Episcopal Cathedral, spoke for many of the clergy who had tried to stop the turbulence from reaching this point:

"We can weep for ourselves, for each other, and for our city. But we cannot weep forever. There comes the time when we must pick up the pieces and begin to make this city the City of Good Abode for all the people who live here....In the anxious days of the immediate past and even last night under the shadow of the guards I found men and women—white and black—who reached out in love for a new life for all of us...St. Paul made clear that until men learned to accept each other, they had not learned Christ. Nor have we. But we still may...."

But we still may....

In the rain outside of Parkway Gardens Presbyterian Church, Rev. Darrell Doughty, white, wearing his Sunday suit, labored to change a tire on his car. Protecting him with an umbrella from the rain stood a church elder, black, wearing his Sunday suit. Modean Thompson, black, wrote a letter to all the women, white, she had grown to know at the Rearing Children of Good Will workshop. "Perhaps we can find in each other some hope..." Another of the workshop participants, white, reported, "The first phone call I got after being caught in the march breakup was from a black lady I'd met. She wanted to make sure I was okay."

The pain was on all of them, black and white, who had fumbled in the miasma of racial prejudice and confused solution, who even now could not clearly break through to one another.

The strange, passing ties. There were women who paid their maids a dollar an hour, yet who called to offer their employees' entire families sanctuary in their East Memphis homes if they were frightened in their own neighborhoods.

No longer enough to build on. Not now. Yet a sub-strata that somehow even in failing continued to testify to possibility.

Dr. King preached that Sunday night at the National Cathedral in Washington, invited by that church's own clergy to explain the objectives of the Poor People's Campaign. The crowd, overflowing the splendid Gothic cathedral, heard again the resonant call for justice and brotherhood and the raising of the dark vision of a country torn apart if it still failed to respond to the cry of the poor and hurt.

President Lyndon Johnson that same night, with 510,000 American troops in Vietnam, came before a national radio and television audience to announce that he would not be a candidate again for president. His near-defeat in the New Hampshire presidential primary earlier that month by opponents of the Vietnam War, galvanized into united action by the candidacy of Sen. Eugene McCarthy, and then the entry into the race of Bobby Kennedy, bearing with him all the nostalgic longings and unmet hopes of the years of John F. Kennedy, signaled a Democratic Party that was falling into chaos. And Lyndon Johnson withdrew. The high hopes of an America with no poverty, no war, no hate, were falling back, overwhelmed by violence at home and in Vietnam, in a disorganized retreat whose full extent, mercifully, was not fully visible.

Jericho Road

12

> *"The Jericho Road is a dangerous road."*
> *Martin Luther King, Jr.*

That weekend Rev. James Jordan had a dream. It was understandable. His church, Beale Street Baptist, had been in the center of the disturbance area, which was enough to upset anyone's equilibrium, and Rev. Jordan was a believer in dreams and prophecies even in the best of times. And from that first meeting with white ministers in February leading to the St. Mary's talks, he had been absorbed in the strike effort.

Now he received a phone call from a man who refused to identify himself, but who expressed fears for Dr. King's life if he returned to Memphis. Rev. Jordan tended to dismiss the call, not sure if it had been made out of concern or mischief.

"That night I went to bed early…and I woke up between 2:00 and 2:30 A.M. twice. The first time I woke up I was crying, just crying for no reason at all. I woke myself up crying. I got up and I said, 'Lord, what is this?' I sat on the side of the bed. And I thought about my wife who was visiting in Atlanta. I went back to sleep and woke up again doing the same thing. I said, 'Lord, what is this?' Dr. King's picture came before me just as big. And so I saw the Lord had shown me Dr. King's death."

The dream would have been forgotten except he took it with him the next day to a meeting of black clergy and later to a much larger group that included several of the SCLC leaders who were by now in Memphis. "I told them I had had this happening, that the Lord had shown this, and that I feared for Dr. King's life....I asked, couldn't we let Dr. King stay out of town, and solve this ourselves, because I feared for his life....Can't he give us instructions from Atlanta?"

Response was what might be expected. "This big fellow, big dark fellow, beard...he said, 'You don't have to worry about any white people doing anything to Dr. King. That cat's safe around them. When he gets it, it'll be from some black!' " related Rev. Jordan. "And Jim Bevel said, 'Dr. King's great because he's brave. If there was a man across the street with a gun and hollered out a window, "I'm gonna kill King," and if Dr. King was on his way and we called him and said, "Doc, don't come cause there's a man across the street says he's gonna kill you," you think he would stop? He would come on anyhow.' ...So that was that," concluded Rev. Jordan.

"He was sincerely disturbed," related Maxine Smith, who was at the meeting. "To say to this group 'Do you have to march?' was pretty ridiculous because to this group the march was the thing. He was bluntly answered, and I felt a little sorry for him. I felt we had to march, too...I was trying to say to Rev. Jordan that if someone's going to get you, I don't think they're going to call and tell you. I was trying to comfort him, not to be as blunt as some of the others."

It was easy enough to put down Rev. Jordan's fears. Dreams come and go in the night, substantial only to those who dream them. But concern such as that expressed by Rev. Kyles had to be dealt with. "I said I am not prepared to lead women and children...out into a group like that again unless I am convinced that black people are together...unless I am convinced that militants and everybody else mean for us to have a peaceful march."

Obviously what was necessary to bring about public confidence in a new march was a public reuniting of all forces across the black community.

Dr. King was still in Atlanta, but by the first of the week SCLC staff were in Memphis, among them ministers James Bevel, Jesse Jackson of Chicago's Operation Breadbasket, James Orange, and Hosea Williams, all veterans of SCLC organizing. "They were a nice bunch of people, but they were arrogant beyond belief," said one of the local union representatives working with them. The SCLC staff were professionals. They did know a great deal about organizing, and local people did tend to rely on their experience and judgments, regarding SCLC as a sort of *deus ex machina*.

The immediate aim was to see that the next march was successful and that Dr. King would move smoothly through Memphis. Meetings began to try to reach the young militants.

"The fact was pointed out that there were other elements that had to be included," noted Bobby Doctor, of the civil rights commission, who was helping with the meetings. "There were the boys off Beale Street, the prostitutes, the pimps, the hustlers. It was suggested that Dr. King go into the Beale Street area, in the pool halls and the barber shops, and talk to them there and try to solicit their support."

By midweek some progress had been made, the BOP/ Invaders preparing to cooperate but still seeking some leverage within the situation that would bring prestige and SCLC support for their own specific program.

The march was definitely set for the following Monday, April 8. In New York, Bayard Rustin and Victor Gotbaum, the executive director of District Council 37 of AFSCME, announced they would come to Memphis and bring six thousand union members from across the country. Rustin also offered his personal services in helping organize the upcoming demonstrations as he had done the giant march on Washington in 1963. Other labor and civil rights groups were announcing their support.

The strikers continued to trudge up Main Street and back.

Larry Payne was buried that Tuesday in an intermittent rain

which turned the new gravesite into mud. As there had been confusion over his death, so there was confusion over his funeral. Originally to have been held in his father's church, services were finally held in Clayborn Temple because, said Rev. Harold Middlebrook, "We really felt his death was related to the movement."

Grief broke out at the end of the funeral. "They shot you down like a dog," Mrs. Payne was heard to cry. Several teen-age girls fainted passing the open casket. Like green grass that grows and is cut down before it is tall was the boy, the pastor said. No matter now how he died or how his name would be used. He was sixteen years old and dead. In the rain, those who had known him walked away from the grave.

Mayor Loeb announced the end of the curfew on Monday. Units of the National Guard gradually began pulling out. Little black kids, who had circled them warily at shopping centers, parks, attracted by the helmets, boots, the weapons, until their mothers hustled them away, saw them go with regret. Local units were the last to be released and members of the Memphis Guard finally got home in time for dinner on Wednesday.

But with the forthcoming King march, "We were definitely told not to stow ourselves away, to be ready...we were prepared to be called again," said Guardsman McGinnis. Officials reported the force could be activated again within hours if necessary.

Sheriff's deputies and state highway patrolmen were also gone, and the county court, with little discussion, voted $46,000 to the county sheriff for new riot control equipment.

The Memphis Police Department remained on emergency status. "We don't know when we'll be able to return to normal operations," said Commissioner Holloman. The one cheerful note around the police department was that routine daily crime was off dramatically. The whole scene, curfew, Guard, police saturation, was just too much for the petty crooks to cope with.

Business was off downtown. Councilman Philip Perel, from his Main Street jewelry shop, reported that business had been off at least twenty-five percent before the most recent disturbances. Attorney Thomas F. Turley, Jr., in a letter to the mayor and city council urging them to break the strike by hiring replacement workers, estimated downtown retail trade had been off by forty-five percent for the past few weeks. Easter was only two weeks away, and to have the peak of the spring buying season muddled by marches and demonstrations put great strain on the places of business, especially those with no suburban outlets to take up the slack.

Yet the business community had continued public support for the mayor. It was, then, with some surprise that slippage among the city's smaller businessmen was noted. The heads of a television service operation and of a sewing appliances center came to the city council meeting on Tuesday, April 2, to say that their own businesses were hurting and that many more small businessmen were facing the same problem.

"But if we give in on this, where are you going to draw the line?" asked Councilman Chandler. "Mr. Chandler," answered the owner of the appliances center, "we have just about reached the line…We are not big businessmen like Mr. Pryor or Mr. James. I had salesmen who had to go home the other night without paychecks. If I could find a way to sell my business and leave Memphis, I would do it."

"I can remember very well telling Loeb that—as normal political judgment—you can count on the businessman till his profit column begins to be hurt and then you've got to watch out for him because he'll turn on you. And the first crack in that element was, of course, the downtown merchants…the boycott had cut them up," said Ned Cook.

The city council, however, contented itself with passing another resolution, at the private urging of mediator Frank Miles, calling for the immediate resumption of mediation talks. The council also had other things on its mind, among them whether the east-west interstate could be built through the city's large and lovely Overton Park.

But there were unquiet thoughts. Plans for the Cotton

Carnival in May, the city's great tourist-attracting celebration of King Cotton, were rolling along. But parades and street carnivals, even the parties of the secret societies, could hardly be enjoyed if the racially tense atmosphere continued to lie over the city. Suppose someone tried to disrupt the Cotton Carnival? When was the damn strike going to end?

Galvanized by the rioting and the prospect of Dr. King's return, there were new attempts to bring about meetings of community leaders. The old Memphis Committee on Community Relations made its first public utterance of the strike, calling on all parties to return to negotiating, but MCCR as a body had waited too long to be effective. Auto dealer John T. Fisher was trying, with no success, to set up a personal meeting between Mayor Loeb and Rev. Lawson.

The regular monthly meeting of the ministers association recommended a summit meeting of bishops, senior clergy, and leading citizens. But the white and black ministers themselves had not yet been able to get together—an ill omen for expanding peacemaking—so a smaller meeting was planned for two days later to iron out details.

Tommy Powell, president of the AFL-CIO labor council, was inviting some thirty business, civic, and religious leaders to a meeting with labor leaders to be held that Thursday, April 4, and John Spence, of the civil rights commission, was into more elaborate preparations. Special delivery letters went out to twenty-five business and civic leaders inviting them to a series of small discussion groups to be held April 5 and 6, each to also be attended by "responsible leaders" of the union, the black churches, business and education, and each staffed by a member of the commission. The meetings were to be kept confidential. There was a lot of duplication on Powell and Spence's lists. The chamber of commerce, Future Memphis, Inc., and the Downtown Association had just issued a joint call for the city to stop mass demonstrations that might endanger life or property.

Frank Miles, meanwhile, was preparing to get the mediation sessions between city and union representatives going again.

His feeling was that both sides were now ready, that casual willingness to meet had become real desire. He was also picking up a hint here and there that the city's opposition to dues deduction through the credit union might be softening.

But he ran into unexpected difficulties with AFSCME president Jerry Wurf. Wurf wanted to be at the meetings, and Miles thought he should be, but when they talked, Wurf was leaving for the airport. Miles was a little disturbed. "He's needing to go to Chicago and he has a commitment in Iowa of some kind to speak before a teachers' convention or something…he was sort of putting me off." But Wurf assured him that he and the union committee would be ready to talk on Friday, so the next mediation session was scheduled for April 5.

Miles would have been more disturbed at that point if he had known that the union was setting in motion a plan to circumvent the mediation sessions, for some of the union representatives privately were now convinced that the city would not bargain in good faith and that future meetings would be futile. With public pressure as great as it was, neither side could afford to break off mediation permanently. The mediation strategy would have to be played out, but meanwhile the union was casting around for some other opening.

On Monday afternoon, April 1, Marx Borod, an attorney who specialized in labor law, whose reputation was that of a conservative, and whose clients were management, received a call from union representative P. J. Ciampa. The union's attorney, Anthony Sabella, had suggested Borod might act as an intermediary in settling the strike and union officials wanted to talk with him, said Ciampa. Borod was surprised. While he handled labor law matters, his clients invariably were employers, he told Ciampa, and he was in no position to represent AFSCME. However, he added, he would as a private citizen be willing to help because the strike was a matter of public interest, as long as it was understood there would be no lawyer-client relationship.

He met with Ciampa and Bill Lucy about a half-hour later at The Peabody hotel where they gave him the list of demands and copies of their membership agreement and checkoff authorization forms, and filled him in on the strike background as they saw it. Borod suggested that a much more limited meeting than the existing Miles' mediation committee, perhaps with two city and two union representatives, be set up. But first, he said, he must have some encouragement from Mayor Loeb to proceed.

He couldn't reach Loeb, but late the next afternoon Myron Halle, Jr., one of the city attorneys on the mediation team, returned his call. Halle flatly rejected Borod's proposal. "We've won the strike. Nothing more needs to be done." Borod was irritated. "I observed that I did not agree with him, that the community was being torn up, and that unless a more realistic attitude was taken in this matter, we were in for a lot of trouble. I also observed that Mr. Halle was obviously living in a fool's paradise."

Shortly afterwards, Loeb also called. He wasn't buying any new plan. But later that evening at home Borod got another call from Loeb in which he explained his stand on the dues checkoff and, while still refusing any go-ahead, he did give Borod his private phone number.

Borod took this as at least a glimmer of encouragement and set up another meeting with the union people. He also obtained material on the present civil service procedures and coverage and on the format of the unclassified credit union. Then he began hammering out a union proposal covering everything except wages, feeling that the wage settlement probably could be made on the mayor's terms.

Borod's proposed settlement called for agreement by the city that employees could make arrangements with the unclassified credit union to pay union dues: in effect, the dues checkoff. It also called for Local 1733, AFSCME, to negotiate to resolve problems relating to wages, hours and conditions of employment for certain classifications of employees in the public works department: in effect, union recognition; and it spelled out a grievance procedure. There was a guarantee against any union member being fired as a result of participation in the strike,

although Borod was careful to state that this protection did not
give the employee immunity for any violation of law.

The few city officials who knew what Borod was doing simply
averted their eyes. Borod was on his own.[1]

The city legal staff was concentrating on blocking the next
march. "We were trying to stop the parade," explained Memphis City Attorney Frank Gianotti. "But the right to assemble
and the right to speak are part of our fundamental rights and
whenever you want to move in on them you must go very
slowly. You don't just barge in....The basis of our bill was that
we were obligated to protect the rights of merchants and other
people who were being subjected to all the turmoil and
everything." The city lawyers decided to move in federal rather
than local court because they believed the SCLC leaders would
be more responsive to federal court directives.

On Wednesday morning, April 3, Gianotti appeared in the
U. S. District Court, Judge Bailey Brown sitting, with a bill of
complaint asking for a temporary restraining order against
out-of-state residents Dr. King, Ralph Abernathy, Hosea
Williams, James Bevel, James Orange, and Bernard Lee and
their "servants, agents, employees and those in concert with
them from organizing in or engaging in a massive parade or
march in the city of Memphis." This action was asked only
against nonresidents.

They hoped the march to be led by Dr. King would be stopped
altogether, but if it could be merely postponed there was a belief
that momentum for it would die. And if not stopped, at least the
court might set restrictions and controls.

City lawyers Gianotti, James Manire, E. Brady Bartusch, and
Frierson Graves requested the restraining order be issued at
once.

At the same time Judge Brown was hearing the petition,
attorney Walter Bailey over in his law office was taking a call from
the NAACP Legal Defense Fund in New York which asked the
local integrated firm headed by Louis Lucas to get onto the
injunction case immediately and to stay with it. Bailey and Lucas

immediately headed for the Federal Building.

Judge Brown did issue the temporary restraining order, limited to ten days. He would, however, he told the defense attorneys, stand by to hear their motion to dissolve the order upon an hour's notice.

At about the same time, attorney Lucius Burch was brought into the case. He had received a call from Rev. Lawson earlier that morning which requested he appear in court to represent King on behalf of COME. Almost simultaneously he had a call from Atlanta from the American Civil Liberties Union, which he had long supported, asking him to represent King. "To be perfectly frank," said Burch, "as I was with Rev. Lawson, I wished at that time he had gone anywhere else in the city of Memphis rather than to call me because it did involve a great deal of unpleasantness as the thing went along and subsequently, too...."

"My clientele is mostly composed of fairly responsible business people, business organizations....This was not the sort of thing they like to see their lawyer engaged in. Then, too, there is a very large and active reactionary group here, and aside from the irritation that they give you by calling up saying they are going to burn your house and kidnap your children and shoot you and all that sort of stuff which is of no consequence, you never know when you are going to get one of those people on a jury....Anybody would not be very intelligent at least if they didn't think about those sort of things. And I assure you that I did think about them."

And although he had known and respected Rev. Lawson for some time, he, too, had heard all the stories about Lawson, "that he's been to Vietnam or Poland or some place and that the FBI thinks he's a Communist and all that sort of junk...so that I thought I ought not to rely entirely on what he told me." He needed to talk to King personally.

Wednesday, April 3, was unseasonably warm and skittishly cloudy with showers heading in. Dr. King was again late. The flight from Atlanta had been delayed in takeoff while baggage was checked for bombs, threatened by an anonymous caller. He was met at the airport by Jesse Epps, and driven straight to Rev. Lawson's church on McLemore street.

Here were converging a large group of people closely connected with the new march, including the SCLC staff, union men, a group of ministers with whom King was to meet, lawyers Lucas and Bailey, as well as reporters and police. County human relations director Jerry Fanion was immeasurably relieved to spot the police. A day or so before, Commissioner Holloman had gotten in touch with Fanion to request that he be told when Dr. King was returning. "He said, 'We have gotten some threats that he is going to be killed if he comes back to Memphis,'" Fanion reported. Now, as he cut across the church parking lot, Fanion saw Inspector Joe Gagliano and knew there must be unmarked police cars in the area. "I was very happy to see that...even though King wouldn't want this....There were police around. I saw them."

The police were extremely uneasy about protection for Dr. King. The tempo and volume of threats against him were increasing, and there was little or no official cooperation from the SCLC staff. Dr. King did not want to be surrounded by police. "In part, it's got to be the way King wanted to live...rather than behind the steel plate, and you can't fault him for that," mused one observer.

"He wasn't the kind just to play and flirt with death," explained Rev. Kyles. "But, by the same token, he wouldn't try to live secretively. There were always threats. He lived with it."

Nonetheless, Dr. King's calm did not carry over to all of those who knew him and it certainly did not carry over to the uniformed police and plain-clothes men who were assigned to him in Memphis. They were to protect him—and to keep reports on where he went and to whom he talked for inclusion in the unending intelligence files, his supporters charged—but they had to carry out their task from a distance, following, squinting, getting information on his coming and going from peripheral sources.

Among the routine and unimaginative threats coming in was
one down at the *Commercial Appeal* office where a quarter-
page ad was accepted, paid for in cash, and scheduled to run the
morning of April 4. It included the old photo of Dr. King at a
meeting at the Highlander Folk School, a picture that had been
making the rounds of the South for a decade to prove his
Communist connections, with inflammatory headline and copy.
When advertising manager Jim Cherry saw it, he refused to run
it, despite the threat of "Don't be surprised if something
happens to the newspaper office and you."[2]

Dr. King went into one of the church halls, a big, barren room
with folding chairs. He spoke briefly and quietly to his fellow
ministers, emphasizing again the need for unity in the march,
and Jesse Jackson followed with an enthusiastic description of
Operation Breadbasket. Reporters got a few quotes. "We are
not going to be stopped by Mace or injunctions," said Dr. King,
adding that "We stand on the First Amendment. In the past on
the basis of conscience we have had to break injunctions and if
necessary we may do it (in Memphis). We'll cross that bridge
when we come to it."

He then went immediately into Lawson's office to meet with
attorneys Lucas and Bailey who brought him up-to-date on the
restraining order. Lucas then telephoned to inform federal
marshals where they could find Dr. King and serve the injunction. "He agreed to stay around a few minutes to give the
marshals time enough to get there," said Bailey. "However,
there was some delay....Dr. King had another meeting later and
he and Dr. Abernathy wanted to eat. They told us that they were
going to the Lorraine and eat....

"King, of course, had anticipated the injunction. He was a
man of great humility and he was very professional in his
approach to problems...he'd been through this before."

Burch and three younger lawyers from his firm, David
Caywood, Michael Cody, and Charles Newman, missed meeting King at the church by a few minutes, but they stayed to

confer with Bailey and Lucas to determine initial legal strategy.
They agreed to join forces and as a group represent all the parties
involved, Dr. King, SCLC, COME, the ACLU, and the
NAACP Legal Defense Fund. Then they, too, drove over to the
Lorraine Motel. "There were plenty of policemen around,"
Caywood observed as he saw them sitting in parked cars in the
streets around the Lorraine.

The Lorraine Motel was a two-story, cinder-block complex at
406 Mulberry, set in the shabby warehouse, garage, and
rooming house section just five blocks south of Beale Street and
a block east of Main. It was black-owned and black-operated,
and before integration had served as the stopping place of black
church notables, gospel and jazz musicians, and businessmen
who came through the city. It was the grand functioning dream
of Walter (Bill) Bailey (no relation to the attorney) and his wife
Lorraine—he had named it after her. They had scrabbled to
finance it and keep it going since 1955 when they had first taken
over the existing fourteen room structure, sprucing it up and
adding nearly fifty new units and a swimming pool.

Bill and Lorraine Bailey had begun inn-keeping by renting
rooms for seventy-five cents a night in a rooming house on
nearby Vance. "We were trying to go places," said Bailey. "She
(Mrs. Bailey) would get up in the morning with me if I needed
her. She would stay up until seven o'clock the next morning and
get right back up at eight. We cooked together. We washed
dishes together. We did everything together...She was always
saying, 'We gotta be there to fix this hamburger. We gotta be
there to wash the linen. We gotta be there to watch the money.'"

"This is a family motel," Bill Bailey would say proudly.
"People felt they was at home. They would come back in the
kitchen. They could pick their own room to stay in." He and
Lorraine Bailey were still doing much of the work around the
place themselves; they specialized in "home cooked food" and
business was good.

Dr. King had stayed at the Lorraine several times before, the last in mid-March. This trip he had Room 306 on the second floor, a fact casually made known to anyone watching the television newscast that evening on Channel 5, as the cameraman caught him entering the clearly marked doorway of the room from the balcony. After that telecast there was some talk that perhaps his room should be changed, but no one got around to it. His balcony looked over the combination parking lot and courtyard, the small empty swimming pool, and over the high block wall surrounding the complex, across Mulberry to a grassy rise and the rear of a few shabby buildings that fronted on Main. The Lorraine was conveniently located, within walking distance of Clayborn Temple, a short ride to Mason Temple, an easy gathering place for those in the movement. And for thirteen dollars a night, no one bothered about the view.

There was a hominess about the place. Dr. King was with friends. His SCLC aides had rooms there. James Laue, a representative of the community relations division of the Justice Department and a long-time acquaintance, had checked in. So had television cameraman Joe Lowe who was working on a Public Broadcasting System documentary on preparations for the Poor People's Campaign and had been traveling with King since January. Bill Bailey and his wife were glad to welcome King back. Everywhere were smiles and handshakes.

Dr. King was eating in the motel dining room with a group of young blacks when the lawyers arrived. The marshals had also found him there and he had walked out onto the driveway to meet them, listen politely and accept the injunction. His codefendants had also been notified.

The lawyers met with him in his room. "He was introduced to Burch and the others," said attorney Bailey. "Burch was very direct with it. We other lawyers just sort of took back seats to Burch's forwardness…He just said, 'Dr. King, I'm going to get right to the point….We want to assure you that we are going to give you the best representation that we can possibly muster. Now I want to ask a few questions and find out a few things.'...Abernathy had come up with fish or chicken on a paper plate and he was still eating...It was very informal."

"I hadn't met Dr. King before," said Burch. "The substance of my conversation was to check out from him personally the things that I had heard about and I believed about the nonviolent nature of his objectives....These assurances were not legally necessary....I wanted to be sure myself that these people were what they purported to be....

"Dr. King made it very clear to me that his *whole* future depended on having a nonviolent march in Memphis. He represented the riot as a complete fiasco as far as he was concerned, that it was the result of poor planning, and he wasn't reluctant about laying the blame on the people here in Memphis....He was simple and seemed to be straightforward.

"About this time I began to get more closely thrown with Andrew Young who, in my opinion formed at that time, is one of the ablest young men in this country....Young completely assured me that it (the march)...was just exactly what it was represented to be—the right of those people to express by assembly and petition and demonstration what they felt was a just grievance. And so after that I had no second thoughts or looking back....The white community didn't realize that Martin Luther King was the best friend anybody had. He was the answer to the fire bombing and he was the answer to the looting and he was the answer to Black Power."

"I think," said Bailey, "that Burch asked indirectly if the injunction were not lifted, would Dr. King march anyway, and I think Dr. King said yes, he would." But King was ready to leave the legal case in the hands of his lawyers, and he had immediately liked and put confidence in Lucius Burch, so the lawyers adjourned to Burch's law office. Late that afternoon they met with Judge Bailey Brown and the city attorneys in the Judge's chambers and a hearing on the injunction was set for the next morning.

Now the backstage legal maneuvering to reach some accommodation about the march began. It was evident to all the

attorneys that, based on past court decisions, the march probably would be allowed. The teams of lawyers thought "something could be worked out about the march," said Bailey,
although the city lawyers didn't want to put themselves on the
spot by agreeing and King's lawyers aimed their legal research
at getting the injunction lifted.

King's lawyers worked in Burch's office throughout the
evening. They decided Rev. Andrew Young would testify for
SCLC and Rev. Lawson for COME. It was 3:00 A.M. Thursday
morning when they straggled home, "except for Burch," said
Bailey. "I think he slept in his office."

Still, there were hints of uncertainty about the wider course
King was following. With Lyndon Johnson's withdrawal from
the presidential race had come renewed pressure to hold up on
the Poor People's Campaign, to see in which direction the
Democratic Party would now move on the war and social and
economic issues. Might there not be a chance that Bobby
Kennedy could accomplish their objectives, and that the Poor
People's Campaign would only aid Richard Nixon, already the
Republicans' clear-cut choice of a candidate? Could even the
march for public works employees in Memphis be backed away
from if there were any assurances that the strike could be settled?
King did not, after all, have to march in Memphis if the simple
threat of his marching looked as if it might bring a settlement.
Or did he?

That same Wednesday morning in Washington, Congressman Dan Kuykendall got a call from the minorities division of
the Republican National Committee. King's people wanted a
face-saving way out of Memphis, Kuykendall was told. Would
he be willing to meet with someone to discuss that? The next call
on the matter was to come April 5.

In Memphis mediator Frank Miles got a call that Wednesday
afternoon from Tom Robinson, the U. S. district attorney, who
informed him that a representative of U. S. Attorney General
Ramsey Clark was then in his office, that he had talked to the

union and that he was "kind of considering going over and talking to the mayor." The justice department was concerned that the next march and confrontation would set off violence. They felt if the strike could be settled, "the whole thing would just…wash itself out," said Miles. But Ramsey Clark's man was trying to move tactfully and he was wondering if a talk with the mayor might help the whole situation. "My immediate reaction," related Miles, "was that it was not going to help and that the only thing it would do would be probably hurt the image of the attorney general's office."

Later that evening at home in his bedroom, Miles received another call from a friend suggesting that Miles and a representative of the community relations division of the justice department needed to talk to each other. There was a feeling around, the caller said, that King might decide not to march if he could have any assurances that Miles' mediation might resolve the dispute.

A short time later the community relations division representative himself called. Dr. King was uneasy about the whole situation, he told Miles. He would rather retire from it if there was a good chance the strike could be settled. Miles was somewhat incredulous. "I don't see how, in God's name, Dr. King could ever back away from this situation gracefully or any other way." No, the man assured him, he knew what he was talking about. He could almost write the script of what would be said. He wanted to arrange a meeting between Miles and Dr. King's people the next day, maybe in the evening. Still dubious, Miles agreed and went on to bed.

Rev. Frank McRae had lunch with the mayor in his office that same day. Known among the strike-concerned ministers as Loeb's friend, McRae did not defend his actions as mayor but he did defend Henry Loeb the man, and it was of great sadness to him that others could not make this distinction. "Henry Loeb would have felt exactly the same way if the union had been ninety-seven percent white and three percent black. I did not feel from beginning to end that Henry's attitude had anything to do with a racial question. Henry Loeb is not that kind of a man!"

He and Henry lunched with the police guards. "The people surrounding the mayor were all saying basically the same thing to him. 'Mr. Mayor, everything's under control. We have no worry, no fear; there's nothing to really get excited about.' But I'd been to Clayborn Temple and seen the spirit. I'd been with the union. And everyone was saying to Henry, 'Henry, boy, don't give up the ship. You're doing a great job.' And I kept saying, 'Henry, you're sitting on a powder keg. Please realize this.'

"But I didn't feel Henry really heard this. He heard—maybe what he wanted to hear. He heard what the people there were telling him. Everything was breezing along at City Hall. It was business as usual."

Over at St. Mary's Episcopal Cathedral the long-postponed meeting between black and white clergy was finally getting underway. McRae came to it after lunching with the mayor. It had been hoped by the planners that this would be a frank gathering and that some sort of reconciliation between the black and white communities might be achieved through the clergy. Perhaps the ministers believed this was still possible. Certainly many of the white ministers did. But by the end of that abrasive meeting, few had any illusions left.

"It was unbelievable, unbelievable," said one minister of that meeting. "Rabbi Wax got up, opened the meeting, and said, 'I think we ought to limit this discussion to try to find out what the issues are.' And Ralph Jackson came unwound...He jumped up and said, 'You've tricked me! I thought at long last my white brothers had decided to help their poor black brothers. You not only tricked me, you insult me by saying what we're going to discuss is what the issues are. Why, hell, while you have sat on your [backsides] and not done a damn thing, we've had thirteen hundred starving families. That's the issue...And then...you call me over here and ask what the issues are!'"

"The atmosphere...you could just cut it. And finally Ralph, when he quit, said 'Damn you!' and headed for the door. Someone caught him. And he stayed.

"Then one of the old saints, an old Christian minister who's been here for years, got up and said, 'Now, my dear brethren, we've got to be Christian about this. We must love. If our nigra brethren...' And when he said this Zeke Bell jumped up and said 'You're an old man and you ought to know better. You've got an education. The word N-E-G-R-O is not nigra, it's knee-grow...You ministers talk about love, and black people can't even get in the doors of your churches!'

"And this poor old man's chin was just trembling, and he said, 'Forgive me, brethren!' Then a few other ministers got up and said something, then a few others...Oh, my God!'"

To Father Greenspun, this scene of ministers baring their souls and other ministers beating them down was "awful."

"Then," said the first minister, "Frank McRae got up and said, 'I propose we get up and march to City Hall. That, first, we go tell the mayor what we think and, second, that we do it in the language that our black brothers can understand—the language of marching. We have no strategy of our own, so I feel we should accept the strategy of our black brethren—to take decisive action to pressure the mayor. The mayor is a man I trust. He'll receive you gladly.' "

"I felt," said McRae himself in retrospect, "Henry needed this from the men who were in the group."

"And listen," continued the first minister, "his idea just caught on. I thought we were gone. I was shocked, surprised! There was some discussion. Here, suddenly, you see the Church at its worst and best...One of the high moments was Frank McRae's proposal—just laying his ministry and his friendship for the mayor on the line. I know Methodists here and I know how radical that would have been for them.

"Then here's this other brother—'Now, brethren, I'm for this, but there are grave questions to consider here. Do you realize that the mayor's office is the highest office that we have in our power to confer upon one of our citizens? And what we do to this office, we do to ourselves. And I do not think that it is proper or right—and I'm for marching—to go to the mayor's office without first calling and making an appointment!' "

"And did you know that a lot of the other brethren had been looking for a hole to crawl in. This gave them a chance…and they decided to do it Friday and they'd get a bigger crowd!"

Father Greenspun was again a little more succinct. "As soon as a march was suggested, some white ministers began leaving the room like rats off a sinking ship."

"So I have the feeling…in this power-charged meeting, that if they had gone over that afternoon and had been as close and talked to Loeb, I think it would have been like throwing a stick of dynamite in his office," concluded the first minister.

In retrospect Frank McRae wished that they had gone quietly that afternoon to say to the mayor, "This is what we believe." But it was decided that the ministers would meet again the next morning, this time in a black church, to make further plans for a march to the mayor's office.

That night Rev. McRae called the mayor to tell him of the proposed visit on Friday. "Henry said, 'Fine. Be glad to see you, Frank, but you're going to waste your time and all you're going to do is get yourselves in trouble with your congregations, and you're going to be misunderstood. And you're not going to change my mind one way or another. I know how I feel.' I said, 'Well, that's fine, but I think we need to say to this community that we as ministers have this concern.' So Henry said, 'Fine. Be glad to see you.' "

By early that evening storms were rolling and tossing across the city, piles of white-streaked gray and purple clouds, storm light deepening the green of grass and shrubs, then heavy sullen blackness. Thunder could be heard off to the west, down the bluff, across the river, the first rain running ahead of the lightening, the muggy constricting air beginning to loosen and cool.

The crowd that had come to hear Dr. King speak was heavy with public works men, shaking water off their jackets, looking sparse in the vastness of Mason Temple as they arranged themselves in the center seats up near the platform. Three thousand people, at most, had come out into the storm. On the platform preachers and union people conferred, and as Dr. Ralph Abernathy entered the side door of the auditorium and was recognized, applause began as the audience searched for Dr. King behind him. But they could not find him, and the applause trailed off on a puzzled note.

Abernathy was alone. Dr. King was tired. He wanted to stay at the motel and rest, talk to a few people, and since the storm seemed to presage a scanty crowd, Rev. Abernathy was dispatched to fill in with the main speech. "But he never even started to speak," said Rev. Middlebrook. "He just looked at the crowd." Ralph Abernathy had been number two man for a long time, "and I had sense enough to know that this was not my crowd." Where was the phone? he asked Middlebrook, and the two of them made their way around the side of the auditorium to the telephone in the vestibule. "When he called Dr. King," said Middlebrook, "he told him, 'Your people are here and you ought to come and talk to them. This isn't my crowd. It's your crowd. I can look at them and tell you. They didn't come tonight just to hear Abernathy. They came tonight in this storm to hear King.'

"Abernathy related, 'He said, "I'll do whatever you say. If you say come, I will be there." I said, "Come." ' "

While they waited for Dr. King, other ministers stepped into the pulpit to speak. "There were a couple of times when there was quite a clap of thunder and wind and rain. As I stood in the pulpit and looked up above the galleries these very high windows up in the top would rattle and shake," recounted Rev. Malcolm Blackburn.

Tornado warnings were out now, the eerie wail of the civil defense sirens sounding across the city as the storms swept out of Arkansas and across Tennessee and Kentucky, leveling houses, barns, utility lines, trees. Twelve people would be dead and a hundred injured throughout the wide area before the storm was done. At 10:00 P.M. a tornado would swing down on a trailer court twenty miles north of Memphis. Power went out in some areas.

Dr. King came into Mason Temple out of the storm about 9:00 P.M. to a roaring crowd competing with the thunder outside. "I thought he looked harrowed and tired and worn and rushed," commented Rev. Middlebrook. But King grinned at the crowd and took his seat on the platform as Abernathy rose to introduce him. "Sometimes," said Abernathy, "we get in too big a hurry to introduce a man like Dr. King, but tonight I just want to take my time." He did. The introductory remarks ran twenty-five minutes. "I started off at the cradle and I ended up with that particular day, April 3," said Abernathy. He sat down to the jokes and jibes of his fellow ministers, remembered Middlebrook, adding, "You could hear the storm just bellowing. There were two large window fans, very large things, and we could hear them just rumbling."

Dr. King began to speak.

> Something is happening in Memphis
> Something is happening in our world.

The crowd was small, but it was his crowd. With "Yeah" and "Yes, sir," it moved him on. It laughed with him and applause rose and fell.

> If I were standing at the beginning of time...
> And the Almighty said to me,
> Martin Luther King,
> Which age would you like to live in?...
> Strangely enough,
> I would turn to the Almighty and say,
> If you allow me to live just a few years
> In the second half of the twentieth century,

I WILL be happy.
Now that's a strange statement to make
Because the world is all messed up.
The nation is sick.
Trouble is in the land,
Confusion all around.
That's a strange statement.
But I know
Somehow
That ONLY WHEN IT IS DARK ENOUGH
Can you see the stars.
And I see God working
In this period of the twentieth century
In a way that men in some STRANGE way are responding to.
Something is happening in our world.
The masses of people are rising up.
And wherever they are assembled today,
Whether they are in Johannesburg South Africa Nairobi Kenya Accra
Ghana New York City Atlanta Georgia Jackson Mississippi or
Memphis Tennessee
The cry is always the same.
WE WANT TO BE FREE!

"I'm not a religious fanatic," said Jesse Epps. "But at some high points where there should have been applause, there was a real severe flash of lightning and a real loud clap of thunder that sort of hushed the crowd."

We've got to give ourselves to this struggle
Until the end.
Nothing would be more tragic
Than to stop at this point in Memphis.
We've got to see it through.

When we have our march
You need to be there,
If it means leaving work,
If it means leaving school,
Be there.
Be concerned about your brother.
You may not be on strike,
But either we go up together
Or we go down together.
Let us develop a kind of dangerous unselfishness.

"I walked off the platform to catch a phone call at the back of the church and I sat on the steps back there and listened to the last twenty minutes," said Rev. Lawson. "I was kind of enamored by it all...very pleased...a wonderful kind of feeling....On the one hand the thunder had been going on and the rain and the lightning, but on the inside were three or four thousand people who felt very much at home with each other and with the world even though we were in the midst of a great struggle and tension...a great feeling of oneness...a great warmth. I was basking in this feeling...of kinship and warmth and the struggle."

One day a man came to Jesus...
And he said to Jesus,
Who is my neighbor?
That question could have easily ended up
In a philosophical and theological debate.
But Jesus immediately pulled that question from mid-air,
Placed it on a dangerous curve
Between Jerusalem and Jericho...
The Jericho Road is a dangerous road...
The first question that the priest asked
The first question that the Levite asked,
If I stop to help this man,
What will happen to me?
But then the Good Samaritan came by.

And he reversed the question.
If I do not stop to help this man,
What will happen to him?
That's the question before you tonight...
If I do not stop to help the sanitation workers,
What will happen to them?

Rev. Middlebrook on the platform watched with a preacher's admiration. "Where can the man go next to climax this thing? All of us sitting there started asking....When he got to a point where he could have climaxed, he didn't...He was just an old Baptist preacher with eloquence and insight...and prophecy...And we said, 'Where is the man? How is he going to climax?' "

> And they were telling me—Now it doesn't matter now—It really doesn't matter what happens now.
> I left Atlanta this morning and as we got started on the plane—there were six of us—the pilot said over the public address system, 'We're sorry for the delay. But we have Dr. Martin Luther King on the plane. And to be sure that all of the bags were checked, and to be sure that nothing would be wrong on the plane, we had to check out everything carefully. And we've had the plane protected and guarded all night.'
> And then I got into Memphis. And some began to say the threats or talk about the threats that were out, about what would happen to me from some of our sick white brothers.
> Well, I don't know what will happen now. We've got some difficult days ahead. But it really doesn't matter with me now. Because I've been to the mountain top.
> I don't mind. Like anybody, I would like to live
> A long life.
> Longevity has its place.
> But I'm not concerned about that now.

I just want to do God's will.
And he's allowed me to go up to the mountain
And I've looked over
    And I've seen the Promised Land.
    I may not get there with you.
But I want you to know tonight
THAT WE AS A PEOPLE WILL GET TO THE
PROMISED LAND.
    So I'm happy tonight.
I'm not worried about any thing.
I'm not fearing any man.
    MINE EYES HAVE SEEN THE GLORY OF THE
    COMING OF THE LORD!

The sound of the crowd comes up, engulfs, surrounds, pushes, catches, threatens, all turning on him, lifting him up.

He turned abruptly, tears in his eyes, and walked to his seat. "Do you want water?" Harold Middlebrook kept pressing him. "I don't. No. Uh-uh." Middlebrook hovered over him. "He just sat there."

His audience, caught between tears and applause, was on its feet. "I saw ministers who ordinarily would keep their composure just break down," murmured Rev. Kyles, looking down from the platform. "You could hear one minister crying all over the building, just at the top of his voice," added Rev. Jordan.

The moment held, bewildered. Then it broke. And the crowd let go, some pulling on their jackets and raincoats, others moving toward the platform, toward Dr. King. "Usually he would like to get away from the meeting so he wouldn't be swarmed by the crowd," said Middlebrook. "But that night he just didn't want to leave. He just wanted to stay there and meet people and shake their hands and talk to them."

Outside the storm was over, the rain steady and muted. It was late, nearly midnight, when the COME strategy committee met. Dr. King was at the home of his old friend Judge Ben Hooks. The only surprise at the meeting was the unexpected arrival of Rev. A. D. King, Dr. King's younger brother who pastored a church in Louisville, Kentucky. Driving back from a meeting in Florida, he decided on impulse to swing by Memphis and see Martin.

Maxine Smith had been at an NAACP gathering and missed Dr. King's speech. "At the meeting several people remarked about how unusual it was...but I didn't attach any significance."

Darkest Day

13

"This is the darkest day I've ever
seen. I am sad, sad, sad."
Downing Pryor

The fifty-third day of the strike, Thursday, April 4, slid in soggy and chilly but quiet after the upheaval of the night before. Jim Lawson drove to The Peabody hotel for his usual strategy breakfast with Jesse Epps and Rev. Ralph Jackson. Over at the Lorraine, Martin King was sleeping late. It was a year to the day since his influential speech against the Vietnam War at New York's Riverside Church, when he had cried out, "Somehow this madness must cease. I speak as a child of God and brother to the suffering poor of Vietnam and the poor of America who are paying the double price of smashed hopes at home and death and corruption in Vietnam."

White and black ministers met that morning at Elder Blair Hunt's Mississippi Boulevard Christian Church in South Memphis in a loose continuation of the gathering of the day before. There were far fewer white clergy present, "no more than a dozen," said Father Greenspun. And this meeting, which had hoped to plan the presentation of a statement to the Mayor, also got bogged down in roundabout discussion.

Rabbi Wax stated flatly that he would not take part in any march to the mayor and that he felt such a gesture would be futile. "Negro ministers did not take keenly to my idea of not marching or appearing," noted the Rabbi.

"There was hedging, hawing, and hemming," said Greenspun. "I said to myself again that this march will never get off the ground."

But the meeting inched a little farther along. Wax and Rev. Starks agreed to appoint men from their respective ministerial groups to draw up the statement. That afternoon Rev. Bill Aldridge got a call from Wax. "He said, 'Would you take over the writing of the statement and the march? McRae doesn't want to because of his personal relationship with Loeb.' " Aldridge agreed. Dr. Carl Walters, professor of Bible at Southwestern, was eager to help, and Dean Dimmick volunteered his curate Bob Watson, chaplain of the University of Tennessee medical units. Rev. Dick Wells had been recruited by Rev. Starks. They agreed to meet with Rev. Starks and write the statement during the mass meeting and speech by Dr. King that night.

Meanwhile, Episcopalian clergy met with their bishop, VanderHorst, to consider the ministers' proposed march. Bishop VanderHorst's position was traditionally *via media*; his blessings would be on those who marched and on those who did not. And Rev. Ezekiel Bell, rhetorical conjuror of dark doom and destruction upon the collective head of white Memphis, was busy getting into the mail letters inviting a number of whites to become part of an integrated congregation at his Parkway Gardens Presbyterian Church.

In Judge Bailey Brown's crowded federal courtroom began the legal skirmishing over whether or not the massive march scheduled for the next Monday would proceed under Dr. King's leadership.[1] Attorneys Burch, Lucas, Bailey, Caywood, Cody, and Newman came into court asking for dismissal or modification of the restraining order. They also provided the court with a proposed plan for restrictions on the march in the event it was allowed to go on. "We thought King wanted as many restrictions as possible that would protect the march and let it go on," explained Caywood. "We took guidelines from the Selma march that were in a reported case and adapted them to our own situation and added a few." These restrictions included such things as liaison between march leaders and city officials, thorough training of marshals, and the presence of "adequate police forces to accompany the march and to maintain moving and stationary positions between the marchers and the side-walks."

With Mayor Loeb among the spectators for a short time, city attorney Gianotti offered only two options—a riotous march or no march at all. The city's three witnesses were Fire and Police Commissioner Holloman, Chief of Police Macdonald, and Assistant Chief Lux, each telling again of the disorders of the week before, the lack of control by leaders, and the lack of enough police to handle widespread violence.

Holloman added that he knew that outsiders would come into the city if another march were held, and he had received information from a Ku Klux Klan member that the Klan planned to march on the same day. He noted that Dr. King had met with a Black Power group at the Rivermont. He had definite information that Negroes had been buying guns and ammuni-tion in wholesale in adjoining Arkansas, and there had been a theft of guns and ammunition from a city sporting goods store the very night before. He was worried about the welfare of Dr. King, Rev. Lawson, and other leaders "in view of the reports and rumors and threats against their lives."

All three lawmen were convinced that any new demonstration would again lead to rioting and looting, and that neither the city nor its citizens could be adequately protected. Burch moved into a strategy of alternatives. Assuming the court extended the temporary restraining order to an injunction and Dr. King and his staff said they would obey that injunction "and pack up and go back to Atlanta" and that others, not acting in concert with Dr. King, held a march, "do you think that that would be a better situation than it would be to have the march carried out Monday with Dr. King and his people at least in leadership under some court-imposed special restrictions?"

And the three law officials would finally, reluctantly agree that if a mass march were to be held—an alternative they continued to deplore—its best chance for success would be under the aegis of nonviolent leaders.

Chauncey Eskridge, Dr. King's personal attorney and friend, arrived from Chicago and joined Lucas' group. After a lunch break, the court session resumed with Rev. Lawson and Rev. Andrew Young, an ordained United Church of Christ minister and executive vice-president of SCLC with "authority" to speak for Dr. King, testifying. Burch was seeking to establish four main points: the defendants' commitment to nonviolence, the place of demonstrations in nonviolent social change, the need to march again in Memphis, and the importance to Dr. King and SCLC of a peaceful march.

Both Lawson and Young testified that mass marches called attention to injustices in a visible way, served as a controlled outlet for pent-up emotions on the part of poor people who had no equal access to the communications media, and offered hope for social change. Both ministers reiterated that the march was centered on the demands of the sanitation workers.

Judge Brown, with the precedents of freedom of speech, assembly, and petition and the problems of prior restraint before him, concluded the hearing by stating that he wished to see the lawyers in his chambers and that he would give his written opinion the next morning. It was about 4:00 P.M.

"Judge Brown told us, 'I am going to let this march go...with the restrictions that are set forth in Dr. King's answer,'" related Caywood.

Like the union, the city was not putting all its trust into mediation or legal maneuvers. Scuttlebutt around City Hall was that opposed to the "radical" preachers, there were a number of blacks trying to defuse the strike issue. "These were the people we were trying to reach, to talk to," explained Ned Cook. "We had a preacher named Jonathan Rodgers..."

Rev. Rodgers, a black radio revivalist, had drawn large racially
mixed crowds to revivals the preceding fall. Now he announced
he was scheduling a "peace" meeting for the coming Sunday,
April 7. The world had social problems, believed Rodgers, and
the church needed to do something about them, but the
greatest problem was loss of religion. "All of us would like to see
the men who work hard get better pay. But you don't get this
with the approaches they (ministers preaching hate) are using."

"He's a very, very fine individual," said Ned Cook, "and
probably, I'd say, one of the best true pure preachers. ...The
meeting (for Sunday) was all well arranged...and I think that
would have been the end of the strike. The strike would have
collapsed."

Cook met with the preacher that afternoon and had come
back to Loeb's office for another rundown on the situation. "I
think the responsible element of the Negro community thought
the thing was getting out of hand. And it had gotten out of
hand! And they were just ready to get the thing over with."
Before learning of the results of the court hearing, there was a
brightening in the mayor's office.

It had brightened outside, too. Both the daily strikers' march
and the ninety-five garbage trucks on the street moved in cool
sunshine; the lowering clouds of early morning were gone.

Frank Miles, late that morning, received a second call from his
contact man in the justice department about the march being
called off. He was sitting in on the injunction hearing, he told
Miles, and during a recess had spoken to Rev. Andy Young out
in the hall. "Young is in agreement that we should have a
meeting. I'll be in touch with you later." Miles replied that he
still needed more to go on if he were to meet with Dr. King's
people and be able to honestly tell them that a settlement was
in the offing. He decided to get back to Downing Pryor and the
council to see again if they could take some further action.

The council, with Blanchard and Patterson out of town, was

meeting in special session again over the controversial route of
Interstate 40. Pryor confidentially asked several of the councilmen to remain after the session to confer unofficially with Miles
at the Claridge Hotel.

Still pursuing his independent course toward a settlement,
attorney Marx Borod finally contacted Miles about 4:00 P.M.,
a course which several people had urged, fearing that Borod's
moves might scuttle the official negotiations under Miles. "I
told him of my meetings with the union and my effort to meet
with the mayor," said Borod. "At first Mr. Miles responded with
a threat to call the newspapers and resign. He recovered his
composure, and agreed to meet me downtown to look over the
proposal." They met at a downtown garage at about 4:30 P.M.,
and Borod handed Miles a copy of the proposal he had worked
out by himself. "Miles asked that I not disclose it to anyone else
until he could reconvene the (mediation) meeting."

Miles then went on over to the suite of rooms at the Claridge
for his meeting with council members. He now, more than any
other person, was caught in all of the crosscurrents swirling
around the attempt at strike settlement, in Jerry Wurf's distrust
of his own official mediation sessions, in Marx Borod's end run,
in the justice department's pressure to find Dr. King a graceful
exit, in the council's inability to act. Despite rumors that Loeb
was softening on the dues checkoff, these rumors were not
substantial enough to act on, and if another march by Dr. King
would further muddy the waters, time was getting short. If the
council could at this juncture be of any help, Miles had to know
at once.

Councilmen Pryor, Donelson, Netters, Hyman, and Davis
walked over from City Hall to meet him. It didn't make much
sense, Miles told them, but there was word that Dr. King wanted
out of the march. Could they give him any assurances that if the
mediation sessions were able to resolve the dues checkoff
question, the council would then authorize it for the union? But
the men present could not give him that guarantee; they were
not sure about corralling the votes. They continued to talk.

Outside the hotel the late afternoon exodus of workers and shoppers from downtown was underway.

At about the same time, eighteen of the city's businessmen gathered at The Peabody hotel in response to labor council president Tommy Powell's invitation. The racial problems would relax, Powell told them, if the strike could be settled and he suggested a committee call upon the city council to demand compulsory arbitration.

"It was a cold audience," said labor council secretary Bill Ross, "…and a last ditch desperate attempt." The meeting accomplished nothing.

In John Spence's civil rights commission office several members of the Tennessee advisory group also were meeting. They decided to begin gathering information and to hold a closed hearing on the charges of alleged police brutality stemming from the disturbances of the weekend before.

In the fourth floor radio dispatch center at police headquarters at least a modicum of relaxation had descended, in decided contrast to the night before when, said Lieutenant Frank J. Kallaher who was in charge of the 3:00 P.M. shift, the switchboard had been lit up like a Christmas tree during the tornado. Dispatch had known Dr. King had been speaking at Mason Temple at the time, but their concern was the storm, and Lieutenant Kallaher had stayed on duty extra hours to help out. Dispatch had also lost track of Dr. King for a period of time on the day before, but now he was under surveillance. In addition to the small group of men assigned in cars or on foot in the Lorraine Motel area, the locker room at Firestation #2, at 484 S. Main, which was at the back of the station and faced the Lorraine courtyard across Mulberry, was being used as an observation point. The day before Detective Ed Redditt and another black policeman, Patrolman W. B. Richmond, had arrived at the station, covered the window of the back door in the locker room with paper, and equipped with binoculars aimed through slits in the paper were keeping a record of the movements of Dr. King and his associates as they moved back and forth to different rooms along the balcony.

There had been a flurry over Detective Redditt earlier Thursday. As a black lawman, Redditt had been badly overused as an undercover man in the strike, and strike leaders now recognized him, not without hostility. Both he and Richmond had been at Mason Temple the night before, but there was some apparent animosity toward them and they left early. Later that night Floyd Newsum, a veteran fireman who was the one black man in his shift at Firestation #2 and who had been working with the strike movement, was called and told to temporarily report to a station up in Frayser at the northern edge of the city the next morning. Newsum believed the temporary transfer was because he had reported Redditt's presence at the fire station to strike leaders. The next morning Redditt got a threatening phone call at the station, and Police Commissioner Holloman pulled him off the observation assignment.

But Richmond was still at his post. King was still covered. Now, in late afternoon, the daily march had gone smoothly, the TAC units were functioning routinely, and early rush hour traffic was presenting no special problems. The threat of mobilization for another giant march hung over the police department, but there was still hope the march would be blocked by court order and no actual police deployment plans were underway. And up in radio dispatch, Lieutenant Kallaher was juggling the supper schedule for his three dispatchers and operators.

The day rolled gently on. In late morning Dr. King had talked again with a few of the militants and by noon he and Dr. Abernathy were cheerfully sharing a catfish lunch in their room, eating from the same plate because the motel waitress didn't get the order straight. Martin and his brother A. D. carried on a joking long distance phone conversation with their mother in Atlanta. And for the next several hours there was an impromptu SCLC meeting, centering not on the prospective march but upon the importance of nonviolence itself and their unified commitment to it. There had been some talk, said Rev.

Middlebrook, of putting a couple of Invaders on the SCLC staff. "Maybe exposure to Dr. King and the staff would give them the idea of being nonviolent. Dr. King was saying he could not envision putting any man on the SCLC staff who had violent attitudes...so Hosea Williams started talking about tactical violence. And Dr. King said that he could not appreciate any man who had not at least learned to accept nonviolence as a tactic if not a way of life. He went on to dwell on this thing. He actually got up...and walked around preaching to the staff."

It was a comfortable meeting though, a continuation of scores of similar meetings among a closely knit group of men who had set out to redeem the time and who, along the way, had learned to rely on one another. Memphis was racking them; so were the plans for Washington, but beneath all of the doubts and problems lay the belief that their way was ultimately right, even righteous. King, even in his tormented moments, stood on this bedrock belief and continued to transmit it to those who worked closest to him.

The meeting broke up with the same joking and jiving with which it had begun, old movement stories and reminiscences, back-slapping. Abernathy ducked out of the way for a quick nap, but King and some of the others continued talking and laughing, and there was continuous coming and going from room to room within the motel. Supporters drifted in from the noon union meeting. Chicago's Operation Breadbasket bandleader, Ben Branch, got the small band together in one of the rooms to rehearse for the mass meeting that night. Branch was out of Memphis, his first playing done in clubs around town. Union representative Bill Lucy moved between the Lorraine and the Minimum Salary Building. "We were trying to make sure we had a good crowd (that night) and that Dr. King would be able to have the feeling there was lots of support and he could carry on."

Rev. Billy Kyles reached the Lorraine in midafternoon. Dr. King and a number of his aides were invited to the Kyles' home for dinner that evening before the mass meeting. At home,

Gwen Kyles, beautiful, mother of four, was getting ready. "There was so much moving around, no home-cooked meals, restaurant food, having a plate brought over from the hotel, sandwiches," she said with concern. "So Billy came home and told me about it and we set out to get all of the soul food we could find." About fifteen guests were expected, including A. D. King, SCLC staff, Maxine and Vasco Smith. And Gwen Kyles turned to some of the best cooks in her husband's Monumental Baptist Church for contributions.

The variety of food coming in was staggering: roast beef, chitlins, neck bones, potatoes, ham, macaroni and cheese, spaghetti, greens, candied sweet potatoes, tossed salad, potato salad, slaw, cornbread, corn muffins, corn pone, rolls, cakes, pies, ice cream, lemonade, iced tea, coffee. "We had the mood set where they could just relax," smiled Gwen Kyles.

Rev. Kyles, knowing how tense Dr. King had been, planned on getting him out to his house as early as possible, but three o'clock was way too early, and Kyles, hearing music coming from upstairs at the Lorraine, wandered up to find Jesse Jackson singing with the Breadbasket band. Kyles and other arriving ministers joined in, singing "Yield Not to Temptation" and "I'm So Glad Trouble Don't Last Always" and "I've Been 'Buked and I've Been Scorned."

Rev. Andy Young and Chauncey Eskridge returned to report to Dr. King on the court hearing. Hotel manager Mrs. Loree Bailey ran into Dr. King in the hallway and he stood joking with her. "I'm getting ready to go to Dr. Kyles. If he don't have good food out there, like that catfish we had, I'm going to come back and eat here." "All right, Doctor," beamed Mrs. Bailey. The staff members invited to the dinner slowly scattered to their motel rooms to dress and television sets were tuned in to catch the national coverage of Dr. King's speech of the night before.

Rev. Kyles joined Dr. King and Rev. Abernathy in their room around 5:30 P.M. (He has told the story so many times now that it comes to his lips automatically, a verbatim repeat of the last time he told it. Only when he comes to describe the wound will he falter and keep lifting his hand to the side of his face.)

"Ralph was dressed when I got in and Martin was still dressing...Ralph said, 'All right now, Billy. I don't want you fooling me tonight. Are we going to have soul food? Now if we go over there and get some filet mignon or T-bone, you're going to flunk. We don't want no filet mignon.' Martin says, 'Yeah, we don't want it to be like that preacher's house we went to in Atlanta, that great big house. We went over there for dinner and had some ham—a ham bone—and there wasn't no meat on it. We had Kool Aid and it wasn't even sweet. And if that's the kind of dinner we're going to, we'll stay here.' I said, 'You just get ready. You're late.' I had told them five o'clock and I told my wife six. I said, 'Hurry up. Let's go.'

"They were teasing me about the dinner...And Ralph said, 'You know, your wife is real pretty. I'm gonna put some cologne and stuff on.' ...And Martin said, 'Yes, she's so pretty. Can she really cook soul food? Course, she'd have to be pretty to be married to a fashion plate like you.' "

Kyles, who prided himself on being an impeccable dresser, leaned back in a chair and stretched out his long legs. Dr. King was still dressing and Abernathy was wandering between the room and the bath.

"Ralph mentioned about needing somebody to do a revival at his church...We really just talked preaching—preachers talk. And they started talking about Martin's father. Martin spoke very kindly toward his father. Ralph said, 'How old is Dad?' Martin named the year he was born and Ralph said, 'He's got lots of spunk left in him.' Martin said, 'Yeah. You know, Dad is really something. When he was courting Mama, not only did Dad get the daughter, but he got the church, too.' Martin's grandfather was the minister of a church.

"He was in a real good mood...It may have been from what they accomplished in the staff meeting...When Martin's relaxed...he's relaxed. I hear many people say they didn't know that side of him and I guess they wouldn't, but he always was relaxed in our group. He'd put his shirt on. He couldn't find his tie. And he thought that the staff was playing games with him, but we did find it in the drawer. When he put the shirt on, it was too tight. And I said, 'Oh, Doctor, you're getting fat!' He said, 'Yeah, I'm doing that.' And he couldn't button it, so he took it off…and put another shirt on and a tie.

"Meanwhile, we were talking, and he said, 'Billy, what do you think brought the Negroes together in Memphis? Why do you think so many people got involved in the sanitation thing?' I said I guessed every Negro can identify with the sanitation worker aspect…And Martin said, 'This is like the old movement days, isn't it? That first speech here! When I got to the Temple and saw all those people—you couldn't have squeezed two more in there if you tried. This really is the old movement spirit.'

"Ralph said, 'I better put some more of this good-smelling stuff on me.' He went to Martin's open case and took out some of this aeromist and was putting some on. I was sitting in a chair. Martin opened the door to the balcony and went out and was greeting people. 'Hi! Hey! Hi!' He said, 'All right, load up. We're getting ready to go.' "

It was only a few feet to the railing of the balcony.

Below in the motel courtyard Solomon Jones, the driver loaned along with a large white Cadillac for King's stay in Memphis by the R. S. Lewis and Sons Funeral Home, stood by the car. In another car bandleader Ben Branch's two children waited for their father as he stood talking to Jesse Jackson. In the courtyard were SCLC aides Andy Young, Hosea Williams, James Bevel, Bernard Lee, and James Orange. Attorney Chauncey Eskridge stood nearby; so did other motel guests, including several youngsters outside to get a glimpse of Dr. King.

At Firestation #2, Patrolman Richmond watched. One of the TAC units, three cars and a dozen men, back from monitoring the daily march, had pulled in on the Main Street side of the station for a rest break and the police were milling about, talking, getting drinks of water. It was a half-hour before sunset, a few minutes before six o'clock, and the light was still good.

"Ralph called, 'Martin, tell Jesse we're not going to take that whole (Breadbasket) band to Billy's house. I know he hasn't got room for all them folks. Tell Jesse—don't invite the whole band now.' So Martin said, 'Hey, Jesse, don't take the whole band now.' I said, 'Well, you can't leave Jesse out. He was the instigator of this thing.' He said, 'No, but we're not going to feed that whole band. My goodness. We'll feed them at the hotel.' ...And he came back into the room.

"Ralph was still doing something. He's very slow. And we went back out together, Dr. King and myself, and stood side by side...Solomon Jones said something about it was getting cool and to get your coat...I was greeting some of the people I had not seen...Martin was leaning over the railing. Jesse said, 'Hey, you remember Ben Branch?' He said, 'Hi, Ben.' "

"He'd heard us play 'Precious Lord' up in Chicago," said Branch. "So he told me, 'Man, tonight'—you know he talks real slow anyway—'tonight I want you to play that "Precious Lord" like you've never played it before.' And I said, 'Dr. King, you know I do that all the time.' He said, 'But tonight especially for me. I want you to play it real pretty.' "

Kyles continued, "I called to Ralph to come on. They were getting ready to load up. I said, 'I'll come down. Wait a minute. Somebody can ride with me.' As I turned and got maybe five steps away this noise sounded. Like a firecracker.

"The noise sounded as if it came from the courtyard and I looked over the rail...I thought someone was playing games...And then people began to duck, ducked behind cars...The people who were looking up knew....Somebody screamed, 'Oh, Lord, they've shot Martin.' ...I wheeled around...I didn't see him hit. I didn't see it. He had fallen on his back when I got to him...He had a crushed cigarette in his hand. The knot in his tie was blown off...And I looked at this tremendous wound. All this was just pouring out from his chin here to his cheek. He looked like he was trying to say something. His eyes moved."

There was screaming and shouting in the courtyard and frenzied running, some toward the balcony and some toward the street from which the shot must have come. Top SCLC

leadership were all exposed in the courtyard. Abernathy rushed
from the room and knelt beside Dr. King, patting him gently
and talking to him. Jim Laue, of the justice department's
community relations division, crawled along the balcony with
a towel to staunch the blood, now thick and heavy. A bedspread
was laid over him. Billy Kyles was like a madman, screaming into
Room 306's telephone at the motel's unattended switchboard
and beating his head and hands against the wall.

Patrolman Richmond had seen King fall, and at his shouts
police officers poured out of the firestation and toward the
Lorraine, panicking still further some of those in the courtyard
who now thought they were being attacked by a mob of police.

At police dispatch the first call came in at 6:03 P.M. with a
special service unit breaking in on routine broadcasts to report
it had information Dr. King had been shot. Stunned, the
dispatchers turned to Lieutenant Kallaher. Almost simultaneously an outside call was put through on the extreme emergency
line, and Kallaher grabbed it. "A hysterical female voice said,
'Somebody has shot and killed Dr. King. Send an ambulance,'
and hung up." The dispatchers moved. Both from police
dispatch and the firestation went out the call for a fire department ambulance to the Lorraine. "Verify that report," came the
terse order from Chief Macdonald's office. Within minutes
TAC units raced to seal off the motel area and the brick building
west of the Lorraine Motel from which the shot was now
reported to have come. Police had in hand a rifle with a
telescopic sight and a box of shells, covered by a bedspread and
dropped in front of Canipe's Amusement Center, just south of
the entrance to a shabby rooming house on Main. The suspect
was described as a young white male who had hurriedly left the
area in a white Mustang. Both the Arkansas and Mississippi state
lines were within a few minutes.

On the Lorraine balcony, Martin Luther King was lifted onto
a stretcher and carried carefully down the stairs to the ambulance. "His color had changed," said Billy Kyles despairingly.
Abernathy, still beside his friend, climbed into the ambulance.

Lee, Young, and Eskridge followed in the car with driver Solomon Jones, as the police escort screamed through the streets to St. Joseph Hospital, just north of downtown. The "loop lights," red lights to halt all cross traffic downtown in an emergency, were thrown on as the ambulance sped through.

Reports of the shooting ricocheted quickly from the Lorraine and as more police cars poured into the area the story was spreading by word of mouth along the streets. County human relations director Jerry Fanion was already heading toward the motel when "four cars of policemen passed me—flying. And then somebody hollered across the street, 'King has been shot.' ...I got right behind the police cars and I went. They had got the ambulance and were just pulling off. And the blood and everything was still there."

Maxine Smith was driving through the area, hurried, already late for the dinner with Dr. King at the Kyles home. "As we stopped for a traffic light, a patrol car sped by, and I jokingly said, 'Let's follow this car....I think they're going to Dr. King's hotel now.' We were on Third Street then.

"A few yards down the street I see John Henry Ferguson running very excitedly. When I see John Henry, I get concerned because when the police see him they almost automatically start hitting him. He's one of those who's been arrested probably eight times in the strike. I said, 'What is John Henry up to?' He had run out of his shoes; he had his shoes in his hand. And he was outrunning cars. I stopped in the middle of the street and hollered, 'John Henry, what's wrong with you?' And he said, 'They've shot Dr. King.' So I said, 'Get in the car, John Henry.' ...We got to the hotel just as they were having to seal it off and we couldn't get in.

"I don't know....I remember parking the car and just running. I don't know where I was running or why I was running...."

Mayor Henry Loeb was also in a car, his heading south toward Mississippi on Interstate 55 where he was scheduled that evening to speak to Ole Miss law students. With him were a couple of old friends and two plain-clothes men. Following his usual pattern, Loeb was using his car phone to return calls that had come in during the day when suddenly they spotted sheriff Bill Morris' car. "Did you hear that Dr. King has just been shot?" Loeb immediately contacted Commissioner Holloman to confirm the report. His car swung around, back toward Memphis.

In the *Commercial Appeal* city room a few reporters were finishing their last pieces of copy for the first edition deadline, still nearly an hour away. The police radio, monitored by the metro desk, chattered softly away. In front of the Tri-State teletype machine Calvin Taylor rapped casually with a new copy boy. On one of the phones, an assistant editor was briefing Memphis Congressman Dan Kuykendall, who had called from Washington, about the court hearing on Dr. King's next march. "All of a sudden," said Congressman Kuykendall, "a lot of noise broke loose...I could hear it in the background...I said, 'What's going on?' They hollered back, said King had been shot."

"Everybody—policemen on the radio, people at the paper—was screaming and hollering 'Was he dead?' " said Taylor. And much the same scene was being enacted upstairs at the *Press-Scimitar.* As police reports were repeated, editors began to move, photographers swinging up cameras and reporters hurriedly grabbing up paper and pencils and heading out, calls going out to bring the papers' top management back to the building and to reach and dispatch other reporters and photographers already at home. And intern Calvin Taylor hit the streets on his first assignment, a bona fide *Commercial Appeal* reporter who was, still unbeknown to most of his fellow workers, one of the leaders of the Invaders.

Congressman Kuykendall could learn nothing at the *Commercial Appeal* in those early confused moments, so he hung up and tried the newsroom at WMC/TV, Channel 5, NBC's Memphis affiliate, hoping he could just be tuned onto the police band radio. "Somebody answered in the newsroom and the first thing I said was 'Is he dead?' They said, 'What are you talking about?' I said, 'Is Dr. King dead?' 'We don't know what you are talking about.' I said, 'He's been shot.' They didn't know...I couldn't find out anything." Frustrated, the congressman turned to his Washington television set.

WMC/TV newscaster Dave Patterson was on the air with the 6:00 P.M. half-hour local news roundup when the first United Press International bulletins on the shooting cleared the wire and were rushed to him by the now-alerted newsroom. Ashen-faced, he read it out. At WHBQ (ABC) and WREC (CBS) announcers broke into "Rawhide" and reruns of "I Love Lucy" with the same bulletin catching thousands of Memphians at home for supper. Radio stations were now picking it up.

"There is an unconfirmed report that Dr. Martin Luther King has been shot."

At 6:19 P.M., police at the hospital radioed the Emergency Room report to headquarters. "Condition critical."

Gwen Kyles, chattering gaily with some church friends who had dropped by to admire the soul food tables, got the call from her husband as the ambulance was pulling out of the Lorraine. "I went just numb. I just felt like somebody had knocked all my senses out. I mean, the light just went out...just everything drained out. I couldn't cry. I couldn't do anything. I just went stiff, and when I finally came to myself, I was just walking the floor and I remember saying, 'They've torn it now.' " She paced past the empty, waiting chairs, the silent tables.

On the television was a report that Dr. King had walked into surgery, holding a towel to his face.

Rev. Jim Lawson had reached home around 6:00 P.M.; despite meetings, he tried to get home for that meal hour with his wife and small sons. Peripherally, for he was not watching television closely, he caught the bulletin that Dr. King had been shot. Unbelieving, he moved over to the set, as the trailer again passed across the bottom of the screen. Lawson's overriding thought was that he must get to radio station WDIA, center of the black community's communications, and put out the call for calm. At the radio station he found the wire reports showed Dr.

King badly wounded but alive, and Lawson began cutting the first tape of many that night.

Stay calm. Don't listen to rumors. At this moment we only know that he is wounded. Pray. We must adhere to nonviolence. As soon as we find out his condition, we'll be letting you know. Pray. Keep faith in his life and works. We must go on with the struggle. There will be the usual march tomorrow. Stay calm. Stay calm.

The meeting of the councilmen and Frank Miles at the Claridge was continuing. At about 6:20 P.M., Downing Pryor called his wife about the delay. "My wife said, 'There's an awful thing on television!'" The hotel suite's television set verified the shooting. "Oh, my God, this is the end," moaned Rev. Netters. "So unnecessary, so foolish," Billy Hyman kept repeating. "You feel kind of sick with a tug at your stomach." Stunned, the council members and Miles left the hotel. Across the street at City Hall they separated, Donelson, Hyman, and Miles heading to their homes, the others hurrying to the office of the mayor.

The labor people were caught by the news at various places. Jesse Epps had left the Lorraine shortly before and stopped by the Minimum Salary Building to pick up some materials, and P. J. Ciampa was with him as they drove on down to their rooms at The Peabody hotel. "When I was getting out of my car, the boy at the door said, 'I heard over the news that Dr. King has been shot. Is there any truth in it?' And I said, 'No, I just left him.' But he said, 'No, just a minute ago.' And then I turned on my heels and drove back down to the Lorraine."

"We got there before the police blocked us out," said Ciampa. "Neither one of us served any useful purpose except to say, 'I saw them load the body.' We talked to some of the SCLC who were in an absolute state of shock, infuriation…We played the role of saying, you know, 'He may not be dead—he may just—time will tell—this isn't the time.' That kind of thing."

Bill Lucy, Rev. Ralph Jackson, and several others caught the news at the Minimum Salary Building as sirens wailed on the nearby streets. They, too, rushed to the Lorraine.

T. O. Jones, at first refusing to believe the reports, and then fearful of a widespread plot, locked the doors to his room at The Peabody.

In the produce department of a large Pic Pac grocery store catering to both black and white customers, Eddie Jenkins, of the Black Students Association, was at his regular job. "Things slowed down. People were saying, 'Something's happened. We don't know what it is, but something's happened.' People felt it immediately. But what? Had another riot broke loose? There was a rumor. 'Dr. King is hurt.' I said, 'Oh, no,' but I figured somebody's probably thrown a rock or something. Somebody said he'd gotten shot. I figured if he's shot, he's probably not shot bad. They wouldn't let that happen to Dr. King. Whitey's not that crazy. Somebody said he'd gotten shot in the head. Everybody was saying, 'No.' Then everybody was saying, 'Oh, I hope not.' It finally dawned on us that Dr. King was hurt."

Seventeen guests were arriving at the home of jeweler Fred Dreifus and his wife Myra. Among them were Rabbi and Mrs. Wax and friends who had helped Myra Dreifus found and carry on the Fund for Needy Schoolchildren, so helpful in providing hot food and clothing in ghetto schools. They never sat down at the dinner table. In the city's more exclusive restaurants, managers and waiters moved quietly from table to table informing guests, and the exodus began.

As the news spread, Memphis lay stunned and unbelieving. After the troubles of the week before, the shooting was too much to grasp, to comprehend. The city held, waited.

The team of doctors at St. Joseph Hospital fought to keep him alive nearly an hour while outside police sealed off the hospital, prevented all entrance without identification, and watched the crowd gathering at the front doors, not a belligerent crowd, but a crowd that simply stood there, muttering, keeping watch, waiting. Emergency had been notified a gunshot victim was on the way: no one knew it was Dr. King until the ambulance arrived and police swarmed in, followed by Dr. King's aides.

Upstairs neurosurgeon Dr. Frederick Gioia, Geneva-trained, was finishing up some paper work when his phone rang. "It was a physician who told me that Dr. King was in the Emergency Room and had been shot." He rushed to Emergency. "The waiting room was like walking into Grand Central Station with a multitude of armed men, the likes of which force I have never seen outside of the army...This is usually a busy time of the evening in Emergency. That's when the doctors' offices are closed and all normal things become emergencies when you can't get the family doctor....But there were several hundred people in the Emergency waiting room...It was jammed...I remember one woman, out in the waiting room, trying to get in, who yelled out, 'If they can treat King, there's no damned reason they can't treat me.' ...The nurses had their hands full between patients and detectives and FBI and armed men.

"Then I was fully aware that it had really happened....The police stopped me....I told them I had been called....There was a physician right there waiting....He said, 'Come quickly.' ...I went in there and saw Dr. King."

There were four or five doctors working on Dr. King. Dr. Rufus Brown, surgery resident on emergency duty, was already into the life-saving procedures, a tracheotomy to open breathing passages, restoration of fluids, the monitoring of heart and brain waves. Dr. Jerome Barrasso, surgeon on duty, was there. And STAT, or emergency, intercom calls for specialists rang softly through other parts of the hospital.

The doctors worked feverishly, although they knew, as the autopsy was later to show, that the high-velocity bullet had slammed through the chin and neck at a downward angle, severing the spinal cord in both the lower neck and upper chest regions, that vital linkage of the central nervous system with the nerve tissue at the bottom of the brain controlling respiration, circulation, and other bodily functions. Yet his heart continued to beat.

Upstairs in surgery, fourth-term University of Tennessee medical student Fred Williams, an extern every fourth night at

St. Joseph's, had changed into his scrub suit. When he walked out into the hall, usually quiet as the hospital began settling down for the night, news was flying among the staff and those patients who had television sets on that Dr. King was wounded and downstairs in the hospital. In the surgery hall a nurse told him, 'Martin Luther King's down in the Emergency Room and they have us on standby.' …I asked the nurse, 'Are they gonna bring him up here?' And she said, 'No.' …I realized it was pretty serious if they couldn't get him up to surgery….About that time the phone rang and the nurse said they needed a surgery lamp downstairs…So I got this big surgical lamp and we pushed it out to the elevator…One of the nurses there said she'd heard that he was shot through the head, half of his face gone. I still didn't put too much stock in that 'cause you know how rumors are.

"As soon as the elevator opened…somebody said, 'Make way.' …And I pushed this lamp in and everybody turned around, got out of my way and lights flashed and I heard cameras…So I pushed the lamp in the room and there were a lot of cops back there…doctors, too…There was this old colored guy, colored cop. Oh, he was big. He was 6'6", 6'8", something like that, and he was guarding the Emergency Room door…And I saw Dr. King laying there and the report was right. Just like they said."

The hospital's assistant administrator Paul Hess, already at home and called back, arrived at about 6:45 P.M. He found "a mass of reporters in the Emergency Room lobby. They were all milling around. There were about two or three telephones in that area…and there was always somebody at a phone…The press did not present a problem to us…under the circumstances they were quite contained."

Fire department and ambulance services had been notified that all emergencies were to be taken to other hospitals; the St. Joseph Emergency Room was closed. Police manned the Emergency Room phones, taking incoming calls and keeping in contact by special radio with headquarters. In an anteroom Rev. Andy Young and Chauncey Eskridge kept watch. Within the small room where Dr. King lay on the table surrounded by doctors and monitoring equipment, Rev. Ralph Abernathy and Bernard Lee stood quietly against the wall, waiting. "I spoke to Dr. Abernathy," said Dr. Gioia, "...very much like I've done on many other occasions with a concerned parent or guardian or friend about the bad prognosis. Of course, he reacted like any good friend would...I couldn't give him any hope."

"I was sent back upstairs for a surgeon's head lamp," said extern Williams. "When I got back down, they didn't need that either."

The heartbeat, his final life function, stopped at last. Despite the legal implications raised by such medical advances as heart transplants, most hospitals required a cessation of both heart and brain activity before death was declared. Now, at St. Joseph, they had both.

Dr. Martin Luther King, Jr., was dead.

Police were notified instantly. Mayor Loeb learned the final news over the police intercom amplified in his office. "What a lonely sight this was," recalled Downing Pryor. "Other than security people, there were only the councilmen and the mayor. There was an awful shock in the room...awful tragedy. Not only the man's having to die, but what this was going to do to the world...Memphis and America damned to hell all over the world...the man who was recognized as the Negro leader of all the leaders, slain, assassinated. Just a modern form of lynching."

"Loeb was just stunned," said Councilman Fred Davis. "We tried to comfort him a lot and I pulled myself together pretty good and he talked about God. Loeb had Rev. Netters pray...And I just started crying uncontrollably...Netters broke down...I was crying and I couldn't stop and at the same time I was trying to stop. I just didn't want to do that there. Then Loeb broke down...I just told them to leave me alone and I went out into an anteroom and just sat there until I got myself together."

"I broke down without any restraint," remembered Rev. Netters. "Actually, the mayor and all of the aides there were attempting to console Fred and me...I don't think he would like me to say this, but I saw the mayor cry...He said he was sorry that it had to happen like this, but he hoped that in some way I could understand that he had to take some stand as mayor...I guess I broke down even more with this. I repeated something like, 'If they had only listened. I tried to tell them, over and over and over again that this would be the result. Now whatever happens, I hope that we all live to see it straightened out.' I knew the danger that was in the making for all of us."

It was the only time anyone saw Loeb break, this small moment when he faced at close quarter the pain of other men. He had held his principles as a shield before him and would continue to do so. Within minutes he would be on the phone to the governor of the state, demanding the National Guard, and would order a strict curfew to again close down his entire city. But, for that moment, his own anguish came through, and for these two black men who saw, he became more, not less, of a man for it.

Father Coleman Bergard, St. Joseph's chaplain, reached the Emergency Room a few minutes later. He had not been called earlier partially because of the confusion and partially because Dr. King was not a Catholic and was accompanied by his own ministers. Now, alone with the body, he bent over, gave conditional absolution, prayed for his departed soul, and gently closed Dr. King's eyes.

In the anteroom, Dr. King's aides also prayed.

In Atlanta, Mrs. Coretta King, news of the shooting already broken by calls from Jesse Jackson and Andy Young and waiting even then to board a plane for Memphis, was told of her husband's death. She returned home—to her four children.

A delay in the formal announcement of Dr. King's death, ostensibly for the preparing of the official wording, also gave Memphis police time to alert their forces and to secure the hospital more tightly, for there was genuine official fear that some sort of outburst might occur there. Once again officialdom had misjudged Memphis blacks; there were no demonstrations against the hospital where Dr. King died.

Assistant administrator Paul Hess stepped before the cameras and microphones. His announcement was brief and he would answer no questions at that time. "At 7:00 P.M., Dr. Martin Luther King expired in the Emergency Room of a gunshot wound in the neck." Newsmen broke for the phones, but they really had known already. Now it was official.

At the Lorraine, where a number of Dr. King's friends had remained, reporters and television newsmen as well as police went over the field of the shooting again and again. As Rev. Kyles, who had spent much of the time since the shooting in Dr. King's room, walked over to the motel office, "There was a UPI man on the public phone, and I heard him say, 'Is that official?' And they called the time. And he said that Dr. King had died."

Jim Lawson was still at WDIA radio, and Bert Ferguson, the white station owner, finding the staff in a state of shock, was personally reading the news bulletins over the air.

"The first tape I had made was playing on the radio when we got over the teletype the news that Dr. King was dead," said Lawson. "Since I was in the radio station...I took it calmly...I did another tape...again a call for calm, that since he was dead we would want to honor him by seeking to live out what he lived for and died for."

Alone in his car Lawson almost did break down. "But then I said Martin would expect the movement to go on and I better be sure that's going to happen." The years of self-discipline took over. No guilt about the death, about his bringing King to Memphis. The risk had been everywhere, like the hate, Memphis no more nor less.

He found criminal courts judge Ben Hooks, behind him now the judicial neutrality that he had tried to maintain publicly during the strike, and together they agreed to head for the television stations to broadcast calls for calm.

Lawson's message would say, "It would be a compounding of this death if now Negro people or white people around our country should despair and decide that now is the time to let loose an orgy of violence. It would not be a tribute to Dr. King but a denial of his life and work."

Judge Hooks struck the same note, adding that he was vastly concerned over the strike settlement and that he hoped now that the news media would take a deeper look at the causes that had brought it on. He called for prayer and reflection.

On the streets some scattered glass-breaking and looting had begun and crowds of blacks were beginning to gather on street corners. Trouble was minor at first, said one policeman, "like when you burn your finger, it takes a couple of seconds for the pain to reach your brain." Chief Henry Lux said, "I didn't have time to think about a tragedy or anything. My first feeling was that, my God, we've got to get organized because all hell's gonna break loose...we were in for another riot."[2]

The police were caught in a frightful situation during the first hour after Dr. King's death as the trouble mounted. All available manpower was needed in the hunt for the murderer, and the false reports over a civilian radio band of the chase of a white Mustang, supposedly connected with the shooting, across the northern part of the city shortly after 6:30 P.M. had shaken up everyone at headquarters. Still, the trail was so hot and police on the scene so quickly, it seemed impossible that whoever had fired the shot had been able to get away.

If heavy rioting were to begin in the black community—and police officers were convinced it would—the only way of stopping it would be to throw in massive forces at the outset. But there would be no massive forces until the National Guard could be moved onto the streets. And if any black violence turned against whites, would whites retaliate? Even men who would never think of using guns except on hunting trips into the dry stubbly fields were glad the guns were there, in cases, on racks, in closets. Police knew the quick disposition of the National Guard would be as important in convincing some whites that they did not have to turn vigilante, that law enforcement forces were in control, as it would be in keeping actual order in the black neighborhoods, although the real fate of Memphis depended on which way the black community would go as the news that Dr. King was, indeed, dead shuddered across it.

A breakdown in telephone communications, especially in the central city, as thousands tried to make phone calls added to the tension. In some exchanges callers were unable to even get dial tones for as long as fifteen minutes and then were unable to complete calls. During a three-and-a-half-hour period that night, thirty thousand more long distance calls than would normally be handled went in and out of the city.

Numbers of blacks were now converging on Mason Temple, announced site of that night's mass meeting at which Dr. King was to have spoken. Some did not know that the curfew had been called and the meeting canceled; some had come despite the ban. "I found my brothers there…" said one of the militants. "And there was an old lady there. She was as crippled as any duck. She was ready to go out and fight. She said, 'The Lord has deserted us.' …Every hope that any black man ever had of obtaining any kind of equality and justice, it was shattered."

Rev. Starks, at the Temple, was extremely concerned. The "mood was turning ugly."

"And people were saying, 'Let's go do this,' and 'Let's go do that,' " continued the militant. "We said, 'Just respect the man enough not to go out and do it tonight. Wait till he's buried. Don't you know the policemen are out there waiting for you? …That's just what the honkies want us to do. Come right out there like a bunch of wild Indians and they could wipe us out like they did the Indians. Don't do it.' And the ladies were asking, 'What do we do now?' And we told them, 'Go home. Just go home and when we call you, be ready.' …They went home.

"We didn't do the rioting. We had made a promise to Dr. King that the march would be successful and we had said that night if that march was held ten years from today, every one of you black s.o.b's better do right. No kidding…Everybody quieted down…But for me it meant we didn't have any choice now. We used to have a choice. We could wait for Dr. King to carry out his program and if it didn't work, we could use ours, but now it was as if white people didn't want any other program but ours."

P. J. Ciampa and others had gone to the Temple "to tell the people they better get home and off the streets. And we got out there and then the people we were telling that to were telling us to go to hell, because it's their night for revenge. And we said, 'It's impossible.' "

Attorney David Caywood also reached Mason Temple. "They (some of King's staff) were having a terrific argument with a bunch of young Negroes...trying to talk them out of burning the town down....And they did a fairly good job of it." But *Press-Scimitar* reporters heading for Mason Temple never got there. A group of kids broke out their back window with bricks and bottles.

At 8:15 P.M. police with calls of "less than emergency nature" were ordered to stay off the police radio and officers were ordered to disregard broken windows and ringing burglar alarms. Rock-throwing incidents were spreading. Sniping reports were coming in and fires were breaking out. By 9:00 P.M. several policemen reported they were pinned down by sniper fire in North Memphis, and aid was sent. By 10:00 P.M. the biggest fire of the night, at a building supplies company just north of downtown, was raging among piles of roofing and barrels of tar, and flames were a hundred feet in the air. Smaller fires were started at scattered locations over the inner city, both north and south. Liquor stores were again targets, and 26-year-old Ellis Tate, later discovered to have a record for assault and robbery, was critically wounded at a liquor store after police said he fired a rifle at them from the shadows. Tate would die in the hospital early Saturday morning.

"From the radio room it was a panicky situation," said Lieutenant Kallaher in police dispatch. Commissioner Holloman, reporting that "rioting and looting is rampant," went on television with County Sheriff William Morris to call for restraint. Every resource, he said, was being used "to identify and apprehend the person or persons responsible for this heinous crime.

"Remain calm, and cooperate with the law enforcement officers who are doing everything possible at this time to handle the situation...remain off the streets...leave this matter in the hands of your law enforcement officers...We are in a very critical emergency situation."

Local FBI representatives were already working with the police on Dr. King's killing, and as Holloman spoke, the first contingents of four thousand National Guardsmen were moving in the streets, joining the police, sheriff's deputies, highway patrol, and fifty Arkansas Highway Patrol officers sent over to help. The entire Tennessee National Guard was on alert and a large contingent was being sent into Nashville.

During the first hour of the curfew it had been almost impossible to clear the streets. People caught away from their homes headed there, and as cars would draw up next to each other at stop lights, their occupants would eye each other uneasily, unsure. Initially, there had been some stoning of cars with whites in the inner city. Nighttime stores and businesses sent their employees home. Some employers had the foresight to provide their people with notes explaining their presence on the streets; some did not, and police in certain black areas were stopping cars and checking occupants. Emergency installations such as hospitals found themselves without employees on the late-night shifts unless earlier staff voluntarily stayed on to work through the night. Some employees came through the curfew, angry at being stopped by police. But the checking of cars was a sometime thing. Some blacks drove through the curfew without ever seeing police. Others were stopped, checked, and warned to get off the streets and in some cases, when hot words broke out, arrested. There seemed to be no checkpoints in white areas, and reports on police brutality would again flood the NAACP office.

As news of Dr. King's death had spread, blacks had poured out of their homes, some to curse, some to wring their hands, but all to find what sustenance they could from each other. Groups of kids gathered, moving up the streets, first in one direction, then in another, no clear purpose other than that even moving was doing something. Gradually, most drifted back inside, leaving the streets to a few of the young, to the TAC units with their darkened vehicles, to the police, ambulance, and firetruck sirens which wailed across the night. National Guard helicopters were used for surveillance, to pinpoint trouble and fires.

Like the week before, the assessment of the seriousness of the rioting depended on where one stood. To a policeman it seemed at first that the whole city was likely to go up and police reacted accordingly. To a black, simply trying to get home, it seemed as if a police state had been established. There were rumors, panic, and a growing suspicion among blacks—completely unfounded—that the Memphis police had, in fact, been accessories to Dr. King's murder.

Those of Dr. King's friends grouped at the Lorraine still struggled to accept the horror now two hours old in time. His brother, Rev. A. D. King, had been in the shower when the shooting occurred. "He was hurrying up and dressing so he could come out and see if somebody was sick or something," said Rev. Middlebrook, who rushed toward A. D.'s room as the ambulance left and spent most of the evening with him while they waited for word from the hospital and A. D. kept in contact with his parents in Atlanta.

"We were trying to keep A. D. away from newsmen," said Rev. Kyles, "from the stupid questions they can ask at a time like this....I went down to his room. He said, 'Well, Billy, they got my brother. They got him. They got my brother.' And he just kept saying that."

Now the sobering news swept through the motel that the co-owner Mrs. Loree Bailey had suffered a stroke. "We were out in the kitchen when we heard the noise (of the shot)," Bailey said. "She said, 'Oh, yeah, Daddy, somebody done hit that truck.'

But we heard so much commotion going on, and somebody said, 'Dr. King got shot.' She hit her head with her hand. We walked on back around there and she said, 'Why? Why? Why?' We went on back to the kitchen, and then she went back outside and stood out there. She wasn't even crying, wasn't even saying nothing." About 9:00 P.M. Mrs. Bailey, lying down in her room, could not be roused, and he held her in his arms while they waited for the ambulance.

But Mrs. Bailey had suffered a cerebral hemorrhage. She would die in the hospital the following Tuesday, as the funeral for Dr. King began in Atlanta.

Finally Rev. Kyles took Dr. King's brother out to his home. "The soul food dinner was still set up." They sat quietly in the Kyles home, watching scene after scene of Martin King and the movement as the television specials memorializing his life flickered across the screen. Hosea Williams, Andy Young, Judge Ben Hooks, and others came in, out of the rapidly cooling curfew night.

In Washington, AFSCME president Jerry Wurf, called out of a meeting by news that King had been shot, had rushed home. "They didn't want to tell me he was dead…" His wife broke the full story. "You first think, how could such a thing happen? How could King be killed? And at this point, of course, we thought it was directly related to the strike. What's happening to our people in Memphis? Where are they? Are they dead? Are they alive? There was this great fear of what was happening to our people…I had the same feeling as when John Kennedy was killed. Why? How? What kind of world are we living in? This whole dreadful feeling. What the hell are we all doing?"

Wurf and his aides were on the phones all night trying to track down people both in Memphis and Washington. And he was determined to get some kind of federal presence into Memphis to deal with the strike. He finally got a call through to Vice-President Hubert Humphrey's assistant Bill Welch. "I remember saying, 'Bill, I don't know what button to press, but, goddammit, Memphis is going to burn!' I don't realize the whole country is going to burn…I said, 'Bill, for Christ's sake!' Bill said, 'I'm on it.' …I think the message was conveyed…I wanted responsible third parties to deal with the situation…The government (now) had a responsibility."

He also talked to Tennessee Governor Buford Ellington, whom Wurf suspected of playing politics with the strike. "But Ellington understood clearly that we couldn't let Loeb go on with his intransigence…I was reassured by the conversation only because it seemed to me that only a maniac would allow Loeb to remain in control."

On other phones AFSCME aides were calling on organized labor to pressure politically for some sort of end to the strike. "And we know we can't end it in a defeat because then King's death…on and on forever," mused Wurf. He left for Memphis the next morning.

At the White House a strained and heartsick Lyndon Johnson, destined now to leave office almost as traumatically as he had come into it, called upon his fellow citizens "to reject the blind violence that has struck down Dr. King, who lived by nonviolence," knowing that vandalism and looting were reaching within blocks of the White House. The shock waves out of Memphis were rolling across the country, and angry blacks were moving destructively through the streets in Detroit, Nashville, Minneapolis, Chicago, Harlem, Boston, through North Carolina, even in Itta Bena, Mississippi. And the second night would be worse than the first.

But not in Memphis. There the peak of the trouble was passing.

To most blacks in Memphis the shooting of Martin King was a direct and open attack on the black community itself. He had come to help them and now he was dead. A few strategists and militants might veer away from King, but the bulk of the black community strongly identified with him. "I didn't even know him, but I felt like he belonged to our family." They might not agree with everything he did. They might chuckle silently to themselves over his high-flown flights of rhetoric that so impressed whites. But they delighted in him. They were comfortable with him. He not only represented black, he was black as they were. For that reason he had been killed and it was as if the gun had been turned on all of them.[3]

The immediate attempted sealing off and patrolling of the black community by police and the Guard was almost unbelievable to them. They knew about the young cats out doing the damage. They understood that burning and looting had to be stopped. They, too, were fearful and prey to rumors. They didn't want their community torn up. But they had not expected the massive cold hostility that they sensed under the guise of professional law enforcement. It was not decent. They were in mourning. Dr. King had been shot, they were sure, by a white man, but it was their sons and husbands who were being looked at as if they were guilty.

As the reality closed in, "I wanted to cry, but I was all choked up and my surroundings seemed to have been closing in on me. I had to escape and try to catch my breath and to allow time for my thoughts to clear," said a Hamilton high school boy.

To those few more advantaged younger blacks, who had gone through adolescence playing football or cheerleading, working on projects for the science fairs, cramming for college entrance exams during those few years in the sixties when the visible barriers to segregation were falling and it seemed a breakthrough in race relations was being made, the killing was devastating. "Now I hate Memphis as much as the thought of Mississippi," said one of them. "This once great, beautiful city of Memphis could sink into the current of the Mississippi River for all I care," said another. Like most adults, the less advantaged kids never had too many illusions.

With the hurt came anger and the desire to lash back. Almost every black who spoke of reactions to the death of Dr. King mentioned anger. The young were the most explicit, but they had no monopoly. "I cried, Oh, God, have mercy! I wish that

Stokely Carmichael and the other Black Power advocates would come and burn Memphis down!" Or "Truthfully, I wanted to go out and shoot, mangle, or kill every white person I chanced to meet!"

What was done with the anger made the difference. Outside of a few who used the occasion to try to grab a little loot or pop off a shot or two in the direction of police just for the hell of it, small groups of angry young people were on the streets that night starting fires, breaking windows, throwing stones and crude Molotov cocktails, defying police, under the twisted notion of "getting even with whitey." They represented a greater number who felt such disruption was the only adequate response to the murder but who themselves, either through fear or because they felt strategically this was not the right time, stayed off the streets.

At the other end of the spectrum were the great number of blacks committed to Dr. King not only by race but by belief in his message of love and nonviolence, and this also included many young people. They felt the same anger, but they tried to deal with it in the ways that Dr. King had taught.

One of the white girls in "The Death of Bessie Smith" cast stood in the Green Room in the Memphis State theater building. A black cleaning woman walked in. "I turned around and looked at her and I said, 'I'm sorry.' I started to cry. She put her arm around me and she said, 'Don't cry, honey. It was just a minority. I don't hate you and I know you don't hate me.' We stood for a good ten minutes."

The years of black Christianity helped, the leadership of the black ministers, but these were primarily very personal crises as those who believed in Dr. King came into violent betrayal and despair, into the very real fact of Martin King with a gaping hole in his neck. Yet, as they had believed his way was true while he lived, many would continue to believe stubbornly in that way now he was dead.

But the steady building of a truly just society now seemed futile. Nat Turner had resorted to blood and gone mad.

Frederick Douglass had appealed to American decency and lived to see blacks resegregated throughout the South. Booker T. Washington had gone, subtly and with a multitude of motives, into accommodation. DuBois and the NAACP had relied on brains and legality, black entrepreneurs on power through capital, the Harlem Renaissance on creativity. King had tried *satyagraha* and confrontation and demanded that America face its conscience and its Jesus on the race issue and now he was murdered. And the basic problem still existed. They were still black citizens in a republic that was consciously and proudly white, and as long as that republic remained both conscious and proud of its whiteness, as if that whiteness carried virtue within itself, so long would blacks be in trouble. Blacks that night struggled with these frustrations on different levels, and even those who knew no black history other than the tales or myths of their people that had come down through the years out of cotton fields and sharecrop cabins and through a welter of newspaper headlines felt that with King's death, another avenue of escape from some of the worst conditions of black life had been closed to them.

They responded to calls for calm not from Frank Holloman but from their own leaders and out of respect for the body of Dr. King which lay among them. But that night they could not bring themselves to forgive either the man who actually pulled the trigger or the white society which he represented to them. Yet they held their anger, suffered it side by side with their grief.

Different analysts tried to understand why the city, already tense with the strike, did not reach the massive explosion point. Memphis blacks were, in general, too cowed to really riot. "Our" blacks were basically law-abiding. The militants were not strong. There were no high-rise ghettos. The disturbances of the week before had taken the edge off rioting. The temperature was too cool. The National Guard saturated the streets before mass rioting could get started. The mobility of TAC units prevented any concentration of trouble makers. There was some truth in all of this, but it was incomplete truth which did not acknowledge the great reservoirs of spiritual strength still contained within the black community that even this killing could not transform into vengeance.

The white community again lay protected behind its front line of police and Guardsmen, the hard facts of what was happening in the inner city filtered by the media or by the stories of those few whites who reported they had run the "gauntlet." There was also an unreality about the night for those who never heard glass breaking, watched flames suddenly shooting from a pile of trash, or saw the TAC squads in action. Real fear of blacks invading white residential neighborhoods, the same fear as was felt the week before, was quieted quickly, although the direst rumors of entire shopping centers being set ablaze or whites being stabbed on street corners persisted.

An Episcopal priest told of escorting home a frightened widow and of her next-door neighbor coming over with a plan to attach a line with a bell between the two houses so she could signal in case of trouble. "I'm taking no chances," said the neighbor. "I've an arsenal in my house. Don't you want a gun to take home to protect yourself and your children, Father?" The priest declined.

Most whites were stunned by the news. The immediate official response of the city to the murder was horror and regret, and city leaders spoke out that night deploring the crime. Council Chairman Downing Pryor would say, "This is the darkest day I've ever seen. I am sad, sad, sad." A great majority of the white citizens were against such violence regardless of the reasons or the identity of the victim. There was rather wan hope that the man who pulled the trigger would turn out to be an outsider and not someone with Memphis connections, though the most common opinion was that the assassination was in some way involved with the sanitation strike. And that involvement seemed to presage, if not a Memphis killer, at least a Memphis tie-in, despite an occasional denial such as that of one life-long and elderly Memphis lady, "I just can't believe there is any white person here in Memphis who is capable of doing such a thing unless he was paid to do it."

But it was apparent from widespread remarks made by many white people in Memphis during this period that they did not consider the murder a tragedy in itself. The real tragedy was that it had happened in Memphis and the city could be "misjudged."

Everyone deplored the killing per se. But having paid theoretical lip service to "Thou shalt not kill," some went on to explain why, in fact, the killing of Dr. King was not such a bad thing. "The night Martin Luther King was killed I was glad someone got him. All my friends felt the same way. We even drank to it," said a 21-year-old student who would later admit that he had known little about the civil rights leader.

> Ashes to ashes,
> Dust to dust;
> If he'd stayed out of Memphis
> This wouldn't have happened to us

went a verse. The sick jokes began to appear. What's black and slower than a speeding bullet? Satisfaction was voiced as people talked privately together; it was overheard in barber shops and supermarkets and schools and gas stations.

Some of it was vituperative enough to send Memphians who were not at all sympathetic to Dr. King to his defense, or at least into overt opposition to the twisted hates that produced the remarks. The murder itself had awakened some and forced them to examine their racial feelings; the knowledge that numbers of people actually were glad it had happened jolted still more.

It would take most concerned whites a while to determine which way they could best move, but a few responded to Dr. King's death instantly and in their own individual ways that night. Artist Dolph Smith, highly regarded in art circles in the Mid-South and beyond for his water colors of stark, deserted southern buildings, shacks, barns, remnants of an agricultural sharecrop civilization, went almost immediately into his studio.

There were already several canvasses stretched and ready to paint, but Dolph Smith did not paint. Instead he began working with an American flag, tearing it and fraying edges, patching sections back together, draping and pasting it down on a large canvas. Down the rents in the flag, spilling from top to bottom, he affixed small contact prints, moments and scenes that had caught his attention in various places around the South. At the apex his own small son stood holding a cap pistol; here and there could be glimpsed a print of feet in shabby shoes, of the old train depot, of empty buildings. At the bottom, red paint washed out of the red stripes of the flag like a continuous flow of blood. Dolph Smith would remain in his studio almost continuously for the next five days working on the collage. But he did not call it a collage; he called it an "outburst" and titled it "And the Veil of the Temple Was Rent in Two."

Young auto dealer John T. Fisher, who had spent so much time in the past few weeks trying vainly to get some whites to listen to black leaders, was getting phone calls from friends saying, "Somebody's got to do something." A few considered marching, but Fisher himself was still not convinced of the necessity of the union. As they talked, they began kicking around the idea of some sort of an open, city-wide meeting that would give all Memphians a chance to express regret over the violence and the breakdown of black-white relationships without committing them to a position on the strike.

The white ministers who were to write the statement to take to Mayor Loeb were determined to keep their appointment with Rev. Starks at Mason Temple that night despite murder, curfew, and trouble. Bob Watson, Carl Walters, and Bill Aldridge caught Starks there. "Thank goodness, he was still there," said Aldridge. "It was sticky for white men at Mason Temple that night. It was the only time I'd seen Starks lose his composure. He was worried for us and made us get out of there." But they conferred long enough to be able to write the statement at Walters' home, where the phone continued to ring all night. Dean Dimmick agreed to have a memorial service for Dr. King at St. Mary's and the plan was then to "proceed" to the mayor. Very early in the morning they began calling church leaders though it was apparent the blacks would not be able to get their people together. "Bob and Carl and I decided if there weren't but three of us, we'd march," said Aldridge.

At City Hall there were fears for the safety of Mayor Loeb himself. Threatening calls came in all evening. When *Commercial Appeal* reporter Joe Sweat, assigned to stick with Loeb throughout the night, arrived, he found plain-clothes men, one armed with a riot gun, in both inner and outer offices. All outside doors to the building were locked and shades on the outside windows of the mayor's office were drawn; a screen had been placed by his desk to cut the shadowy view through the translucent glass panel to the outer office. The television set was on.

Ned Cook had already taken care to protect Loeb's family. As soon as he heard of the shooting, Cook remembered, "I went to Loeb's house and got his wife and children and took them out to my house and they spent the night....Mary Loeb wasn't frightened. She didn't want to go. And I said, 'Hell, get the kids and let's go. Let's not take any chances.' I talked to Loeb on the phone and I said, 'I've got your family out here, so you can relax'...But we had a washwoman who had been with us for a number of years, and she said, 'I ain't gonna make beds for Mayor Loeb's wife, and quit. We haven't seen her since."

The mayor had issued official regrets and was upset that they were not being broadcast by the television stations. The stations were, of course, fighting their way out of bedlam as they attempted to set up adequate local and network feed coverage of Dr. King's death and the accompanying grief, the police hunt for the murderer, and the rioting. Station managers also were very conscious that a possible massive riot situation existed. "We made a conscious effort to 'cool it,' " wrote WMC news editor Norm Brewer in the next edition of *Scripps-Howard News*. "We did not broadcast the specific details or specific locations of disturbances. Restraint was a byword."

Against police advice, Loeb went to each television station to personally express regrets, and to call for three days of mourning and for the flying of flags at half-mast. He also insisted on checking by the National Guard Armory and police headquarters. "Holloman was very worried," said Sweat. "At the police station…guns were being passed out, policemen were running everywhere, taking off in cars."

As they sped through the deserted streets in an unmarked police car and accompanied by two policemen, Sweat added, "It was certainly in the back of my mind that this man was such a perfect target for all the people who were upset about King's death. Loeb was realistic about it. He realized that there was danger, a grave danger, to his life. But he didn't exhibit anything I saw as fear. He was carrying a gun, incidentally. He had showed it to me…It was a pearl-handle revolver that the police had given him and had requested or suggested he carry. He carried it in his pants pocket…In fact, it was always falling out…He said, 'I wish you wouldn't say anything about this because I told them I didn't want it, but they insisted I carry the damn thing, so I will.' So he kept it in his pocket."

Loeb slept very little during those two days, grabbing rest when and where he could. He was groggy and punchy by late the next day, noted Ned Cook, who watched the pressures on him mount.

In the early hours of Friday morning SCLC staff members and some of the Memphis people gathered again in Room 306. The things that had to be done immediately had been done. The autopsy at John Gaston hospital by Dr. Jerry Francisco, the county medical examiner, had been long and thorough to preclude any of the type of suspicions that had arisen at Dallas. Now Martin King's body rested in the hands of the embalmers at R. S. Lewis and Sons Funeral Home, the somber wait in the chapel there kept by only a few out-of-town newsmen. There had been constant communication with the King family in Atlanta, getting the necessary permission for the autopsy, sorting out the confusion of when Coretta King would arrive in Memphis to escort the body back home, some talk of how the funeral should go.

Jesse Jackson had already left for Chicago as stories of northern rioting continued to pour in. Other members of the SCLC affiliates were heading into Memphis to gather around the staff and help escort the body back to Atlanta.

The men closest to Dr. King were still dazed, their grief restricted to the privacy of their own rooms as every so often throughout the night one or two of them would slip away from the others. "It was something you expect and you might think you're prepared for it, but when it comes, you're never pre-pared," said Rev. Kyles. They tried to maintain balance for each other. Bernard Lee silently packed Martin King's suitcase for the last time.

Rev. Ralph Abernathy would now head the Southern Chris-tian Leadership Conference. There was no question about that. Not only had it been Dr. King's wish, but Abernathy was constitutionally the SCLC vice president. "What the staff did that night literally was to pledge themselves to Dr. Abernathy," said Rev. Kyles.

SCLC aide Jim Bevel talked. "He said, 'As sorry as we are, we can't be down in the graveyard. Martin's dead,' " recalled Kyles. " 'And we've got to deal with that…Everything that we planned has to go on.' " The Poor People's Campaign would go on. And the Memphis men were determined that the sanitation workers would march again that day.

"There was a great sense of unity," said Rev. Lawson. "A great sense of realization that Martin had died on behalf of all of us."

Outside, said Rev. Middlebrook, "the tanks were rolling up and down, and there were rumors of riots in Washington, Kentucky, Chicago, all across the country…How now do we speak to all of these problems when the most nonviolent leader in the history of the country has been shot down? You know, how do you do this?"

At the end they prayed together. And sang "We Shall Overcome."

In the hour before dawn two carloads of the staff went to the funeral home. "I took one load," said Rev. Kyles. "We had to pick out a casket....They went to see the body. I wouldn't go. They were working on the body at that point."

There was one more thing to do. Some SCLC leaders, said Kyles, wanted the blood, to try to preserve it. "There was quite a pool of it on the balcony and we got it up. We scooped it up on a piece of cardboard and put it in a jar." The rites of sanctification had begun.

Greater Laws

14

*"There are laws that are greater
than the laws of Memphis and Tennessee."*
James Wax

He was laid out among his own people in the black section of
the city. And his people came in a steady stream, old men, maids
and clerk typists and day laborers dressed for work, families with
their children, men with button-down collars and teen-agers in
blue jeans, a pitiful handful of whites among them, across the
streets where just a week before violence had spattered after the
march breakup, across grass thick with spring in the bright chill
morning wind. No public viewing of the body had been
planned, but from early morning on the people had come,
standing quietly in front of the Lewis funeral home on Vance,
moving slowly past the body, some leaning forward to touch his
face. Not so much in the purple draped chapel, its tawdry and
pathetic defiance of death lifted in the cross of stained glass, as
outside in the open air would sobs be heard, would heavy old
women seem to give up and stumble and lean on others.

The SCLC staff members found the people when they arrived
to escort the body to the airport, the people solid and sure, the
words that had just been spoken at the Lorraine press conference about carrying on Dr. King's work already translucent,

fading. That impression would carry throughout the next four days. Of the millions of words spoken over this death, only a few would be remembered. But memory of the masses of people would remain and the movement of their grief.

Dr. Abernathy led an impromptu service in the chapel. "The Lord is my light and my salvation; whom shall I fear? The Lord is the strength of my life; of whom shall I be afraid?" There was silence everywhere, said Rev. Kyles. "I am the resurrection and the life." Camera lights flashed. "I made the announcement that I was very sorry that we couldn't let all the people come inside, but that Mrs. King was due to arrive at the airport in ten minutes and that it just wouldn't be fair to have her waiting on his body. And they understood," said Rev. Kyles.

The lid came down on the bronze casket. It was loaded into the hearse, and the long procession of cars, escorted by police, turned to the Memphis Metropolitan Airport.

Flags flew at half-mast at the airport, and the National Guard and police were there with shotguns and riot sticks. Conference rooms had been set aside while those accompanying the body waited for it to be lifted on the plane, and Attorney General of the United States, Ramsey Clark, moved about, talking quietly to SCLC staff. Clark had arrived earlier that morning, sent in by President Johnson to confer with law enforcement officials. Mrs. King, who had brought her children with her, never left the Electra prop jet in which she arrived from Atlanta, and Clark spent some time on the plane with her. Rev. Andy Young spoke again to the press. "I don't care what happened, his faith in nonviolence was never affected and he would plead with us all the time, don't ever let anybody make you hate, that the world just can't live on hate. And unless men learn to get along together and love one another, then human life is impossible. He'd always say, 'I'm not gonna let anybody make me hate.' " Outside a crowd of several hundred watched and waited, shifting between the silent pressure of the Guard and the whine of jet engines.

There was no official city representative at the airport to meet

Mrs. King and this omission angered black leaders even further. "We offered city representation and Mrs. King's representatives told us they didn't want it," explained Ned Cook, as chairman of the citizen airport commission. "We were told 'No.' They didn't want anybody. They'd take care of it themselves...I know that I instructed Captain Bob Wood (director of the airport) to be there...to get hold of them and find out anything they wanted...We did every possible thing we could to expedite it and help them."

But Cook seems to have been talking about the mechanics of moving the body, not about an official expression of sympathy to Mrs. King from the city. "This was an absolute slip on the part of the council or the mayor's office," admitted council Chairman Downing Pryor, "and I was just as guilty as anybody."

At the edge of the field the crowd tried to sing "We Shall Overcome." It trailed off. They could not get through it. At 10:40 A.M., the casket was lifted on the plane, A. D. King and SCLC staff already aboard. In the racking whine of the jet noise the crowd again tried to sing "We Shall Overcome." The plane was airborne. For a moment blacks watched, then, tired, they turned back to Memphis.

It was easier to ritualize Dr. King's death in the memorial service held for LeMoyne College that morning, for the body, scarf hiding the torn neck, was not present. The LeMoyne chaplain, Edward F. Ouellette, elderly and scholarly, had spent the night organizing the program to be held at the Second Congregational Church and intended for the college community and for any other citizens, black or white, who might wish to come. Dr. Hollis Price, LeMoyne president, was helping set up extra folding chairs and as the crowd of mourners grew, a number of them were forced to stand outside the sanctuary. An ABC-TV crew positioned its cameras.

Mrs. Margaret Valient, LeMoyne Gardens public housing project's sole white resident, bore armloads of flowering branches into the church and to the altar. Several years before she and two little black girls from the project had brought flowers to Dr. King as he spoke at a church meeting, remembering, she said, "how the people of the Indian countryside would take their neighborhood flowers to Gandhi when he passed their villages." But that had been in August, in the brightness of flowers. Now in early April, having already viewed the broken windows near the project and been informed by young blacks that they still intended to "burn it down," she carried in the pale, shimmering branches.

The congregation was far more middle class, middle age, than poor or young. There were a few whites and being there had not been simple for them. The church stood in the heart of the black south side and there were still reports of trouble. There was hesitancy about intruding and calling attention to themselves as grieving whites, fear they would appear as hypocrites. "We felt the need to go somewhere and express something," said Midge Wade, wife of a professor of music at Memphis State. "But who would want to see a white face at a time like this? ...But I felt it really didn't matter if no one wanted us there; we'd just go."

The difficulty of openly sharing grief is more a middle-class than a white phenomenon. Grief was tight-lipped that morning and only in the relative anonymity of the hymns, the quickly pieced-together college choir breaking down on "Lord, I want to be a Christian in my heart, in my heart," did tears come.

"The mood had shifted," said Ms. Wade. "Afterwards, people clasped hands, reached out, touched, clung briefly...still miserable but at least together."

Something of the same feeling of release would occur at other church services. Bishop Joseph Durick returned to Memphis to lead a memorial mass among his shattered social action Catholics. This time the congregation would be mostly white and the ubiquitous television lights caught their faces even as they moved to the communion rail itself in vaulted Immaculate Conception Church. But they sang "Kumbaya" as they moved forward and as they commended Martin King to God so they commended themselves to a peace of sorts.

For those ministers, priests, and rabbis gathered at St. Mary's Episcopal Cathedral for their own memorial service that Friday morning, it was over and done. The vascillation, the qualms, the struggle between conscience and rationalization were finished.

Those who had spoken out knew they had not spoken loud enough. And there were many who had not spoken at all. Those who had marched knew they had not marched far enough. And most had not marched at all.

Their brother in the Lord High God, Martin, had moved through the deep waters while they argued in committees, spoke timidly, tested their positions, looked away. Not even the comfortable words of the liturgy could cover that.

Jim Lawson came before them and his voice was quiet.

> He was despised and rejected of men; a man of sorrows and acquainted with grief; and we hid as it were our faces from him; he was despised, and we esteemed him not....
>
> But he was wounded for our transgressions; he was bruised for our iniquities; the chastisement of our peace was upon him; and with his stripes we are healed.
>
> ...because he hath poured out his soul unto death.

When the passage from Isaiah was finished, he simply closed the book and turned away.

In the crowded parish hall Father Nicholas Vieron, pastor of the Greek Orthodox Church, went down on his knees before Henry Starks. "Will my black brother forgive me?" he asked. It was a symbolic act for them all.

And Rev. Starks, who had marched every day with the sanitation workers, could only raise him up wordlessly.

Rabbi Wax stood in the front of the room. "Gentlemen, we have a statement to be read." Bill Aldridge read the statement drawn up to present to Mayor Loeb.

"We, as ministers of God...mourn with deep sorrow and a sense of unspeakable loss the murder of our brother, Dr. Martin Luther King...We implore our mayor and city council to address themselves with swift dispatch to the forging of a mutually acceptable solution including agreement upon union recognition and dues checkoff..."

"Gentlemen, you have a statement before you," said Rabbi Wax. "What will you do with it?" The statement was moved and seconded. A few of the ministers then started asking questions. The Rabbi cut them off.

"Gentlemen, you have a statement before you. How do you vote?" A chorus of "ayes" shouted the motion in.

"There were quite a few 'no's in the back," Aldridge noted, "but they were so quiet it passed as unanimous."

"Gentlemen," said Rabbi Wax, "we will proceed to the sidewalk and Rev. Lawson and Rev. Starks will line us up."

Some of the ministers now stepped to the side, disapproving. "They're not really going to go. They're not really going to march to the mayor," one prominent clergyman kept repeating. "I was elated to see those who had the courage—my white brothers—to march," said Rev. Starks. "And then I was appalled at the number of clergy who didn't have the courage, who for reasons best known to them had business elsewhere, but yet who would come to a memorial service." The crowd of marching ministers simply moved past them.

Spontaneously Dean Dimmick caught up the gold processional cross and moved to the front. Now they were actually moving, something like relief came over them. They began to talk, to smile. Father Greenspun was next to a black minister who had been in Memphis for forty years. Greenspun said, "I think this is the first redemptive fruits," and the old preacher kept saying, "That's right. That's right. I haven't seen anything like this in forty years."

Two-by-two they moved onto the sidewalk. Rabbi Wax, no questions now whether he should march or not, walked with Rev. Starks. Frank McRae was next to Rev. J. A. McDaniel, head of the Urban League. The two white Baptists present, Brooks Ramsey and Bob Troutman, moved into line.

"Dean Dimmick was a real crusader—out in front all by

himself with the cross," chuckled Monsignor Leppert. "He stayed within calling distance of the rest of us though."

At the corner three squad cars with officers in battle gear met and began to move with them along Poplar and down Main to City Hall. The ministers themselves never called it a march; they called it a "procession," a "walk," a "stroll," and pointed out that they stayed two-by-two on the sidewalk and observed all the traffic rules, fine distinctions that did little to placate some of their irate parishoners.

What was their thought? They went as a tribute to Dr. King, as a show of solidarity with the black ministers, in the hope that their action would give Mayor Loeb an excuse to change, and, as Monsignor Leppert would say, because they were "heartsick over the amount of sacrifice necessary to bring justice," and, finally, because they could see no other recourse, to call for the end of the strike through union recognition and the dues checkoff if that was what the solution required. "I was quite willing not to go on the march if anyone could show me any other means of action at all," said Ted Hoover, Memphis State's Episcopal chaplain.

They passed the beds of blowing tulips in front of City Hall. Downing Pryor and Gwen Awsumb were standing outside. "Several of our clergy, these being true Episcopalians, got out of line to go up and shake hands," grinned Hoover who was at the end of the long line. "In the mayor's anteroom there were some men checking through the crowd to make certain all people were validly ordained ministers of one sort or another. They did pull out five or six people who had come into the line as it went down the street."

The mayor's large office was crowded with ministers; they overflowed into the outer room. "Loeb was very dignified, ostensibly cordial," continued Hoover. "He made a very fine appearance. He was back of his desk, television cameras on him. He looked as if we were people coming to congratulate him rather than people coming to deliver an ultimatum....Frankly, I felt for the man."

The mayor listened quietly to the ministers' statement, formally read by Rev. Aldridge, and he started to speak, to thank them for coming, to assure them he would take their words into consideration. The television cameras whirred. Before him stood Rabbi Wax, the leader of his old faith; Dean Dimmick with the cross, defender of his new; Frank McRae, his friend. In the crowd were the dark faces of Rev. Jackson, Starks, Lawson. And his response was not enough for them.

Rev. James Jordan, of Beale Street Baptist, suddenly began to speak. He had had a vision of what the mayor must do to bring Christ to the city, and for the moment the world of signs and portents wheeled above their heads. The stern voice of Rabbi Wax cut in, thirty-five hundred years now since Sinai and the tablets, "What we come here for this morning, sir, is to appeal to you out of the fervor of our hearts that this city shall be ruled with justice, and justice for all. I realize we live in a society of law and order. We must have laws. But I would remind you most respectfully, sir, that there are laws that are greater than the laws of Memphis and Tennessee—the laws of God."

"Yes. Yes," came the black voices.

"Let us not hide behind legal technicalities. Let us not wrap ourselves up in slogans. Let us do the will of God for the good of this city…that every person in this city can live with dignity and self-respect."

Then Rev. Ralph Jackson was there, his broad black forehead wrinkling, his voice beginning to rise. "We have asked you today in that petition and you have not promised it to us. We are asking you, will you please agree to give union recognition and the dues checkoff? We would like an answer. Let others negotiate on finances and everything, but *we* have come to ask you or plead with you today."

"Well, Reverend," Loeb began.

"Put it on us. Put it on the preachers. Put it on anybody, sir." Calling now, "For God's sake, come down!"

"Reverend…."

"And help our people. I'm pleading with you." His voice

broke.

"Well, in equal sincerity and in equal desire to get this behind us, I assure you, Reverend, that we have intended, but we will intend more, to sit down…I think it might prejudice what we do in getting together to talk about it before we get together. But I promise you and each of the men in this room that we're going to do our best…"

There was some embarrassment in the room. Speaking as an Episcopalian again, recounted Ted Hoover, "We wanted to go in there in a very dignified manner, present this thing, and leave." Others were upset not so much by the lack of protocol as by the resultant lack of publicity given their statement by the media. All across the country that night Rabbi Wax was seen on television like an Old Testament prophet before the erring king, but the words of the statement, that statement the ministers had hoped would in some way alleviate the Memphis crisis, were not there.

Ted Hoover continued, "There was a little more back-and-forth kind of talk and finally one of the ministers up front said, 'We are grateful for your time and we thank you for receiving us. We know you have other things to do, and now if you'll allow us to excuse ourselves.' I'd been talking in little side conversations to Dick Moon and he had just been talking to Lawson. We were close together. I said to Dick, 'Well, I think this is as far as we can go on this.'"

Suddenly Rev. Moon's voice went out over the room before anyone could get out the door. "Gentlemen, we have just heard the mayor say the same thing he has been saying for the last eight weeks. He has not changed his mind. He is not going to change his mind. I, for one, am going to stay in his office until he changes his mind. Until the strike is over, I'm going to stay without eating. Anyone who wants to join me, can!"

There was a moment of shocked silence from everyone, mayor, media, ministers. "They had turned to leave," said Dick Moon. "And I was afraid they felt their job was done, and that was the reason I all of a sudden found myself with my mouth open....It wasn't so much a response to the mayor as it was a response to the ministers....I just felt that this was about all they were going to do. And I wanted there to be some kind of reminder to the ministers that they had been there and also a reminder to the mayor that they had been there. I was going to remind them daily with my presence."

It seemed to Moon that consciences, neither his nor those of the other men in that room, should be quieted so easily. And he stood there, a round-faced, prematurely balding figure, as his fellow ministers departed, some to speak to him first and press his hand, others to avert their eyes and push past, irritated that his lone action might mar their collective one and bothered by their own irritation. Only one person came to stand with him—a slim, middle-aged nun, Sister Adrien Marie Hofstetter, a professor of biology at Siena College, who had been supporting the strikers for weeks. "Then all of a sudden out of nowhere came a towboat worker named Edward M. Carter, Jr., a former Memphis State student who was working on the boats," said Moon. "His parents are members of a Presbyterian church here in the city. I don't know how he got there...he followed us in, I guess." Now there were three.

They offered to stay in the outer office, "but the mayor came over. I was sitting on a couch and he squatted down and told me, 'No, this is your office. This is the city's office. You're more than welcome to stay.'" They stayed. Other people came by or sent word. That afternoon they were joined by two young men, Jimmy Gates, Memphis State student, and Richard Geller, creative writing instructor at the university. Throughout that harried day, through the meetings, the consultations with councilmen, police, aides, the various pressures from Washington, the five of them sat in Loeb's office. Evening came and City Hall closed.

"That was the first time I can really recall Loeb showing real strain," said reporter Joe Sweat. "And he was a bit shaken because he asked me several times what I thought he should do about allowing those people to stay in City Hall. And I said, 'I'm sorry, but I am not going to say...I am here as a reporter.'...He was very worried about Sister Adrien Marie's safety, about the safety of them all....And he said, 'We can't put this nun out. We can't just throw them out of City Hall.' Police Inspector Soule said, 'You can't let them stay here.' Soule was very, very firm....The building had to be completely secure....Loeb was saying, 'Why can't they stay downstairs? I don't see any reason putting them outside. There is no place for them to go to the bathroom....We can't throw a nun out on the street!' "

"They had a powwow in his inner office," said Rev. Moon. "And the first man out was one of the inspectors from the police department. He said, 'No, Mr. Mayor! No!' ...and came storming out and said, 'All right, you come with me!' We said, "Where are we going?' And he said, 'Outside.' "

There was, recalled Sweat, "a little bit of a tug back and forth between Soule and the mayor. The mayor was trying to go down to the front door...Soule had the mayor's arm and was trying to pull him back up the stairs and saying, 'Leave them alone. You need to stay inside.' And the mayor was saying, 'No, I just can't. I want to talk to them one more time. She shouldn't be out there.' ...It was very confused....Soule ordered him back into the office, almost physically made the mayor go back....Soule was worried about the mayor's safety and the mayor was worried about perhaps a number of things, how this would look publicly to kick a nun out on the street, his own feeling of compassion."

Outside, with frost warnings out for the night, Dick Moon and the three other men finally succeeded in convincing Sister Adrien Marie to go home. Shortly after she left, the doors to City Hall were opened and they were allowed back inside for the night, to sleep on the long benches in the lobby in the company of two police detectives.

They remained inside the closed building throughout the next day, Saturday, but that night they were evicted. By then sleeping bags had been brought so they quite literally camped out at City Hall for the next seven days, renting a nearby hotel room in order to change clothes and take baths. In the mornings

they would fold their sleeping bags in front of City Hall, move
around to the back to greet Mayor Loeb as he came by, council
members coming in and out, reporters, students, and friends
checking to see if they needed anything.

Because the hunger fast had begun so precipitously, there had
been no physical or psychological preparation for it, but they
struggled through for a week, until Saturday, April 13, supported by Sister Adrien and eight Southwestern students in the
community. Then at home Dick Moon went on to a liquid and
vitamin supplement diet until the strike was settled. His weight
dropped twenty-two pounds. What others made of his gesture
was out of his hands.

For the ordinary citizen, black or white, Friday was an
apprehensive, disjointed day.[1] Businesses, stores, and banks
were open, but schools were closed. Children ran and shouted
in the cool, sunny streets, but parents watched them more
intently and tried to keep them closer to home. Memphis State
University moved its spring vacation forward a week amid
rumors that buildings on campus were about to be blown up.
Meetings and social events of all description were postponed,
including the planned Saturday night crowning of the King and
Queen of the Cotton Carnival at the Crown and Sceptre Ball.
Memphis Transit Authority buses made their regular runs, but
stopped at 6:30 P.M. Fifty-six buses had been slightly damaged,
mostly by rocks, the night before. At grocery stores shoppers
stocked up on food as if they feared siege. Garbage was being
picked up in the east central section of the city, but the workers
were feeling none too comfortable out on the streets.

At midmorning another flurry of reports crackled over police
radios that roving bands of armed youths were looting, but by
afternoon Police Commissioner Holloman said that while
spurts of looting were still occurring in some neighborhoods,
the situation in the city overall was under control. At dark,
trouble began to pick up, but it remained minor compared to
the night before.

The massive manhunt for Dr. King's killer under the direction of local and state law agencies and the FBI "has already spread several hundred miles from the boundaries of Tennessee now," said U. S. Attorney General Ramsey Clark, who had several justice department aides and the assistant director of the FBI, Cartha D. DeLoach, with him in Memphis. "We are getting close." Police were in possession of a great amount of physical evidence in the bundle containing the rifle that the still unidentified assassin had dropped, and all of it had been sent to Washington for analysis by the FBI. Local law enforcement men were painstakingly following up every Memphis lead, chagrined that the killer had managed so easily to slip through their hands. Police were very conscious that the whole country was watching how they handled Dr. King's murder.

Attorney General Clark spent the day conferring with law enforcement officials and touched base with community leaders as well. In an afternoon press conference, he would declare there was "no evidence of a widespread plot," a statement that was questioned as premature at the time and that would continue to rankle those who believed in a wider conspiracy even, or especially, after two-bit criminal James Earl Ray pleaded guilty to the murder a year later. Clark's "no conspiracy" theory was greeted with some relief by local residents who felt more prepared mentally to deal with a single racist killer than with some sort of secret organization—right wing? radical? foreign?—whose tentacles reached even into Memphis. Clark, having pulled some of the loose ends together in Memphis from the federal standpoint, flew back to Washington that evening.

There was a great deal of support among white citizens for the police and National Guard during this period. People brought food to the police stations. National Guardsmen found themselves offered sandwiches and doughnuts and even money and cut prices in stores, especially after it became known that while some Guardsmen received full salary from their employers while on active duty, a few got nothing and others received the difference between their regular salary and the Guard pay.

There was feeling that citizens should stand by their city in this

hour of crisis. Charles Holmes, public relations director of
Memphis State, had volunteered to act as liaison between Police
Commissioner Holloman and the press. The corps of out-of-
town reporters by then in Memphis numbered about 150. In
addition to the Americans, Holmes was working with newsmen
from Japan, Yugoslavia, Sweden, England, Australia, and France.

"Holloman hadn't been to bed when I came in (Friday
morning)," said Holmes. "When he had his first press conference I could tell he was just about out on his feet…he had been
moving and making decision after decision and he was just
about whipped. He was almost numb. His reactions were very
slow…Someone would ask him a question and he would stare
at the person. You could see he was just struggling to try to catch
the question in his mind and dissect it and then get an answer."

But the situation was not as grim in Memphis as it was in the
great urban ghettos across the nation. By late Friday afternoon
at least forty cities were in trouble. In Chicago young blacks
walked out of schools and before alerted Guardsmen could hit
the streets, the fires had begun, stretching finally nearly thirty
blocks along West Madison street, out of control, and with
water pressure low; looting was reaching the Loop, and Mayor
Richard J. Daley was pleading for order. Before it was over, there
would be federal troops in Chicago and other cities. In New
York City, Mayor John Lindsay personally went into the ghettos
to talk to crowds. New York's worst time had been Thursday
night. Nashville was under curfew but quieting. On Saturday
Baltimore and Pittsburgh would join the stricken list.

The horrified television eyes of the nation were on Washington by Friday night. Morning there had been sluggish after the
outbreaks of Thursday night. With the 1968 Civil Rights Bill
still bottled up in Congress, President Johnson met early with
twenty-one civil rights leaders from across the country and then
attended services for Dr. King at the National Cathedral. By late
afternoon fires were again burning and smoke hung over the
White House while pillaging and glass-breaking crowds, many
laughing and cheering, hit stores only blocks away. The Presi-

dent called in regular army troops to aid the National Guard, the first to be called into Washington since the Bonus March of the thirties. In the night a hundred fires were raging and soldiers in combat fatigues stood watch over the White House and Capitol Hill. The next day paratroopers would come in.

That night in Memphis the heavy curfew was on again from 7:00 P.M. to 5:00 A.M. and only those civilians involved in emergency services were to be allowed on the streets. Officials in adjoining Arkansas and Mississippi also declared curfews.

The Memphis City Council was in almost continuous session throughout the day. A resolution expressing sympathy to Dr. King's family was passed, which also affirmed the council's dedication to the principle of nonviolence and urged fellow citizens to that same dedication. The council guaranteed to underwrite $50,000 in reward money for information leading to the capture and conviction of Dr. King's killer, joining the *Commercial Appeal* and the Scripps-Howard publishers who had each pledged $25,000. Lewis Dolelson's resolution putting the city on record as a model fair employment opportunities and practices employer, that same resolution which had been in and out of council discussion for a month, was passed.

But the council was in an emotional state. Billy Hyman's lumberyard on North Hollywood would be firebombed three times during the disturbances. J. O. Patterson didn't reach the meeting until noon because he had been at the airport with Dr. King's body. There were conflicting feelings, unexpressed but underlying, not only over what they should do now but over what they should have done weeks ago.

And there was a new plan for stopping the strike. An anonymous businessman, or group of businessmen, were offering $25,000 to pay union dues for a six-month cooling-off period if the strikers would return to their jobs while city and union continued in negotiations. If no contract were drawn up, the men would be free to strike again.

"I loved that," said Councilman James sarcastically. "The

guy's blood hadn't congealed good yet. There we were mixing a murder with facts that had nothing, absolutely nothing, to do with the strike…We are letting somebody come in on a sharing basis and inject themselves into a strike settlement that we said we had nothing to do with in the first place by public decree."

The resolution on this cooling-off period was never officially introduced for vote in council. Councilmen Davis and Netters would not agree to its introduction unless Patterson approved and Patterson did not.

Pressure from the city's businessmen on Mayor Loeb to end the strike took on a different quality. Some business leaders saw Loeb, said Ned Cook, to say, "Listen, the fat's in the fire….They told Henry that the strike had to be settled now…that the business community insisted that it be settled at once…And Loeb's answer was, 'Well, we're going to settle, but we're not going to settle and shoot with a scared stick and just bend over and let them have the whole city and do something that's idiotic. We'll proceed with negotiations on a rational basis.' " But, said Cook, "The pressure was put on from every conceivable source."

Councilman James observed, "I saw the change take place in the mayor the morning after Martin Luther King was murdered. I knew that he was going to give in then…He wasn't nearly as determined or adamant."

The Monday mass march would be allowed to go on, came the word out of U. S. District Court as Judge Bailey Brown publicly announced the legal decision he had reached just before Dr. King's death. The city had withdrawn all legal objection. The march would be subject to those restrictions suggested by Dr. King's lawyers. The march would become a crusade for those who planned and those who marched.

No one knew how many people would pour into Memphis from around the country before going on to Atlanta for the funeral there the day after, nor, for that matter, how many Memphians would walk, but forty thousand seemed a reasonable figure to work with. There would be meetings of march planners with city officials and police, endless checklists, the training of marshals. Speakers had to be confirmed and a platform assured for the rally in front of City Hall. There would have to be doctors and nurses available and mobile toilets. Placards had to be printed and march instructions, and liaison set up with unions all across the country who would send representatives. All through the weekend planning for the march went forward.

Meanwhile the long row of strikers with their placards moved slowly up Main Street on their regular daily marches. Law enforcement officials were not happy. It seemed madness to allow the union marches, but in the face of strike leaders' determination that the march on Friday would go even if every man were arrested as he stepped into line, police allowed the march.

L. C. Reed of sewers and drains told it. "Ralph Jackson asked us after the tragedy did happen, were we still willing to stick together, and we all agreed that we was and we wasn't going to stop marching."

His wife nodded. "Mens are mens these days no matter what color they are."

Efforts to resume strike mediation again lurched forward. Marx Borod's proposal was now in the hands of mediator Frank Miles, and Miles told Borod that official negotiation sessions were to begin again. It was the last news Borod had of his written plan for settlement until the actual end of the strike.

Jerry Wurf flew into Memphis that Friday afternoon on a plane out of Washington that also carried Bayard Rustin, fresh from the emergency meeting of civil rights leaders with President Johnson. Rustin had not been back in Memphis since his speech there to the mass meeting in early March, but he had been speaking about the strike and raising funds. He was returning now at the request of Rev. Lawson and labor leaders to help plan the memorial march.

Wurf's deep anger and frustration of the night before had not

been assuaged, and, if anything, his determination to establish
the Memphis union went even deeper. "You couldn't kill King
and then destroy the union. That would have been too much.
That would have been too much for Loeb, which that fool
couldn't understand. Do you understand what could have
happened to that city had they destroyed the union?"

In this mood he was hardly even startled by what he considered Bayard Rustin's uncharacteristic response to Memphis as
they drove in from the airport. "Many of our blacks consider
Rustin a sellout...an apologist for the worst elements in the
American labor movement...But he's a man of moderation,
committed to nonviolence totally, whatever other faults he may
have. Bayard looked around and said, 'My black brothers simply
haven't carried out their mission. There's too much of this town
standing.' ...He didn't really mean it...but it was descriptive."
Somberly, they watched the streets of Memphis move past the
car windows.

Undersecretary of Labor James Reynolds followed them in
from Washington a few hours later. At the department of labor
he had become through the years involved in many disputes that
concerned the national welfare and had taken on the role of a
sort of special mediator in difficult cases that had frustrated the
efforts of usual mediation channels.

Late Friday morning in his Washington office he had a call
from President Johnson. Why aren't you in Memphis settling
the garbage strike? the president wanted to know. "And I told
him," said Reynolds, " 'Mr. President, the reason I am not down
there is because you must understand the federal government
does not involve itself in labor disputes which concern municipalities or the counties or states and their employees. And we
never get involved unless we are specifically asked to do so.'

" 'I don't care whether you're asked to do it,' he said. 'I am
telling you I want you to go down there. And you may say that
you are down there at my direction to do everything possible to
bring that strike to an end. When you get down there, call
Governor Buford Ellington to tell him you are in the state so he

will know. And then the rest is up to you.' "

Reynolds left directly for the airport. As the plane swung out, the passengers looked out of the windows to see smoke rising from 14th Street. Washington was burning.

He arrived in early evening, found Memphis "crowded with half-tracks and soldiers," and went directly to The Peabody hotel. He checked with Governor Ellington in Nashville, as the President had instructed.

And then, Reynolds continued, "I called Mayor Loeb…reached him at home…and told the mayor that I had been sent there by the president to do everything I could to assist in resolving the difficulty and that I would like very much to seee him immediately. And the mayor pleaded that he had been up all the previous night…and would I mind waiting until early the following morning." The meeting was set for 7:30 A.M.

Next Reynolds hunted out Jerry Wurf, and met with Wurf and Bill Lucy. "The mayor had, in Mr. Wurf's opinion, positioned himself in such a very clearly defined manner that to retreat from that was going to be extremely difficult for him…Mr. Wurf was quite bitter in his comments about the mayor, of course…They regarded him as a very serious, violent racist…But I didn't accept that. I wanted to appraise the mayor on my own terms, by my own yardstick."

Reynolds also learned of Frank Miles' efforts at mediation and that night the two men met and spent several hours together reviewing the strike. Like Miles, Reynolds came out of a background that included both labor and management. He had left a seat on the New York Stock Exchange to learn the steel business, working his way up from a molder's helper at a foundry in Bessemer, Alabama, into management. He got into labor relations in the navy department during World War II, and after the war was appointed to the National Labor Relations Board by President Harry Truman. Under John Kennedy, he came in as assistant secretary of labor, eventually becoming undersecretary.

"Just from the first day we met we hit it off as a team and we worked as a team. The most enjoyable association I ever had as a mediatior was with this fellow," Miles would say. Reynolds put it, "From the time I contacted him until the thing was resolved, Mr. Miles worked very closely with me and he was a great assistance…I had a feeling that the union people respected him as well as the management people, so this was a great help."

In a strike where so much had gone wrong, the working together of Miles and Reynolds was one of the best things that happened.

Early the next morning, Saturday, Miles sent out telegrams calling both union and city representatives back into negotiation. Reynolds would participate. And Reynolds headed for his appointment with Mayor Loeb.

"Walking up Main Street very early in the morning, a beautiful Saturday morning, I do recall looking around. It was the first time I had ever been in Memphis…There were very few people on the streets, but there were some soldiers about…Main Street looked prosperous. It didn't seem possible to me that there could be such deep bitterness and racial differences of this sort in that city. But I went to City Hall…and as I walked up, there were guards, armed guards, outside the City Hall with rifles and pistols, and I came up and identified myself, and word had been given that I was to be permitted in. So the armed guards let me in, and there at the foot of the stairs were two more armed guards…city police or deputies, because some of them were in civilian clothes, but with pistols. Two had rifles…There was an atmosphere of great tension. I was directed up to the mayor's office and there sitting outside his door were two more armed guards." Inside the office were two more.

The mayor was sitting behind his desk in shirt sleeves. "I said, 'Do you mind if I take my coat off, too?' …and I rolled up my sleeves as he had his rolled up. I said, 'Let me get something very straight, Mr. Mayor. I have been sent here by the president, *but* having said that, let me tell you that there is no intention of anybody in the federal government coming down here to try to dictate and direct the terms of the settlement. You are the man who has to run the city and you are the man who is going to have to live with it—and the people are. And I am not going to come here and be an intruder thinking I know all the answers. But I am here to try to help you—to try to help the city—to terminate this thing in as quick and as peaceful and as logical and honorable way as we can.'

"And, you know, he said, 'I think I like you.' And he said, 'How about a Coke?' And I said, 'Yes, that will be nice. Let's have a Coke.' So he said to one of the sergeants, 'Go and get a couple of Cokes,' and the guard jumped up and said, 'O.K., Mayor baby. O.K.' And I thought for a moment I was in the midst of a Tennessee Williams' play. I just couldn't believe the rapport and the informality.

"The Cokes came and I asked the mayor to then tell me please what the problem was. And he said the problem was, 'We are not ever going to recognize this union.' …Well, that was a pretty difficult point to start from."

Before the official afternoon negotiations, "We had a session up in Jim Reynolds' room with Mr. Wurf and Mayor Loeb and Mr. Reynolds and myself," said Frank Miles. "We were trying to explore the possibilities…but it also served the definite purpose of bringing Henry and Wurf back together."

The second series of mediation sessions began at the Claridge. Assistant city attorney James Manire had been added to the city team, and Rev. Ralph Jackson, the black community representative on the union side, was out helping organize the memorial march, but otherwise participants were the same as the two weeks before. "Reynolds said that the eyes of the world were there on that table, whether the people at that table realized it or not," said Miles.

The groups began working within the concept of a memorandum of understanding, clarification of and agreement to that framework having come out of Miles' earlier meetings. They met until after midnight on Saturday, reconvened on Sunday, and worked until early Monday morning, recessing then for the memorial march and Dr. King's funeral the next day in Atlanta.

Any optimism that the strike would be immediately settled soon dissipated. Even after all that had happened, reaching agreement between the city and union was going to be a long haul.

Meanwhile John T. Fisher was pursuing support for the idea of a city-wide public gathering on Sunday, April 7, to express the anguish he was sure many Memphians were feeling. What he intended was to bring ordinary black and white citizens together in a neutral setting where they could express a concern, a caring for each other that would transcend all the horror and violence and mistrust in which they now found themselves. The problems in holding such a meeting in Memphis at that point seemed insurmountable. There was the danger of violence in bringing any large group of people together. There was no guarantee that both black and white citizens would attend and if the gathering were not integrated, it would serve no purpose. There was the shortage of time. By the time supporters of the gathering, now named "Memphis Cares," had convinced people as wide apart as Police Commissioner Holloman, business leaders, and Rev. Lawson that such a meeting should—and could—take place, less than twenty-four hours remained.

By Saturday afternoon seventy-five volunteers were working out of the board of education building, opened to them by school board president and businessman Edgar Bailey. Committees were handling stadium, publicity, speakers, program, and statement. Hundreds of phone calls were going out to invite people to attend.

"We said, 'All right. Each committee is autonomous,' " explained Fisher, hardly believing everything was pulling together. " 'You don't have to report back. Go out and do your job.' The first time I saw the stage was when I walked in. I didn't know if it would be ready or not."

Concourse of Witnesses

15

*"Would to God this great concourse
of witnesses could have been with
him on that last Thursday..."*
Ben Hooks

The palm fronds swayed in the high Christian churches, and congregations in triumph welcomed the Christ into Jerusalem, down the long green arch toward Golgotha. On public buildings flags flew at half-staff. That Palm Sunday, April 7, was the national day of mourning for Martin Luther King, and all across the country the preachers, those caring, went before their people, black and white, to try to make sense of it all—Jesus, love, sacrifice, justice, Martin. So they did, too, in Memphis, some of them, finding parallels in Christ's love for the city and King's concern, the weeping over the city then and the weeping now. In some of the churches the Memphis Cares gathering was announced and pastors encouraged their people to join them there. In other churches only Jesus went his way.

Driving past the National Guard Armory, Rev. Dick Wells found flags at full staff. A jeep pulled out with a colonel and a driver. "I rolled my window down and he anticipated me with a cheery 'Good morning.' I said, 'Colonel, why aren't your flags at half-mast?' 'I thought that was yesterday,' answered the

colonel and drove off.' " Wells took time to make some
protesting phone calls to police and the Guard liaison. The flags
were lowered.

Memphis Cares early that afternoon was not one gathering; it
was many. Pictures of it are deceiving, for they show rows of
people on the south bleachers in old Crump Stadium, all
looking toward the football field and the American flag hung
with black streamers, all hearing the speakers as if, indeed, they
all were focused sight and sound on one point. Some had come
in actual fear of what might now happen in any large grouping
of blacks and whites. Many left their children at home out of that
fear, although artist Dolph Smith and his wife Jessie, as uneasy
as any, purposely brought their children as a token of faith that
violence would not occur. People had come, seven or eight
thousand of them, perhaps a third of them black, in memorial
and tribute to Martin Luther King. No? Not for that? They had
come as part of their civic responsibility, called by their leaders
to demonstrate the concern of Memphis for all the media and
country to see. No? Well, then, because this was an acceptable
way to call for an end to the strike. No? They had come because
there was a chance that this might presage a new direction for
the city...because they felt guilty that events had reached this
point while they sat by...because this was as good a place as any
to begin involvement? Yes? No? For some or none or all these
reasons they had come.

A strong wind rammed around the microphones. "Come,
Holy Spirit, and fill the hearts of your faithful," intoned
Monsignor Leppert. The planners had expected Rev. Zeke Bell
for the invocation; he did not appear. "Where there is injury, let
us sow pardon; sorrow, joy..." went on the dry voice of the old
monsignor. The rain was holding off but it would come. The
skies were leaden. "Our shelter from the stormy blast," sang the
assembly in defiance of both man and fate.

Dr. David Alexander, president of Southwestern at Memphis,
defined their common ground, Memphians concerned about

one another. On the platform John T. Fisher hurriedly scribbled notes for what he would say. Rev. Lawson had arrived; Fisher was relieved about that and about the sizable crowd. That many of his friends and acquaintances would think he was crazy for even getting mixed up with an idea like Memphis Cares was something he would have to deal with later. Now he stood at the microphone, voice rising against the wind. "The time has come when you must stand and be counted. Make up your own mind. Choose your ground. And stand on it…or we have more trouble than we imagine."

A black physician, Dr. E. W. Reed, spoke next, and for the first time the name of Martin Luther King was spoken aloud. The taboo was broken. The audience could look at the name now, mentally touch it, acknowledge that it was among them. Dr. Reed was calling for change. "A good place to start is an immediate settlement of the garbage strike." There was scattered applause. The second taboo fell. So it was not to be an indefinable meeting for community uplift. Episcopal Bishop VanderHorst came forward to speak and then high school teacher Ms. Mary Collier who had worked with the strike.

Outside the stadium, sirens sounded and the audience shifted uneasily. The long wailing shimmered across the football field and passed, echoing off toward the hospital complex.

"For it was to Memphis he came, to the people in need…" spoke Tommy Powell, of the labor council. "Working men have the right to form a recognized union." The clapping kept breaking in on him.

John Fisher shifted uncomfortably. He was not exactly sure what kind of speeches he had anticipated, but these were edging into controversy. A piece of paper was passing around the platform. Signed by a black political faction leader, it said that Memphis Cares was going to raise money for a King memorial and to get the new expressway named for him. "I couldn't even breathe when I read that. I thought, if somebody gets up there and says that, I don't know what I'll do. I'll have to say something. I didn't come here to try and build any memorial to

Martin Luther King. I came here to talk about Memphis. It was bad enough what I had to listen to…but this! Boy! I was in the lion's den."

The next speaker, Judge Ben Hooks, was to lead him firmly to the lion's jaws. Judge Hooks had just returned from Atlanta, from the body and the public manifestation of grief. The applause was long as he was introduced, as he stood there, and it was to interrupt him constantly. "We come today to pay tribute to the passing of a great man, Martin Luther King, Jr. We come belatedly. Would to God this great concourse of witnesses could have been with him on that last Thursday…."

Hooks was not the judge now but the Baptist preacher, voice rising and falling, cadenced, stressed. Down near the front a black woman began to moan and wail and friends surrounded her, a distracting huddle of movement. In the audience the uneasiness rose. "For all I know he thought that he was in a memorial service for Martin Luther King," thought John Fisher grimly. "That's what his speech was about."

Magnified by the microphones, his voice echoed across the old football field. In the stands several groups of white people stood up angrily and began to leave. "I thought to myself, 'Man, alive, if that Ben Hooks doesn't be quiet and sit down…' " remembered Fisher. "People felt like 'Wait, this ain't what I thought it was going to be. It's not quite the deal!' "

Judge Hooks pushed on. "And I call today on the mayor of this city to settle the sanitation strike and to do it now…or there cannot be peace…And if it mark us for death to speak the truth, then let it come, but the truth must be told."

A few more whites were leaving. "I could see the next speaker Tom O'Ryan down there, and he was getting madder by the minute and I didn't know whether he was going to get mad enough to walk off or to do something," said Fisher.

"…When we can, black and white, join in singing 'Free at last. Free at last. Thank God Almighty, I'm free at last!' "

The shouting voice echoed off and half of the crowd responded to him in anger and resentment or in approval and

faith, but he had broken them open. They remained collected,
but the variegated emotions that had brought them there and
had lain below so shallow a surface were now out in the air.

Into this sudden breach now stepped the most extraordinary
speaker of a whole extraordinary afternoon—Tom O'Ryan.
"Tom O'Ryan was my saving grace," murmured John Fisher.
O'Ryan was an Irishman who had emigrated to America as a
young man, worked on construction of New York subway
tunnels, gone into transit advertising, and finally owned his own
advertising agency in Memphis. He worked hard on numerous
civic charities, and he had supported the idea of Memphis Cares.

But for Tom O'Ryan, the tone of the gathering was amiss and
he would set it right. His brogue was thick, lovely in an
outlandish way in the setting, another contradiction. "I deeply
regret...that you weren't born in a foreign country...that many
of you here who get emotionally disturbed and fight—or holler
rather—had not been the victims of oppression in a foreign
country. I was born in a foreign country. I was born when...foreign
soldiers walked our land."

The audience was quiet, watching, ready to follow but unsure.
"Hollering?"

"America is the greatest country in the world." There was
applause, some heartfelt, some dutiful. "With great privilege
comes obligation...to love your fellow man in the sense that you
want them to love you." Another smattering of applause, mostly
puzzled silence. "You cannot burn down and loot—even
though it's only a fraction of the community. The total community should not bear the ills of a few."

The final proscription was violated. He had picked this
moment to lecture to blacks. There was more movement in the
stands. Some blacks were walking out on him, still not quite sure
of his ultimate point but somehow insulted, resenting the tone,
refusing to listen. They missed his final statement, the statement
he had come to so badly.

"I recognize the white people have a tremendous obligation,
but the obligation alone is not on the whites. The obligation

rests on the total community, not a segment of the community."

He had, indeed, balanced the program. He had represented those whites who were at Memphis Cares not because they chose to beat their breasts over their past actions but because they were willing to try to make a fresh start on equal terms with blacks, but who felt the fresh start could never be made without blacks acknowledging that they, too, bore some of the responsibility for where the city now stood. It was a reasonable response. Reason there had to be, but now more than reason was required. Reason alone could not lift murder into reconciliation.

Rev. Lawson stood now at the microphone in long silence, a black opposition leader called upon by whites yet another time to speak to gatherings that were predominantly white. What did they want of him? Symbolic forgiveness from the black community? He could not speak to that. Black denunciation to bring white emotional catharsis? He did not play at that. Or were they in some strange way testing him, waiting for his faith in them to fail?

"I decided to come this afternoon after a great deal of hesitation....As I understand our coming together, it is not only that we are sorrowful but because we know that the events that we have seen over the last few days in Memphis call us together.

"Crucifixion is a terrible sign. We have witnessed crucifixion in the city of Memphis...Is the crucifixion which occurred here on Thursday and which still takes place in our city—is this crucifixion a sign from God? If it is a sign, it is an awful and a shattering one...God's judgment on you and me and upon our city and our land that it is already too late. That the time is now upon us when not one stone will be left upon another stone in this place, but that this city and this nation which we love dearly will become nothing more than a roost for vultures and a smoldering heap of debris."

The darkness was on them. Another siren wailed across Memphis streets. Chicago and Washington still tasted the acrid smell of smoke.

"If this crucifixion is a sign from God, it may not only be a word of judgment but, pray God, that it would also be a word of healing. For if it is a word of judgment, then it is a call to repentance.

"Now repentance is not illustrated by some of the things that I've heard over the last couple of days...I've heard people laughing that this man, this human being like you and I, in the full prime of his life, is dead, shot down, executed in cold blood. That is not repentance. Repentance is not being concerned whether or not business moves away from Memphis. Repentance is not being concerned whether or not people outside of our city will have a good feeling about us.

"How can anyone have a good feeling about Memphis when one of the finest sons of this world of ours was shot down in her streets?"

John T. Fisher had given up. "Thoughts were expressed later that they (some of the speakers) double-crossed us and it didn't go, this harmony and platitude and atmosphere and 'We're gonna do better' and all. My own thoughts were that at first. By later that afternoon...it became to me very clear that...the best thing about that meeting was that it was honest and truthful and righteous."

Jim Lawson would speak long. "And no matter how much we try, from now on until there is no longer any written history, Memphis will be known as the place where Martin Luther King was crucified...

"But if we have come here because...we are determined that we will repent, that we will turn the corner and turn the ways of our city, then God can make out of this act our healing and the healing of the life of this city and this land..."

At the end the assembly, in hope because hope dies last of all, stood and read the Memphis Cares pledge and sang "God Bless America." Rabbi Harry Danziger gave the benediction. The crowd broke, swirled across the grass and dirt toward their cars, spiraled prism-like toward every section of the city. Whether

Memphis Cares meant everything or nothing, no one dared to say.

John Fisher wrestled with his experience there for a long time. Several days later he would make the necessary follow-up and speak of it and the need for involvement by the business community to the Rotary Club, reaching there the most powerful business leaders in the city. "Man," he told a friend, "I wouldn't trade a world for this Memphis Cares (experience), because I got out of it alive this time…But I'll tell you one thing. You'll never show me up like that again in my life. I'm not going to be caught up there in just that neat little 'don't get involved' group…If I want a place to walk in the world, then I had better get around creating that place."

Final plans for the mass memorial march went on throughout that day and far into the night. Downtown merchants were unable to agree on a unified statement explaining why they would all close during the march. A few of the store managers wanted to stay open and "take their chances," though there seemed small chance of doing much retail business. Almost all of them finally did remain closed, but suburban stores were open.

Ned Cook spent Sunday at the airport. Planes bringing in marchers were arriving from all parts of the country. "We had to get the Federal Aviation Administration and block off part of the air space… I don't know how many buses had been ordered and told to go to the airport. Well, where at the airport? And we had all these charter flights, running from Electras to DC-8s…It was a real crowded situation." Additional marchers were arriving from all around by car.

Bayard Rustin sat in on the important meetings with city officials in the march planning while union and COME people did most of the leg work. "I don't know how much sleep Rustin got, if any at all, on Sunday night," said John Spence, of the civil rights commission. "But I went with him that night over the route of the march, block by block and step by step."

The park commission built a low platform in front of City Hall that night, said Rev. Dick Moon from his hunger strike vantage point at the building. "Bayard Rustin and Lawson came by and some of the others and said, 'This isn't tall enough.' Then about 12:30 that morning, we were all asleep and all of a sudden this army moved in and people were laughing and screaming and tearing things up. I was afraid to open my eyes. I thought they were coming to get us. But here were about twenty people tearing down this platform, and madly, and in about thirty minutes they had it down. And trucks moved in and they had all this equipment and they put up this big superstructure for a platform. They worked all through the night."

By 10:00 P.M. that Sunday, the period of violence in Memphis was over. Statistically, the city was comparatively lucky. The report of the international chiefs of police showed finally three civilian deaths, forty-seven fairly serious injuries, property damage at around $900,000, 275 stores looted, and fires, characterized as occasional, confined to the "ghetto" areas. Like fire, violence had begun in a quick burst and ended in a sputter.[1]

City Councilman Jerred Blanchard flew in from Houston at 1:00 A.M. that dark Monday. Nobody was moving on the streets. The taxi driver bringing him in from the airport was gloomy and pessimistic. "And the air was gloomy and pessimistic," said Blanchard. "I couldn't sleep. I didn't want to march. I really didn't want to be alive that day. I guess it's really about that simple. We had a little whiskey. I bought the *Commercial Appeal*, read all about it, drank the whiskey, read the paper, drank the whiskey, got more and more sober. Went to bed about three and tossed till five. Got up, stewing and fretting.

"It was a gray day, and God didn't make great decisions...on gray days. I went downtown and tried to practice law. Couldn't practice law because the Temple was calling. And I knew it...So I went on down to Clayborn Temple (rallying point for the march)."

He had stopped to talk to National Guardsmen during the week before. "These were my kind of guys...white guys...from

Harrison, Martin, Dresden and everywhere…I'm a soldier and the military I understand and like…I've fought two wars with them. That morning walking down to the Temple, boy, it was different! …all those tanks around and those personnel carriers around, every crossing. You could scarcely get to the Temple.

"So I get down there and I shuffle around. Can't make up my mind whether to go home and cry or—so finally the heart says, 'Well, you gonna march?' I hadn't decided yet. You would like it that way. Later I can say all about the moral bases, right and wrong.

"But on that great, tired, weary, hungover Monday morning, it was my mother speaking and my wife. I'm not trying to be dramatic, but what I'm really trying to say is that decency said, 'You get your old south end in that march, bud, and go on. To hell with the country club.'"

In the rain-threatened streets of Memphis the great, quiet Memorial March moved, Hernando to Linden, Linden to Main, to City Hall, preceded by police escorts, sound trucks, a flat-bed truck for photographers, and a row of marshals stretching hand-in-hand across the street. Other marshals, among them the Invaders keeping their promise to Dr. King, moved along the sides of the march. National Guard lined the streets and clustered at intersections at parade rest with bayonets attached to unloaded rifles. "We asked for the cooperation of people not to open the windows and to stay back from windows and not to get on the roofs. We ran people off of roofs," said Assistant Chief Lux. Overhead the two police and Guard helicopters circled, loud because the march was silent. Another thousand Guardsmen had been brought in for the march; they now totaled five thousand, and M-48 tanks were in use for the first time. "Persons intent on discord may attempt to enter the city," Commissioner Holloman had warned.

There were few spectators. Some store windows had protective boards across them; others showed floral displays for Dr. King in their entrances, either in tribute or to ward off any "destructive impulses" on the part of marchers. Outside of the downtown area, Memphians, expecting the worst from the whole affair and wishing alternately that it was all over or happening elsewhere, tried to go about their normal routines, but schools were still closed and over radio and television came periodic reports on how the march and rally were progressing.

The march moved forward in stops and starts. Mrs. King and her three older children joined the front rank at Main and Beale. She had come, she would tell the crowd later, because when it was impossible for her husband to be where he was needed, he would sometimes send her. "I felt he would have wanted me to be here." Police Commissioner Holloman, deeply concerned about her safety in an open march, stayed by her throughout; so did Lux, so close that any sniper would have had to knock them out of the way to reach her. The television cameras caught Holloman scanning buildings, watching from side to side.

Eight abreast came the marchers, another sign added to their lexicon.

HONOR KING—END RACISM

In the front rows were the well-known SCLC leaders; Walter Reuther, president of the United Auto Workers, who would himself soon die in a plane crash, and Leonard Woodcock, UAW vice president; Bishop John Hines, presiding bishop of the Episcopal Church of the United States; Dr. Abraham Heschel, of the Jewish Theological Seminary in New York; Tennessee Catholic Bishop Joseph Durick; Percy Sutton, borough president of Manhattan; Albert Shanker, president of the American Federation of Teachers; anti-war hero Dr. Benjamin Spock. Singer Harry Belafonte walked by Mrs. King; Bill Cosby and his popular "I Spy" television show co-star Robert Culp slipped into the procession farther back. James Brown marched and Sidney Poitier and Ossie Davis, and a representative from Actors Equity. As in Selma, there were men from the race and civil rights divisions of the national religious denominations; the

AFL-CIO civil rights division officials were there.

"The town was full of labor people," Bill Ross of the labor council would say, identifying marchers from more than a dozen international unions, as well as Cesar Chavez' farmworkers. AFSCME locals across the country sent in people, some two or three, some large contingents. The union delegations carried signs.

MICHIGAN PUBLIC WORKERS
NEW YORK TEACHERS

Police reported the crowd at nineteen thousand, based, they said, on their line-by-line count. National newscasters were estimating thirty-five thousand to forty thousand. Bayard Rustin set the figure at forty-two thousand. Whatever the number, the march stretched from City Hall nine blocks down Main to Linden and around the corner without ending, a great, moving mass.

The bulk of the marchers were Memphis blacks, men and women and youngsters from all segments of the community. Spread among them were the whites. By the end of the strike, white Memphians who had publicly supported it were almost all mildly paranoid.

Many, both black and white, marched with trepidation. Episcopal chaplain Ted Hoover would laugh about it afterwards, but that morning he got out his will and left it in his secretary's hands before he went off to march. It seemed inconceivable that there could be any trouble with a third of Tennessee's National Guard surrounding them, but blacks were leery of the Guard itself and whites found themselves with mixed feelings, on the one hand grateful the Guard was there and on the other outraged, as one would say, that in a free country one had to walk between bayonets to express an opinion about a strike and assassination.

"I wasn't really scared that day," mused Councilman Blanchard. "I was in the fifteenth rank. Why should I be scared?

Holloman though—he's right up there at the front. Every time that blasted parade would stop and the voices would start to rise, then you couldn't help but think 'Oh,' and then you'd tense a little…I was looking around for a place to run. And then I'd look up there and there's Holloman just standing there." He mused further. "And the mayor's missing it all. It's really his kind of show, too."

Closely packed together at City Hall Plaza and spilling off into surrounding streets, the marchers listened to the rally's main speeches and to those who came by to "just say a few words." The program lasted for three hours.

Mrs. King spoke first, the long ovation a tribute to her own courage in coming that day as well as to her husband.[2] Women in the crowd sobbed quietly; others stood with wet eyes. "My husband was a loving man…devoted to nonviolence…able to instill much of this into his family. We want to carry on in the best way we can…We loved him dearly…and we know that his spirit will never die…The campaign for the poor must go on." Only at the end did her anguish show. "How many more must die before we can really have a free and true and peaceful society? How long will it take?"

Ralph Abernathy took their sadness and worked with it, exhorting, shouting, with old Baptist oratory. Nobody gonna turn us around…I'm gonna drink from the springs of freedom in Canaan land. I'm gonna eat from the vines in Canaan land…I'm gonna lead to victory.

"Freedom," shouted the crowd. "Free…dom! Freedom!" Roaring, clapping, laughing.

Jerry Wurf, the dry New York accent, reviewed the strike for them. He had been in mediation sessions until six o'clock that morning with still no success in reaching settlement. "As a white trade unionist, I say to you with shame that only the black community cared.…I pledge to you this…we'll go back to these meetings…not with hate but with love…That so long as we shall live we shall not forget our struggle to be men, our struggle to stop being 'boys.' …and until we have justice and decency and morality, we will not go back to work!"

UAW president Walter Reuther, pledging to "drag (Henry Loeb) into the twentieth century," held high a $50,000 check from the UAW to Local 1733. And P. J. Ciampa, on the platform, came to life, still not believing that all those days of trying to find money to keep the strike going were now behind him. Ciampa had also been at the all-night session. "I was so exhausted...And Walter Reuther came with his $50,000 check. And I wanted to make sure that Walter didn't pull out—'Here's the check, folks!'—and put it back in his pocket. So I staged T. O. and some other guy so that the minute he says 'the check' to stand up and say 'Yes, sir.' And grab the check. Walter says, 'For God's sake, I want to make a speech!' But T. O. had the check."

Through all the speeches the crowd stood and cheered, not flaking off around the edges until the very end. As the march returned to Clayborn Temple, down Second, people began moving out of it, slipping down side streets toward their cars or toward the streets they would walk home. Back at the Temple the march would scatter.

But the marchers had done what they set out to do. They had marched peacefully in Memphis. In their own way, they had honored Dr. King and supported continuation of the union struggle.

There was one final rite of passage for Dr. King and obliquely for Memphis. That was the funeral in Atlanta the next day, 100,000 people marching behind the mule-drawn caisson to the campus of Morehouse College. Memphis black leaders went to Atlanta, several churches sent buses, and an AFSCME contingent of strikers and their wives, led by T. O. Jones, went over.[3] The city sent as its official representatives hospitals director Odell Horton, who had been in college at Morehouse with Dr. King, Councilmen Fred Davis and James Netters, and council Chairman Downing Pryor. They flew to Atlanta in Ned Cook's jet, and Cook had arranged for a car and driver to get them to the Morehouse campus.

They arrived at the campus two hours ahead of the scheduled time for the service. Downing Pryor was distinctly uneasy in the huge crowd. He stayed till almost the end of the orations, then still feeling somewhat edgy, he squeezed out of the crowd and walked down the street to where a black family had allowed them to park the car in a side yard.

"I asked if I could sit on the porch for a minute. They said they were watching the end of the service on TV and to come on in and sit with them. There were about seven or eight Negroes in the room...A very handsome, very large man there was a minister...I apologized for intruding and they made me feel very comfortable."

On the television the Morehouse alma mater was being sung and the people in the room stood up. "I stood up with them. Then they got into holding hands and singing 'We Shall Overcome.' And there was one verse in it about black and white blending together...and when it was over, I said that I really felt like I had added to it. I was a stranger, but they said, 'No, we think it's nice that you were here. Where are you from?' Then I just said Tennessee. 'Where in Tennessee?' I said, 'I am from Memphis.' And he said, 'Well, I am surprised that you would come today.'"

The chairman of the Memphis City Council paused. "But he made me feel very comfortable and very good."

I Am a Man

16

"I Am a Man. They meant it. It was a real thing."
James Reynolds

Around the negotiation table at the Claridge, members of the city and union delegations met and argued, separated and met again while Frank Miles and Jim Reynolds worked into exhaustion to bring about the strike settlement. The mechanics of the meetings were the same ones that Miles had initially set up.

"One group met in one room and one in another until there was really something to say and something to agree on, because there was no point in them sitting across the table, because the more you did that the more bitterness was growing up, building and building," said Reynolds. "So it was a question of going back and forth and back and forth and then, occasionally, bringing Loeb and Wurf together."

The city knew now that if there was going to be a settlement, there was going to be a recognized union. There was no help for that. "We bargained with a gun at our head...not that we thought it was the right thing to do but to relieve the situation....They had the ball game won and even though we had these pressures put upon us, we didn't feel like we could capitulate and give them carte blanche the rape of the city which is what they wanted," said Tom Todd. "We had to make out as best we could." Todd represented the city's attitude at the extreme, but all of the city representatives were determined to hold the line as best they could, even though that line was in retreat, and to, almost in a protective sense, stand by the mayor, who would say "...after Dr. King was killed, I thought that we simply had to get this thing behind us...in the country's interest and for many other reasons...There wasn't any deviation in it or a sellout. The only change was this horrible thing of Dr. King killed in Memphis."

"There is a way here," Reynolds would assure them again and again at the beginning when cities were still burning and "No! No!" was the only response in bargaining. "This isn't unique. There are other municipalities that have been confronted with efforts to organize and to have people speak for employees. Please think of this within the welfare of Memphis, but please recognize that what you are doing has an impact all over the country."

The union team, convinced as never before that some sort of victory was at hand, grew more and more frustrated as the bargaining dragged on. There was nothing Wurf could report back to the union and the black community as a breakthrough. But Reynolds, knowing that Wurf also had to hold his own small group of negotiators together, remained firm. "We're not going to stop. We're going to keep at it day and night if necessary and we are going to settle it!"

Reynolds realized the mayor was in a difficult position, too. Once, he recalled, "the mayor expressed his deep regret that the murder of Dr. King had occurred. And there was sullen but deep hurt on the part of the fellows on the other side of the table. Almost afraid to answer any expressions of sympathy from Mayor Loeb because they distrusted him, they disliked him...It had all the ingredients of a disaster. Everybody would walk out and that would be the end of it."

No one did walk out. Mayor Loeb, within the confines of his opposition to the union, remained unfailingly cooperative with the mediators. He trusted both Reynolds and Miles. Several members of the city team proved moderating influences. Wurf held himself and his men in check. Gradually, substantive terms began to emerge in a memorandum of understanding that read remarkably like the one drawn up by Marx Borod.

First agreement came on use of the word "recognition." It had become a symbolic word not just a legalistic one. The union was not to be "acknowledged" or "accepted"; it was to be "recognized." That was the word Rev. Ralph Jackson on behalf of the black community movement had insisted on. The mediators perceived this and what lay beneath it.

Reynolds never told Wurf or Loeb, but he would strike up conversations with the picketing workers on Main Street. How long had they worked? How much were they earning? He knew, on the basis of salaries in other southern cities, that they were underpaid. But he also found that more important to them was what they had come to regard as the dignity of being "recognized."

"I Am a Man! They meant it. They wanted—for the first time—even though they were the men who picked up garbage and threw it into trucks—they wanted somebody to say, 'You are a man!' It was a real thing." We have got to get some recognition for these people; it's a basic matter of dignity, he told Miles.

The final memorandum would read:

> The City of Memphis recognizes the American Federa-
> tion of State County and Municipal Employees, AFL-
> CIO, Local 1733, as the designated representative for
> certain employees in the Division of Public Works, for the
> purpose of negotiations on wages, hours and conditions of
> employment to the full extent and authority provided by
> the Charter of the City of Memphis and the laws of the
> State of Tennessee. The term "certain employees" as used
> herein places no limitations or restrictions on the right of
> any employee to belong and be represented by the union.

This was not exclusive recognition, but it was recognition enough.

There was easy compromise on fringe benefits, insurance, vacations, sick leave, overtime, and on pensions. The city would simply list such present benefits with the understanding that discussion on them would continue.

The clause on promotions was short. "The City shall make promotions on the basis of seniority and competency." Mayor Loeb reported there was never any question about that. No time was spent on it.

Nor was much time spent on the "non discrimination" clause that "no member of the Union shall be discriminated against or discharged because of the present work stoppage or subsequent Union activities, including the utilization of the grievance procedure outlined herein, and there shall be no discrimination against any employee because of age, sex, marital status, race, religion, national origin, or political affiliation." However, this would provide no immunity for strikers for any law violations that happened during the strike.

Essentially this clause guaranteed that all the men who had gone on strike would be rehired. Since Mayor Loeb had promised that none of the replacement workers would be left without work when the strikers returned, this left the city with an overload of 350 to 400 workers in public works, and would raise problems for several months until some of the new workers could be shifted to other departments or found jobs in private industry and until the natural attrition of public works unclassified workers again lowered the total.

The agreement on the grievance procedure left the mayor with the final decision after acknowledging union representation at all stages of a complicated process of investigating and reporting. A three-man arbitration panel would make recommendations to the mayor.

A no-strike clause was included. The city insisted on it, but Wurf did not fight it.

Throughout the negotiating, Jim Reynolds kept in touch with Washington, reporting back to the secretary of labor on how the settlement was going. Washington was not concerned about details but about an end to the dispute. "One night I was close to Reynolds when he hung up the phone and he said, 'That was the president,' " Miles related. " 'He wants to know when in the hell you and I are going to get this strike settled. I tried to tell him we are working as hard as we can on it.' ...By the end we were numb...played out emotionally."

The tough issues of the dues checkoff and the wage increase dragged on, the dues checkoff because of the complicated mechanics of it and the pay hike because of the lack of money in the city budget.

"Any idea of the city engaging (directly) in a checkoff was out of the question," said Reynolds. Wurf had modified that demand almost immediately, when he had suggested in mid-February that the employees' credit union be utilized for deducting dues. All attempts throughout the strike to settle it had swung around this idea. Loeb had fought it almost until the end, ideologically and administratively. But the Public Works Federal Credit Union, Charter No. 15433, was a wholly separate corporation chartered and operated under federal statutes. The city had no control over what monies were deducted from the credit union members' checks nor over what those monies were used for once an employee had authorized the credit union to act for him, as long as such deduction and payment was consistent with federal credit union policy.

Working out the mechanics of the checkoff through the credit union was involved. AFSCME paid the initial credit union membership dues for the men who did not belong, and this, too, would be deducted. The union was insisting that the checkoff authorization forms the men had already signed were sufficient and that no new forms were necessary. "This is where Jim Reynolds is really helpful," said Miles. "He gets hold of a man in Washington in whatever department it is that heads the whole thing up, and he can get some answers...he can unlock

doors real quick." The board of directors of the local public
works credit union, half of them on strike, had to be brought
together to approve the plan. The area director of credit unions
had to approve. "In some instances," said Miles, "we had to go
as far as Washington to get approval of some of the mechanics
that were being worked out."

The dues checkoff, after recognition the most exacerbating
issue of the whole strike, was finally worked out. The union
would stand on a firm financial footing in Memphis. Local 1733
dues would be four dollars per month, with one dollar of that
sent to the international union. Additionally, Wurf announced,
for the duration of that first memorandum of understanding,
the international would send its one-dollar-a-month dues from
each Local 1733 worker back to Memphis to be used in
"worthwhile community projects among the poor." It was
Wurf's last futile attempt to say that AFSCME might care about
more than lining its international pockets.

In the end, negotiations became a matter of dealing with the
economics of the pay raise. Both Reynolds and Miles thought
a fifteen-cents-an-hour package would be required, ten at the
beginning and five cents later. That figure had been bandied
about throughout the strike and it did not appear the strike
could be settled for less. Their recommendation was that the ten
cents be made effective on May 1 and the subsequent five cents
on September 1.[1]

The mayor had agreed to a pay raise in the next fiscal budget
beginning July 1, but not before that. In fact, he was talking in
terms of a total raise of five percent, which was less than the
package. And "it would be awfully difficult for these men to
bring a termination to the strike without any increase at all at this
time," said Reynolds.

Estimates were that the public works raises would total around
$558,000 for the coming fiscal year. That amount could be
included in the new budget. The trouble was, Miles reported,
the city actually had no money to give raises before that. At this

impasse, civic and cultural philanthropist Abe Plough, who sixty years before on a borrowed $125 began to build the multi-million dollar pharmaceutical firm of Plough, Inc., offered his assistance. He would contribute to the city the money to pay the raises before July 1, but insisted that his name not be made public.[2]

"It could have presented an almost insurmountable problem had he not come forth with it," said Miles. "He placed his confidence in me to handle it in the best interest of the city and in his interest as well in protecting his funds. And I tried in every way possible to protect the interest of both."

The amount Plough contributed and which the city agreed to accept and then use for the pay raises for two months was originally estimated at $50,000. However, it finally figured out nearer $60,000 and Abe Plough increased his gift by another $10,000.

"I had never heard of such a thing," commented Reynolds. "I think it was one of the most remarkable and noble gestures that I have ever heard of."

The last mountain had been climbed. The memorandum of understanding was drawn up to run until June 30, 1969, end of the next fiscal period.[3]

In the morning of Tuesday, April 16, city and union committees met jointly for the last time in what Reynolds labeled "a spirit of reasonable good will." City negotiators then left for the executive session of the city council and the union men for a meeting with black community leaders before presenting the agreement to the men on strike for their vote.

" 'This has been your fight as well as our fight,' Wurf told them. 'We think this should be recommended to the men for approval. If, however, you don't think it should be, you are welcome to…say what you will. We want you to.' And I, and every other union official, got out of the room while they discussed it. They agreed unanimously that it was worthy of recommendation."

That afternoon the city council, in regular session, adopted the memorandum of understanding as city policy, knowing that now the mayor believed it must be done. Only Bob James voted against it, still holding that the council was violating the city charter by the vote. The mayor, who would retire from political office after his term was over, was never in an official position of supporting the memorandum of understanding. Final praise or blame rested on the council.

The moment of the long struggle that was Memphis was over now. It lay behind all of those who had the great responsibilities and views and ideologies and who, whether by choice or chance, had come to share in it—the leaders of the greatest mass movement for social change of the century, the leaders of national politics, of labor, of religion, even the presidency itself.

It had been about principalities and powers, decency and justice and true honor, but the torn symbols it would leave in a nation's consciousness would be simple and concrete. The scuffed I AM A MAN signs. The mapped trajectory of a bullet from a cheap rooming house to the Lorraine Motel. Tanks in city streets. Scraps of garbage.

In the end, the strike would come again into the hands of the men where it had begun.

The union meeting was cheers and shouts of joy, praise the Lord, and singing, great loud laughter and sudden tears.

They had won. They had the union, the pay raise, the dues checkoff.

They had won. They had become part of the process of determining their own lives, their employment conditions.

They had won. They listened carefully to the reading of the agreement, every clause, every explanation. And they voted. In a roar. They danced in the aisles. They rushed the platform and engulfed their leaders—the local union stewards, T. O. Jones, Wurf, Lucy, Ciampa, Epps, Lawson, Jackson, all the ministers,

Jesse Turner of the NAACP. They grabbed each other's hands and slapped each other's backs.

They had won.

That knowing they would always have.

Martin King was dead and the cost beyond counting.

But they had won.

Early the next morning—sixty-five days it had been—they went back to work.

A   P   R   I   L   1   6   ,   1   9   6   8

On Making the Book

This book comes out of the work of the Memphis Search for Meaning Committee although it in no way officially represents that project.

The ad hoc Search for Meaning Committee came into being in those disjointed April 1968 days immediately after the assassination of Martin Luther King and even before the final settlement of the public works strike which brought him into Memphis.

Its members understood only dimly *what* had gone wrong and even less *how* and *why* the drama of labor dispute to racial crisis to catastrophe had played out all around them. But two things they were sure of. They had been witness to an important moment in American history. And it was crucial both for themselves and for their city to understand what had happened.

Their first move was to begin to analyze the local newspaper coverage of the strike period. But as word of their project spread, several unexpected things happened. First, all sorts of related material—letters, television news outtake film, a bloodied I AM A MAN sign—began to come in from other people and the committee found itself an unplanned repository of files of material reflecting community attitudes and actions during the strike.

More important, within three weeks the decision had been made to begin taped interviews of people involved in the strike and assassination period. The committee begged and borrowed several large reel tape recorders and set out. Some one hundred fifty people were interviewed and taped during the summer and fall of 1968. Caught in sharp focus on these tapes are the thoughts and feelings of those days, before time could blur, soften, or change recollection.

The committee of some eighty people was, for its purposes, the right group in the right place at the right time. Its members had ties to many parts of the community, both black and white. There were a number of people with media experience. The entire project was headed by David Yellin, then professor of radio/television broadcasting at Memphis State University, and his wife Carol Lynn, an editor of the *Reader's Digest* book division. There were several professional historians. But there was also a wide range of others—lawyers, businessmen, housewives, teachers, an Episcopal priest, a medical student, the owner of a women's dress shop, even a junior high school student who would grow up to become an architectural photographer.

The entire effort was volunteer. Memphis State University loaned office space. The Pepper Tanner recording studios contributed tapes. The *Reader's Digest* book division made a small grant which helped carry the project through its first six months. But for the next two years a small core of people struggled to get the tapes transcribed and to organize the great mass of materials.

Finally, two large grants were obtained from the National Endowment for the Humanities for the professional collation of the entire collection through Memphis State. Now titled "The Sanitation Strike Project," the collection includes 364 audio tapes, film, newspaper files, photographs, some art, and printed materials of all types. It is housed in the Mississippi Valley Collection of the university library. From all over the country scholars and writers on media, civil rights, race relations, labor, politics, southern history, and Dr. King have come in to use the material.

I joined the Search for Meaning project in its second week of existence in April 1968 and stayed with it until the collection went to the university. This book was begun during that early period.

Insofar as possible, the story is told in the words of the people who were the story. There is no quotation in this book that cannot be found in the research collection, in the interviews, newspaper reports, on film, in writing. The *Commercial Appeal* and the *Memphis Press-Scimitar* news columns were invaluable in following the chronology of the strike period and for their coverage of public city activities and policy. But the taped interviews were the key to the real story. An extensive list of tapes and sources can be found at the end of this book.

The rapid advances in printing technology made publishing the book in Memphis feasible. *At The River I Stand* was published in softcover in October 1985 under the logo of B & W Books. My husband Jack and I did the selling and distribution ourselves and allowed the book to run out of print after three thousand copies had been sold and orders were still coming in.

In 1989, Ralph Carlson, of the new Carlson Publishing, Inc., reprinted the book in hardcover as one of the eighteen volumes in his major studies series on "Martin Luther King, Jr. and the Civil Rights Movement." The series, with David J. Garrow as overall editor, is aimed at academic libraries.

This St. Lukes edition, then, is the story's third.

Over the years a great many people have believed in this book and among the many a few must be named. First of all is Edith Fox, who painted the figure of the sanitation worker used throughout and who contributed her work. Next my thanks go to Queen Esther Morrell who mothered my children in those early years; to Jim Simmons, Phyllis Tickle, and Roger Easson for their professional advice; to Bill and Charlene DeLoach for their computer and so much more; to Fred Wimmer at the first production point; to David Bowman, Walter Wade, George McDaniel, Charles and Linda Raiteri, Charlotte Schultz, and Ed Weathers for reading parts of the manuscript; and to Frank Wranovix for his understanding.

But most of all I am beholden to Dave and Carol Lynn Yellin, Jerry Viar Thomas, Tom Beckner, and Bill Thomas at the source, and to my husband Jack and to our five children who grew up surrounded by pieces of research and manuscript, John, Jill, Joellen, Nan and Kate.

Joan Turner Beifuss
February 1990

Notes

Chapter 1: Fertile Ground

1. Ciampa had been in Memphis in the preceding summer to explore chances of any of the mayoral candidates supporting union recognition. He found no support.
2. The deficit was cut. By June 1968 it had been reduced to a little less than $800,000. By June 1969 it was around $25,000. By the end of Loeb's term, the budget was balanced.
3. Local black hero Tom Lee, who rescued thirty-two people from a sinking river steamer in 1925 by making repeated trips back and forth from shore in a small skiff, was rewarded by the city, which gave him a steady job in the garbage department, bought him a house, supported him in his last years, and erected a thirty-foot high granite obelisk in his honor on the riverfront.
4. At the time the city put its workers under Social Security, those employees who had been paying into the city pension plan had the choice of staying in the plan, going under Social Security, or belonging to neither. All new unclassified employees were to come under Social Security. In sanitation all but thirty of the men voted to withdraw from the pension plan because the monies they had paid into it were refunded.
5. Eyewitness reports are drawn from the *Commercial Appeal* and *Press-Scimitar*, Feb. 2, 1968.
6. Mayor Loeb's "kitchen cabinet" would at times include Tom Prewitt, Walter F. Armstrong, Jr., John Heiskell, Myron Halle, Frank Gianotti, Tom Todd, Harry Woodbury, and E. W. (Ned) Cook.

See taped interviews with C. Blackburn, J. Cherry, M. Cherry, Ciampa, Epps, Gianotti, Gillis, Hyman, Jones, Kuykendall, Lucy, Manire, Powell, Reed, Ross, Sisson, Todd, Wurf.

Chapter 2: Garbage Is Going To Be Picked Up

1. Direct quotations from Loeb and Ciampa during the first set of negotiations at City Hall; from Loeb and union leaders addressing strikers at the Auditorium; and exchanges between labor leaders and city council members several days later are drawn from the *Commercial Appeal* and *Press-Scimitar*, Feb. 13–17, 1968.
2. Reports on early meetings at the union hall are also drawn from the notes of Police Det. Ed Redditt, assigned to cover the union meetings from the first day on. He subsequently testified to his information at the chancery court hearing of Mar. 6. Cf. "City of Memphis vs. Local 1733, AFSCME, AFL-CIO, et al, 69415-1 R.D."
3. For details on this particularly gruesome case, cf. William Miller, *Memphis During the Progressive Era*, p.10 ff.
4. As late as 1973, Harold Jones, field representative for the Office of Minority Enterprise, U.S. Dept. of Commerce, estimated that while blacks owned ten percent of Memphis businesses—eleven hundred—of them, most had less than two hundred dollars a week gross income. Cf. Susan Adler's articles on Memphis black business, *Press-Scimitar*, Jan. 2–3, 1973.
5. The magnitude of the poverty problem was reflected in the statistics of MAP-South, the War on Poverty multi-service program in the old neighborhood stretching south from downtown where the largest concentration of poverty was found. There were some fifty thousand people centered in ten thousand families. Median family income in the area was $2,600, but sixty-seven percent of the families were earning less than $2,100. MAP-South

estimated eighty percent of the housing was substandard. Thirty-nine percent of children between fourteen and sixteen were not in school. Seventy-two percent of the young men called up from the area failed the selective service examination. Illegitimate births ran three times higher than the city rate and infant mortality was significantly higher. When a supplemental food program for a small group of children was begun under the auspices of St. Jude Children's Research Hospital, actual malnutrition was found in families whose staple diet was fatback, beans, and overcooked greens.

Based on census figures for Shelby County, Jacques Wilmore of the U.S. Civil Rights Commission reported in 1966 that median black family income in the county stood at $2,666 with white income at $6,031; that 51.1 percent of blacks were found in service and laboring jobs; and that 57.2 percent of black families earned less than $3,000 per year compared with a white percentage of 13.8.

The Regional Economic Development Center at Memphis State University in 1968 estimated that forty-seven thousand to forty-eight thousand households in Memphis and the county were still below the $3,000 poverty line.

In 1967 the Fund for Needy Schoolchildren estimated that children from some forty thousand families were eligible for free or partially paid lunches in the public schools because their total family income was less than $3,000. Cf. reports of United Way, 1972; Tenn. Advisory Commission to the U.S. Commission on Civil Rights, 1967; Hammer, 1969; MAP-South, 1968; Stewart, 1966; and War on Poverty, 1966–67.

6. For a vivid picture of the Yellow Fever epidemics in Memphis, cf. Gerald Capers, *Biography of a River Town*, and novelists Charles Turner, *The Celebrant*, and Edward Hatcher, Jr., *Gayoso Bayou*.

7. For an overview of black politics in the 1950s and particularly the 1959 election, cf. William Wright, *Memphis Politics: A Study in Racial Bloc Voting*.

8. A forerunner had been a race relations committee begun in 1956, but composed of separate white and black groups. Since some of the white members at that time did not choose to meet with blacks, special representatives of each group were chosen to meet together. Out of these meetings the integrated MCCR would eventually come.

9. Other candidates in the mayoral campaign were Commissioner of Public Works, Pete Sisson; Commissioner of Public Service, Hunter Lane; Shelby County Sheriff, William Morris; and Ms. O.E. Oxley, co-owner of a flying service.

10. Cf. Arthur Crowns, "A Case Study Analysis of Police Relations During the Summer of 1967 in Memphis, Tennessee."

See taped interviews with Ahlgren, Burch, Ciampa, Crowns, Davis, Epps, Gianotti, Gillis, Holloman, Hooks, Jones, Kyles, Lucy, Manire, Ray, Reed, Sabella, Sisson, Smith, Stimbert, Sugarmon, Turner, Wax.

Chapter 3: Contempt in My Heart

1 Among the men working with Rev. Jordan were the Revs. J.W. Williams, W.E. Ragsdale, Brady Johnson, A.C. Jackson, and W.M. Brown.

2. Cf. tape, P.J. Ciampa meets with Memphis Ministers Assn., Feb. 16, 1968.

3. Cf. tape, negotiations under auspices of Memphis Ministers Assn., Feb. 18–20, 1968.

See taped interviews with Ahlgren, Aldridge, Awsumb, Bell, Blanchard, Bryant, Chandler, Ciampa, Davis, Dimmick, Donelson, Fanion, Gianotti, Hyman, James, Jenkins, Jones, Jordan, Lucy, McAdams, McRae, Netters, J.O. Patterson, Perel, Pollard, Pryor, Todd, Wax, Wurf.

Chapter 4: Planted by the Waterside

1. Direct quotations from the Fred Davis committee hearing are drawn from reports in the *Commercial Appeal* and *Press-Scimitar*, Feb. 22–23, 1968.
2. Direct quotations from the meeting in the Auditorium, Feb. 23, are drawn from the *Commercial Appeal* and *Press-Scimitar*, Feb. 24, 1968.
3. Mace was squirted from an aerosol can. The active irritant in the spray was a tear gas affecting eyes. But another chemical had been added to break down the oily protective skin coating to allow the tear gas to work directly on nerve endings on the face and hands. A direct hit with the spray caused pain and a feeling of burning, blinding, disorientation and loss of balance, and shortness of breath. Mace was then being adopted by police departments across the country as a crowd-control device though the range of the spray was only about twenty feet. But reports were already being gathered on skin burns, minor eye damage, and allergic reactions that resulted, and there was a question whether the resultant reduced respiration might not prove fatal to anyone already suffering from respiratory difficulties. In 1971 the Memphis Police Dept. discontinued the use of Mace.
4. The grand jury in mid-March indicted eight men for nightriding and disorderly conduct on Feb. 23, among them John Kearney of the green sweater and T.O. Jones.

See taped interviews with Awsumb, Bell, Blanchard, Bryant, Carpenter, Caywood, Chandler, Ciampa, Davis, Doctor, Donelson, Epps, Fanion, Gillis, Harris, Holloman, Hooks, Hyman, Jackson, James, Jones, Kyles, Lawson, Lucy, Lux, Middlebrook, Moon, Netters, J.O. Patterson, Pryor, Sengstacke family, Starks, Todd, Turner, Wilmore, Wurf.

Chapter 5: Nothing but the Strike

1. Also listed in the injunction were union stewards and leaders Nelson Jones, J.L. McClain, Joe Warren, Booker T. Bonds, Oscar Middleton, Lent Willis, Alvin Turner, James Jordan, Lee Washington, and Peter Parker.
2. Cf. David Tucker, *Black Pastors and Leaders.*
3. For example, churches turning in bulk contributions the first night were Ward Chapel, Progressive Baptist, Bethel Methodist, St. James AME, Oak Grove Baptist, Mt. Olive CME Cathedral, Mt. Zion AME, St. Mark Missionary Baptist, Beulah Baptist, Olivet Baptist, and Pentecostal Temple. COME kept records of all contributions.
4. Quotations from strikers are from the *Commercial Appeal.*
5. Before expansion, the strategy committee was composed of Rev. Lawson, Jesse Turner, Ms. Cornelia Crenshaw, Ms. Thomas C. Matthews, and the Revs. G.E. Patterson, P.L. Rowe, Henry L. Starks, Harold Middlebrook, Ezekiel Bell and H. Ralph Jackson.
6. Cf. "City of Memphis vs. 1733, AFSCME, AFL-CIO, et al."69415-1 R.D., Mar. 5, 1968.

See taped interviews with Bell, C. Blackburn, M. Blackburn, Blair, Ciampa, Cook, Epps, Hooks, Jackson, Jones, Jordan, Lawson, Lucy, Moon, G. Patterson, Powell, Reed, Sabella, Spence, Starks, Weintraub, Wurf.

Chapter 6: No Easy Riders Here

1. *Commercial Appeal* political editor William Street asked rhetorically in his Feb. 28 column, "When does a labor problem become the politics of race?" and answered 1) when all the necessary ingredients are there as in the strike, 2) when there is money to be raised and

power to be gained by expanding labor into civil rights, and 3) when a strike is all-Negro and the opportunity arises to attack the white power structure. "There are sagging reputations to be bolstered...depleted financial reserves to be shored up." The Shelby County Democratic Club, the Unity League Democratic Council, the NAACP, and "other groups hastily formed to make hay...now supply the cheerleader qualities." Street specifically named Jesse Turner, Vasco Smith, O.Z. Evers, O.W. Pickett, A.W. Willis, Rev. Ezekiel Bell, and Rev. James Lawson. Each has his own ax to grind, he wrote. Each must out-promise, out-shout and out-condemn so that "on another day they can say, 'We spoke for you.' He also deplored the "distortion of truth" by some of the preachers in their reports on the Macing and in their implications that "Mayor Loeb is taking a stubborn stand because he is dealing with a union of Negro employees."

2. The report on this incident, as well as some other material on the mass meetings, is found in J. Edwin Stanfield, *In Memphis: More Than a Garbage Strike.*

3. The Nashville group, headed by Kelly Miller Smith, included students who would later become well known in the civil rights movement—James Bevel, Diane Nash, Bernard Lafayette, Marion Barry, and John Lewis.

4. Cf. James M. Lawson, Jr., "We Are Trying to Raise the 'Moral Issue,' " address at SNCC conference, Raleigh, N.C., April 1960, in Broderick and Meier, *Negro Protest Thought in the Twentieth Century.*

5. The FOR team also included Geneva pastor and underground leader against the Nazis Andre Trocme and German pastor and anti-Nazi leader Martin Niemoeller. The FOR report was widely circulated in U.S. church circles. Cf. Alfred Hassler, *Saigon. U.S.A.*

See taped interviews with Allen, M. Blackburn, Bryant, Cook, Cooper, Doctor, Fisher, Holloman, Ivy, Jackson, James, Jemison, Jenkins, Kallaher, Lawson, Lux, Middlebrook, Starks, Taylor, Turner, Wilkins, Wilmore, Wurf.

Chapter 7: Down Where We Are

1. Cf. *Commercial Appeal* and *Press-Scimitar* reports, Feb. 28, 1968.

2. Walter Chandler's place in history would be secured because of his part in the Supreme Court's "one man, one vote" decision. There had been no reapportionment in the Tennessee State Legislature for nearly sixty years. As chief counsel of Baker vs. Carr (Shelby County Court chairman Charles W. Baker vs. Tennessee Secretary of State Joe C. Carr) Chandler would spearhead the case. In March 1962 the U.S. Supreme Court handed down its far-reaching decision breaking the hold of rural forces over the cities in numerous state legislatures and opening "one man, one vote" challenges in other political areas. Cf. Gene Graham, *One Man, One Vote.*

3. Cf. *Commercial Appeal* and *Press-Scimitar* reports, Mar. 6, 1968.

See taped interviews with Awsumb, Bell, M. Blackburn, Blanchard, Caywood, Chandler, Cook, Davis, Donelson, Hyman, James, Kyles, Lawson, Lux, McAdams, Middlebrook, Miles, Moon, Moore, Netters, J.O. Patterson, Perel, Pryor, Smith, Starks, Sweat, Todd, Wurf.

Chapter 8: Mats and Spittoons

1. Signed by Aldridge, Dr. John Morgan, James Simpson, and Taylor Blair, this letter caused considerable perturbation in Presbyterian circles. The governing body of Aldridge's own church, Idlewild, wrote an overture to the Presbytery asking whether the Christian

Relations Committee had overstepped its authority. On Apr. 23, 1968, the Presbytery ruled that perhaps it had, but complimented members on their attempt to be a reconciling force in the community.

See taped interviews with Aldridge, Awsumb, Blair, Blanchard, Burch, Casey, Caywood, Chandler, J. Cherry, Cook, Dimmick, Donelson, Doughty, Durick, Fisher, Geary, Greenspun, Hooks, Hyman, Lawson, Leppert, Manire, McRae, Miles, Moon, Pryor, Ross, Southwestern students, Spence, Starks, Tolleson, Wax, Wilmore, Wurf.

Chapter 9: Here Comes Dr. King

1. "Hambone's Meditations" officially ceased to exist on Apr. 30, 1968, cartoonist Alley acknowledging regretfully that Hambone had outlasted his time.

See taped interviews with Ahlgren, Awsumb, Blair, Blanchard, Bryant, Donelson, Durick, Hooks, Hyman, Ivy, James, Jones, Lawson, Leppert, Lucy, Middlebrook, Miles, Moon, Netters, J.O. Patterson, Pryor, Ray, Reed, Ross, Smith, Starks, Stimbert, Woodbury, Yellin.

Chapter 10: Situation out of Control

1. Although most reports of the march and disruption come from other sources, also cf. *Press-Scimitar* Mar. 28–30, and *Commercial Appeal*, Mar. 29–31, 1968.
2. For the feelings of younger blacks in the march, cf. "The Memphis Riot," ninety-seven eyewitness accounts by LeMoyne College students. Also note Paul Barnett and Ray Sherman radio tapes.
3. Officers were supposed to wear identification badges at all times, said Asst. Police Chief Henry Lux. But on Mar. 28, police were still in their heavy winter uniforms and when they took off their coats, many did not transfer their badges. Badge numbers were also carried on officers' hats, but not on helmets. In other cases, police were fearful that badges served as targets for snipers and removed them.
4. Description of the fatal shooting of Larry Payne is drawn primarily from court testimony in the civil suit brought by his parents against Patrolman L.D. Jones and the city in U.S. District Court in 1971. The Shelby County Grand Jury had failed to indict Jones in June 1968. The federal court decision went against the Paynes in their 1971 suit. Cf. "Mason Payne and Lizzie Mae Payne vs. Leslie Dean (L.D.) Jones and the city of Memphis, defendants." C–69–87.

See taped interviews with Aldridge, Awsumb, Bailey, Bell, Berry, M. Blackburn, Blanchard, Bryant, Caywood, Ciampa, Crowns, Davis, Doctor, Doughty, Epps, Fanion, Geary, Gillis, Greenspun, Harris, Holloman, Ivy, Jackson, Jenkins, Jones, Jordan, Kallaher, Kyles, Lawson, Leppert, Lucy, Lux, Middlebrook, Moon, Netters, Palmer, G. Patterson, J.O. Patterson, Powell, Reed, Ross, Sengstacke family, Smith, Southwestern students, Spence, Starks, Stimbert, Taylor, Tolleson, Turner, Walker, Wells, Wilmore.

Chapter 11: Mission Accomplished

See taped interviews with Blanchard, Bryant, Ciampa, Dimmick, Donelson, Doughty, Epps, Kyles, Lawson, Leppert, Lux, McGinnis, McRae, Miles, Moon, Stimbert, Taylor, Wells, Wurf.

Chapter 12: Jericho Road

1. Cf. Marx Borod resumé of attempts to end strike.
2. Only later would Cherry remember the Dallas newspaper which printed a right-wing ad attacking John Kennedy on the morning of Nov. 22, 1963.

See taped interviews with Bailey, Walter (Bill) Bailey, Bryant, Burch, Caywood, Cherry, Ciampa, Cook, Doctor, Epps, Fanion, Fisher, Gianotti, Greenspun, Holloman, Hoover, Ivy, Jackson, Jordan, Kuykendall, Kyles, Lawson, Lucy, Lux, Manire, McGinnis, McRae, Middlebrook, Miles, Perel, Ross, Sengstacke family, Smith, Spence, Starks, Taylor, Wax, Wurf.

Chapter 13: Darkest Day

1. Cf. "City of Memphis vs. Martin Luther King, Hosea Williams, Rev. James Bevel, Rev. James Orange, Ralph Abernathy, Bernard Lee..." C–68–80.
2. For further descriptions of trouble on the streets, cf. *Press-Scimitar*, Apr. 5–6, and *Commercial Appeal*, Apr. 5–7, 1968.
3. Cf. "Reactions to Assassination." No actual polls were taken in Memphis that spring on reaction to the killing of Dr. King, but several informal surveys were made, particularly at Memphis State University. Because most of the students were commuters, the response may give some indication of how feeling was running in the community, or at least in the white community since most of the MSU students were white. No attempt was made to differentiate between black and white respondents. The MSU surveys were done in a basic psychology lecture class of 75 students and two sophomore history classes with 98 students, a total of 173. The question was "What was your reaction to the assassination of Martin Luther King, Jr.?" One hundred five students, or 61 percent, expressed disapproval of the killing; 35, or 20 percent, many of them deploring killing per se, generally approved of this killing; and 33 students, 19 percent, didn't care one way or the other. The same question was asked of 53 students at suburban Millington High School north of Memphis, primarily white. Among these students, 55 percent disapproved of the assassination; 28 percent approved; and 17 percent were neutral. Both samplings are too small and unscientific to base any conclusions on. Results are cited here only to give some slight indication of opinions surrounding the assassination in the city where it happened.

See taped interviews with Aldridge, Bailey, Walter (Bill) Bailey, Bell, Branch, Burch, Caywood, Chandler, Ciampa, Cook, Davis, "Death of Bessie Smith" cast, Donelson, Dreifus, Epps, Fanion, Ferguson, Fisher, Gianotti, Gioia, Greenspun, Hess, Holloman, Hooks, Hoover, Hyman, Jackson, Jenkins, Jones, Kallaher, G. Kyles, S.B. Kyles, Kuykendall, Lawson, Lucy, Lux, Middlebrook, Miles, Netters, Newsum, Pryor, Ross, D. Smith, M. Smith, Spence, Starks, Taylor, Wax, Wells, Williams, Wurf.

Chapter 14: Greater Laws

1. Cf. *Press-Scimitar*, Apr. 5–6, and *Commercial Appeal*, Apr. 5–7, 1968.

See taped interviews with Aldridge, Cook, Dimmick, Donelson, Durick, Fisher, Greenspun, Holloman, Holmes, Hoover, James, Jordan, Kyles, Lawson, Leppert, Lucy, Manire, McRae, Miles, Moon, J.O. Patterson, Pryor, Reed, Reynolds, Starks, Sweat, Valient, Wax, Wurf.

Chapter 15: Concourse of Witnesses

1. Cf. "Civil Disorders After Action Reports," p. 326. The NAACP filed with the Justice Dept. sixty-six affidavits charging police brutality during March and April 1968. Cf. NAACP local branch affidavits on brutality.
2. For quotations from Memorial March speeches, cf. *Commercial Appeal* and *Press-Scimitar*, Apr. 8–9, 1968.
3. For an account of the strikers' bus trip to the King funeral, cf. Garry Wills, "Martin Luther King is *still on the case.*" *Esquire*, Aug. 1968.

See taped interviews with Blanchard, Ciampa, Dimmick, Fisher, Hooks, Hoover, Lawson, Leppert, Lux, Moon, Pryor, Ross, D. Smith, Spence, Wells.

Chapter 16: I Am a Man

1. The money saved in wages in public works during the strike had been almost exactly offset by overtime pay for police and firemen, according to Jerrold Moore, Mayor Loeb's administrative assistant.
2. Those men privy to the arrangement, Loeb, Reynolds, and Miles, scrupulously respected Abe Plough's wish for anonymity. However, his identity after a time was common knowledge both inside and outside City Hall.
3. Cf. "Memorandum of Agreement between City of Memphis and Local 1733, AFSCME (AFL-CIO)." Apr. 16, 1968.

See taped interviews with C. Blackburn, Blanchard, Chandler, Gianotti, Hooks, James, Jones, Lawson, Lucy, Manire, Miles, Moore, Pryor, Reynolds, Ross, Todd, Wurf.

Sources

All source material is to be found in the Sanitation Strike Project of the Mississippi Valley Collection at Memphis State University.

Taped Interviews and Transcripts
(Individuals are identified by positions held in 1968.)

COME = Community on the Move for Equality, the black community movement supporting the strike.
AFSCME = the American Federation of State, County and Municipal Employees

Ahlgren, Frank: publisher, *Commercial Appeal*
Aldridge, John W.: assistant pastor, Idlewild Presbyterian Church
Allen, Linda: member, Memphis Junior League
Awsumb, Gwen: member, Memphis City Council
Bailey, Walter: attorney
Bailey, Walter (Bill): owner, Lorraine Motel
Bell, Ezekiel: pastor, Parkway Gardens Presbyterian Church; COME
Berry, Lewis: resident, Fowler Homes
Blackburn, Charles: director, Memphis Public Works Department
Blackburn, Malcolm: pastor, Clayborn Temple; COME
Blair, Taylor: international representative, International Brotherhood of Electrical Workers
Blanchard, Jerred: member, Memphis City Council
Branch, Ben: band director, Operation Breadbasket, Chicago
Bryant, Baxton: executive director, Tennessee Council on Human Relations, Nashville
Burch, Lucius: attorney
Carpenter, Gladys: marcher
Caywood, David: attorney
Chandler, Wyeth: member, Memphis City Council
Cherry, James: advertising manager, Memphis Publishing Co.; and Marge Cherry
Ciampa, P.J.: director of field services, AFSCME, Washington
Clark, Glenn: physician, City of Memphis hospitals
Cook, E.W. (Ned): chairman, Cook Industries
Cook, Luella: domestic
Cooper, Peter: professor, LeMoyne College
Crowns, Arthur: professor, Memphis State University
Davis, Fred: member, Memphis City Council
"Death of Bessie Smith" cast, Memphis State University
Dimmick, William: dean, St. Mary's Episcopal Cathedral
Doctor, Bobby: field representative, U.S. Civil Rights Commission
Donelson, Lewis: member, Memphis City Council
Doughty, Darrell: professor, Southwestern at Memphis
Dreifus, Myra: founder, Fund for Needy Schoolchildren
Durick, Joseph: apostolic administrator (acting bishop), Roman Catholic diocese of Nashville (including Memphis), Nashville
Epps, Jesse: field representative, AFSCME, Washington
Fanion, Gerald: director, Shelby County Human Relations Commission
Ferguson, Burt: owner, WDIA radio
Fisher, John T.: chairman, Fisher Motors
Geary, Ann: member, Catholic Human Relations Council

Gianotti, Frank: Memphis City Attorney

Gillis, Ed: striker, Local 1733, AFSCME

Gioia, Frederick: neurosurgeon, St. Joseph Hospital

Greenspun, William: director, Paulist inner-city project, St. Patrick Church

Hess, Paul: assistant administrator, St. Joseph Hospital

Holloman, Frank: director, Memphis Fire and Police Department

Holmes, Charles: public relations director, Memphis State University

Hooks, Benjamin L.: judge, Criminal Courts; pastor, Middle Baptist Church

Ivy, Ron: founder, Black Students Association, Memphis State University

Jackson, H. Ralph: director, Minimum Salary Division, African Methodist Episcopal Church; COME

James, Robert: member, Memphis City Council

Jemison, Peggy: member, Memphis Junior League

Jenkins, Eddie: member, Black Students Association, Memphis State University

Jones, T.O.: organizer and president, Local 1733, AFSCME

Jordan, James: pastor, Beale Street Baptist Church; COME

Kallaher, Frank J.: lieutenant, Memphis Police Department

Kuykendall, Dan: U.S. House of Representatives, 9th Tennessee District

Kyles, Gwen: COME

Kyles, S.B. (Billy): pastor, Monumental Baptist Church; COME

Lawson, James M., Jr.: chairman, COME strategy committee; pastor, Centenary United Methodist Church

Leppert, Joseph: pastor, St. Therese of the Little Flower Church

Lucy, Bill: director of legislation, AFSCME, Washington

Lux, Henry: assistant chief, Memphis Police Department

Manire, James: Assistant City Attorney

McAdams, W.T.: member, Memphis City Council

McGinnis, James: member, Tennessee National Guard; instructor, Christian Brothers College

McRae, Frank: Memphis district superintendent, United Methodist Church

Memphis Search for Meaning Committee discussion of marches: Joan Beifuss, Ted and Virginia Hoover, Charles and Joyce Palmer, Judy Schulz, Carol Lynn and David Yellin

Middlebrook, Harold: assistant pastor, Middle Baptist Church; COME

Miles, Frank: labor relations director, E.L. Bruce Co.

Moon, Richard: Presbyterian chaplain, Memphis State University; COME

Moore, Jerrold: administrative assistant to Memphis mayor Henry Loeb

Netters, James: member, Memphis City Council

Newsum, Floyd: fireman, Memphis Fire Department

Patterson, Gilbert: pastor, Holy Temple Church of God in Christ; COME

Patterson, J.O., Jr.: member, Memphis City Council, Tennessee State Legislature

Perel, Philip: member, Memphis City Council

Pollard, Ramsey: pastor, Bellevue Baptist Church

Powell, Dan: director, Committee on Political Education, AFL-CIO

Ray, Ed: managing editor, *Memphis Press-Scimitar*

Reed, L.C.: striker, Local 1733, AFSCME

Reynolds, James: U.S. undersecretary of labor, Washington

Ross, Bill: executive secretary, Memphis AFL-CIO labor council

Sabella, Anthony: attorney

Sengstacke, Whittier: editor, *Tri-State Defender*; Mattie Sengstacke; Whittier Sengstacke, Jr., *Tri-State Defender* reporter; Ethel Sengstacke; and Ed Harris, *Tri-State Defender* photographer

Sisson, Pete: former director, Memphis Public Works Department
Smith, Dolph: artist; and Jessie Smith
Smith, Maxine: executive secretary, Memphis NAACP
Southwestern at Memphis Students; Bill Casey, editor of *Sou'wester*; Marty Frisch and Dale
 Worsley, reporters
Spence, John: assistant director, U.S. Civil Rights Commission, southern field office,
 (Memphis)
Starks, Henry: pastor, St. James AME Church; COME
Stimbert, E.C.: superintendent, Memphis City Schools
Sugarmon, Russell: attorney; member, Tennessee State Senate
Sweat, Joseph: reporter, *Commercial Appeal*
Taylor, Calvin: member, Black Organizing Project
Todd, Thomas: member, Memphis City Council
Tolleson, Mary Kay: member, Catholic Human Relations Council
Turner, Jesse: president, Memphis NAACP
Valient, Margaret: resident, LeMoyne Gardens
Walker, Mose: assistant principal, Booker T. Washington High School
Wax, James: rabbi, Temple Israel; president, Memphis Ministers Association
Weintraub, Sam: attorney
Wells, Richard: professor, Memphis Theological Seminary
Wilkins, Roy: national executive director, NAACP, New York
Williams, Fred: student, University of Tennessee Medical School
Wilmore, Jacques: director, U.S. Civil Rights Commission, southern field office, (Memphis)
Woodbury, Harry: director, Memphis Public Service Department
Wurf, Jerry: international president, AFSCME, Washington

Additional Tapes

P.J. Ciampa meets with Memphis Ministers Assn. members, Feb. 16, 1968.
Negotiations between city and union under auspices of Memphis Ministers Assn., Feb. 18–20,
 1968.
Eyewitness reports, Mar. 28, 1968. Paul Barnett. WREC Radio.
Eyewitness reports, Mar. 28, 1968. Ray Sherman. WMPS Radio.
WREC Radio general strike and assassination coverage.
WMPS Radio general strike and assassination coverage.
Martin Luther King, Jr. speech, Mason Temple, Mar. 18, 1968.
Martin Luther King, Jr. "Mountaintop" speech, Mason Temple, Apr. 3, 1968.

Videotape and film

WMC-TV (NBC Memphis affiliate) assorted strike and assassination footage.

Newspapers

(The *Memphis Press-Scimitar* ceased publication in the fall of 1983.)

Commercial Appeal. July 3–29, 1967; election coverage, Sept. through Nov., 1967; day-by-
 day Feb. 1–May 31, 1968. Memphis Publishing Company (Scripps-Howard).
Memphis Press-Scimitar. July 3–29, 1967; election coverage, Sept. through Nov., 1967; day-
 by-day (no Sunday edition), Feb. 1–May 31, 1968. Memphis Publishing Company
 (Scripps-Howard).
The Sou'wester, weekly student newspaper, Southwestern at Memphis, Jan.–May 1968. Also
 working papers and notebooks of staff.

The Tiger Rag, twice-weekly student newspaper, Memphis State University, Jan.–May 1968.
The Tri-State Defender, weekly newspaper. Jan.–May 1968. Sengstacke Publishing Co.,
   Chicago. Edited in Memphis.

Pamphlets, Reports, Articles, Notes

1. Adams, Null, "Boss Crump." *Press-Scimitar* sesquicentennial edition, May 28, 1969.
2. "AFSCME Stands for Service." American Federation of State, County and Municipal
   Employees.
3. Bennett, Lerone, Jr., "The Making of Black America: The Black Worker." *Ebony*. Nov.
   1972. Chicago: Johnson Publishing Co.
4. Bevier, Thomas, "James Lawson: His Creed Non-Violence; His Aim Progress." *Commercial Appeal*, April 9, 1969.
5. "Black Thesis," occasional mimeographed publication of Black Students Assn., Memphis
   State University. Vols. I, II, 1968.
6. Born, Kate, "The Negro in Twentieth Century Memphis." Research paper for Joint University Center, Memphis State University and University of Tennessee.
7. Borod, Marx. Resumé of attempts to end strike and a proposed settlement. Apr. 1–4,
   1968.
8. Brewer, Norman, "Riot Coverage in Detail, WMC Stations." *Scripps-Howard News.* June
   1968.
9. Christy, George, "Memphis: Boom Town on the River." *Town & Country.* May 1970.
10. "Citizens Study Committee, Priority Report for Health and Welfare Services for SUN and
    the Health and Welfare Planning Council of Memphis-Shelby County in Co-operation
    with the Mid-South Medical Council." 1972.
11. "City of Memphis vs. Local 1733, AFSCME, AFL-CIO, et al." 69415-1 R.D., Mar. 5,
    1968. Chancery Court of Shelby County, Tennessee.
12. "City of Memphis vs. Martin Luther King, Hosea Williams, Rev. James Bevel, Rev. James
    Orange, Ralph Abernathy, Bernard Lee, all non-residents of the State of Tennessee." C-
    68-80. Apr. 4, 1968. U.S. District Court, Western District of Tennessee, Western
    Division.
13. "Civil Disorders After-Action Reports: A Report to the Attorney General of the United
    States Reviewing the Experiences of Eight American Cities During the Civil Disorders of
    March–April 1968." Professional Standards Division, International Association of Chiefs
    of Police.
14. Coe, Frances, "Schools." Preliminary papers and summaries. LeMoyne College Race Re-
    lations Conference, Nov. 12, 1966.
15. Crowns, Arthur, "A Case Study Analysis of Police Relations during the Hot Summer of
    1967 in Memphis, Tennessee." Memphis State University, 1967.
16. DuBois, Barney, "The Power Structure." *Commercial Appeal*. Sept. 20–24, 1970.
17. "Employment, Administration of Justice and Health Services in Memphis-Shelby
    County, Tennessee." Tennessee State Advisory Committee to U.S. Commission on Civil
    Rights, August 1967.
18. Hammer, Philip, "Action Line-Memphis: An Economic Overview Prepared for the
    Memphis Area Chamber of Commerce." Hammer, Green, Siler Associates (Washington-
    Atlanta), 1969.
19. Kilpatrick, James, "Mr. Crump and the Organization." *Commercial Appeal* sesquicen-
    tennial edition, May 25, 1969.
20. King, Martin Luther, Jr., speeches to Southern Christian Leadership Conference
    Ministers Leadership Training Conference. Miami Beach, Feb. 19–23, 1968.
21. Levine, Richard J., "Public Employees Group Grows Rapidly, Plans Stepped Up

Organizing." *Wall Street Journal*, June 3, 1968.

22. *Mainstream*, Vol. I, No. 1. January 1968. National Business League.

23. "Mason Payne and Lizzie Mae Payne vs. Leslie Dean (L.D.) Jones and the City of Memphis, defendants." C–69–87. Feb. 1971. U.S. District Court, Western District of Tennessee. Also working notes, documentation, depositions of attorneys for the plaintiff, Henry Sutton and Irving Salky, and for the defense, John Thomason.

24. "Memorandum of Agreement between the City of Memphis and Local 1733, American Federation of State, County and Municipal Employees (AFL-CIO)" Apr. 16, 1968.

25. Memphis Area Chamber of Commerce brochures: "Memphis 1968," "Memphis Digest," "Facts for Use in Making Visitors Welcome and for Introducing Memphis to Newcomers, 1967."

26. "Memphis in the 70's." Division of Continuing Studies and Institute of Urban Development, with the Memphis Area Chamber of Commerce and the Memphis and Shelby County Planning Commission.

27. "The Memphis Riot." Ninety-seven eyewitness accounts of events in Memphis, Mar. 28–Apr. 1, 1968, by students in History 202 and 304, LeMoyne College, Memphis.

28. "MAP-South Annual Report, 1968." MAP-South (Memphis anti-poverty agency).

29. Mitchell, Henry, editorial on Dr. Martin Luther King, Jr. in *The Delta Review*, May 1968.

30. Muse, Benjamin. "Memphis." Southern Regional Council, 1964.

31. National Association for the Advancement of Colored People, Memphis branch, "Annual Reports," 1964–1968; affidavits (sixty-six) on police brutality compiled Mar. and Apr. 1968; surveys on Negro employment in Memphis city government and Shelby County government, August 1967.

32. "Public Employee Unions: Rights and Responsibilities." Policy statement adopted by the international executive board, American Federation of State, County and Municipal Employees, AFL-CIO, July 26, 1966.

33. "Reactions to the Assassination," 27 students from Hamilton High School; "How I Heard of the Assassination," members of the Memphis Search for Meaning Committee; survey of 173 students in psychology and history classes at Memphis State University and of 53 students at Millington High School.

34. "Riot Data Review #2." Lemburg Center for Study of Violence, Brandeis University, Aug. 1968.

35. Stanfield, J. Edwin, "In Memphis More Than a Garbage Strike." Southern Regional Council, Mar. 22, 1968.

36. _____, "In Memphis More Than A Garbage Strike" (a compilation of the earlier reports). Southern Regional Council, June 28, 1968.

37. _____, "In Memphis, Tragedy Unaverted." Southern Regional Council, Apr. 3, 1968.

38. Steiber, Jack, "Employee Organization in State and Local Government." International Symposium on Public Employment Labor Relations. May 3–5, 1971.

39. Stewart, Donald D. "Poverty in Memphis and Shelby County." Memphis State University, departments of sociology and anthropology and Bureau of Social Research. 1966.

40. Tucker, David M., "Black Pride and Negro Business in the 1920's: George Washington Lee of Memphis." *Business History Review*. Vol. XLIII, No.4, Winter, 1969. Harvard University.

41. "War on Poverty Committee of Memphis and Shelby County Annual Report 1966–67." War on Poverty Committee, Memphis and Shelby County.

42. Wills, Garry, "Martin Luther King is *still on the case!*" *Esquire*. Aug. 1968.

43. Wurf, Jerry, "An Address to the Mayors." United States Conference of Mayors, Honolulu, June 19, 1967.

44. Yglesias, Jose, "Dr. King's March on Washington, Part II." *New York Times Magazine*, Mar. 31, 1968.

Additional Bibliography

1. Baker, Thomas Harrison, *The Memphis Commercial Appeal: The History of a Southern Newspaper*. Baton Rouge: Louisiana Univ. Press, 1971.
2. Bennett, Lerone, Jr., *What Manner of Man?* Chicago: Johnson Pub. Co, Inc., 1964.
3. Bishop, Jim, *The Days of Martin Luther King*. New York: G.P. Putnam's Sons, 1971.
4. Blair, Clay, Jr., *The Strange Case of James Earl Ray*. New York: Bantam Books, 1969.
5. Boles, John B., *The Great Revival, 1787–1805: The Origins of the Southern Evangelical Mind*. Univ. Press of Kentucky, 1972.
6. Botkin, B.A., ed., *Lay My Burden Down: A Folk History of Southern Slavery*. Chicago: Univ. of Chicago Press, 1945.
7. Branch, Taylor, *Parting the Waters: America in the King Years, 1954-1963*. New York: Simon and Schuster, 1988.
8. Broderick, Francis L. and August Meier, eds., *Negro Protest Thought in the Twentieth Century*. Indianapolis: Bobbs Merrill Co., Inc., 1965.
9. Capers, Gerald, *Biography of a River Town: Memphis' Heroic Age*. 2nd ed. Gerald Capers. Tulane University, 1966.
10. Cash, Wilbur J., *The Mind of the South*. New York: Alfred A. Knopf, 1941.
11. Cortner, Richard C., *The Apportionment Cases*. Knoxville: Univ. of Tennessee Press, 1970.
12. Davis, James D., *The History of the City of Memphis*. 1873. Facsimile edition of the West Tennessee Historical Society, 1970.
13. Douglas, James W., *The Non-Violent Cross*. New York: Macmillan Co., 1969.
14. Dulles, Foster R., *Labor in America*. New York: Thomas Y. Crowell, 1949.
15. Erikson, Erik H., *Gandhi's Truth: On the Origins of Militant Non Violence*. New York: W.W. Norton Co., 1969.
16. Farmer, James, *Lay Bare the Heart: An Autobiography of the Civil Rights Movement*. New York: Arbor House, 1985.
17. Frank, Gerold, *An American Death*. Garden City: Doubleday & Co., Inc., 1972.
18. Garrow, David J., *The FBI and Martin Luther King*. New York: Penguin Books, 1983.
19. _____, *Bearing the Cross: Martin Luther King, Jr., and the Southern Christian Leadership Conference*. New York: William Morrow and Company, Inc., 1986.
20. Genovese, Eugene D., *Roll, Jordan, Roll: The World the Slaves Made*. New York: Pantheon, 1974.
21. Goulden, Joseph C., *Jerry Wurf*. New York: Athenaeum, 1982.
22. _____, *Meany: The Unchallenged Strong Man of American Labor*. New York: Athenaeum, 1972.
23. Graham, Gene, *One Man, One Vote: Baker v. Carr and the American Levellers*. Boston: Atlantic Monthly Press, Little Brown and Co., 1972.
24. Graham, Hugh Davis, *Crisis in Print; Desegregation and the Press in Tennessee*. Nashville: Vanderbilt Univ. Press, 1967.
25. Graham, Hugh Davis and Ted Robert Gurr, eds., *Violence in America: Historical and Comparative Perspectives*. Report to the National Commission on the Causes and Prevention of Violence. New York: Bantam Books, 1969.
26. Grand, Joanne, ed., *Black Protest: History, Documents and Analysis from 1619 to the Present*. New York: Fawcett, 1968.
27. Hassler, Alfred, *Saigon. U.S.A.* New York: Richard W. Baron, 1970.
28. Hatcher, Edward, Jr., *Gayoso Bayou*. Memphis: St. Lukes Press, 1982.

29. Hawkins, John, *Metropolis on the American Nile*. Woodland Hills, Cal.: Windsor, 1982.
30. Huie, William Bradford, *He Slew the Dreamer*. New York: Delacorte Press, 1968.
31. Hutchins, Fred L., *What Happened in Memphis*. Privately printed in Memphis, 1965.
32. Jackson, Kenneth T., *The Ku Klux Klan in the City, 1915–1930*. New York: Oxford Univ. Press, 1967.
33. Jacobson, Julius, ed., *The Negro and the American Labor Movement*. Garden City: Doubleday, Anchor Books, 1968.
34. King, Coretta Scott, *My Life with Martin Luther King, Jr.* New York: Holt, Rinehart & Winston, 1969.
35. King, Martin Luther, Jr., *Strength to Love*. New York: Harper & Row, 1963.
36. _____, *Stride Toward Freedom: The Montgomery Story*. New York: Harper & Row, 1957.
37. _____, *Where Do We Go From Here: Chaos or Community?* New York: Harper & Row, 1967.
38. _____, *Why We Can't Wait*. New York: Harper & Row, 1964.
39. Lee, George W., *Beale Street: Where the Blues Began*. New York: Robert O. Ballou, 1934.
40. Lewis, Anthony, *Portrait of a Decade: The Second American Revolution*. New York: Random House, 1964.
41. Lewis, David L., *King: A Critical Biography*. New York: Praeger Publishers, 1970.
42. Martin, Ralph G., *The Bosses*. New York: G.P. Putnam's Sons, 1964.
43. Miller, William D., *Memphis During the Progressive Era. 1900–1917*. Memphis: Memphis State Univ. Press, 1957.
44. _____, *Mr. Crump of Memphis*. Baton Rouge: Louisiana State Press, 1964.
45. Miller, William Robert, *Martin Luther King, Jr.: His Life, Martyrdom and Meaning for the World*. New York: Waybright & Talley, 1968.
46. Oates, Stephen B., *Let the Trumpet Sound: The Life of Martin Luther King*. New York: Harper & Row, 1982.
47. *Report of the National Advisory Commission on Civil Disorders*. New York: Bantam Books, 1968.
48. Riggs, Joseph and Margaret Lawrence, *Everett R. Cook*. Memphis Public Library, 1971.
49. Tucker, David, *Black Pastors and Leaders, 1819–1972*. Memphis: Memphis State Univ. Press, 1975.
50. _____, *Lieutenant Lee of Beale Street: The Biography of a Negro Leader*. Nashville: Vanderbilt Univ. Press, 1971.
51. _____, *Memphis Since Crump. Bossism, Blacks and Civic Reformers. 1948–1968*. Knoxville: Univ. of Tennessee Press, 1980.
52. Turner, Charles, *The Celebrant*. Ann Arbor: Servant Publications, 1982.
53. Walsh, Robert E., ed., *Sorry...No Government Today: Unions vs. City Hall*. Boston: Beacon Press, 1969.
54. Watters, Pat, *Down to Now*. New York: Random House, 1971.
55. Williams, John A., *The King God Didn't Save*. New York: Coward-McCann, 1970.
56. Wright, William E., *Memphis Politics: A Study in Racial Bloc Voting*. Eagleton Inst. of Politics, Rutgers University, 1962.